W9-CSN-730

JARGONAPHASIA

Théophile Alajouanine (1890–1980)

This is a volume in

PERSPECTIVES IN
NEUROLINGUISTICS, NEUROPSYCHOLOGY,
   AND PSYCHOLINGUISTICS

A Series of Monographs and Treatises

A complete list of titles in this series appears at the end of this volume.

JARGONAPHASIA

Edited by

JASON W. BROWN

Institute for Research in Behavioral Neuroscience
New York, New York
and Division of Neuropsychology
Department of Neurology
New York University Medical Center
New York, New York

WITHDRAWN

1981

ACADEMIC PRESS

A Subsidiary of Harcourt Brace Jovanovich, Publishers

New York   London   Toronto   Sydney   San Francisco

COPYRIGHT © 1981, BY ACADEMIC PRESS, INC.
ALL RIGHTS RESERVED.
NO PART OF THIS PUBLICATION MAY BE REPRODUCED OR
TRANSMITTED IN ANY FORM OR BY ANY MEANS, ELECTRONIC
OR MECHANICAL, INCLUDING PHOTOCOPY, RECORDING, OR ANY
INFORMATION STORAGE AND RETRIEVAL SYSTEM, WITHOUT
PERMISSION IN WRITING FROM THE PUBLISHER.

ACADEMIC PRESS, INC.
111 Fifth Avenue, New York, New York 10003

United Kingdom Edition published by
ACADEMIC PRESS, INC. (LONDON) LTD.
24/28 Oval Road, London NW1 7DX

Library of Congress Cataloging in Publication Data
Main entry under title:

Jargonaphasia.

    (Perspectives in neurolinguistics)
    Includes bibliographies and index.
    1. Aphasia. 2. Jargon (Terminology) I. Brown,
Jason W. II. Series. [DNLM: 1. Aphasia. 2. Speech.
WL 340.5 J37]
RC425.J37   616.85'52   80-2328
ISBN 0-12-137580-3

PRINTED IN THE UNITED STATES OF AMERICA

81 82 83 84   9 8 7 6 5 4 3 2 1

616.8552
J287

Contents

Chapter 6

Aphasic Jargon and the Speech Acts of Naming and Judging   125

EUGENE GREEN

Chapter 7

Behavioral Aspects of Jargonaphasia   139

EDWIN A. WEINSTEIN

Chapter 8

Associative Processes in Semantic Jargon and in Schizophrenic Language   151

K. ZAIMOV

List of Contributors

Numbers in parentheses indicate the pages on which the authors' contributions begin.

Samuel W. Anderson (295), Department of Psychiatry, College of Physicians and Surgeons, Columbia University, New York, New York 10032

Jason W. Brown (1, 169, 177), Institute for Research in Behavioral Neuroscience, and Division of Neuropsychology, Department of Neurology, New York University Medical Center, New York, New York 10016

Hugh W. Buckingham, Jr.* (39), Department of Audiology and Speech Sciences, Purdue University, West Lafayette, Indiana 47907

Brian Butterworth† (113), The Psychological Laboratory, University of Cambridge, Cambridge, England

Eugene Green (125), Department of Psychology, Boston Veterans Administration Hospital, Boston, Massachusetts 02130

Malcom Grimston (113), The Psychological Laboratory, University of Cambridge, Cambridge, England

Ginette Lavallée-Huynh (9), Faculté de Médecine, Université de Montréal, Montreal, Quebec, Canada H2W 1T8

* PRESENT ADDRESS: Interdepartmental Program in Linguistics, Department of Speech, Louisiana State University, Baton Rouge, Louisiana 70803

† PRESENT ADDRESS: Department of Psychology, University College London, Gower Street, London WC1 6BT England

Andrew Kertesz (63), Department of Clinical Neurological Sciences, The University of Western Ontario, St. Joseph's Hospital, London, Ontario, Canada N6A 4V2

André Roche Lecours* (9), Faculté de Médecine, Université de Montréal, Montreal, Quebec, Canada H2W 1T8

A. Damien Martin (305), Program in Speech Pathology and Audiology, Department of Communication Arts and Sciences, New York University, New York, New York 10016

Ellen Osborn (9), Escola Paulista de Medicina, São Paulo, Brazil

Ellen Perecman (177), Department of Neurology, New York University Medical Center, New York, New York 10016

Günter Peuser (259), Rheinische Landesklinik für Sprachgestörte, Kaiser-Karl-Ring 20, 5300 Bonn 1, West Germany

Françoise Rouillon (9), Centre de Recherches en Sciences Neurologiques, Université de Montréal, Montreal, Quebec, Canada H2W 1T8

John Swallow (113), The Psychological Laboratory, University of Cambridge, Cambridge, England

Kuno Temp (259), Rheinische Landesklinik für Sprachgestörte, Kaiser-Karl-Ring 20, 5300 Bonn 1, West Germany

Lisa Travis (9), Department of Linguistics, McGill University, Montreal, Quebec, Canada

Edwin A. Weinstein (139), 7306 Holiday Terrace, Bethesda, Maryland 20034

K. Zaimov (151), Chancellor's Department, Medical Academy, Sofia 15, Bulgaria

* PRESENT ADDRESS: Service de Neurologie, Hôtel-Dieu de Montréal, 3840 rue St-Urbain, Montreal, Quebec H2W 1T8 Canada

Preface

This work on jargonaphasia appropriately reflects the interdisciplinary nature of the subject, in that it brings together contributions from linguistics, psychology, speech pathology, and neuroscience around a common theme of considerable importance to aphasia study, namely the sorting out of the different forms of posterior aphasia and the relations of these pathological states to focal brain lesions. In some respects, jargon is the most fascinating of the aphasias, inasmuch as it presents the picture of language disarray in the most perplexing and extravagant manner. Yet one of the major factors that has prevented a fuller understanding of jargonaphasia is the poverty of case material on the subject, and the incompleteness of linguistic description. Most of the early cases are of little present value, and there are still insufficient case reports in the current literature. Moreover, since jargonaphasics can rarely cooperate with the constraints of experimental testing, there are still fewer investigative studies of this disorder. The present volume is intended to help remedy this situation.

I am especially pleased to have contributions from most of the leading workers in this field of research. There is, however, one unfortunate omission that will be evident to all students of aphasia. Some time ago I invited the late Professor Théophile Alajouanine to contribute a chapter, but he was unable to comply because of his age and failing health. Nonetheless, he wrote to me of his continuing interest in jargon as an "anosognosic disintegration of the semantic values of language" and the broad opposition of the asemantic and dysphonetic forms. I am sure he would have been pleased to see that the approach taken by most of the contributors incorporates the distinction of a (disrupted) semantic and/or phonological component. Alajouanine also saw the problem of anosognosia as central to the understanding of jargon, in that awareness for language breaks down in relation to the dissolution of semantic structure. One can infer from this that self-awareness is built up on systems of lexical- and conceptual-meaning relationships, an important idea that I hope can be explored in the future. In the field of jargonaphasia, as in so many other areas of aphasia study, Alajouanine opened up new areas of research and, like the true innovator, left many profound questions for us to struggle with in the years to come.

Finally, I wish to express my appreciation to Harry Whitaker for encouraging me to plan and edit this volume. Support for the project has come from various sources, the Institute for Research in Behavioral Neuroscience, NIH Grant NS 13740, and an award from the Alexander von Humboldt-Stiftung.

Théophile Alajouanine
(1890–1980)

Antonin Joseph Théophile Alajouanine was born on June 12, 1890, in a house situated on the Place de l'Eglise of Verneix, a little village near Montluçon (Allier), in the French province of Bourbonnais, of which he often talked, throughout his life, with great warmth and fondness, and where he managed to spend at least 3 months every year after he had become a Parisian celebrity. He was the only son of Antoine Alajouanine, the *maréchal-serrurier* of Verneix.

After having completed his studies in humanities in Moulins, the prefecture of the Allier department, Théophile Alajouanine went to Paris where, in view of his interest in both literature and medicine, he hesitated for a while between the Ecole Normale Supérieure and the Faculté de Médecine. He finally decided in favor of the latter. He became an Interne des Hôpitaux de Paris in 1914, but his training was soon interrupted by the First World War in which he served with the French army. He resumed his duties as an intern after the war. In 1923 he received the Médaille d'Or de l'Internat. Meanwhile, on June 15, 1920, he married an English woman, Maud Jennings.

Alajouanine's first masters were psychiatrists, some of whom, such as Philippe Chaslin and Jules Ernest Séglas, no doubt communicated to him their interest in pathological language. He later studied under outstanding neurologists such as Achille Alexandre Souques, who had been among the last of Charcot's direct collaborators, Pierre Marie, under whom he worked for a relatively short period, and Charles Foix. Charles Foix was the one whose teachings and friendship Alajouanine appreciated most: Alajouanine once wrote that Foix had been "an incomparable master, an affectionate friend, an eldest brother" (*'un maître incomparable, un ami délicieux, un frère aîné'*). It was nonetheless to the memory of both Pierre Marie and Charles Foix that Alajouanine dedicated his 1968 monograph on aphasia.

Like Joseph Jules Dejerine after Fulgence Raymond, and Pierre Marie after Dejerine, and Georges Guillain after Pierre Marie, Théophile Alajouanine was elected to the Chair of the Clinique des Maladies du Système Nerveux when Guillain retired, thus becoming the fifth successor of Jean-Martin Charcot at la Salpêtrière. This was in 1947, and Alajouanine held the chair until he retired in 1960; his successor to this day is Paul Castaigne. Before 1947, Alajouanine had been a Chef de Clinique (1923–1925), a Médecin des Hôpitaux de Paris (1926), a Professeur Agrégé (1927), and, like Broca, Dejerine, and Pierre Marie before him, he had headed a service of neurology at Bicêtre (1913–1947). He had also been, for several years, the Titular of the Chair of History of Medicine at the Faculté de Paris. (Parisian neurologists still quote the magnificent conferences he hosted during this period on the evolution of ideas and theories concerning aphasia and the mutual relationships of language and the brain.)

Alajouanine's medical research, teachings, and publications bore on practically every aspect of neurology. He was, for instance, the first to describe the pathology of the herniation of nucleus pulposus and to suggest that discoidectomy was an appropriate treatment in certain cases. Although his nearly 600 books and scientific articles show that his interest for neurological and muscular pathology knew no boundaries, he himself listed his own major clinical interests as pain, trophic disorders, and acquired perturbations of speech and language.

As he once said to François Lhermitte, who shared with Paul Castaigne the advantage of being the master's privileged disciple, Alajouanine's thinking about aphasia in the adult was always guided by three postulates which he considered to be empirical: Aphasia in the adult is the perturbation of an already learned and completely organized behavior (*'elle trouble un langage complètement organisé'*); the study of aphasic symptom-complexes open a window on the physiological mechanisms behind psycholinguistic activities; aphasia is the result of focal brain lesions, and the study of these lesions should therefore provide precise information as to the cerebral structures and neural networks that are involved, specifically or not, in the biological control of normal language behavior. Indeed, Alajouanine viewed language not only as a neurologist, that is, as one dealing with clinical manifestations, orthophonic reeducation, and anatomo-clinical correlations, but he also viewed it as a psychopathologist (and there, he did not always share Pierre Marie's somewhat doctrinal ideas, for instance with regard to the intellectual state of aphasics), and as a neurolinguist, which is shown by his pioneering works on the linguistic characteristics of the phonetic disintegration of Broca's aphasics and of the jargons of Wernicke's aphasics.

Théophile Alajouanine neither liked nor even used words such as "aphasiology" and "neurolinguistics": He explained himself on this at the end of 1979, in the preface he wrote to a textbook of aphasiology by Lecours and François Lhermitte. Though others before him—including Jacques Lordat, Paul Broca, Abel Hovelacque (a linguist), John Hughlings Jackson, and Sigmund Freud—had had explicit linguistic preoccupations and opinions apropos of aphasia, he was nevertheless the first to open the doors of neurology wards to a linguist, more precisely to a phonetician. The phonetician was Madame Marguerite Durand. Together with André Ombredane, a psychologist who worked at Bicêtre before the Second World War, Alajouanine and Durand proceeded with an exhaustive neurological, psychometric, linguistic, and, in particular, phonetic study of the disorders characteristically observed in Broca's aphasia. The book they published as an account of this research, which is entitled *Le syndrome de désintégration phonétique dans l'aphasie* (Masson, Paris, 1939), is in our opinion the one publication that marked the birth of neurolinguistics as a well-delineated field of multidisciplinary research and knowledge.

Alajouanine, perhaps still under the influence of Chaslin and Séglas, was fascinated by the discursive behavior of jargonaphasics, which he studied with François Lhermitte, Blanche Ducarne de Ribaucourt, Olivier Sabouraud, Luigi Vignolo, and others. He and his collaborators coined terms such as "phonemic paraphasia" (till then improperly designated as "literal paraphasia") and "semantic paraphasia," and they probably were the first to tackle the problem of a linguistic taxonomy of various types of jargons. Although he disliked and never used the label "conduction aphasia," Alajouanine described the preponderance of phonemic deviations in certain jargons occurring together with a disorder of repetition but without major comprehension difficulties. Furthermore, he attributed phonemic and semantic jargonaphasic disorders to dysfunctions of different anatomo-functional substrata.

Recognized in Europe and America as an authority in the field of neurology, Théophile Alajouanine was particularly appreciated as a scientific speaker in Argentina, Belgium, Brazil, Canada, England (a country he loved), Rumania, Uruguay, and so forth. He counted numerous friends among the international academic community, such as Percival Bailey, Macdonald Critchley, Wilder Penfield, and others: To these friends, as well as to his masters and pupils, and just as to his native Bourbonnais, he remained unfailingly faithful throughout his life.

Until a few weeks before his death, Alajouanine obviously enjoyed life, kept appreciating good food and good wines, and spent the best part of his days reading, writing, and in discussions with visitors in his home library, the shelves of which sheltered, it is said, one of the richest private collections in Paris.

Théophile Alajouanine died quietly, on May 2, 1980. A little more than a month before, he had told or rather repeated to us that, in his opinion, the mutual relationships of brain and language were and would forever remain a mystery. He added with a smile that it was in the nature of things and therefore good that it should be so. Well, he did not insist that we agree with him on this.

ANDRÉ ROCH LECOURS
JEAN-LOUIS SIGNORET

Chapter 1

Introduction

JASON W. BROWN

Historically, jargon was first defined as a series of speech sounds without meaning (Bastian, 1869), later as a combination of verbal (lexical) and literal (sound) errors, either type alone giving rise to the "pure" form of the paraphasic defect (Kussmaul, 1876; Mirallie, 1896; Niessl von Mayendorff, 1911). Wernicke (1874) argued that verbal paraphasia occurred with a lesion of left posterior T1 and T2, and was due to an interruption of a control system modulating Broca's area. Presumably, paraphasia and jargon reflected the extent of interruption in this system. The idea that a left temporal lesion could de-afferent Broca's area, allowing it to "run on" uninhibitedly, constitutes perhaps the first "theory" of jargon production.

However, there have been other views. Niessl von Mayendorff (1911) proposed that paraphasia and jargon resulted from the inferior language ability of the right hemisphere after lesion of the left temporal lobe, a view that predicted an abolition of pre-existing paraphasia by a second lesion in the right Wernicke area. Henschen (1920) gave a critical discussion of this theory. He reported a case with a bilateral lesion of T1 without paraphasia, and suggested that, if the right hemisphere did have a role in the residual jargon or paraphasic speech of an aphasic, this was not necessarily through the mediation of the right temporal lobe. Henschen also reviewed the anatomical cases of jargonaphasia to date (see Kertesz, this volume)

1

JARGONAPHASIA

Copyright © 1981 by Academic Press, Inc.
All rights in any form reserved.
ISBN 0-12-137580-3

and concluded that the disorder was due to a large lesion, generally softening, involving posterior T1 and T2. These were all unilateral lesions
except for one bilateral case reported by Mingazzini (1913). Unfortunately,
these cases were not sufficiently well documented to be certain of the
clinical type of jargon, though it is likely that the majority were neologistic.

There have been several other theories of jargon advanced over the
years, many of which are discussed in this volume. Goldstein (1948) wrote
that paraphasia was due to impaired inner speech; but then, what is the
cause of the impaired inner speech? Jargon has also been attributed to
impaired auditory feedback, inattention, or hyperfluency. Luria wrote of
paraphasia as due to an "equalization of associative strengths," after Pavlov. In certain of these accounts we are left to wonder if the deficit that
is invoked as an "explanation" is not just another manifestation of the
jargon state rather than its cause.

The classification of Alajouanine, Sabouraud, and DeRibaucourt (1952)
was an important advance in that afterward it was no longer sufficient to
speak of jargonaphasia as if it was a unitary deficit. The recognition of
several different, perhaps independent, types of jargon invalidated much
of the older literature in which the form of jargon was left unspecified.
Moreover, with the identification of at least three forms of jargon—asemantic, neologistic, and undifferentiated—a heavy burden was placed on
correlative anatomical studies to explain the qualitative differences. Of
course, the explanation of symptom change and the diversity of symptom
expression has never been the strong point of the Wernicke approach. Yet
other theories of jargon are no less obligated to account for the heterogeneity
of the clinical picture, as well as the links between jargon and other fluent
aphasic disorders.

Turning to the individual chapters, Buckingham (Chapter 3) raises several points to which I would like to respond. The observation that anomia
"deteriorates" to phonemic (conduction) aphasia, or that phonemic aphasia
recovers to anomia, is taken to disconfirm the microgenetic account of
these disorders. The reasoning is unclear to me. The deterioration refers
to a progressive lesion, not a worsening of the aphasia. Indeed, I wonder
if severity is a concept of any meaning whatsoever in language pathology.
It is simply a question of the disturbance "moving" from one state (level)
to another. Buckingham implies that I disavow multiple level deficits, but
the notion of a combined semantic and phonological disturbance is central
to my account of neologistic jargon. Personally, I have no problem with
the idea of an anomia submerged in phonemic aphasia or in neologistic
jargon. The fact that a patient is one moment anomic, the next paraphasic,
is precisely the sort of dynamic change that is captured by the microgenetic
model. What would bother me is the idea that anomia can occur SIMUL-
TANEOUSLY with phonemic or semantic paraphasia.

The anomic deficit—inability to evoke a word, not paraphasia—seems one that is positioned just at the point of lexical selection, displaying that moment where an abstract semantic representation is first isolated out of a background field prior to achieving lexical form. The phonological representation is not evoked and the background semantic content does not achieve full lexical differentiation. This is why the anomic has more diffuse—or less stable—semantic categories than the phonemic aphasic; witness the poor performance of anomics on TOT studies. In a way, the deficit in anomia is comparable to that in amnestic states. In the latter (e.g., Korsakoff syndrome), the failure in evocation is at the semantic level, involving temporally linked experiential events. In my view, this is the same deficit but at a different stage in retrieval.

Butterworth, Swallow, and Grimston (Chapter 5) also claim that there is an anomia in jargon, on the finding of hesitations (lexical search) before neologisms. It is of interest that the hesitations are longest for neologisms, less for phonemic paraphasias, and least for verbal paraphasias. Might this be consistent with the idea that the neologism involves a two-level deficit, semantic plus phonemic, and therefore the latency is greatest before the neologism? In this chapter, the authors find evidence from a study of the gestures of their patient to support the concept of an anomia submerged in the jargonaphasia. However, many neologisms do not show exceptional hesitation, suggesting that anomia may not be an intrinsic aspect of neology.

Probably the anomia, if present at all DURING the paraphasic error, occurs only with ''device-generated'' neologisms. This would account for their aberrant phoneme frequency. In other words, neologisms with normal phoneme frequencies represent phonemic paraphasias superimposed on lexical targets, whether correct or not, as the underlying (?paraphasic) lexical item, being a real word of the language, will, by virtue of WORD frequency effects, constrain the PHONEME frequency of the neologism in the direction of a normal distribution. On the other hand, neologisms that are not determined by semantic intentions (i.e., where there is no underlying lexical frame), will have a phoneme frequency distribution that reflects intrinsic relationships within the sound system itself. Here the neologism, and thus its phoneme frequency distribution, is no longer constrained by the need to realize possible lexical targets. These neologisms might be associated with an anomia, in that they reflect an output of phoneme strings when lexical search has been unsuccessful. This is a possible explanation of the frequency data in our case of phonemic jargon. Of course, why some patients are simply anomic and others fill the anomic ''spaces'' with ''device-generated'' phoneme strings, is another problem entirely. No doubt it has something to do with the pathological locus, to involvement of regions, for example Wernicke's area proper, which mediate phonological realization.

With regard to pathological correlation, few will disagree with Kertesz (Chapter 4) that neologistic jargon is associated with large lesions of left posterior T1 and T2. The localization of semantic jargon, however, is another matter. There are too few cases with pathology to be certain on this point, but such evidence as does exist points to bilateral (basal) temporal lesions. This was present in Green's case, and has been inferred in the majority of clinical reports (Brown, 1979). Several personal cases, all with bilateral pathology, are reported in this collection just to provide some perspective on Kertesz's conclusions.

Kertesz also raises the related issue of the evolution of neologistic jargon. The majority of cases seem to resolve toward semantic jargon. This would argue that the lesion of semantic jargon, is, if anything, smaller than that of neologistic jargon, certainly left-sided. Yet I wonder about this. In my experience, neologistic jargon tends to recover into a state of fluent empty speech with skewed meaning content and occasional paraphasia rather than the semantic anomaly of the typical jargon case. This is not to say that semantic jargon does not occur with a unilateral left lesion, but rather that in true (unintelligible) semantic jargon a bilateral lesion is often present.

Again, with regard to recovery, it is argued that the tendency for neologistic jargon to evolve toward semantic jargon rather than phonemic aphasia disconfirms the concept of a two-level deficit in neologistic jargon. In other words, if neologistic jargon represents a combined semantic and phonological disturbance, why does it recover only to the semantic deficit? The fact is that neologistic jargon evolves in both directions, though admittedly the recovery to phonemic aphasia is less frequent. Why should this be? Presumably, if right hemisphere compensation is involved, this should, because of its presumably better semantic ability, bias recovery toward a residual phonological deficit. A possible explanation is that semantic recovery leads to anomia in most cases, and that it is not possible to have a phonemic paraphasia, as distinct from "device-generated" jargon, superimposed on an empty anomic segment. That is, semantic recovery occurs from incorrect selection (semantic paraphasia) toward correct but incomplete selection (anomia). The deficit in anomia is just prior to full lexical differentiation. How could one have a deficit of phoneme sequencing or selection on empty word frames? This predicts that phonemic (conduction) aphasia would occur ONLY with complete recovery of semantic-lexical intentions. The fact that such recovery is usually incomplete (e.g., anomic) explains the recovery bias. In contrast, recovery of the phonemic disturbance exposes underlying semantic errors. In such cases, lexical realization is adequate from the phonological, but not the semantic, standpoint.

The cases of phonemic (undifferentiated) jargon described by Peuser and Temp (Chapter 11), and by Perecman and myself (Chapter 10), are the first thorough reports of this disorder in the literature. The chapter by Anderson (Chapter 13) which describes the prosodic contours in our case is a valuable addition. There are, however, important differences between these cases which need to be emphasized. The first case produced simple but variegated CV strings in relation to a type of mumbling behavior. This patient had a large central lesion, and seems closer to Alajouanine's case of undifferentiated jargon. Our case had a richer phoneme inventory with more complex clusters, and was more clearly situated among the fluent aphasias, both clinically and anatomically. Conceivably, these cases represent a dissolution within the phonetic and phonemic systems respectively. Alternatively, there could be a continuum between them, leading from mumbling to simplified "Honolulu" utterances as in Pueser's case, to well-articulated complex jargon as in our case. Anatomically, the situation is no less uncertain. I have described a "mumbler" with a large left central lesion (Brown, 1979), yet there is a case—the only other of which I am aware—reported by Kähler and Pick (1879) of mumbling in association with bilateral temporal lesions, as were present in our case of complex jargon.

Zaimov (Chapter 8) provides a somewhat different approach to paraphasia and possible links to schizophrenia. Lecours, Osborn, Travis, and Rouillon (Chapter 2) also discuss structural similarities between schizophrenic and aphasic language. Such similarities are not wholly unexpected, in view of the fact that normal speech errors, and sleep speech and transitional speech, resemble certain types of aphasic utterances. The problem with most studies of schizophrenic speech is that they tend to focus on mild cases, or patients under treatment, where the regression does not penetrate too far into intrasentential material. Like the confabulating Korsakoff patient, the schizophrenic gives the impression of a thought disorder, or a paramnesia. When such cases are then juxtaposed to aphasic disorders such as Broca's aphasia, obviously the similarities are not very striking. However, careful investigations carried out years ago by Kleist and others— and for that matter my own experience with regressed psychotics—point to close relationships between schizophasic and aphasic jargon. These findings are, it seems to me, buttressed by recent work on hemispheric asymmetries in schizophrenia, evidence for limbic-temporal dysfunction, and preliminary PET studies which suggest temporal lobe dysfunction in schizophrenics (Farkas et al., 1980).

My own view is that aphasic and schizophrenic language are structurally identical, and that those who think differently ought to pay closer attention to aphasics such as that described by Green (Chapter 6), where semantic jargon is associated with tangentiality and derailments in thinking reminiscent of schizophrenic cognition (see also Brown, 1972). In this regard, consider the paranoia of the jargonaphasic, and the auditory hallucinations of the word deaf. We learn from such cases that a thought disorder—which is not restricted to a problem in object relations—is in reality an aphasia at a greater degree of depth.

The relation between "word salad" in schizophrenia and semantic jargon in aphasia, and the possible cognitive similarities between certain schizophrenic and jargon cases, suggests that jargonaphasia is more than a language disorder. In fact, in jargon there are changes in affect, behavior, and awareness that are a dramatic—and, in my view, an intrinsic—part of the aphasic disorder. Weinstein's view (Chapter 7) that these are adaptive in nature is reminiscent of Schilder's account of denial as an "organic repression." Alternatively, one can view the change in affect and awareness as reflecting a disruption at a level in the elaboration of these behaviors corresponding to the level of the jargon. In other words, together with language, affect and awareness also undergo a microgenetic development, and this development is attenuated, or prematurely displayed, in the same way that preliminary language is displayed in the jargon. This explains the specificity in a given patient of the anosognosia to the aphasia and not the hemiparetic deficit; it explains why a lack of awareness is specific to aphasia type, even to the type of error. An aphasic may be unaware of a semantic error but aware of a phonological error; that is, awareness is linked to the nature of the utterance at a given moment. This is also true of the affective tone. Presently we are studying a fluent left temporal aphasic with rapid "fatigue." He begins a conversation as an anomic with frustration, self-correction, and word search. Over a few minutes this passes to a stage where neologisms fill the anomic gaps and then to fluent neologistic jargon with euphoria, logorrhea, "hyperfluency," and lack of error awareness. The transformation from anomia to unintelligible jargon is rapid and dramatic in this case, but elements of this change occur moment to moment in most aphasics, as well as in recovery (see below). Such observations cannot be explained along psychodynamic lines, but ARE captured by an account in which these various behaviors are understood as level-specific manifestations of cognitive structure.

This approach supposes an inner bond between the linguistic and paralinguistic aspects of every language disorder. In jargon, the various types of impairments, paraphasia, anosognosia, comprehension deficit, do not point to separate components embraced by an extensive lesion. Rather, they are part of a common level which has been momentarily displayed in the pathological destructuration. The inner relationship between these aspects of language and behavior has been studied in a case of neologistic jargon by Perecman (1980). This patient was followed in our laboratory over a 2½-month period following a stroke. An analysis of his spontaneous speech at 1, 1½, and 2½ months post-onset showed a correspondence between a decrease in neology, a decrease in predilection units, a decrease in fluency, and an increase in hesitation and word search (Fig. 1.1). Moreover, in this evolution a change also occurred from euphoria to frustration with gradual improvement in comprehension.

Case studies of this type are of value in that one can determine the pattern of linguistic change in recovery. Such studies provide essential data for a linguistic typology of jargon, as well as the basis for a rational approach to therapy. Martin (Chapter 11) points out some of the difficulties in the

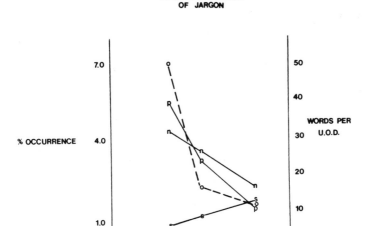

CHANGES IN CONTENT
OF JARGON

MONTHS POST ONSET

Figure 1.1. Change in jargon over time: o = quantity of speech (units of dialogue on right vertical axis); p = predilection units; n = neologisms; s = hesitations and self-corrections.

rehabilitation of the jargonaphasic. Clearly, a knowledge of the spontaneous recovery pattern in specific forms of aphasia, and the means in therapy to facilitate or enhance in some way the transition from one stage to another along NATURAL lines in the microstructure of language, are the first steps in the development of a scientific theory of treatment.

REFERENCES

Alajouanine, T., Sabouraud, O., & Ribaucourt, B. de. Le jargon des aphasiques. *Journal de Psychologique,* 1952, *45,* 158–180; 293–329.
Bastian, C. On the various forms of loss of speech in cerebral disease. *British and Foreign Medical–Chirurgical Review* 1869, *43,* 209–236; 470–492.
Brown, J. W. *Aphasia, apraxia and agnosia.* Springfield, Ill.: Charles C Thomas, 1972.
Brown, J. W. Language representation in the brain. In H. Steklis & M. Raleigh (Eds.), *Neurobiology of social communication in primates.* New York: Academic Press, 1979.
Farkas, T., Wolf, A., Cancro, R., Friedhoff, A., Christman, D., Fowler, J., van Gelder, P., Brown, J. W., & Brill, A. *The application of 18 F-2 deoxy-2 fluoro-D-glucose and positron emission tomography in the study of psychiatric conditions* (Abstract). Twelfth CINP Congress, Goteberg, June 1980.
Goldstein, K. *Language and language disturbances.* New York: Grune and Stratton, 1948.
Henschen, S. (Ed.). *Pathologie des Gehirns* (Vol. 6: *Über sensorische Aphasie*). Stockholm: Nordiska, 1920.

Kähler, O., & Pick, A. *Vierteljahresschrift für practische Heilkunde* 1879, *1*(6).

Kussmaul, A. Die Störungen der Sprache. In *Handb. der spez. Path.* Bd. XII 1876.

Mingazzini, G. In S. Henschen (Ed.), *Pathologie des Gehirns* (Vol. 6). Stockholm: Nordiska, 1920.

Mirallie, C. *L'Aphasie sensorielle*. Paris: Steinheil, 1896.

Niessl von Mayendorff, E. *Die aphasischen Symptome und ihre kortikale Lokalisation.* Leipzig: Barth, 1911.

Perecman, E. *Semantic jargon over time*. Paper presented at the meeting of the International Neuropsychology Society, San Francisco, February 1980.

Wernicke, C. *Der aphasische Symptomenkomplex*. Breslau: Cohn & Weigart, 1874.

Chapter 2

Jargons[1]

ANDRÉ ROCH LECOURS
ELLEN OSBORN
LISA TRAVIS
FRANÇOISE ROUILLON
GINETTE LAVALLÉE-HUYNH

Nowadays, when one labels a patient's language behavior as JARGON-APHASIA, one usually means that this patient is an adult with an acquired brain lesion, that his speech is produced without arthric distortions, that it is fluent, and—hence the label—that it comprises enough DEVIATIONS for the listener to be unable to make conventional sense out of it. This can occur, at one time or another, in the course of the clinical evolution of several forms of aphasia. In most cases, it occurs as a manifestation—although not a necessary one—of either conduction aphasia, Wernicke's aphasia proper, or transcortical sensory aphasia (Lecours & Rouillon, 1976).

In the present context, the term DEVIATION designates any segment of spoken or written language that does not entirely correspond to target, and we are concerned primarily with the deviations observed in the oral language of jargonaphasic subjects. The term PHONEMIC DEVIATIONS regroups phonemic approaches, phonemic paraphasias, phonemic *télescopages,* and formal verbal paraphasias (most of which are paradigmatic verbal substitutions between formally similar dictionary words). The term MORPHEMIC DEVIATIONS designates deviant segments that are made up of at least two bona fide

[1] This work was supported by grant MT-4210 of the Conseil de la Recherche Médicale du Canada.

JARGONAPHASIA

Copyright © 1981 by Academic Press, Inc.
All rights in any form reserved.
ISBN 0-12-137580-3

morphemes and uttered as if they were single words or locutions although they do not occur in the dictionary. The term NEOLOGISMS designates deviant segments that are uttered as if they were single words or locutions although they do not occur in the dictionary, and that can neither be positively identified as phonemic paraphasias, because the listener cannot recognize target words, if any, nor as morphemic deviations, because they are not made of bona fide morphemes. The term VERBAL DEVIATIONS regroups semantic verbal paraphasias (most of which are paradigmatic verbal substitutions between conceptually related words), predilection words (words which occur repeatedly as substitutes for any word of the same lexical category), filler words, syntagmic paraphasias (most of which are paradigmatic substitutions between segments comprising several words), and inadequate circumlocutions. The term PARAGRAMMATIC DEVIATION, finally, is used whenever a deviation, usually a verbal one, causes the clause, phrase, or sentence in which it occurs to transgress one rule or another of normative grammar. All of the above terms have been precisely defined elsewhere (Lecours & Lhermitte, 1979; Lecours & Rouillon, 1976; Lecours & Vanier-Clément, 1976), and all will be exemplified extensively in quotations given in this chapter. These quotations are excerpted from interviews with French-speaking jargonaphasic subjects; conventions followed in transcriptions of the originals and in English translations are summarized in Table 2.1.

This chapter aims at further precision in the typology of JARGONS, with special interest in linguistic typology. It deals with the behavior of eight patients with full-blown jargonaphasia. All were right-handed adults without previous speech or language disorders. In each case, the aphasia directly resulted from an acquired focal brain lesion. Our report bears on the phases of their disease when linguistic anomalies were at their zenith (this is what we mean by "full-blown"). We will first discuss the cases of three patients with forms of jargonaphasia that are well defined, relatively frequent, and generally recognized as clinical entities; these three cases will be considered as prototypes. We will then turn to five other cases, each of which displays one or more unusual features, including some that are usually thought of as indicative of psychiatric rather than neurological disorder. For each of these five cases, a comparison will be made with the prototypes, underlining both similarities and dissimilarities.

CASE 1

The first case is that of Mr. K., an Alsatian engineer who enjoyed good health until the winter of 1970 when, at the age of 76, his language behavior suddenly became grossly abnormal. This occurred to such an extent that his next of kin thought he had just been struck by sudden madness and

TABLE 2.1

Conventions for the Transcription of Jargonaphasic Samples and Their English Translations

	Transcription in French	English translation
Phonemic deviations		
Phonemic approaches	IPA; within oblique slashes	Target word translated; small capitals; oblique slashes[a]
Phonemic paraphasias	IPA; within oblique slashes	Target word translated; small capitals; oblique slashes
Phonemic télescopages	IPA; within oblique slashes	Target words translated; hyphen; small capitals; oblique slashes
Formal verbal paraphasias	IPA; within vertical slashes	Paraphasic word translated; small capitals; vertical slashes
Morphemic paraphasias	IPA; within square brackets; hyphen between morphemes	IPA; within square brakets; hyphen between morphemes
Neologisms	IPA; within square brackets	IPA; within square brackets
Verbal deviations		
Semantic verbal paraphasias	Bold italics	Paraphasic word translated; bold italics
Predilection words	Italics	Predilection word translated; italics
Filler words	Italics	Filler word translated; italics
Circumlocutions	Italics	Circumlocution translated; italics
Paragrammatic deviations	Italics; within parentheses	Deviation roughly translated; italics; within parentheses
Incomplete production, with or without attempted correction	Arrow pointing down	Arrow pointing down

[a] Transcribed as in the French original when target word is not obvious.

decided, somewhat hastily, to have him interned in a lunatic asylum. Mr. K. understood the meaning of this decision and resented it; indeed, he never forgot nor forgave although he later agreed that his verbal protests could hardly have helped. After a week or so at the asylum, he had the good fortune of being visited by a knowledgeable intern. As a consequence, he was transferred to the aphasia unit of *la Salpêtrière* where clinical and paraclinical manifestations of a left posterior sylvian softening were observed. The patient produced fluent jargon without arthric distortions; word-finding difficulties were obvious in both spontaneous speech and naming; attempts at repetition and, to a lesser degree, at reading aloud, led to production of numerous phonemic paraphasias; attempts at writing, either spontaneously or on dictation, led to production of numerous literal paragraphias; comprehension of oral and written language was nearly normal. Mr. K.'s linguistic behavior was therefore labeled as CONDUCTION APHASIA

The following is excerpted from the recording of a conversation with Mr. K. about 3 weeks after his stroke:

RACONTEZ-MOI VOTRE VIE AU COURS DE LA GRANDE GUERRE

J'étais encore au[1]|fɔ̃| ↓ sur le [1]|fɔ̃| ↓ J'étais mobilisé encore sur le ↓ sur le [2]/flɔ̃/ ↓ le [2]/fa/ ↓ le ↓ la ↓ dans ↓ dans la [3]bataille. . . . J'ai été [4]/a/ ↓ [4]/a/ ↓ [4]/ata/ ↓ [4]/a/ ↓ J'ai été ensuite [4]/ata/ ↓ détaché parce que je connaissais très bien l'Allemand. . . . J'ai été ensuite chargé, avec juste quelques autres, quand ↓ euh d'[5]/ɛ̃tɛg/ ↓ de ↓ d'[5]/ɛ̃tɛʀɔg/ ↓ euh de l'[5]/ɛ̃tɛga/ ↓ [5]/gɔ/ ↓ [5]/da/ ↓ de ↓ d'[5]/ɛ̃tɛʀogosi/ ↓ de ↓ —euh [6]je vais trop vite—d'[5]/ɛ̃tɛʀɔ/ ↓ Oui: d'[5]/ɛ̃tɛʀɔge/ des [7]/pe/ ↓ des [7]/pe ↓ des prisonniers allemands. . . . On recevait euh les papiers et tout ce qu'on avait trouvé sur les Allemands tués ou [8]/plitɔne/ et caetera. C'était même pas ↓ pas drôle quelquefois, parce que j'ai eu à faire ↓ j'[9]/a/ ↓ On recevait ça dans des [10]/sk/ ↓ quelquefois des [10]/saʃk/ ↓ [11]*sous* des grands sacs en jute qui [12]/saʀti/ ↓ qui [12]/saʀ/ ↓ qui [12]/saʀt/ ↓ qui sentaient le [13]/tavaʀ/ ↓ le [13]/tʀava/ ↓ les [13]/tɛ/ ↓ les [13]/t/ ↓ le [14]|kavjaʀ|. Non: l'[15]/epuvãtɛt/ [13]/tavaʀ/. Oui: le ↓ le [13]/ka/ ↓ le [13]/kava/ ↓ le [13]/kadʀav/ ↓ le cadavre humain, qui a une [16]/ɛskø/ [17]/fal/ ↓ une odeur [17]/fal/ ↓ euh [17]/fals/ ↓ . . . . (Je suis souvent nerveux) [18]/da/ ↓ depuis quatorze ↓ de ↓ la guerre de [19]/sa/ ↓ la guerre de [20]/kalis| ↓ de [21]|galis| ↓ de ↓ Oui: C'est la [22]/kɛ/ ↓ C'est la [22]/gɛ/ ↓ Depuis la guerre de [19]/kɔz/ ↓ de mille neuf cent [19]/kasɔz/ ↓ [19]/kœ/ ↓ [19]/ka/ ↓ [23]/katʀɔs/. . . . C'est une [24]|tɛʀ| ↓ une ↓ C'est une grande [25]/plɛʀ/ ↓ une grande place, qui s'appelait la Place des [26]/fizɔ/ ↓ des Philosophes.

Given the conventions defined in Table 2.1 the following is the best English translation we can provide:

TELL ME ABOUT YOUR LIFE DURING THE FIRST WORLD WAR

I was still at the [1]|BOTTOM| ↓ on the [1]|BOTTOM| ↓ I was sent again on the ↓ on the [2]/FRONT/ ↓ the [2]/FRONT/ ↓ the ↓ the ↓ in ↓ in the [3]battle. . . . I was [4]/DETACHED/ ↓ [4]/DETACHED/ ↓ [4]/DETACHED/ ↓ [4]/DETACHED/ ↓ I was then [4]/DETACHED/

↓ detached because I spoke German very well. . . . I was then charged, with a few others only, when ↓ hm to ⁵/QUESTION/ ↓ to ↓ to ⁵/QUESTION/ ↓ hm of the ⁵/QUESTIONING/ ↓ ⁵/QUESTIONING/ ↓ to ⁵/QUESTION/ ↓ to ↓ to ⁵/QUESTION/ ↓ —hm ⁶I am talking too fast—to ⁵/QUESTION/ ↓ Yes: to ⁵/QUESTION/ ⁷/PRISONERS/ ↓ ⁷/PRISONERS/ ↓ German prisoners. . . . We received hm the papers and everything that had been found on Germans who had been killed or ⁸/CAPTURED/ et cetera. It was not ↓ not even funny sometimes, because I had to do ↓ I ⁹/HAD/ ↓ We received this in ¹⁰/BAGS/ ↓ sometimes in ¹⁰/BAGS/ ↓ ¹¹*under* large gunny bags which ¹²/SMELLED/ ↓ which ¹²/SMELLED/ ↓ which ¹²/SMELLED/ ↓ which smelled of ¹³/CADAVER/ ↓ of ¹³/CADAVER/ ↓ of ¹³/CADAVER/ ↓ of ¹³/CADAVER/ ↓ of ¹⁴|CAVIAR|. No: the ¹⁵/DREADFUL/ ¹³/CADAVER/. Yes: the ↓ the ¹³/CADAVER/ ↓ the ¹³/CADAVER/ ↓ the ¹³/CADAVER/ ↓ the human cadaver, which has a ¹⁷/FOUL/ ¹⁶/ODOR/ ↓ a ¹⁷/FOUL/ odor ↓ hm ¹⁷/FOUL/ ↓ . . . . (I am often nervous) ¹⁸/SINCE/ ↓ since fourteen ↓ of ↓ the war of ¹⁹/FOURTEEN/ ↓ the war of ²⁰|CHALICE| ↓ of ²¹|GALICIA| ↓ of ↓ Yes: It is the ²²/WAR/ ↓ It is the ²²/WAR/ ↓ Since the war of ¹⁹/FOURTEEN/ ↓ of nineteen hundred and ¹⁹/FOURTEEN/ ↓ ¹⁹/FOURTEEN/ ↓ ¹⁹/FOURTEEN/ ↓ ¹⁹/FOURTEEN/ ↓ ²³/FOURTEEN-ATROCIOUS/. . . . . It is a ²⁴|LAND| ↓ a ↓ It is a large ²⁵/SQUARE-LAND/ ↓ a large square, which was called the Square of the ²⁶/PHILOSOPHERS/ ↓ of the Philosophers.

As is obvious from this quotation, Mr. K.'s conversational behavior was indeed very characteristic of the jargon sometimes observed during the earlier phases of severe conduction aphasia. Besides a major perturbation in the evocation of lexical words, evidenced by hesitations, repetitions of articles and prepositions, and aborted sentences, it comprised an important and nearly exclusive production of phonemic deviations—that is, of phonemic approaches (4,5,7,9,10,12,13,18,19,22,26), of phonemic paraphasias (2,5,8,10,12,13,15,16,17,19)[2], of phonemic *télescopages* [/katɔRz/ + /atrɔs/ → /katRɔs/ in (23); /plas/ + /tɛR/ → /plɛR/ in (25)], and of formal verbal paraphasias (1,14,20,21,24).[3] The difficulty in word finding and the production of phonemic deviations typically affected the same targets, and easy replacement of an involved word by a normally uttered synonym (3), a phenomenon that is not uncommon in such cases, was sometimes observed. The speaker's frequent attempts at correction, as well as other comments (6), showed how conscious he was of the anomalous nature of his discouse; this is the rule in such cases (absence of anosognosia).

It should be noted that, from an exclusively descriptive point of view, the jargon of severe conduction aphasia occasionally comprises stretches that are somewhat reminiscent of the FORMAL GLOSSOMANIA (Lecours & Vanier-Clément, 1976) occurring, in its full-blown form, in the discourse of certain schizophasic subjects. In this respect, Mr. K.'s {*quatorze–*|

---

[2] In (16), one would have had to consider the deviation as a neologism had not the speaker himself correctly uttered the target word in the immediate context.

[3] Verbal deviations such as (11) were not more frequent in this sample than in the conversational speech of nonaphasic ordinary speakers.

kalis|–|galis|–/katrɔs/}   (20,21,23)   and   {|tɛʀ|–/plɛʀ/–*place*}   (24,25)   are
good examples.

Notes

1. Conduction aphasia, including eventually the typical jargon, is sometimes observed immediately at the onset of disease, presumably as the
result of supramarginal lesions, and sometimes it gradually emerges from
the more complex clinical picture of Wernicke's aphasia proper. The latter
perhaps occurred in the case of Mr. K.

2. A computer programmed to simulate the production of phonemic
paraphasias will also produce, without any instructions to do so, a certain
proportion of outputs that are assimilable to formal verbal paraphasias
(Lecours, Deloche, & Lhermitte 1973). One can therefore suggest that in
conduction aphasia the production of both phonemic paraphasias and formal
verbal paraphasias could result from a single dysfunction, possibly that of
a neuronal net dealing essentially with phonemic selection.

3. When the extent of the speech disorder warrants the label JARGON,
some refer to conduction aphasia as PHONEMIC JARGON, therefore avoiding
the issue of physiopathological interpretation, inherent to the term CONDUC-
TION APHASIA since 1874 (Wernicke, 1874), and making explicit mention of
a fundamental linguistic aspect of the disorder. Luigi Vignolo (personal
communication), for instance, talked of phonemic jargon in the case of a
patient whose very fluent discourse could only be perceived as almost
entirely neologistic although his comprehension of oral and written language
was nearly normal; for some reason, Théophile Alajouanine (1968) reserves
the term JARGONAPHASIA for this particular clinical picture.

CASE 2

The second case is that of Mr. Z., a rich Gaulist and industrialist who
lived in the sixteenth ward of Paris, unaware that his florid complexion was
related to Vasquez's disease, rather than *Château-Lafite* input. He was the
victim of a left posterior sylvian softening at the age of 55, during the fall
of 1968 (which was a difficult period for Gaulists, anyway). Apart from a
right visual field defect and some degree of "intellectual deterioration"
(according to psychometrics), this left Mr. Z. with fluent euarthric jargon.
He was seen at *la Salpêtrière* a few weeks later. His jargon persisted; his
written output was very much reduced and dysorthographic; repetition
abilities were normal or nearly so; comprehension of both oral and written
language was severely impaired. Mr. Z.'s linguistic behavior was therefore
given the label of WERNICKE'S APHASIA WITH PRESERVATION OF REPETITION;
some might have talked of TRANSCORTICAL SENSORY APHASIA, or else of ISO-

LATED SPEECH AREA, although these terms are anatomically compromising and do not necessarily imply preservation of fluency.

The following is excerpted from a recording of a conversation with Mr. Z. made a few weeks after the onset of his aphasia:

QUEL EST VOTRE MÉTIER?

Mon métier? Bien, j'ai un métier qui est [1]*à peu près identique à celui des autres* ↓ [1]*à des* ↓ Seulement, [2]*il est* [3]/pRɔ/ ↓ [2]*il est* [4]*professeur.* Enfin! C'est ↓ C'est dur ↓ C'est dur pour moi. Il est difficile parce que euh je suis ↓ Je suis [5]*chargé de* ↓ —Attendez!—Je suis [4]*professeur.* Je suis ↓ Je suis [4]*professeur.* Comment pourrais-je dire? Je fais [6]*rien du tout.* Je suis [5]*chargé de faire mettre de la* ↓ *de la terre cuite en état* euh *pour la* /pRɔp/ ↓ *la plupart des gens* ↓ *pour la plupart des gens.* C'est ça. C'est-à-dire que j'essaie de [5]*leur faire mettre de la terre cuite qui* ↓ *qui soit en état,* quoi. Alors, j'ai deux usines dans le Nord ↓ euh dans le ↓ qui ↓ qui sont là, [7]*à côté de Paris,* et puis une autre, qui est [8]*à peu près* **autour** *de Paris* également, qui est neuve et qui est ↓ qui est susceptible de faire quelque chose de très bien. Et puis alors, en dehors de ça, j'ai deux [9]*usines* ↓ j'ai deux dépôts importants, qui sont des [10]*dépôts* où on [11]*fait* de la ↓ euh où on [11]*fait* de ↓ Je sais pas quoi: de ↓ [12]*toutes sortes de choses.* Seulement, si vous me [13]/di/ ↓ demandez ça pour me [13]/dœ/ ↓ me [14]*demander* ça, ça, c'est ↓ C'est assez compliqué, hein. Ca devient ↓ Ca devient assez compliqué de ↓ de ↓ de [15]*tirer* ça. . . . J'arrive à faire ↓ euh à faire euh que le ↓ que le total [16]*arrive à faire* un certain bien ↓ —Ah là là! là là!—un certain bien et qu'on [16]*arrive à arriver* à ↓ à avoir des ↓ des marchandises.

WHAT IS YOUR TRADE?

My trade? Well, I have a trade that is [1]*nearly identical to that of others* ↓ [1]*to that* ↓ However,[2]*he is* a [3]/PROFESSOR/ ↓ [2]*he is* a [4]*professor.* Well! It is ↓ It is hard ↓ It is hard for me. It is difficult because hm I am ↓ I am [5]*in charge of* ↓ —Wait!—I am a [4]*professor.* I am ↓ I am a [4]*professor.* How can I put it? I do [6]*nothing at all.* I am [5]*in charge of seeing to it that* ↓ *that baked clay is being conditioned for* /MOST/ ↓ *most people* ↓ *for most people.* This is it. The fact is that I try to [5]*see to it that baked clay is being* ↓ *being conditioned for them.* Well. Thus, I have two factories in the North ↓ hm in the ↓ which ↓ which are there, [7]*beside Paris,* and then another, which is also [8]*almost* **around** *Paris.* And then, also, beside that, I have two [9]*factories* ↓ I have two important warehouses, which are [10]*warehouses* where we [11]*manufacture* some ↓ hm where we [11]*manufacture* some ↓ I don't know what: some ↓ [12]*all sorts of things.* However, if you [13]/ASK/ me ↓ ask me that to [13]/ASK/ me ↓ [14]*ask* me that, well, that is ↓ that is quite complicated, eh. It becomes ↓ It becomes quite complicated to ↓ to [15]*draw* that. . . . I manage to do ↓ hm to do hm that the ↓ that the total [16]*manages to do* something good ↓ —Oh dear me! dear me!—something good and that we [16]*manage to manage* to ↓ to have some ↓ some merchandise.

As obvious from this quotation, Mr. Z.'s conversational behavior was characteristic of the jargon sometimes observed in so-called transcortical sensory aphasia. Besides a major difficulty in the evocation of lexical words, evidenced mostly by the abundance of aborted syntagms, it comprised an important and nearly exclusive production of verbal deviations, that is of semantic verbal paraphasias (2,4,8,9,10,11,14,15), of empty circumlocutions (1,5,7,8,16), and of filler expressions (6,12). Many of the verbal paraphasias were paradigmatic word substitutions, as in (4) where Mr. Z. describes himself as a *professeur* rather than a *président-directeur-général;* others were contextual verbal assimilations, usually anterograde as in (9) where "factory" is reiterated and temporarily replaces "warehouse." Character-istically, paragrammatism was absent from the interview, and phonemic paraphasias, phonemic *télescopages,* and neologisms did not occur. A few phonemic approaches were observed (3,5,13), most of them single and corresponding to hesitations related to paraphasic or circumlocutory ut-terances; in any event, approaches were not more numerous than in certain samples from nonaphasic ordinary speakers.

It should be noted that, from an exclusively descriptive point of view, the jargon sometimes observed in so-called transcortical sensory aphasia occasionally comprises stretches that are quite reminiscent of the SEMANTIC GLOSSOMANIA (Lecours & Vanier-Clément, 1976) occurring, in its full-blown form, in the discourse of certain schizophasic subjects. Consider, for in-stance, the use of "jacket" (*veston*), "mantle" (*manteau*), and "peddlar" (*colporteur:* literally, 'collar bearer') in the following quotation from Mr. Z.'s interview:[4]

QUE PENSEZ-VOUS DE LA DERNIÈRE ÉLECTION PRÉSIDENTIELLE AUX ÉTATS-UNIS?

On s'est surtout occupé de la partie intérieure et on s'est aperçu que, partout ailleurs, ils ont mis des petits *colporteurs* et ils ont pu, avec un *veston* . . . avec un *manteau colporté.* . . .

WHAT DO YOU THINK OF THE LAST PRESIDENTIAL ELECTION IN THE UNITED STATES?

Above all, we took care of the internal part and we realized that, everywhere else, they put some little *peddlars* and they were capable, with a *jacket* . . . with a *peddled mantle.* . . .

Notes

1. Considered separately, the manifestations of word-finding difficul-ties in cases such as Mr. Z's are clinically identical to those observed in severe amnestic aphasia.

2. With the possible exception of partial awareness of word-finding

---

[4] Inserted, aborted, and repetitive segments not included in this quotation.

difficulties, patients such as Mr. Z. seem to be very much anosognosic of their aphasia.

3. Although there are cases, such as Mr. Z.'s, in which this form of aphasia occurs without gross quantitative reduction, qualitative reduction is usually obvious (see, for instance, the paraphasic or circumlocutory recurrence of the same lexical words in the first quotation from Mr. Z.'s interview). This might be the reason why Eberhard Bay (1964) chose to call this condition *Einfallsleere*, that is to say, "lack of ideas."

4. Frequent failures in attempts at guessing plausible targets behind the patients' deviant utterances often leave the listener of this type of jargon with an impression of ideational incoherence (see, for instance, the second quotation from Mr. Z's interview). This might be the reason why Henri Hécaen (1972) called this condition *désorganisation attentionnelle* ("attentional disorganization"). Now, perhaps Hécaen has a point there, but it should be remembered, on the other hand, that if there are indeed intended segments that differ from actual utterances, as is the case in positively identified semantic paraphasias, the listener's impression might result from the limits of his own decoding abilities rather than the patient's mode of ideation.

CASE 3

The third case is that of Ms. D., a Parisian lady born in the Sarthes. Ms. D. had long been the underpaid and very efficient secretary of three medical doctors when, in April 1969, at the age of 58, she fell off her motorbike and hit her head on the sidewalk. She was found semicomatose, with a right hemiparesis and Babinski sign, and the three doctors were deeply annoyed. Surgical removal of a left intratemporal hematoma was performed a few hours later. Ms. D. remained comatose for nearly 2 weeks thereafter. When she came to, the right hemiparesis had cleared although the Babinski sign was still present, visual fields were normal, and her conversational behavior was disconcerting. She was sent to the aphasia unit of *la Salpêtrière* where the following were observed: euarthric logorrheic jargon; severely impaired repetition and reading, with paraphasic and neologistic productions; reduced and paragraphic written expression; and impaired comprehension of spoken and written language. Ms. D's condition was therefore considered to be WERNICKE'S APHASIA PROPER.

The following is excerpted from the recording of a conversation with Ms. D. a little less than a month after her head trauma and surgery:

EST-CE QUE VOUS AVEZ DES ENFANTS?

Des enfants où, ¹*Mademoiselle*? . . . Oui, j'ai encore une autre ²*femme* qui est restée depuis le ↓ la ³[bœtʀe] de l'enfant de ⁴(*ma fils*). ⁵*Il* ⁶/a/ ↓ Elle avait dix ans quand [7](*mon* |fɛs|) est mort. Et alors, elle est là maintenant. Elle va sur [8]/syz/ ans. Elle va toujours à l'école puisqu'elle se présente les ↓ Je l'avais envoyée à l'école puisque, moi, je travaillais bien dans les [9][syz] ↓ euh à la [10][faʀmid] de ↓ de ↓ de [9][syz]—[11]n'est-ce pas?—de deux [12][ɛtmiʀ]. Et alors, je ↓ Cette [13]/mwazela/, [14]*Ginette* elle s'appelle, elle ↓ elle [15][abil]. Tous les jours, elle venait à Paris pour euh [16][pale] dans les [17][kɔsig], parce qu'elle prenait pour ↓ aussi pour entrer le ↓ euh le [18]*palais*, le [18]*palais* normal bien entendu, euh le [19][namytyʀ], la [20][tɔktœʀ] et l'[21][ãbœtjɛʀ], pour qu'elle sache [22](*tous ces* ↓ *ces choses* ↓) pour qu'elle [23](*sache à*) bien s'[24][ɛskʀyme] ↓ *à* bien ↓ bien s'[25]/ɛ̃/ ↓ s'[26][ɛ̃kyme]. Et c'est là que je suis [27]*morte*, là, cette année. Elle était ↓ Elle allait toujours à l'école. . . . Ma fille vient deux fois (par semaine) chez moi . . . [28]*Mademoiselle* ↓ . . . alors [28]*celle-là* vient le [29]/ʒødim/, puisqu'elle ne va pas en [30]/klis/, et elle vient le [31]/ʒydi/ ↓ le dimanche, puisque nous faisons bonne [32]*filleule* [33]**ici.**

DO YOU HAVE CHILDREN?[5]

Children where, [1]*Miss* [the interviewer was male]? . . . Yes, I have still another [2]*woman* who has remained since the-M ↓ the-F [3][bœtʀe] of the child of [4](*my*-F *son*-M). [5]*He* [6]/WAS/ ↓ She was ten years old when [7](*my*-M |BUTTOCK|-F) died. And then, she is there now. She will soon be [8]/SIXTEEN/ years old. She is still going to school since she presents herself the ↓ I had sent her to school since I myself was indeed working in the [9][syz] ↓ hm at the [10][faʀmid] of ↓ of ↓ of [9][syz]—[11]is it not?—of two [12][ɛtmiʀ]. And then, I ↓ This [13]/YOUNG LADY/, [14]*Ginette* is her name, she ↓ she [15][abil]. Each day, she came to Paris in order to hm [16][pale] in the [17][kɔsig], because she was taking in order to ↓ also in order to enter, the ↓ hm the [18]*palace,* the normal [18]*palace* of course, hm the [19][namytyʀ], the [20][tɔktœʀ] and the [21][ãbœtjɛʀ], in order that she knows [22](*all*-M *these* ↓ *these things* ↓) in order that she [23](*knows at*) [24][ɛ̃skʀyme] herself correctly ↓ *at* ↓ *at* [25]/ɛ̃/ ↓ [26][ɛ̃kyme] herself correctly. And this is when I [27]*died,* then, this year. She was ↓ She still went to school. . . . My daughter comes twice (a week) at my home. . . . [28]*Miss* ↓ . . . thus [28]*this one*-F comes on [29]/THURSDAYS-SUNDAYS/, since she does not go to [30]/SCHOOL/, and she comes on [31]/THURSDAYS/ ↓ on Sundays, since we make a good [32]*god-daughter* [33]*here.*

As obvious from this quotation, Ms. D.'s conversational behavior was characteristic of the jargon that is quite often observed in Wernicke's aphasia proper. Arthric realization itself was flawless. Speech flow sounded normal, or even conveyed an impression of logorrhea. Although present and rather severe, the manifestations of word-finding difficulties were less immediately apparent than in the two preceding cases. This no doubt resulted from a lesser incidence of aborted sentences, phonemic approaches, and attempted corrections, on the one hand, and, on the other, from a fluent neologistic production which, although it almost exclusively replaced lexical components of discourse (mostly nouns and attributes), was not readily perceived by the listener as the indicator of a perturbation in lexical evo-

---

[5] In the translation, -M indicates French masculine, -F indicates French feminine.

cation. Besides neologisms (3,9,10,12,15,16,17,19,20,21,24,26), Ms. D.'s jargon comprised both phonemic and verbal deviations (Alajouanine, Lhermitte, Ledoux, Renaud, & Vignolo, 1964). Most of the former were phonemic paraphasias (8,13,30,31), that is, there were relatively few recognizable phonemic *télescopages* (29) and formal verbal paraphasias (7), and phonemic approaches (6,25) were not more frequent than in the discourse of certain nonaphasic ordinary speakers. The latter and the rarity of attempted corrections were among manifestations of the patient's anosognosia. Most of the verbal deviations were obvious or probable semantic verbal paraphasias, either paradigmatic substitutions (1,2,14,27,28,33) or wrong choices that were at least partially determined by a contextual factor (5,18,23,32): The former is well illustrated in (2) and (28), where 'daughter' became "woman," then "Miss" and "this one," and in (27), where 'I fell sick' became "I died"; and the latter is well illustrated in (5), where 'she' became "he" in the context of "my son," and in (32), where 'to make a good meal' (*faire bonne chère*) became "to make a good god-daughter" (*faire bonne filleule* /fijœl/) in the context of "daughter" (*fille* /fij/). Some of the verbal deviations led to so-called paragrammatism (4,22,23). There were no circumlocutions of the type observed in the preceding case, and filler words were infrequent (there was no apparent qualitative reduction).

A few compounded deviations could be recognized as such in Ms. D.'s discourse. In (7), for instance, the target word, 'husband,' was retargeted as 'son' (*fils* /fis/) in the context of prepositioned "son," a semantic deviation, and /fis/ was realized as /fɛs/, an obvious phonemic deviation although /fɛs/ happens to be a French word (*fesse* 'buttock'); furthermore, since the deviation followed a masculine possessive, selected no doubt in relation to 'husband' and/or 'son,' the deviation takes a superficial appearance of paragrammatism (French buttocks being feminine). Likewise, (31) is a compounded deviation in which 'Sunday' (*dimanche* /dimãʃ/) was semantically retargeted as 'Thursday' (*jeudi* /ʒødi/) in the context of prepositioned 'Thursday,' with wrongly selected /ʒødi/ phonemically realized as /ʒydi/; the existence of a syllable common to the two words in semantic competition is likely to have played a role in the genesis of this deviation.

Notes

1. Although no variety of full-blown aphasic jargon is really common, the one observed in Wernicke's aphasia proper is the commonest and, in several ways, the most spectacular. Some refer to it as NEOLOGISTIC JARGON APHASIA (Buckingham & Kertesz, 1976).

2. Although anosognosia belongs with the jargon of Wernicke's aphasia proper, and lasts as long as the label jargon itself remains appropriate, this type of jargon typically comprises numerous hesitations (3,10,9,15,16,19, 25,26,31) and inserted comments (11,18) which occur in direct relation with the production of deviant segments and therefore suggest that something

within the speaker's dysfunctioning neuronal nets is somehow aware of dysfunction (Lecours, Travis, & Nespoulous, 1981).

3. The jargon of patients with Wernicke's aphasia proper is often qualified as logorrhea. Word counts have convinced us that this should not be equated with increase in number of words uttered per time unit (the contrary is true in certain cases) (Lecours & Lhermitte, 1979). The main characteristic of logorrhea is rather that the speaker tends to keep talking for long periods in response to minimal stimulation (or no stimulation at all). As far as we know, increased rapidity of the speech flow is a characteristic of mania and hypomania rather than jargonaphasia, whatever the type (Lecours & Lhermitte, 1979).

4. The neologisms occurring in the discourse of patients with Wernicke's aphasia proper usually replace nouns (3,9,10,12,17,19,20,21), less frequently attributes and verbs; they often end on a suffix of the speaker's tongue (3,16,19,20,21,24,26); they sometimes borrow phonemic and perhaps semantic materials from immediate context (9,16) (Buckingham & Kertesz, 1976; Lecours & Rouillon, 1976). The last of these characteristics also holds true for other types of deviant segments in jargonaphasia, and all three are shared by the neologisms observed in the discourse of certain schizophasic speakers (Lecours & Vanier-Clément, 1976).

5. As a rule, paragrammatic (dyssyntactic) deviations are relatively few in the jargon of patients with Wernicke's aphasia proper, whose discourse indeed testifies to preservation of syntax. On the whole, such deviations represent a surface phenomenon: Verbal deviations bearing on grammatical words or groups of words, which account for a large majority of paragrammatic deviations, are of the same nature as those bearing on lexical words or groups of words, that is, they correspond to a disorder in selection, not to one in contextual integration (Jakobson, 1964). Henry Head's (1926) label for this condition, SYNTACTICAL APHASIA, is therefore utterly misleading as it can be taken to mean that syntax is selectively impaired in Wernicke's aphasia proper.

Cases 4–8 were all patients whose language behavior was considered to be Wernicke's aphasia proper because they all had left brain lesions resulting in fluent euarthric jargon, impaired repetition, and impaired comprehension (Geschwind, 1971). In each case, however, one or several aspects of the jargon was unusual enough to raise the possibility of a somewhat different type of jargon.

CASE 4

The fourth case is that of Mr. A., a general in the French army. He was 57 years of age when his career was brutally interrupted by the hazards of his peace time duties. This occurred in April 1967 and took the form of a blow on the head, inflicted by the rotor of his helicopter. This resulted in a left temporo-occipital fracture and contusion which necessitated surgery. He remained comatose for 3 weeks thereafter. When he recovered, he proved to have a complex neurological disorder comprising jargonaphasia and ideational apraxia (the latter was short lasting). Electroencephalograms showed evidence of bilateral brain dysfunction, maximal over the left temporal region. The general was transferred to the aphasia unit of *la Salpêtrière* about 2 months after his accident. Besides florid euarthric logorrheic jargon with anosognosia, his condition then comprised impaired naming, repetition, and reading aloud, jargonagraphia, and impaired comprehension of oral and written language. He was thus considered to have WERNICKE'S APHASIA PROPER.

The following is excerpted from the recording of a conversation with Gen. A. a few days after he was admitted at *la Salpêtrière:*

LE PATIENT RACONTE SA VIE MILITAIRE EN EUROPE ET EN AFRIQUE DU NORD

C'est pas le ↓ le ¹[fɔRs-jal] habituel—²si vous voulez—qui est lent. Il est lent ↓ Il est lent parce qu'il est ↓ il est lent pour tout le monde. . . . Je suis d'infanterie ↓ de ↓ Je ne suis pas des ↓ des ↓ des ³[buRs-jɛl] personnels. . . . Je les ai vus dans le même cas que moi maintenant. C'est ↓ C'est ↓ C'est ⁴/idãtɛk/ des ↓ des ⁵/f/ ↓ des ⁶[fRãs-jɛl], de toute façon. C'est très ⁶[fRãs-jɛl] des Français, ça. C'est ↓ C'est ↓ C'est évident. Tout le monde le ↓ . . . .J'ai été, moi, chez les ⁷[fɔRs-jɛR] ⁸/aliʒaRjɛn/, mais je n'ai pas vécu avec eux longuement. . . . Les artilleurs ont un ⁹*changement* ¹⁰/de/ ↓ différent des ↓ des ¹¹/al/ ↓ ¹²*artilleurs*. Le ¹³/flãbyʒ/ est complètement ¹⁴*modifiant*. . . . Ca n'intéresse personne, les ↓ les ↓ les ¹⁵[blãʃ-aʒ] avec les gens du Sud. Oui—si vous voulez—on y va pour le plaisir ¹⁶(à) tout le monde mais eux, ¹⁷[mɔRs-jal-mã] ↓ personnellement, ne ¹⁸*jouent* pas beaucoup. . . . Les artilleurs ¹⁹[ital-aR], qui sont ↓ qui ont de ↓ . . . Dès que j'aurai des ²⁰[pRɔmn-aʒ], je ↓ je m'y ²¹(*remettra*). . . . Au fond, ce que je ²²*donne* ne donne pas les ↓ les ↓ les ↓ les ²³[bRãf] ↓ les ↓ les ↓ les ²⁴[pRɔm-yR] que j'ai promus. Je ↓ Euh alors, maintenant, on fait ce qu'on peut. On me donne des ↓ des ²⁵[fɔRm-œtyR], mais ↓ mais c'est ↓ c'est pas des ²⁵[fɔRm-œtyR] brillantes. . . . Mon ²⁶[sɔld-aʒ]—²⁷si vous voulez—s'emploie différemment. . . . On remballait à l'arrière. C'était un ²⁸[bal-aʒ] assez dur.

THE PATIENT TELLS ABOUT HIS MILITARY LIFE IN EUROPE AND NORTH AFRICA

It is not the ↓ the usual ¹[fɔRs-jal]—²if you will—which is slow. It is slow ↓ It is slow because it is ↓ it is slow for everybody. . . . I belong to the infantry ↓ to ↓ I do not belong to the ↓ to the ↓ to the personal ³[buRs-jɛl]. I saw them in the same situation as myself now. It is ↓ It is ↓ It is ⁴/IDENTICAL/ of the ↓ of the ⁵/f/ ↓ of the ⁶[fRãs-jɛl], anyway. It is very ⁶[fRãs-jɛl] of the French. It is ↓ It is ↓ It is obvious. Everybody ↓ I went myself with the [8]/ALGERIAN/ [7][fɔʀs-jɛʀ], but I did not live with them very long. . . . The gunners have a [9]*change* that is [10]/DIFFERENT/ ↓ different from the ↓ of the [11]/GUNNERS-GERMANS/ ↓ [12]*gunners*. The [13]/FIRE/ is completely [14]*modifying*. . . . It does not interest anybody, the ↓ the ↓ the [15][blāʃ-aʒ] with the people from the South. Yes— if you will—we go for the pleasure [16](*at*) everybody but themselves, [17][mɔʀs-jal-mā] ↓ personally, do not [18]*play* a lot. . . . The [19][ital-aʀ] gunners, who are ↓ who have some ↓ . . . . As soon as I have some [20][pʀɔmn-aʒ], I ↓ I will [21](*does*) it again. . . . As a matter of fact, what I [22]*give* does not give the ↓ the ↓ the ↓ the [23][bʀāf] ↓ the ↓ the ↓ the [24][pʀɔm-yʀ] whom I promoted. I ↓ Hm then, now, they do what they can. They give me some ↓ some [25][fɔʀmœ-tyʀ] but these are ↓ these are not brilliant [25]]fɔʀmœ-tyʀ]. . . . My [26][sɔld-aʒ]—[27]if you will—is employing itself differently. . . . We were packing behind the lines. It was a rather tough [28][bal-aʒ].

This quotation shows that Gen. A.'s jargon was similar to Ms. D.'s (Case 3) in all but one respect. As in the case of Ms. D., there was production of both phonemic and verbal deviations; specifically,[6] most of the former were phonemic approaches (5,10,11) and paraphasias (4,8,13), and most of the latter were semantic verbal paraphasias (9,12,14,18,22), a few of which led to paragrammatism (16,21). And, as in the case of Ms. D., hesitations of all types (1,3,4,5,6,11,12,15,21,23,24,25) and inserted comments (2,27) often occurred—although anosognosia was otherwise manifest—in direct relation to the production of deviant utterances (and word-finding difficulties).

Given the definitions formulated in the introduction of this chapter, the one difference was that Gen. A. produced morphemic deviations (1,3,6, 7,15,17,19,20,24,25,26,28) rather than the commoner form of neologism (23). More precisely, he produced DERIVATED MORPHEMIC PARAPHASIAS (Lecours & Lhermitte, 1972; Lecours & Vanier-Clément, 1976), which were nearly always made of a single lexical morpheme followed by a single suffix. It is noteworthy, in view of the patient's profession, that the lexical components of his morphemic deviations often belonged to the military paradigm (1,6,7,19,24,25,26,28). In certain cases, the lexical component was borrowed from the immediate context, therefore realizing a deviation of the assimilation type, for example, (6) [fʀās-jɛl] in the context of postpositioned /fʀās-ɛ/ (*Français* 'French'), (24) [pʀɔm-yʀ] in the context of postpositioned /pʀɔm-y/ (*promu* 'promoted'), and (28) [bal-aʒ] in the context of prepositioned /ʀā-bal-ɛ/ (*remballait* 'were packing'). There were also cases in which it was possible to ascertain that choice of the lexical component was determined by a paradigmatic factor, as in certain semantic verbal paraphasias, for instance in (20) [pʀɔmn-aʒ], where the obvious target is 'leisure' (*loisir*)

[6] A compounded deviation occurs in the case of (4): The obvious target word, 'typical' (*typique*), is retargetted as 'identical' (*identique*), a semantically and formally related word, and /idātik/ is phonemically realized as /idātɛk/.

and the lexical component [pRɔmn], as in /pRɔmn-ad/ (*promenade* 'walk').
Although not under this name, the frequent occurrence of morphemic
deviations has long been observed in the discourse of certain schizophasic
subjects (Bleuler, 1966). Together with Marie Vanier, we have reported on
such a case elsewhere (Lecours & Vanier-Clément, 1976). General D., on
the other hand, is the only aphasic we have ever seen whose jargon comprised a copious production of morphemic deviations; René Tissot, from
Geneva, has also observed a similar case (Tissot, personal communication).
It is not at all evident that this deserves a new label, such as "morphemic
jargon," which might be misleading anyway, but it is certainly reasonable
to suggest that Gen. D.'s aphasia did not disrupt his remarkable derivational
abilities. Indeed, he applied derivational laws in morphemic deviations just
as impeccably as jargonaphasics apply phonological laws in phonemic deviations and neologistic productions.

CASE 5

The fifth case is that of Ms. G., a Parisian *concierge* and therefore a
potential police indicator. Ms. G. had long been aware of her mitral disease
and tachyerythmia when she had a stroke, in November 1968, at the age
of 66. She was hospitalized at *la Salpêtrière* where a major neurological
disorder was observed, comprising right hemianopia, apraxia, and aphasia.
The latter included euarthric logorrheic jargon, impaired naming, repetition,
and reading aloud, severely reduced written expression, severely impaired
oral comprehension, and moderately impaired written comprehension. She
was thus considered to have WERNICKE'S APHASIA PROPER (although, as shall
be seen, an important element was missing).

The following is excerpted from the recording of a conversation with
Ms. G. 2 months after her stroke, when she was still very much excited
and logorrheic:

DEPUIS QUAND ÊTES-VOUS MALADE?

Je ↓ J'entends très ¹/mā/ ce que l'on dit ²*à la fille.* Il y a des fois que j'³/ātʀāp/.
. . . . Il y a certains mots, malgré tout, que je comprends un peu. Mais je ne
peux pas parler, vous voyez. Sitôt que je cause un peu, comme ça, de ⁴*figure*,
je peux ⁵*toute seule.* Mais ⁶/p/ ↓ C'est tout. Ça s'arrête là. Je peux ⁷*légèrement*
parler. . . . Mais alors, je peux ⁸|pije|, malgré tout, un tout petit peu. Mais
alors, à cause de cela, je ⁹(*suis arrêtée cela*). Vous voyez. Je ne peux pas.
Je ne ¹⁰/p/ ↓ Aucune ¹¹/paʀlɔʀ/. Par exemple, je ne peux ¹²(*écrire personne*).
Vous ne savez pas! Vous auriez un crayon. ¹³*Je vous verrais* ↓ Vous verriez.
Je ne ¹⁴(*le*) sais absolument ¹⁵/ʀ// ↓ rien ¹⁶(*écrit dessus*). C'est-à-dire que si :
je comprends tout ce qu'¹⁷*il* écrit—vous voyez—mais tout cela me ¹⁸[sut]
complètement la ¹⁹[ʀépʀimi]. . . . Ça m'est venu une nuit, comme ça. Et puis

c'est venu tout seul. Je ↓ Je ↓ Vous savez: par un malaise. J'²⁰*étais* chez le ↓
le ²¹*docteur qui soigne les parents.* Je me suis ²²(*soignée dedans*), et il m'a
été impossible de ²³(*ne plus rien entendre personne*)—vous voyez—de causer,
de ²⁴*ne rien comprendre de ce que* le ²⁵*curé* a dit. . . . Je ne peux rien dire
mais je peux parler ↓ mais je me rappelle aucune parole. Voilà, alors, c'est
ça. C'est ça qui est ²⁶*incompréhensif:* une drôle, drôle de ²⁷*voix* dans ²⁸[tulu].
Y a pas à ²⁹|dʀol|, c'est drôle. . . . Et c'est pas ³⁰/eɡʀeabl/, je vous as-
sure. . . . Vous comprenez ce que je ³¹*comprends,* quand même, un peu?
. . . Je ne peux plus écrire ³²*les gens qu'ils écrivent.* . . . Faut pas ↓ Faut pas
me demander des ↓ beaucoup, beaucoup, beaucoup, et, forcément, des
réflexions. . . . Ah si! Je peux penser. Quand même! . . . puisque tout le
monde essaie maintenant ³³(*à*) être ³⁴*prêtre* de ↓ ³⁵/di/ ↓ euh comme bon ³⁶*curé,*
comme tout partout dans les ↓ Vous voyez! C'est ↓ C'est ↓ C'est la parole
en question, que je suis toujours en train de dire, qui m'énerve assez, que
cette ³⁷*réponse,* que la ↓ "Curé"! ³⁸/tyʀe/ : c'est cette ³⁹*observation!* ⁴⁰(*Est*)
toujours ↓ Pourquoi une ³⁷*réponse* comme ça? Vous voulez me dire? Bon. Et
à chaque fois—à chaque fois!—j'ai cette parole dans la ⁴¹*marque.* Alors, c'est
celle-ci qui ↓ qui a marqué. Et elle ne peut pas s'⁴²[ɔbsi] ↓ ⁴²[ɔbsi]. Rien du
tout! Du tout! Du ⁴³/pʀɛ/ ↓ Rien! Rien! Rien! Non, rien! Et je ⁴⁴[tʀu] ↓ Et j'ai
essayé, justement, ⁴⁵(*le plus que je possible*), ⁴⁶(*sur*) le "curé" que je dis là.
Vous comprenez? Vous voyez? Ce "curé," il ⁴⁷[ʀaplisi] et je me demande
pourquoi ⁴⁸(*cet existe*), pourquoi ⁴⁹(*me résiste*) tout le temps. Mais enfin!

HOW LONG HAVE YOU BEEN SICK?

I ↓ I hear very ¹/ʙaᴅʟʏ/ what is being told ²*to the girl.* There are times when
I ³/ʜᴇaʀ-ᴜɴᴅᴇʀsᴛaɴᴅ/. . . . There are certain words, in spite of all, which I
do understand a little. But I cannot speak, you see. As soon as I chat a little,
like this, ⁴*figuring* you, I can ⁵*all alone.* But ⁶/ɴoᴛ/ ↓ That's all. It stops at
that. I can talk ⁷*lightly.* . . . But then, I can ⁸|sacᴋ|, in spite of it all, but
very little. But then, because of that, I ⁹(*am stopped that*). You see. I cannot.
I do not ¹⁰/sᴘᴇaᴋ/. No ¹¹/ᴜᴛᴛᴇʀaɴcᴇ/. For instance, I can ¹²(*nobody write*). You
do not know! You would have a pencil. ¹³*I would see you* ↓ You would see.
I do not know ¹⁴(*it*) absolutely ¹⁵/ɴoᴛʜɪɴɢ/ ↓ nothing ¹⁶(*written on*). I mean
yes: I do understand all that ¹⁷*he* writes—you see—but all this completely
¹⁸[sut] me the ¹⁹[ʀēᴘʀimi]. . . . It fell on me one night, like that. And then it
came without a cause. I ↓ I ↓ You know: with a fit of faintness. I ²⁰*was* at
the ↓ the ²¹*doctor who treats the parents.* I did ²²(*treat myself in*) and it
became impossible for me to ²³(*no longer nothing hear nobody*)—you see—
to chat, to ²⁴*understand nothing* of what the ²⁵*vicar* said. . . . I cannot say a
thing but I can talk ↓ but I remember no word whatsoever. And that's that,
then, this is it. This is what is ²⁶*uncomprehending:* a funny, funny ²⁷*voice* in
²⁸[tulu]. This goes without ²⁹|ꜰᴜɴɴʏ|, it is funny. . . . And it is not ³⁰/aɢʀᴇᴇ-
aʙʟᴇ/, I assure you. . . . Do you understand what I ³¹*understand,* after all, a
little? . . . I can no longer write ³²*the people whom they write.* . . . One should
not ↓ One should not ask me some ↓ much, much, much, and, above all,
some reflections. . . . Ah yes! I can think! Come now! . . . since everybody
now tries ³³(*at*) be a ³⁴*priest* of ↓ ³⁵/oꜰ/ ↓ like good ³⁶*vicar,* like everywhere

in the ↓ You see! This is ↓ This is ↓ This is the utterance in question, the one I always keep saying, the one that unnerves me so much, that this [37]*response*, that the ↓ "Vicar"! [38]/vɪcaʀ/: it is this [39]*observation*! [40](*Is*) always ↓ Why a [37]*response* like this? Can you explain me? Well. And each time—each time!—I have this utterance in the [41]*mark*. Therefore, it is this one which ↓ which has marked. And it cannot [42][ɔbsi] ↓ [42][ɔbsi] itself. Nothing at all! At all! At [43]/pʀɪᴇsᴛ/ ↓ Nothing! Nothing! Nothing! No, nothing! And I [44][tʀu] ↓ And I have attempted, precisely, [45](*the most I possible*), [46](*on*) the "vicar" that I say there. You understand? You see? This "vicar," it [47][ʀaplisi] and I wonder why [48](*it is existed*), why [49](*offers me resistance*) all the time. Anyway!

As illustrated by this quotation, Ms. G.'s jargon also belonged with the same basic taxonomical group as Ms. D.'s, that is, it coexisted with major perturbation of comprehension and repetition (Geschwind, 1971), and it comprised phonemic deviations and neologisms as well as verbal deviations. Ms. G.'s phonemic deviations included phonemic approaches (6, 10,15,35), phonemic paraphasias (1,11,30,38), phonemic *télescopages* (3)[7] and formal verbal paraphasias (8,29). One of the latter (29), in which the obvious target word, 'to say' (/diʀ/ *dire*), becomes "funny" (/dʀol/ *drôle*) in the immediate context of pre- and postpositioned /dʀol/, showed how a syntagmatic factor sometimes determines, at least in part, the production of a wrongly selected word, that is, of a paradigmatic error (Lecours & Rouillon, 1976).[8] Although present, the production of neologisms (18,19, 28,42,44,47) was not as spectacular in Ms. G.'s discourse as it was in Ms. D.'s. Verbal deviations included numerous semantic verbal paraphasias (2,4,5,7,17,20,24,26,27,31,37,39,41,46,48), syntagmic paraphasias such as (32) and (13), in which 'you would see' becomes "I would see you," and inadequate circumlocutions, such as (21), in which the 'family doctor' becomes the "doctor who treats the parents."

In spite of these basic similarities, Ms. G.'s linguistic behavior differed from Ms. D.'s in three respects. The first was properly linguistic and had to do with an oral production of paragrammatic deviations (9,12,14,16, 22,23,29,33,40,45,46,48,49)[9] which was by far more important than that in any other case we have studied to this day. Of the 450 sentences in the corpus, 92 missed an essential component and 74 comprised at least one paragrammatic deviation (Cyr-Stafford & Boisclair-Papillon, 1974). In such

[7] In (3), the obvious target is 'I understand' (*je comprends* /kɔ̃pʀã/) and the output is "*j'/átʀãp/*," an obvious admixture of 'I understand' and 'I hear' (*j'entends* /ãtã/).

[8] See also (31) and (41). In the latter, the obvious target word, 'mouth', becomes "mark" in the immediate context of postpositioned "marked" (a retrograde verbal assimilation).

[9] By analogy to the structure of phonemic *télescopages*, (45) can be labeled as a verbal *télescopage*, as the paragrammatic utterance "the most I possible" (*le plus que je possible*), obviously results from the concatenation of 'the most I can' (*le plus que je peux*) and 'as much as possible' (*le plus possible*).

a case, and considering only the quantitative aspect of the phenomenon, one might accept the label of DYSSYNTACTIC JARGON (*jargon dyssyntaxique*) used by a few French authors (Ducarne & Preneron, 1976).

The second difference consisted of the recurrent use, in paraphasic verbal substitutions, of five WORDS OF PREDILECTION, all from a same paradigm, which could apparently replace any noun without further conceptual or formal relationships to it. Although she was very much of a Republican, Ms. G.'s words of predilection turned out to be, as is partly illustrated in the quotation (25,34,36,43), 'vicar' (*curé*), 'priest' (*prêtre*), 'father' (*père*), 'abbott' (*abbé*), and 'church' (*église*). Recurrent use of predilection words as verbal substitutes is not really a rarity in the jargon characteristic of the earlier phases of Wernicke's aphasia proper. The verbal paraphasias of Gen. A., for instance, testified to preferential use of words of the military and paramilitary paradigm even when he was not on the subject of his military career. Nonetheless, this phenomenon seldom takes the proportions it took in the discourse of Ms. G., where it was indeed reminiscent of the thematic glossomania sometimes observed in classical schizophasia (Lecours & Vanier-Clément, 1976).

The third and last difference is also the most intriguing. Unlike any other excited logorrheic Wernicke's aphasic we have observed, Ms. G. was fully aware of her aphasia and she kept bemoaning it: In other words, there existed no anosognosia in this case. Moreover, Ms. G.'s awareness of her disordered language was not only global, as it was in a case of paroxysmal dysphasia reported elsewhere (Lecours & Joanette, 1980), but it also bore on various particular aspects of her disease: As is apparent from the first half of the quotation given here, in spite of a grossly paraphasic production, she was for instance aware that she could neither speak nor write properly, and she was aware that her comprehension of written messages was somewhat better than her comprehension of spoken messages (Dejerine, 1914; Wernicke, 1874); similarly, she was very much aware of the anomalous nature of her lapsus-like use of predilection words, as is obvious from the second half of the quotation, and she expressed herself quite clearly as to the obnoxiousness of this particular phenomenon. Again, we do not suggest that this exceptional characteristic deserves a label of its own, but it certainly is of interest to know that full-blown jargon can occur without anosognosia in Wernicke's aphasia proper.

CASE 6

The sixth case is that of Mr. Y., a bachelor and retired salesman from Marseille. Mr. Y. was the victim of a stroke at the age of 71, in November 1971, while he was consulting his lawyer on the possibility of prosecuting a neighbor with whom he had long had an open feud about an oak bordering on their respective estates. He was hospitalized at *l'Hôpital de la Timone* where Professor Michel Poncet examined him. Besides focal electroencephalographical anomalies over the left temporal region, aphasia was the only evidence of neurological disease. Mr. Y.'s aphasia comprised fluent euarthric jargon, a near absolute incapacity to name, repeat, read aloud, or write, and a major deficit in oral as well as written comprehension. The patient's linguistic behavior was therefore labeled as WERNICKE'S APHASIA PROPER, very severe.

The following is excerpted from the recording of a conversation with Mr. Y. a few days after his stroke:

QUEL EST VOTRE NOM? . . . COMMENT ALLEZ-VOUS? . . .

Je suis très heureux de vous ↓ bien heureux—mon Dieu!—je suis très ↓ très bien. Je reconnais que euh—mon Dieu!—j'ai ↓ j'ai ↓ j'aime bien ¹/f/ ↓ parce que—Qu'est-ce que vous voulez?—euh je ²[tʀɛve] ↓ je ³*mettrai* ↓ — N'est-ce pas?—C'est bête, quand même, hein. Je me ⁴*mettrai* à ⁵[beʀɔbi], hein. C'est bête, ça. . . . Alors, je lui ai dit: "Mais, bon sang!, j'ai ↓ " J'ai dit, ⁶*Maître*, et ↓ et j'ai préféré, carrément ↓ Je suis heureux d'avoir ↓ Je suis ⁷/z/ ↓ Je suis bien heureux d'avoir ↓ bien ↓ bien ⁸[abaglia]. Je suis heureux. Ma parole! Monsieur—Voyez!—je ⁹[ʀœʀœpʀe]. Je suis ¹⁰/s/ ↓ Euh j'ai pris—N'est-ce pas?—le bien de ¹¹*maître* ↓ de ↓ de ¹²[pʀetʀi], quoi. Mais—Je veux dire—je ¹³[mɛtʀɛtʀi] ↓ je ¹⁴[mœtʀœtʀi]. . . . Voilà. Alors, on ¹⁵[mɛtʀɛtʀ]. Nous sommes ¹⁶[mɔtʀɔtʀ] et, alors, c'est formidable. Je ¹⁷*mètre* ce ¹⁸*maître*. . . . Je suis ¹⁹*maître*. Je lui ²⁰*mettrai* et je suis, malheureusement ↓ je suis ²¹*maître paie-maître*. Voilà! Voilà! C'est idiot! C'est idiot! . . . Je suis content, ²²*Maître*, parce que—mon Dieu!—je lui ai ²³[tœrtʀe] et, bien entendu, je lui ²⁴*mettrai*, ²⁵*Maître*. J'étais content à ²⁶*mettre*—N'est-ce pas?— . . . . Je ²⁷/ʃ/ ↓ Je ²⁸/m/ ↓ Je ²⁸/m/ ↓ Je crois, malgré tout, euh ↓ Je me devais d'en ²⁹*mettre* deux ³⁰*mètres*. Voilà! C'est idiot! . . . Alors, j'ai ³¹*maître*, bien entendu, et c'est idiot. Alors, représentez-vous ↓ représentez-vous un peu, ³²*Maître*. J'aime bien son ³³*maître*. Je me disais: "J'aime les ³⁴*maîtres*." . . . J'ai voulu ³⁵*mettre* pour voir si j'en avais d'un ³⁶*mètre* et—mon Dieu!—ça m'arrive. Qu'est-ce que je vais faire? Il me reste, ³⁷*Maître*, si j'en arrive ↓ ³⁸*Maître*, j'en arrive, ³⁹*Maître*, à le ⁴⁰*mettre*. Parce que c'est idiot. Je ⁴¹*mètre* un ⁴²*maître*. . . . Il vaut mieux, ⁴³*Maître*, mais c'est du reste ↓ Du reste, je préfère carrément, ⁴⁴*Maître*, lui ⁴⁵*mettre* dehors. . . . Ca, c'est idiot, quand même, ça ⁴⁶[sylbɔk]. Je ↓ Je vais à la ⁴⁷/salpεtjεʀ/. Quand même, la ⁴⁸*salope*! Non, c'est une ⁴⁹*salopette*. Bien oui, ⁵⁰*Maître*, c'est ↓ c'est rien. Alors, si elle avait voulu ⁵¹[patʀœ]. C'est idiot! Ces ⁵²*salopards*! . . . C'est ⁵³*salaud*, hein? . . . Je sais. Je sais. Je sais, ⁵⁴*Maître*. Je sais. Il a ↓ Il ↓ Il a ↓ Il a ↓ Il a dû ⁵⁵*mettre*. Il a le ⁵⁶{/mɛtʀ/}, il a le ⁵⁷{/mɛtʀ/}, et il a le ⁵⁸{/mɛtʀ/}.

WHAT IS YOUR NAME? . . . HOW DO YOU DO? . . .

I am very happy to ↓ very happy—my God!—I am very ↓ very well. I admit that hm—my God!—I have ↓ I have ↓ I like a lot to ¹/f/ ↓ because—What do you want?—hm I [2][tʀɛve] ↓ I [3]*shall put* ↓ —Shall I not?—It is foolish, all the same, eh. I [4]*shall put* myself to [5][beʀɔbi], eh. This is foolish. . . . Then, I told him: "But, good Lord!, I have ↓ " I said, [6]*Maître,* and ↓ and I definitely preferred I am happy to have ↓ I am [7]/HAPPY/ ↓ I am very happy to have ↓ very ↓ very [8][abaglia]. I am happy. Upon my word! Mister,—Look!—I [9][ʀœpʀœpʀœ]. I am [10]/s/ ↓ Hm I took—didn't I?—the property of [11]*master* ↓ of ↓ of [12][pʀetʀi], eh. But—I mean—I [13][mɛtʀɛtʀi] ↓ I [14][mœtʀœtʀi]. . . . That's that. Then, we [15][mɛtʀɛtʀ]. We are [16][mɔtʀɔtʀ] and, then, it is tremendous. I [17]*measure* this [18]*master.* . . . I am [19]*master.* I [20]*shall put* him and I am, unfortunately ↓ I am [21]*master-paymaster.* This is it! This is it! It is idiotic! It is idiotic! . . . I am glad, [22]*Maître,* because—my God!—I have [23][tœʀtʀe] him and, of course, I [24]*shall put* him, [25]*Maître.* I was glad to [26]*put*—Wasn't I?— . . . I [27]/ʃ/ ↓ I [28]/m/ ↓ I [28]/m/ ↓ I believe, in spite of all, hm ↓ I owed it to myself to [29]*put* two [30]*meters* of it. This is it! It is idiotic! . . . Then, I have [31]*master,* of course, and it is idiotic. Then, picture to yourself ↓ picture this to yourself a little, [32]*Maître.* I do like his [33]*master* a lot. I was saying to myself: "I do like the [34]*masters.*" . . . I have wanted to [35]*put* in order to see if I had some that were one [36]*meter* long and—my God!—it happens to me. What am I going to do? It remains for me, [37]*Maître,* if I manage to ↓ [38]*Maître,* I manage [39]*Maître,* to [40]*put* him. Because it is idiotic. I [41]*measure* a [42]*master.* . . . It would be better, [43]*Maître,* and moreover ↓ Moreover, I definitely prefer, [44]*Maître,* to [45]*put* it outside for him. . . . This is indeed idiotic, after all, it [46][sylbɔk]. I ↓ I go to the [47]/SALPÊTRIÈRE/. Hang it all! The [48]*slattern!* No, they are [49]*overalls.* Well, yes, [50]*Maître,* it is ↓ it is nothing. Then, had she wanted to [51][patʀœ]. Now, this is idiotic! The [52]*swines!* . . . It is [53]*filthy,* eh? . . . I know. I know. I know, [54]*Maître.* I know. He has ↓ He ↓ He has ↓ He has ↓ He had to [55]*put.* He has got the [56]{/mɛtʀ/}, he has got the [57]{/mɛtʀ/} and he has got the [58]{/mɛtʀ/}.

This is a most astonishing case. The label of Wernicke's aphasia proper was no doubt justified: On the one hand, a severe language disorder suddenly occurred, which comprised jargon as well as major deficits in repetition and comprehension (Geschwind, 1971) and, on the other hand, there existed clear electrical evidence of a left temporal lesion. From a linguistic point of view, however, Mr. Y.'s jargon differed in several respects from that in other cases of Wernicke's aphasia proper. Phonemic deviations were relatively infrequent and comprised, but for very few exceptions, only phonemic approaches (1,7,10,27,28); in the great majority of the latter, the listener could not recognize target words. A single phonemic paraphasia (47) occurred in the quotation given here, bearing on a proper noun that normal speakers often transform: *Salpêtrière!* Moreover, and although Mr. Y.'s discourse included a great number of verbal deviations, no semantic verbal paraphasias as such could be recognized.

Mr. Y.'s jargon comprised a fair number of neologisms, which is one of the essential characteristics of full-blown jargon in Wernicke's aphasia proper. However, unlike the neologisms in other cases of Wernicke's aphasia proper, of which about 85% typically replace nouns and attributes (cf. Case 3), Mr. Y.'s neologisms functioned as verbs in most cases (2, 5,9,13,14,15,16,23,46,51). In the quotation given, only one neologism occurs in place of noun (12), and only one other in place of participle (8). One might also note that the phonemic constituents of Mr. Y.'s neologisms were somewhat repetitive, a phenomenon we have also observed in a few other cases of neologistic jargon.

The most striking characteristic of Mr. Y.'s discourse is no doubt that it was dominated—in the midst of an overflow of coined expressions such as *mon Dieu! bon sang! n'est-ce pas? vous voyez! qu'est-ce que vous voulez?* and so forth—by a vertiginous play on words that was founded, essentially, on the homophony, in meridienal French, of 'master' (/metʀ/ *maître*) (11,18,19,21,31,33,34,42), 'Maître' (/mɛtʀ/ *Maître*, the vocative for lawyer) (6,22,25,32,37,38,39,43,44,50,54), 'meter' (/mɛtʀ/ *mètre*) (30,36), 'to put' (/mɛtʀ/ *mettre*, infinitive) (26,29,35,40,45,55), and a somewhat obsolete form of 'to measure' (*je* /mɛtʀ/ *je mètre*, first person present indicative) (17,41); use of 'paymaster'(/pɛmɛtʀ/ *paie-maître*) (21) and of 'to put' in the future (*je* /mɛtʀe/ *je mettrai*) (3,4,20,24) was also part of the game, and a fair proportion of the neologisms, such as (13–16), obviously borrowed phonemic components to /mɛtʀ/. The sample we have quoted also comprised a less productive although funnier game founded on the formal kinship between the words /salo/ (*salaud*) (53), /salɔp/ (*salope*) (48), /salɔpɛt/ (*salopette*) (49), /salɔpaʀ/ (*salopard*) (52) and, of all words, /salpɛtʀiɛʀ/ (*Salpêtrière*) (47) (given the context, the first four of these words can be translated, respectively, as 'swine,' 'slattern,' 'dungarees,' and 'filthy'). The dominant element of Mr. Y.'s jargon was therefore full-blown formal glossomania (Lecours & Vanier-Clément, 1976), identical, as far as we can tell, to that sometimes observed in the discourse of psychotic subjects.

Notes

1. With regard to the glossomanic play on /mɛtʀ/, our transcription of Mr. Y.'s discourse was obviously not confident throughout; it was confident enough,[10] however, to substantiate the homonymy phenomenon (95 occurrences of /mɛtʀ/ in the course of a 10 minute interview).

2. Contrary to what occurs in schizophasic glossomania, Mr. Y.'s discourse testified to the existence of tremendous lexical paucity (qualitative reduction in spite of fluency in production). Within the quotation given

[10] Without presumptions as to what the speaker intended to say, syntactic clues often made it possible to distinguish nominal from predicative use of /mɛtʀ/; within the nominal corpus, the vocative 'Maître' was sometimes recognized on prosodic clues; the occurrence of each of the other two nominal possibilities, 'master' and 'meter', was occasionally clear in view of contextual semantic features; syntactic parameters usually permitted identification of the two predicative forms, 'to put' and 'I measure'.

here, for instance, lexical words could have been uttered 141 times: 47 lexical words, most of which bearing little information or telling about the patient's affects ("I am happy," "I am glad," *etc.*) were effectively produced (including 18 recurrences), and 16 more within coined expressions or sentences (including 9 recurrences); aborted segments occurred 24 times; conventional production yielded the way to neologisms 12 times, to /mɛtʀ/ 37 times, and to a word of the /salo/ series 5 times.

3. On the whole, Mr. Y. apparently acted as if he was unaware of the unconventional nature of his discursive behavior. Closer analysis of some of his utterances, however, could be interpreted as indicative of awareness: for instance, exclamations such as "It is foolish!" and "It is idiotic!" frequently occurred, as in the quotation, in immediate relation to the play on /mɛtʀ/; furthermore, sentences such as the last in the quotation (56, 57,58), which we could have transcribed and translated as "He has got the master, he has got the Maître, and he has got the meter," might conceivably be taken to indicate that Mr. Y. was somehow consciously interested in homophony. In other words, we do not know how deep an anosognosia he had for his aphasia.

4. In view of the play on /mɛtʀ/, it is striking that Mr. Y. should have been discussing various metric measures with his lawyer at the moment he had his stroke. Although never in cases of jargonaphasia, as far as we know, similar coincidences have long been known to occur in certain cases of global aphasia with reduction of speech to a single verbal stereotypy (Alajouanine, 1968).

CASE 7

The seventh case is that of Ms. O., a 21-year-old law student in Reims. Lovelorn at the age of 21, she received psychiatric assistance and thereafter, in March 1970, she jumped off a cliff on the Norman coast. This was the cause of a skull fracture and left brain contusion, with extradural and subdural hematomas. Surgery included partial left temporal lobectomy. This was followed by 4 days of coma. When she recovered, her verbal behavior was most puzzling. She was transferred to the aphasia unit of *la Salpêtrière* a month later. Aphasia was by then obvious: Ms. O. could neither name nor repeat normally, both tasks leading to production of phonemic deviations and neologisms; textual reading led to abundant production of neologisms and verbal paraphasias (Lecours & Rouillon, 1976), that is, classical jargonaphasia was manifest in this form of language production; written expression was grossly paragraphic, including a great number of dysorthographic errors; and there existed a rather severe disturbance of oral and written comprehension. As to spontaneous speech, it was fluent, euarthric, and rather bizarre.

The following is excerpted from the recording of a conversation with Ms. O. a few days after her admission to *la Salpêtrière:*

RACONTEZ-MOI COMMENT S'EST PASSÉ CET ACCIDENT

Ce qui s'est passé? Bien, en fin de compte, ça été très ¹/f/ ↓ très ²*faux*, parce que je me suis moi-même blessée, en coupant quelque chose, moi-même; et, quand je me suis blessée, maman m'a envoyée chez un pauvre homme. Et ensuite, je suis arrivée ici. Et je suis là depuis trois mois maintenant. . . . Oh! c'est arrivé très facilement. C'est-à-dire qu'il y avait un pauvre homme qui était en train de ³*moudre* quelque chose dans le ⁴*saint* et, en voyant cet homme qui était en train de ³*moudre,* je l'ai fait moi-même. J'ai ⁵/mu/ ↓ J'ai ⁶*moulu* moi-même et je me suis coupé quelque. . . . C'est très facile, parce que j'ai coupé quelque chose avec un ⁷*blé* et, en coupant, je me suis coupé moi-même une main. Et voilà, ça s'est ⁸/pa/ ↓ ça s'est passé comme ça. Maman m'a envoyée ici et ça été fini. . . . J'ai été blessée parce que mes parents étaient en train de jouer, eux-mêmes, pendant l'été; et, en étant blessés eux-mêmes, ils nous ont fait blesser, moi, mon frère et ma petite soeur aussi. . . . Bien, ça s'est passé très difficilement, parce que mon papa était parti chez ↓ voir des gens, et il était en train de leur dire: "Ah! bien, cette enfant-là va faire telle chose." Et effectivement, moi, qui venais voir mon père, j'ai fait telle chose, c'est-à-dire que je suis partie dans les ↓ dans les endroits où je dois passer moi-même. Et il y a un ⁹*saint* qui est venu et qui m'a tondue. Et c'est là que je suis mal tombée et que ↓ Vraiment, ça va mal depuis. Et alors, quand je suis sortie de là, cet ↓ ce ↓ ce ¹⁰*saint* m'a emmenée voir mon père et lui a dit: "Bien, voilà, vous avez votre enfant. Elle a fait telle chose et, maintenant, ça va mal. Faut faire quelque chose vous aussi." . . . Mon accident? Oh! ça été très difficile parce que c'était avec papa et il a lui-même pris sa ↓ sa ¹¹*biche*—si vous voulez—et il a essayé de tirer dans la Marne. Et, à ce moment, il n'a pas fait attention: c'est moi qui étais dans la Marne et c'est sur moi qu'il a tiré. Et, en fin de compte, ça va beaucoup plus mal depuis, parce que j'¹²(*ai*) beaucoup de mal à re-connaître comment il ¹²(*avait*) fait.

TELL ME WHAT HAPPENED WHEN YOU HAD YOUR ACCIDENT (SAME QUESTION SEVERAL TIMES)

What happened? Well, all things considered, it was very ¹/FALSE/ ↓ very ²*false*, because I wounded myself by cutting something, myself; and, when I wounded myself, mother sent me to a poor man. And then, I arrived here. And I have been here for three months now. . . . Oh! it occurred very easily. There was a poor man who was in the process of ³*milling* something in the ⁴*saint* and, as I saw this man who was in the process of ³*milling*, I did it myself. I ⁵/ MILLED/ ↓ I ⁶*milled*, myself, and I amputated myself somewhere. . . . It is very easy, because I cut something with a ⁷*corn* and, thus cutting, I amputated one of my own hands. And this is it, this is how it ⁸/HAPPENED/ ↓ how it happened. Mother sent me here and it was finished. . . . I was wounded because my parents were themselves playing, during the summer; and, being themselves wounded, they had us wounded, myself, my brother and also my little sister. . . . Well, it happened with the greatest difficulty, because my daddy had left to ↓ to see some people, and he was in the process of telling them: "Ah! well, this child is going to do such and such a thing." And indeed, I, who was coming to see my father, I did such and such a thing, meaning that I left for the ↓ for the places where I must travel myself. And there was a ⁹*saint* who came and cropped my hair. And this is when I made a bad fall and ↓ Really, there has been something wrong ever since. And then, when I got out of there, this ↓ this ↓ this ¹⁰*saint* took me to see my father and he told him: "Well, this is it. You have your child. She did such and such a thing and now something is wrong. You also must do something." . . . My accident? Oh! it was very difficult because it was with daddy and he himself took his ↓ his ¹¹*doe*—if you will—and he tried to shoot in the Marne. And, at this very moment, he was not careful: it was me who was in the Marne and it is me whom he shot. And, all things considered, it has gone from bad to worse ever since, because I find it very difficult to recognize how he ¹²(*had done*) it.

Ms. O. was considered to have WERNICKE'S APHASIA PROPER: This label was clearly justified both by surgical observations and by the results of aphasia testing (impaired naming, repetition and comprehension as well as typical jargon in textual reading).[11] Her spontaneous discourse, however, did not qualify as typical Wernicke's jargonaphasia (although standard listeners could certainly not derive standard information from it). Ms. O.'s conversational productions did comprise occasional phonemic and semantic paraphasias, and also a few neologisms; there were none in the passages we have quoted, where the only identifiable deviations were three phonemic approaches (1,5,8) and one paragrammatic error (12), which could have occurred in a comparable sample of ordinary speech. Intriguing word choices were frequent, nonetheless, some of which are marked in the transcription (2,3,4,6,7,9,10,11),[12] but there was no indication that they did not match the patient's thoughts (Lecours & Vanier-Clément, 1976): In other words, paraphasic transformation of a trivial message was not at all the dominant aspect of Ms. O.'s discourse. Indeed, this discourse was the rather well-structured—however repetitive—production of mystic, contradictory, and at times hair-raising reports of what she called her "accident," and of her dramatic relationships with real as well as imaginary members of her immediate family. This sounded very much like a psychotic discourse, one perfectly adapted to the speaker's modes of ideation.

[11] For instance, "*comme un clavier sensible aux pressions acoustiques*" ('like a keyboard responding to acoustic pressures') was read "*comme un symbole* [maʀsje] *aux* [tʀefɔʀm] *théoriques*" ("like a [maʀsje] symbol with theoretical [tʀefɔʀm]").
[12] One might have been inclined to mention *tondu*, following (9), within this list; however, ths patient's hair had indeed been cropped for neurosurgery.

CASE 8

The eighth case is that of Mr. J., a retired schoolteacher from Auvergne who fluently spoke both French and his provincial dialect. Mr. J. had a stroke at the end of August 1966, when he was 79-years-old. This resulted at first in a mild right hemiparesis and in suppression of speech. The hemiparesis lasted only a few days and 6 weeks later, when the patient was seen at the aphasia unit of *la Salpêtrière,* he presented fluent euarthric jargon. Aphasia testing showed that Mr. J. could not name repeat or read, that he could neither copy nor write on dictation, that spontaneous writing was reduced to repetitive production of a few letters and of two grammatical words (*le* and *de*); it also showed very deep impairment of both oral and written comprehension. It was therefore considered that Mr. J. had a severe form of WERNICKE'S APHASIA PROPER. There existed electroencephalographical and gammaencephalographical evidence of a left temporal softening.

The following is excerpted from the recording of a long "conversation" with Mr. J. about 2 months after his stroke:

ET ALORS?

[ge ¹telɛktɔʀe ²ɛlge ³kɔ̃tɛgɔʀe ⁴dǿte ⁵dito ⁶dɔlɔʀe dybwa ⁷dɔlɔʀe]. [de ⁸logelœʀe ge getʀɔ̃pʀe dœbɛʀ]. [ɛl ⁹ɛlge ¹⁰detɔ̃ ¹¹kɔ̃tɛgɔʀe ¹²ditɔ̃ ¹³kɔ̃tɛdœʀe napɔʀtœme a ¹⁴ādɛsmā]. Ah! Ce n'est pas cą. [bɛlœʀi gatɔ̃dyis ilabe legalɛ̃de kaʀdibʀɛt]. Finalement ↓ Ah! Et pourtant, je l'avais ↓ [¹⁵ɛlge ¹⁶detā mitœdil ¹⁷ātibɛ̃ digitɛʀ ¹⁸dɛltaʀe dis pil ¹⁹tilɛlœʀi ²⁰tɛlœʀe dɔmɛtʀ]. [a tʀā ²¹kātɛgɔʀe dibʀɛkœ ²²dulɔʀe ²³geʀe di ²⁴gɔʀitɔʀe ²⁵dylotœʀe diledu]. [lydotɔʃi aʀātʀɛʃœ ²⁶gigolɔʀe si ki kita ²⁷dɔlɔʀe divā lœ lœ do ²⁸dɔlɔʀe.

QUEL EST VOTRE MÉTIER?

[²⁹lege gœdœ tɔ̃bālœbe ³⁰eteʀe die gudutābi gylɔ̃te debyʀo]. [otɛʀ dɛʀve ³¹dolœdo ³²dɔlodɔʀœʀe gi lyā ³³tolɔ̃teʀe difɔ̃ ³⁴dœlɔ̃ ³⁵deʀe ³⁶dyʀe ³⁷dœlyʀi].

DEPUIS QUAND HABITEZ-VOUS PARIS?

Oui, [ɛle dikelimɛtʀ ³⁸ɛdœʀe ³⁹ɛlge ⁴⁰detɔʀe ⁴¹ʀedɔʀe gil kɔ̃tɔ̃ tɔ̃ ⁴²tɔ̃tegœʀe di dibɛʀtɔ̃te idɔʀbɛ̃ ɔteʀɔʀ]. [ʀɔtɛ̃plyʀgœ til ⁴³āge detɔ̃bɛʀ ⁴⁴edeɔʀe dypatʀ e dikte lœ dœlɔtʀ tʀibyʀ ⁴⁵dɔlɔʀe].

. . . .

ÇA FAIT DE LONGUES ÉTUDES, ÇA

Eh oui! [depœtɛlde lœ ⁴⁶deʀyd ⁴⁷delyd ⁴⁸yd tipǿ dilœdepe ⁴⁹dypo ⁵⁰lybeʀǿd ʀɔmɛd ⁵¹dydœ ⁵²ʀydik ⁵³kilvedākʀe ⁵⁴kikādeʀe ⁵⁵dœdābeʀe gɔte ⁵⁶ābelɔ̃ ⁵⁷ādeʀa] et aussi [ɛldyi vidale]. Il ↓ il [didepe ⁵⁸yldœtābuʀ ⁵⁹dœtā ikɔ̃depe ⁶⁰ādʀœtuʀ ⁶¹dybaʀa ⁶²tādœʀa]. [⁶³edeʀe] et ils ont [dʀese sildatʀɛne ⁶⁴ditā ⁶⁵geloteʀe]. Heureusement, ce n'est pas ↓ et ↓ et [ilipe dāledɔ̃ʀœpu ildelœbʀi dālœkuʀ dœʀœbe].

In English, without repeating the neologistic components, this may be translated as:

AND THEN?

> [. . .]. [. . .]. [. . .]. Ah! This is not it. [. . .]. Finally ↓ Ah! And yet, I did have ↓ [. . .]. [. . .]. [. . .].

WHAT IS YOUR TRADE?

> [. . .]. [. . .].

HOW LONG HAVE YOU BEEN LIVING IN PARIS?

> Yes, [. . .]. [. . .].

THIS MEANS LONG STUDIES, EH?

> Oh yes! [. . .] and also [. . .]. He ↓ he [. . .]. [. . .] and they have [. . .]. Fortunately, it is not ↓ and ↓ and [. . .].

As illustrated in this quotation, Mr. J.'s discourse was characterized by near absolute absence of standard verbal components, especially of lexical ones, and by fluent production that came very close to being entirely neologistic.[13] This is a most uncommon behavior among the jargonaphasics and, as far as we know, it occurs only in the elderly (Lecours & Vanier-Clément, 1976). We have personally observed only one other case (Lecours, Travis, & Osborne, 1980), and Anna Mazzucchi (personal communication), from Parma, has recorded the discourse of another. In Chapter 10 of this volume, Ellen Perecman and Jason Brown report on their thorough study of a similar patient; their label for this condition is PHONEMIC JARGON, which would be quite adequate if this term did not happen to have already been used (Alajouanine *et al.*, 1964; Lecours & Lhermitte, 1979) to designate another form of jargonaphasia (cf. Case 1).

Discourses that are almost entirely neologistic have long been known to occur in certain schizophasic subjects (Bobon, 1952; Cénac, 1925), and they are common among believers in a strong and active Holy Ghost (Samarin, 1972). There are also poets and entertainers who have become famous for their neologistic productions. In all of these cases, this behavior is known as GLOSSOLALIA. Thus, borrowing from psychiatrists, who in turn borrowed from the vocabulary of Christian religions, we refer to the discourse of patients such as Mr. J. under the name of GLOSSOLALIA or GLOSSOLALIC JARGONAPHASIA. The main reason for this choice is that this particular type of Wernicke's jargonaphasia is, in certain respect, closer to schizo-

---

[13] The problems inherent to transcription and segmentation of this type of material have been discussed elsewhere (Lecours *et al.*, 1980).

phasic and charismatic glossolalia than it is to other varieties of Wernicke's jargonaphasia.

There are of course differences between glossolalic jargonaphasia and the glossolalia observed in schizophasic and charismatic speakers. The most significant are the following: The former witnesses the existence of a brain lesion, the latter does not; the former is an exclusive residual behavior, whereas the latter is episodical, coexisting with a capacity for standard language production; the aphasic subject remains apparently unaware (anosognosia), whereas the schizophasic and charismatic are admittedly aware of the unconventional nature of glossolalic discourse; although this is sometimes denied and very seldom acknowledged, glossolalic production is deliberate in the schizophasic and charismatic, whereas it obviously is not in the aphasic; and finally, aphasic glossolalia occurs in the context of dialogues, whereas schizophasic and charismatic glossolalia nearly always occur as monologues (Lecours et al., 1980).

On the other hand, there exist certain very striking similarities between glossolalic productions of all types. We have reviewed them elsewhere (Lecours et al., 1980), after studying the discourse of eleven glossolalic speakers (two aphasics, one schizophasic, five charismatics, two simulators, and one poet). Most of these similarities were amply illustrated by Mr. J.'s discourse:

1. On the whole, constitutive phonemes were those of the mother tongue.

2. The frequency of individual phonemes could differ widely from that in representative samples of the mother tongue (Léon & Léon, 1964), a fact we have not observed in any other case of jargonaphasia or schizophasia. In Mr. J.'s production, the three voiced stops (/b/, /d/ and /g/), for instance, were overemployed, as were /e/ and /o/, whereas /s/, /a/ and /j/, for instance, were underemployed.

3. Although phonologically rule governed (Lecours & Vanier-Clément, 1976), Mr. J.'s discourse comprised frequent recurrence of phonemic combinations that are relatively infrequent in the mother tongue. Furthermore, the frequency of consonantic clusters was far less than in control samples.

4. Reciprocal structural influences between consecutive word-like segments were often obvious (19–20) (31–32) (34–37) (40–41) (58–59) (61–62). Apparently, interventions of the interlocutor could also exert influence on Mr. J.'s phonemic choices: After the interlocutor had used the word /etyd/ (études 'studies'), several of Mr. J.'s word-like segments comprised the phonemes /y/ and /d/ (46–52,58).

5. Mr. J.'s discourse—and this is, in our opinion, one of the primary characteristics shared by all glossolalic productions—comprised families of word-like segments which exhibited the same types of structural relationships that one observes between phonemic paraphasias and corresponding

target words (Lecours & Lhermitte, 1969). This was manifest even in short stretches of his discourse such as the one we have quoted here (4,5,10, 12,16,59,64) (3,11,13,21) (2,29, and possibly other segments such as /ge/ preceding 1, /gi/ following 32, /geʀe/ in 23, and so forth) (6,22) (61 and /debyʀo/ following 30). Neither in Mr. J.'s discourse nor in any other glossolalic sample have we found evidence that these families of word-like segments could be assimilated to some form of declension.

6. Predilection use of segments of all degrees of complexity was present (from phonemes and syllables to word-like and phrase-like segments). At the level of word-like segments, for instance, this point is illustrated by recurrence of /dɔlɔʀe/ (6,7,27,28,45) and /ɛlge/ (2,9,15,39)—both with variants—in the quotation given here.

7. In view of its structure, Mr. J.'s discourse could be interpreted as comprising a few properly morphological elements borrowed from mother tongue. In the sample quoted, this is illustrated, for instance, by recurrent use of prefix-like /ā/ (14,17,43,56,57) and suffix-like /ʀe/ (1,3,6–8,11,13,18, 20–28,30,32,33,35,36,38,40–42,44,45,53–55,63,65).

Similar phenomena, some of which do not occur in comparable samples of spontaneous natural languages (poetry is excluded), were observed in all of the glossolalic samples we have studied so far, whether or not from aphasic speakers. For reasons we have discussed elsewhere (Lecours *et al.*, 1980), they have led us to suggest that glossolalic behavior is not targeted, that is, that it does not represent maximal paraphasic transformation of conventional language.[14] They have also led us to suggest that isolated application of morphophonological laws occurs in glossolalia, without semantic investment other than that inherent to sound and prosody.

SUMMARY AND CONCLUSION

Anyone with an active interest in jargon-lore is likely to reserve a fair-sized drawer in which to put notes on cases that do not really fit his/her own conceptions, preconceptions, and teachings. These cases, like unsolved problems, are all too often ultimately forgotten. Given the topic of this volume, we thought it appropriate to describe five cases from our own drawer, comparing their jargons to those of three patients with more standard manifestations of aphasia.

Given the geographical limitations of contemporary aphasiological terminology, we gave our definition of the word JARGONAPHASIA, insisting on

[14] The study of Mr. J.'s discourse provides an interesting argument in this respect: Had his production been paraphasic, and given a known tendency to unvoicening of voiced consonants in phonemic paraphasia (Blumstein, 1973; Lecours *et al.*, 1973), one would have expected relative increase in the frequency of the unmarked /p,t,k/ rather than the observed increase in the frequency of the marked /b,d,g/.

the fact that it implies both a severe primary encoding disorder in a speaker with a brain lesion, and a secondary decoding difficulty in anyone listening to this speaker. The main varieties of aphasic deviations were then exemplified in verbatim quotations excerpted from conversations with each patient. These quotations were chosen in order to show, in addition to better known aspects of jargon, that all varieties of aphasic deviations, from semantic and phonemic paraphasias to neologisms, at times involve loans of formal and/or semic elements from the immediate context (Buckingham & Kertesz, 1976; Lecours & Rouillon, 1976).[15]

With regard to Cases 4–8, who represent a small proportion of the jargonaphasic population, we showed that each displayed something in his conversational discourse that was reminiscent of one aspect or another of psychotic discourse, in particular of schizophasia (Lecours & Vanier-Clément, 1976).[16] We believe that one should not draw any conclusion from this without having first pondered a few facts: (a) in each of these five patients, the jargon behavior was a direct result of acquired focal brain lesions; (b) in all five, deviant speech production represented a residual behavior; (c) anosognosia—although the definition of this term might be reconsidered—existed in four cases, Ms. G. remaining a most intriguing exception; and, finally, (d) with the possible exception of Ms. O., whose discourse and modes of ideation were perhaps in concordance, none of these patients showed evidence of deliberateness in deviation. As far as we know, these four characteristics do not apply to schizophasia (Lecours & Vanier-Clément, 1976).

Given available data, we have no reason to believe that nature, localization, and extent of lesions, on the one hand, and degree of functional lateralization for language, on the other, had any explanatory value in relation to the unexpected semiological aspects of these five cases. Age, as we have suggested, was possibly of importance in the last case. Having once observed a jargonaphasic nun who remained quite good at praying and related verbal activities, we wonder to what extent cultural background, that is, premorbid learning, talents, habits, and preoccupations can determine the linguistic characteristics of jargonaphasia. In this respect, and concerning the five patients we have presented, one might consider it significant that Gen. A. was very much interested in the forms of language and had written several books and articles dealing with theoretical military tactics, that Ms. G.'s very republicanism, if standard, no doubt led her to be preoccupied with priestly activities, that Mr. Y., besides having had his stroke in the circumstances we described, was a known punner, which is more likely in a salesman from Marseille than, say, in a physician from Göteborg, that Ms. O.'s familial preoccupations quite possibly led to rather than resulted from her brain lesion, and that Mr. J. had long been engrossed in writing and reading poetry before his stroke and subsequent glossolalia.

---

[15] The interventions of an interlocutor can also be a source of loans.

[16] Schizophasia is itself an uncommon form of language behavior among the schizophrenics.

REFERENCES

Alajouanine, Th. *L'aphasie et le langage pathologique.* Paris: Baillière, 1968.

Alajouanine, Th., Lhermitte, F., Ledoux, M., Renaud, D., & Vignolo, L. Les composantes phonémiques et sémantiques de la jargonaphasie. *Revue Neurologique,* 1964, *11,* 5–20.

Bay, E. Principles of classification and their influence on our concepts of aphasia. In A. V. S. de Reuck & M. O'Connor (Eds.), *Disorders of language.* London: Churchill, 1964. Pp. 122–142.

Bleuler, E. *Dementia praecox or the group of the schizophrenias.* New York: International Universities Press, 1966. (Translation of the 1911 German edition.)

Blumstein, S. E. *A phonological investigation of aphasic speech.* The Hague: Mouton, 1973.

Bobon, J. *Contribution historique à l'étude des néologismes et des glossolalies en psychopathologie.* Paris: Masson, 1952.

Buckingham, H. W., Jr., & Kertesz, A. *Neologistic jargon aphasia (Neurolinguistics 3).* Amsterdam: Swets & Zeitlinger, 1976.

Cénac, M. *De certains langages créés par les aliénés : contribution à l'étude des glossolalies.* Paris: Jouve, 1925.

Cyr-Stafford, C., & Boisclair-Papillon, R. *La dyssyntaxie : essai de définition.* Unpublished doctoral dissertation, University of Montreal, 1974.

Dejerine, J. *Sémiologie des affections du système nerveaux.* Paris: Masson, 1914.

Ducarne, B., & Preneron, C. La dyssyntaxie. *La linguistique,* 1976, *12,* 33–54.

Geschwind, N. Aphasia. *New England Journal of Medicine,* 1971, *284,* 654–656.

Head, H. *Aphasia and kindred disorders of speech.* London: Cambridge University Press, 1926.

Hécaen, H. *Introduction à la neuropsychologie.* Paris: Larousse, 1972.

Jakobson, R. Towards a linguistic typology of aphasic impairments. In A. V. S. de Reuck & M. O'Connor (Eds.), *Disorders of language.* London: Churchill, 1964. Pp. 21–46.

Lecours, A. R., Deloche, G., & Lhermitte, F. Paraphasies phonémiques: description et simulation sur ordinateur. In *Colloques I.R.I.A. — Informatique médicale (Vol. 1).* Rocquencourt: Institut de Recherche d'Informatique et d'Automatique, 1973. Pp. 311–350.

Lecours, A. R., & Joanette, Y. Linguistic and other psychological aspects of paroxysmal aphasia. *Brain and Language,* 1980, *10,* 1–23.

Lecours, A. R., & Lhermitte, F. Phonemic paraphasias: Linguistic structures and tentative hypotheses. *Cortex,* 1969, *5,* 193–228.

Lecours, A. R., & Lhermitte, F. Recherches sur le langage des aphasiques: 4. Analyse d'un corpus de néologismes; notion de paraphasie monémique. *Encéphale,* 1972, *61,* 295–315.

Lecours, A. R., & Lhermitte, F. *L'aphasie.* Paris: Flammarion, 1979.

Lecours, A. R., & Rouillon, F. Neurolinguistic analysis of jargonaphasia and jargonagraphia. In H. Whitaker & H. Whitaker (Eds.), *Studies in neurolinguistics (Vol. 2).* New York: Academic Press, 1976. Pp. 95–144.

Lecours, A. R., Travis, L., & Nespoulous, J.-L. Néologismes et Amosoymosie, *Grammatica,* 1981, in press.

Lecours, A. R., Travis, L., & Osborn, E. Glossolalia as a manifestation of Wernicke's aphasia: A comparison to glossolalia in schizophasia and in possession. In M. Taylor-Sarno & O. Höök (Eds.), *Aphasia: Concepts of analysis and management.* Stockholm: Almquist and Wiksell, 1980. Pp. 212–230.

Lecours, A. R., & Vanier-Clément, M. Schizophasia and jargonaphasia: A comparative description with comments on Chaika's and Fromkin's respective looks at "schizophrenic" language. *Brain and Language,* 1976, *3,* 516–565.

Léon, P., & Léon, M. *Introduction à la phonétique corrective.* Paris: Hachette and Larousse, 1964.

Samarin, W. *Tongues of men and angels.* New York: Macmillan, 1972.

Wernicke, C. *Der aphasische Symptomenkomplex.* Breslau: Cohn & Weigert, 1874.

Chapter 3

Where Do Neologisms Come From?

HUGH W. BUCKINGHAM, JR.

INTRODUCTION

In this chapter I address the question of where neologisms come from. I will first define the term NEOLOGISM, and discuss the components of the neologism, the conditions under which it can appear, and its possible functions. I will then outline three approaches, or models, to the analysis of neologisms and will point to the similarities and differences among them. The three models I will treat are (*a*) the linguistic model of word formation sketched in Halle (1973), which with certain modifications can be used to describe the formation of neologisms in aphasia; (*b*) the evolutionary-recovery models presented in Alajouanine (1956), Green (1969), Kertesz and Benson (1970), Lecours and Rouillon (1970), and Weinstein and Puig-Antich (1974); and (*c*) the microgenetic model outlined by Brown (1977).

DEFINITIONS

The term NEOLOGISM, used to describe a lexical form, has always implied novelty of some sort, but difficulties have arisen over its definition. Some

JARGONAPHASIA

Copyright © 1981 by Academic Press, Inc.
All rights in any form reserved.
ISBN 0-12-137580-3

writers have chosen to emphasize only the innovative quality of the form, whereas others have used the term to imply that the word is unintelligible or unidentifiable. Other terms such as WORD SALAD, NONSENSICAL, or GIBBERISH have been used to describe words or strings of words having no meaning for the listener (Buckingham, 1979, p. 282). Those neologisms which arise from the blending of two root forms or from the unacceptable affixation of some bound morpheme onto a root form are not necessarily unrecognizable to the listener provided that the blended parts of the hybrid are traceable to their target sources. Table 3.1 lists some examples drawn from the literature. These forms have been referred to at times as BLENDS, HYBRIDS, CONTAMINATIONS, or TÉLESCOPAGES, but they are far from unrecognizable. They could quite logically arise from: (*a*) incorrect affixation (1); (*b*) simultaneous encoding of two phonologically related lexical items having no semantic similarity (2, 3); (*c*) simultaneous encoding of two semantically related words which may also be phonological associates (4), but need not be (5); or (*d*) perseveration or anticipation of part of a word in the sentential string (6). Although the forms in Table 3.1 are made up of recognizable units, the processes that give rise to them may also play an important role in the production of completely unrecognizable neologisms. It is these unrecognizable forms that are of interest here. For the purposes of the remaining discussion, I will define a neologism as Andrew Kertesz and I did in our recent monograph (Buckingham & Kertesz, 1976) on jargonaphasia: "a phonological form produced by the patient for which it is impossible to recover with any reasonable degree of certainty some single item or items in the vocabulary of the subject's language as it presumably existed prior to the onset of the disease [p. 13]." As we stated in the monograph, it will often be possible to relate a neologism or part of one to some other neologism in the subject's corpus, but this is possible only on the basis of phonological similarity—not on the basis of any meaningful semantic variable. In Table 3.2, I have provided some examples of neologisms in their sentential contexts.

LINGUISTIC WORD FORMATION RULES

One way we might approach the genesis of neologisms is with reference to a model of word formation such as that proposed by Morris Halle (1973). The model is presented in Figure 3.1. Note first that the model has a "list of morphemes" AND a "dictionary of words." The list of morphemes includes content-word roots, function words, stems and affixes; that is, it contains bound and free morphemes in isolation. These are the input to the "rules of word formation" which then construct polymorphemic forms with the morphemes properly concatenated—the roots serving as the bases for the rules. From this component we will generate lexical items such as

TABLE 3.1
Examples of "Hybrid" Lexical Errors Formed through the Coalescence of Two Words

1. *conclusion* → *concludement* (Fromkin, 1971)
2. *apfel* 'apple' + *affe* 'ape' → *apfe* (Freud, 1901)
3. *silab* 'syllabary' + *frikativ* 'fricative' → *silabativ* (Lecours and Vanier-Clément, 1976)
4. *gripping* + *grasping* → *grisping* (Fay and Cutler, 1977)
5. *heritage* + *legacy* → *heresy* (Fay and Cutler, 1977)
6. (Jargon sequence) *field field fliel flood flood* (Buckingham and Kertesz, 1974)

derivation as well as **arrivation; arrival* as well as **derival*. Very general rules of word formation will apply across the board in this component; the systematic gaps and irregular forms will be disallowed at this point by a filter and consequently will not get into the "dictionary of words." At times the root form will have no meaning and will not occur in isolation; thus the word formation rules may apply to "meaningless morphemes," for example: **agress* + *ion* = *agression: *incise* + *ive* = *incisive; *valedict* + *ory* = *valedictory* (Aronoff, 1976, p. 28). The dotted line between the dictionary and the word formation rule component indicates that certain

TABLE 3.2
Selected Examples of Neologisms in Their Sentential Contexts

1. *I* [spóli] *but the labor of the speaker down here in New York.*
2. *You know, it's quite a* [dìsɔ̀pài] *the way I talked with him.*
3. (Same patient)
   (a) *I had this* [néipʃə] *on my head.* (8/30/73)
   (b) *After I was sick, I had a* [wɛ́d nɛ́bi] *on my head.* (10/5/73)
   (c) *I had this* [blei] *on my head.* (10/5/73)
   (d) *I* [fɔ:t] *my* [blóigən] *head.* (10/5/73)
4. *What is that* [fǽnəti] *that* [fɪts]?
5. *I'd write the* [mɛd] *a* [lɛ́di] *at the paper to the* [ǽtəčəbi] *at the* [téisɔ̀mǽdɪk].
6. *The leg* [víltəd] *from here down.*
7. *He* [vʌ́ntəd] *the* [dɔ́rsɪŋ].
8. *I had the* [brǽšə] *lunch for dinner.*
9. *But they did have to* [væn] *my toes.*
10. *The man could make the* [írəkoin].
11. *I never always forget the name of the* [péiðə] *when I call it.*
12. (Reading printed word *inhuman* aloud) [ǽkwiɪb] [ǽkwiɛb] . . . *a woman is* [éikwǽkɪd] . . . *I don't know. I wonder if I'm* [ǽkwìbì]?
13. *I can't even make* [ɪs] . . . *write up the* [mǽsəpəkígələ] *to write about the* [pǽnəsǽpɪkəl].
14. *This is the* [kréibəkrǽks] *where the* [fɔ́jəz] *get out after the* [čuw].
15. *I used to be on* [dízɪks] *on a* [zídɪk] *on a* [vízɪks].
16. *I guess the* [búlwi] *the* [wǽlɪk] *and the* [bíli] *is exactly, and then, of course, the* [gífku].
17. *No, it is not just a* [dɔ́ič], *it's not a* [bɔ́it] *or a* [bívɪk].
18. *I don't know whether she's natural or* [láywər] *or* [θéwən] *or* [kɔ́lwən]. . . . *But I mean, well she might've been* [gɔ́rišt], *too,* [tɔ́iš]. *She might've been* [dérɪš], *too.*
19. *That was one of the nicest* [fɛ́ndlɔz] *that I* [nɛg].

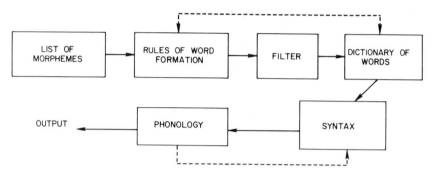

Figure 3.1. Model of word formation (after Halle, 1973, p. 8).

of these rules need to know the category of the word to which they apply. For example, the morpheme -al may be added to a root in order to form a noun only if that root is a verb. Alternatively, we may suppose that root forms in the list of morphemes are bracketed with major lexical category labels. For reasons we need not go into here, the rules of word formation also need recourse to the output of the phonological component.

Now, in the normal case, we can consider that speakers simply select items from the dictionary for insertion into sentential matrices. Halle (1973) writes that "it is possible to suppose that a large part of the dictionary is stored in the speaker's permanent memory and that he needs to invoke the word formation component only when he hears an unfamiliar word or uses a word freely invented [p. 16]."[1] This capacity for novel construction likewise pertains to the aphasic—and in the current context—the neologistic jargon patient. First, it is clear that neologisms are root or stem forms which often have affixes attached to them. In all instances neologisms function as nouns, verbs, adjectives, or adverbs. It therefore seems that, whether brain damaged or not, speakers are restricted as to types of new words. Aronoff (1976) writes that "the only classes of words to which new words can be added by coining are the major lexical categories: noun (N), adjective (Adj), verb (V), adverb (Adv) [p. 19]." From my experience, I have found that the affixes are most often inflectional—not derivational. Quite often the neologistic stem will pick up a correct affix for its sentential function, but other times it will not. Caplan, Keller, and Locke (1972) presented an example where a neologism /pərsét/ was incorrectly inflected with third person singular morpheme when occurring with the first person

---

[1] Other models with dictionaries of fully specified forms allow the irregular or abnormal uses of words to have recourse to the actual rule components of morphology. For instance, Vennemann (1974) writes that "the normal function of the lexicon is to supply words in the construction of sentences, and to identify words in the analysis of sentences; the generative use of the rules is limited to the spontaneous creation of new words and their analysis, the adaptation of foreign words, and pathological application (speech errors) [pp. 368–369]." Aronoff (1976) expresses similar views.

singular pronoun *I*. It is always the case, however, that the phonetic re-alization of affixed morphemes on neologisms is normal and abides by the language specific morphophonemic constraints. Furthermore, neologisms are marked for certain content word grammatical categories and as such fit into proper syntactic slots within grammatical matrices, which are usually well-formed, as shown in Buckingham and Kertesz (1976). Root morphemes clearly have a different status regarding retrievability than do bound affixal morphemes. In Halle's (1973) model, the dictionary contains fully specified forms. In those instances where a neologism is said to result from severe phonemic paraphasia, the paraphasic process could have transformed the root and stem of the full form as it was in the process of being selected from the dictionary. However, I find it difficult to conceive of a phonological distortion process that takes as its input a fully specified polymorphemic string from the dictionary and selectively distorts just the root leaving the affixes untouched. This linguistic sensitivity of the error mechanism for neologisms almost completely rules out any motor-oriented apraxic theory for neologisms. In addition (see Appendix 1), neologisms will resolve and yet the patient will STILL show a tongue apraxia on testing. I believe we should consider that the neologism is formed BEFORE application of word formation rules. Therefore, the neologistic jargon aphasic will be initially selecting from the "list of morphemes," and will show a selective deficit THERE with roots as they exist in their isolated forms. Subsequently, the word formation rules will apply, the neologism will be inserted into the syntactic frame and will then enter the phonological component. It could also be that when NO word is forthcoming, the patient still has recourse to syllable unit selection or formation, where the only constraint that must be abided by is that the syllables obey the language-specific syllable struc-ture laws. One or several syllable units may be randomly generated and strung together in order to fill the slot for the grammatical category of the blocked lexical item.[2] Because it carries its categorial label, the neologism will be ready to enter the word formation rule component, where it most likely will pick up its proper affixation. If it turns into a stereotype, it may get stored in the dictionary for later use. Of course, we need to postulate an aphasic breakdown in the filter in order to let the neologism through. A filter malfunction would also have to be assumed for the production of hybrid lexical forms like those shown in Table 3.1. So, it is not unreasonable to assume some breakdown in the filter to permit neologistic productions as well.

Before leaving the linguistic model I would like to make a distinction

[2] The notion of something like a "random syllable generator" is certainly plausible. For example, a severe conduction aphasic with neologistic jargon was asked to repeat the word *clock* whereupon he produced a string of well-formed, totally random syllables, [howp] [wʊf] [wɪf] [ɛvi].I see no reason to rule out this possibility in ongoing speech where the patient has word-finding blocks.

which is often not appreciated in the aphasiological literature on neologisms.
It has been hypothesized that neologisms may arise through phonological
distortion—but just what type of phonological distortion are we talking
about? First, we are NOT dealing with low-level phonological processes, as
all neologistic forms are composed of permissible syllabic sequences with
properly formed phonetically conditioned allophones. Furthermore, as I
mentioned earlier, the morphophonemic rules are not disturbed, although
at times an incorrect affix may be attached at a level prior to the phonological specification of allomorphs. Consider the pluralized neologism
[féndlɔz] in Sentence (19) of Table 3.2. In English, a noun in the context
one of the nicest _____ must be plural. The fact that the neologism ended
with a [z] and not with a [s] must be accounted for at the morphophonemic
level, as nothing in the phonetic syllable structure constraints of English
would disallow a final [s] preceded by the low, back vowel [ɔ], as in *boss,
floss,* or *Ross* [-ɔs]. Therefore, even if we hypothesize a phonological breakdown for the genesis of neologisms, we must be careful to specify WHICH
aspects of the phonology are distorted, or more properly which linguistic
units are subject to what type of phonological distortion. Consequently, I
feel that the phonological component in Halle's (1973) model is intact for
the neologistic jargon patient, and it assures us that the neologism will be
a phonologically acceptable string in the language and will have expected
morphophonemic realizations. The aphasic "phonological" distortion
mechanism must be located somewhere in the lexicon or at least at some
point higher than the phonological component in the Halle (1973) model
and must not involve allophonics or allomorphy.

We are now entering a crucial area in the theory of neology, as most
researchers have felt that to a great extent neologisms are the result of
severe phonological distortions of target words. If the conditions are right,
then this theory is certainly a logical possibility, but we must be clear in
stating the conditions. That is, if a neologism stems from phonemic transformations, to what forms do these transformations apply—to the desired
lexical item? to some other item? If the phonemic transformation applies
to some other item, is that item somehow related to the original target?
Does there have to be any necessarily related phonological or semantic
entity in the underlying form for a neologism? For instance, in the sentence
I wonder if I'm [ǽkwɪbì]? shown in (12) of Table 3.2, do we necessarily
want to claim that [ǽkwɪbì] comes from phonologically distorting the word
inhuman in its underlying form or from phonologically distorting some other
word semantically related to *inhuman?* What if another condition existed?
That is, what about the condition where there is a complete word block?
How might the syntactic slot be filled, and with what? To answer these
questions, I will begin by drawing from the description of recovery patterns;
I would like to turn to this now.

RECOVERY PHENOMENA

Alajouanine (1956) wrote that "the evolution of jargon aphasia tends to be from an undifferentiated jargon to asemantic jargon and thence to paraphasic jargon of 'one word for another' type [p. 34]." By this he meant that the patient would resolve from severely unintelligible speech with repetitive stereotypic utterances with little phonemic variation (Kertesz and Benson, 1970) to a neologistic jargon of the type shown in Table 3.2. This would eventually clear into speech output characterized by recognizable verbal selection errors. Alajouanine went no further at this time in his recovery scheme to see if there was further resolution to other types of output disorders, but I believe it is safe to say that, at each of the three plateaus he DID describe, the patient had lexical selection difficulties.

Green (1969) has also compared the various recovery levels of a jargonaphasic. He noted that there was a significant decrease—over a period of approximately a year—in the occurrence of jargon episodes, neologisms, and unrelated verbal paraphasias. Literal paraphasias and semantic verbal paraphasias were more numerous in the final interviews, and increased numbers of indefinite pronouns were produced by the patient (cf. Appendix 1). Specifically, Green observed that after a year the neologisms had decreased from 48 on the 1st interview to 0 on the 11th, whereas the indefinite pronouns grew in number from 18 to 238. Green's Chi Square Test for the difference in distribution of neologisms throughout the interviews was significant to the $p < 0.005$ level. These findings, I believe, make it clear that throughout the recovery period the patient had severe lexical retrieval deficits. The conditions were the same—access difficulties; the manifestations of the condition were distinct.

In addition, Kertesz and Benson (1970) discussed evolution in jargon-aphasia and showed that the clinical picture often follows a regular pattern throughout stages of recovery. They state (1970) that "the clinical picture changes from the more severe stage of jargon, where most of the speech is neologistic, to semantic jargon, where most words are recognizable, although inappropriate, and finally to anomic circumlocutory speech with meaningful sentences which are deficient, however, in information-containing words (p. 383–384)." Once again, I do not believe that the patients' word-finding problems are exclusively restricted to the late stages of their disease, but rather they have been there all along.

In our monograph, Andrew Kertesz and I (1976) held that a significant parallel could be drawn between this interpretation of evolution in jargon-aphasia and that presented by Weinstein and Puig-Antich (1974). According to Weinstein and Puig-Antich, jargon resolves to forms of idiomatic speech such as clichés, malapropisms, and puns. These speech forms are "analogues" of the jargon; they are most often elicited in answer to the same types of questions that had educed jargon responses at earlier stages. The analogues still reflect the lack of referential meaning originally apparent with the jargon. As in our interpretation, meaning voids continue to exist but are manifested differently at the later stages of recovery.

A study by Lecours[3] and Rouillon (1976) provides still another description of stages in the resolution of neologistic jargonaphasia. They note that after a period of time "the verbal and phonemic paraphasias get closer and closer to target words [p. 114]." Furthermore, "the number of neologisms gradually decreases . . . [p. 115]." In fact, they often disappear from the patient's discourse altogether. (This is precisely what happened to Green's, 1969, patient, as was mentioned earlier.) Once the neologisms begin to resolve, semantic paraphasias and circumlocutions will appear for a while. Ultimately "the patient's word-finding difficulty may become more apparent in view of the greater number of pauses, hesitations, and repetitions of articles, prepositions, etc., that are not followed by production of a neologistic segment [p. 115]." Presumably, the words "more apparent" mean that the authors believe the word-finding difficulty was present at the early stages as well. According to Lecours and Rouillon, "the most striking facts of evolution . . . are the total disappearance of neologisms AND OF

[3] Lecours has noted that in certain of his jargon patients, a neologistic string will often be produced, immediately preceded by a hesitation, after a determiner or by several repetitions of a determiner (personal communication). I have also observed this on occasion, although by no means for all cases of neology. For instance, one jargon patient I studied, B.F. (Buckingham & Kertesz, 1976), produced the following episodes:

(a) *An, yeah, and it's . . . an . . . a . . . a . . .* [pánəbəl ətmɛh ǽktiyə péndəl bánəbəl] *such that he was using a five inch tan.*

(b) [While holding a ball and trying to name it] *It's a . . . it does some pet . . . a . . .* [bám slébi] *like a* [kə́mp skə́diŋ mayǽnəməl pítswa:].

Butterworth (1979), reporting on his in-depth study of hesitation phenemona in jargonaphasia, observed that neologisms occur after pauses and concluded that this indicated a word-finding difficulty (see also Chapter 5, this volume). Not only do Butterworth's findings pose serious problems for "disinhibition" theories of neologistic jargonaphasia, but they also provide some of the strongest evidence yet for doubting that a "conduction theory" (Buckingham, 1977) accounts for all neologisms.

Lecours has also noted that, at times, immediately following a neologistic stretch of speech, the patient will follow with some sort of justificative phrase such as *if you will* or *so to speak.* I have observed this phenomenon as well and have provided two instances of it below:

(a) *They were invented* [kǽstərz wɪs kístək ən níčəz ɪk hǽmpəs fər nɛ́kstəs ən tɛ́rəs] **an' so on.**

(b) [Looking at a ring and trying to name it] *Very pretty . . . looks like* [bǽčəhǽn bǽnčəhǽŋyə bǽŋəháčəpi] **but it isn't that, is it?**

[Sentence (a) was produced by patient B.F.; Sentence (b) comes from data collected from patient J.T. (Buckingham, Whitaker, & Whitaker, 1979).]

PHONEMIC PARAPHASIAS and the greater obviousness of the word-finding difficulty as marked by hesitations, circumlocutions, semantic paraphasias, and use of semantically weak words [p. 118, emphasis added]." Again, I think one is justified in positing word-finding deficits throughout ALL the stages—from neologism to hesitation.

Essentially, then, what we learn from recovery studies of neologistic jargon is that at the endstage the patients exhibit the symptoms that usually characterize anomia.

MICROGENETIC MODEL

Brown (1972, 1975, 1977) proposes a microgenetic model of language production where the normal linguistic utterance ("the final language act," 1977, p. 45) is the endstage of an unfolding process from limbic cortex through generalized neocortex to strongly lateralized focal neocortex. Anterior and posterior linguistic systems arise simultaneously and in parallel and interact throughout microgenesis by means of subcortical white matter fiber tracts which, in Brown's (1975) model "link up temporally transformations occurring at different points in the microgenetic sequence [p. 29]." For Brown, brain damage can lead to an aphasic syndrome which may be viewed as some earlier stage of microgenesis actually becoming a final speech product. As my concern is with neologisms, I will restrict my remarks to Brown's discussions of posterior system microgenesis.

Content word encoding is one of the principal functions of the posterior language system. Roughly, the encoding stages are divided into semantic, nominal, and phonemic levels. Before any specific target lexical item is selected, a set of semantic associates is aroused. The nominal task is to select from among this group the target word. The phonemic endstage involves the abstract sound specification of the target, which then must be evoked and finally linked up in parallel with the motor program in the anterior system.

A breakdown at the semantic level will give rise to lexical selection errors that are semantically unrelated to the target (semantic paraphasia—JWB). (The clear-cut within-class verbal paraphasia of the nominal level is actually intermediate between the semantic paraphasia and an anomia proper, according to Brown [1977, p. 36]) For the aphasic with semantic disorders, this early semantic stage will thus become the final speech product. If the phonemic specification is undisturbed, the patient's lexical output should be recognizable although bizarrely inappropriate. Brown (1977) reasons that, if these lexical paraphasias themselves "do not achieve correct phonemic realization [p. 43]," a form will be produced that may not be at all recognizable and would thus be classified as a neologism. This notion of a "two-stage" error had been proposed previously, but unlike Brown, most authors also allowed an in-class error to undergo subsequent phonemic distortion. Brown, himself, in his 1972 monograph on *Aphasia, Agnosia, and Apraxia* wrote that "neologistic jargon is a phonemic distortion of severe verbal paraphasia [p. 62]," although in Brown (1977) he distinguishes between verbal paraphasia (within-class) and semantic paraphasia. In 1972, Lecours and Lhermitte stated that "one could suggest that these neologisms stem from monemic paraphasias where the lexical material is subsequently the location of a phonemic transformation [pp. 304–305]." Two years earlier, Luria (1970, p. 296) had reasoned that simultaneous semantic and phonological errors would produce a paraphasia that was "quite complex." At this level, the neologism cannot logically be mapped onto the correct target word, because an incorrectly selected lexical item has been postulated as the underlying source. Since for Brown the lexical errors at the "semantic" level are only marginally, if that, related to the target word (i.e., *chair → engine,* or *chair → Argentinian*), the subsequent phonemic paraphasia would not have to be very complex to render the form unrecognizable to the listener, given that the context of the utterance would not provide any information concerning the underlying form.

At the nominal level, the patient has much firmer control of the full meaning of words; if he makes a lexical error here, it will be a close semantic associate of the target. His principal problem, according to Brown, is that of evoking the underlying phonological form. The patient may hesitate, produce a large quantity of indefinite pronouns. Often the word retrieval deficit is so severe that the output actually becomes nonfluent. The nature of the nominal level, as characterized by Brown, is such that no neologisms are produced. But, while it is certainly true that the anomic does not produce neologisms, nonetheless, like the patient with neologisms which are not properly mappable onto an intended target, the anomic has selectional–retrieval deficits. Furthermore, I see some theoretical difficulties, as there is no principled reason why the patient with verbal paraphasia at the nominal level could not also have phonemic problems. In that case, verbal paraphasia would be produced that would not achieve correct phonemic realization. Yet Brown apparently rules this out, as the only two-stage error for him involves a semantic paraphasia plus phonemic distortion.

For normal lexical production, the speaker successfully traverses the semantic and the nominal levels and lastly he achieves correct phonemic realization. The aphasic disturbance at this endstage level involves phonemic realization of properly selected lexical forms—not of semantic paraphasias. If the phonemic transformations are severe enough, it is not unreasonable to assume that recognizability of target words will be obliterated. In this case the neologism would not logically involve a word-finding problem, but, rather, an abstract phonological realization problem.

For Brown, then, neologisms may stem from phonological distortions of bizarre lexical errors, from severe phonological distortion at the point of selection of correct target words[4] or from CLANG ASSOCIATIONS and WORD FUSIONS. He does not, however, discuss in any detail the underlying conditions that must exist for the CLANG neologisms, nor does he discuss whether or not—or under what conditions—word fusions should even be considered neologistic. It would seem logical, though, that the hybrid neologisms whose components are recognizable must be produced at the level of phonemic realization. Clang neologisms, on the other hand, most likely arise when there are word-finding deficits which leave space in the syntax to be filled.

COMPARISON OF RECOVERY STUDIES AND MICROGENETIC STUDIES

If we now compare the recovery studies with Brown's model, we note that practically all of the former show resolution sequences from neologistic jargon to semantic jargon with paraphasia and from there to an anomic endstage. Brown's model, on the other hand, allows the neologistic jargon to resolve in either of two ways: It may clear to semantic jargon if the hypothesized phonemic problem disappears or it may clear to some sort of conduction or phonemic aphasia if the semantic selection problem disappears. (It is strange that we do not find this phonemic or conduction endstage with the recovery studies.) The recovery studies would predict that Brown's patients who had improved from neologistic jargon to semantic jargon would continue to improve to an anomic stage. Of course, on Brown's model, once the patient would reach this level there would be no way to further clear to a phonemic aphasia because the phonemic problem would have already cleared. The microgenetic model thus forces us to consider a change from anomia to phonemic aphasia as a deterioration. I find this notion of deterioration puzzling, given that, succeeding with proper selection, albeit with phonemic distortion, would seem to be CLOSER to the final endstage of the normally produced "language act," as both the semantic and nominal levels would have been traversed. Therefore, phonemic aphasia would seem to be in the direction of improvement from nominal aphasia. Furthermore, with an anomia there is no underlying target word selected from the lexicon to work off of, so how can this situation deteriorate

[4] It is interesting to note here that Merrill Garrett (1975, p. 155) observed that segmental exchanges and other types of phonemic-level slips of the tongue in normals only occur with content words—not with function words. He postulated a prelexical syntactic matrix structured with the function words, and then hypothesized that the phonemic slips occurred at the point of content word selection and insertion. Apparently, this notion was arrived at independently by Brown and Garrett.

to another aphasic form (phonemic aphasia) where the target has to be selected in order for it to be phonemically distorted? We end up saying that the patient gets better in order to become worse.

The neologisms that are produced as part of phonemic or conduction aphasia are created at the point of lexical selection and as such do not represent a problem with word finding but rather with word execution. This is in contrast to the neologisms that are produced as part of the syndrome called neologistic jargonaphasia, which occur with patients who have severe lexical access deficits.

Finally, compartmentalized and highly differentiated models such as Brown's bring on confusions due to the fact that most aphasics straddle levels even at ONE point in time. In Appendix 1 there is a patient who appeared to be a conduction aphasic in the later stages (March 15, June 7) of his aphasia; he was fluent, had improved comprehension, but could not repeat at all. His neologistic component had resolved quite a bit. However, in no way had this patient traversed the nominal level. Patient J.T. in Appendix 3 had improved comprehension by November 1 and would likely be considered a conduction aphasic. She was very fluent, showed neologistic paraphasia on the referential task of naming, and could not repeat at all. Nevertheless, in no way could she be said to have traversed the nominal level, as would be expected with a conduction aphasic as characterized by Brown.

CONCLUSION

To return now to my original question of where neologisms come from, I think it is safe to say that they may come from several sources, and they do not only arise in patients labeled as neologistic jargonaphasics. First of all, as defined here, a neologism should be unrecognizable, and thus our search for its source will entail no little speculation. As a result, the explanations put forth will be LOGICAL possibilities supported by reasonable indirect evidence. The first logical possibility is that properly selected lexical items do not achieve correct phonemic realization. The phonemic paraphasic processes usually implicated in transforming the input are substitution, deletion, addition, anticipation, and perseveration. Lecours and Lhermitte (1969) paid very close attention to linear phonemic transformations in aphasia, and wrote that "abnormal levels of pre- or post-activation could have something to do with the production of phonemic transformations in jargon aphasia [p. 102]." For phonemic transformation of proper target words to be considered as an explanation for neologisms in some patient, that patient should NOT be simultaneously producing verbal paraphasia at other points in his speech output, or we could never, in principle, rule them out as possible inputs to the phonemic transformations.

Furthermore, that patient should also be producing some phonemic para-phasias which do not totally obliterate recognizability. In addition, he should not otherwise show word-finding difficulties.

Another reasonable source for a neologism would be some phonemic transformation of a lexical form already incorrectly selected. For this to be a reasonable account for the neologisms of some patient, he should, at other places in his speech, be producing verbal paraphasias as well as phonemic paraphasias which do not obliterate the recognizability of the underlying target word. This patient should have severe word-finding def-icits. When these conditions are met, it is not unlikely that many of his neologisms are the result of the "two-stage error." Just how complex the phonemic distortion here needs to be is not well understood, but it should be obvious that, as the context will not facilitate recognition, a rather simple phonemic switch could very well render the lexical paraphasia unrecog-nizable. That is, in order to produce an unrecognizable word, the degree of phonemic paraphasia applied to a lexical paraphasia need not be as severe as the degree of phonemic paraphasia applied to the proper target form. This is especially true where the phonemic transformation distorts a bizarre lexical error (semantic paraphasia of Brown) which is not even a semantic associate of the target word.

Still another possible source for a neologism is some previously uttered material which is perseverated. For instance, if instead of the full example in (12) of Table 3.2 we had only the sentence, *I wonder if I'm* [ǽkwĭbì], we could only speculate as to the source of the neologism. However, we can readily see that it is composed of prior units recombined at this later point. This does not mean that the patient did not have the semantic–cognitive aspects of the word *inhuman* when encoding this sentence. When she said this, it was clear that she was joking with the examiner; she even laughed a bit afterward. What the patient did not have recourse to was the pho-nological shape of the word *inhuman;* the perseverated syllables filled in the void and therefore are not to be mapped onto any underling form for *inhuman.* Processes such as perseveration and anticipation may very log-ically bring together syllables that form a totally meaningless lexical item. For this to be a plausible hypothesis, the patient should clearly, at other points, perseverate and anticipate on items where the result is not totally meaningless. More importantly, the patient should show word-finding def-icits. This condition of word blocking is necessary, because the neologistic perseveration needs a syntactic slot in which to appear. Furthermore, I think it is significant that the perseverates fill content word grammatical categories—most often nouns, although in (12) of Table 3.2 the neologism is functioning as a predicate adjective.

Logically, one might then wish to locate the INITIAL occurrence of the material that is later perseverated, for we must offer a different account of its source (Buckingham, 1977, p. 183). The original material may very well be a segment or a syllable of some proper response or a phonemic error. Or, as I suggested earlier, perhaps the original syllables were produced *de novo* by the speaker from the stock of possible syllables or syllable strings in the language. Alternatively, we have found (Buckingham, Whitaker, & Whitaker, 1979) that initial occurrences of perseverated units were often—but did not need to be—correct responses or parts of a correct response. Nevertheless, these dynamic perseverative and anticipatory processes are, I believe, a real contributor to the formation of neologisms, where the prerequisite condition is a word-finding problem.

Shattuck-Hufnagel and Klatt (1979) suggest a model for normal speech production which includes a "buffer" level where the phonological units are in a readied state. A "scan copier" copies the elements into their slots, and a "bookkeeper" checks off segments that have been copied. We can take this model and ask what conditions would need to obtain where errors would be unavoidable. This, of course, brings us to the interface between aphasic errors and normal slips-of he ongue. In any event, a problem with the scan copy mechanism would lead to anticipatory errors by "looking ahead" too soon. A failure of the bookkeeper to check off an item already copied would lead to perseverative errors. Now, if I may extend the metaphorical description a bit further, I would ask what would happen if nothing got to the buffer. At this point, a random syllable generator could place some segments into the buffer, and speech production could proceed. Any ensuing malfunction of the scan copier and bookkeeper could lead to further errors of a linear nature and in general to the alliteration and assonance (Buckingham, Whitaker, & Whitaker, 1978) observed so often in neologistic jargon aphasia.

Just as I have had to establish some sort of random syllable generator, Butterworth (1979) felt it "necessary to postulate a 'device' which generated neologisms [p. 145]." Although this device's "properties are as yet mysterious [p. 147]," Butterworth conceives of it "as a subsystem with a buffer [p. 152]," where phoneme-size units are "selected randomly or arbitrarily and strung together in the buffer in a phonotactically regular manner . . . [p. 152]." A generator (or device) that worked in terms of SYLLABLE-SIZE units, however, would not have to worry about the phonotactics of its output, as that information would be "built in" automatically within the syllables themselves. The problem rests with the notion of "random" generation. With phoneme-size units, the mechanism that insures proper phonotactics will have a very heavy burden given the enormous range of generatable but nonpermissible strings of English phonemes. If the units that the device generates are syllable size, and if we adopt the view that phonotactic constraints are specified within the domain of the syllable, then this information is automatically accounted for at that level. Consequently, the neologisms produced will abide by the language-specific phonotactics. For example, Butterworth's device could theoretically turn out two initial phonemes /pt-/, only to be disallowed by the mechanism that "edits out" nonpermissible strings. A device that generates syllable-size units, on the other hand, could not theoretically produce initial /pt-/ because there are no English syllables that begin with this cluster. In any event, both Butterworth and I have come upon the need for somehow producing neologistic forms where the input to the production device is NOT the phonological material of the target word.

Finally, in those cases where neologisms occur in a patient with word-finding disturbances, I believe we are justified in considering them as masking (Buckingham, 1979, p. 285) these selectional blocks by filling in syntactic space which in the pure anomic syndrome is often left open by hesitation or filled with some indefinite pronoun or circumlocutory material. This is in complete accordance with the descriptions of Lecours and Rouillon (1976, pp. 106, 114, 118, 123). If there is one overriding similarity among the posterior fluent aphasias, I believe it is difficulty in retrieving substantives for placement in the buffer. What I believe we must do is show how distinct types of errors all point to this primary deficit. Neologistic productions for the most part point to that deficit; I have tried to suggest some possible sources for them.

APPENDIX 1. DESCRIPTIONS OF THE BOSTON "COOKIE THEFT" PICTURE (GOODGLASS AND KAPLAN, 1972).

Patient C.B. at the Indianapolis VA Hospital, in Indianapolis, Indiana, is a severely involved posterior fluent aphasic with no frontal motor involvement. In the early stages of his disease his low comprehension scores kept him out of the "conduction" aphasic category. The patient had his stroke in July 1978 and has shown general improvement since but still has severe word-finding difficulties. Moreover, he cannot even repeat single syllabic items and cannot willfully manipulate his tongue to command, although he improves on visual imitation. His diadochokinetic rate (as tested on Schuell's, 1965, examination) was very rapid, but he could not switch place of articulation with any accuracy whatsoever. This problem remained unchanged even at testing on June 7, 1979. The repeated segments /pa pa pa/ were easier than /pa ta ka/, although even for the bilabial group the patient would switch [voice] and [nasal] rather indiscriminately. It is quite interesting to note that, despite the diminishing neology, C.B. still has the severe tongue apraxia. This makes it difficult to claim that the apraxia was the causal factor for the neologisms. This posterior tongue apraxic syndrome would be in line with the theories of Kimura (1976) and of Mateer and Kimura (1977). Finally, note the gradual increase in indefinite anaphora—especially on March 15, 1979. Because C.B. provided such a short description of the "Cookie Theft" picture on June 7, I have also included for that date a transcription of his description of the Schuell (1965) stick picture of the yard scene with a pond, a tree with a kite caught in it, a house, *etc*. Again, note the plethora of indefinites.

October 26, 1978 (Interview carried out by Hugh Buckingham)

Q: *What do you see going on in this picture?*

CB: [Looking at left side of picture—the cookie theft] *You mean like this boy? I mean* [noy], *and this, uh,* [mɛoy]. *This is a* [kénət] [kákən]. *I don't say it. I'm not getting anything from it. I'm getting, I'm dime from it, but I'm getting from it. These were* [ɛkspréšəz], [əgrǽšənz] *and with the type of mechanic is standing like this . . . and then the . . . I don't know what she* [gɔ́in] *other than* [?]. *And this is* [déli] *this one is the one and this one and this one and . . . I don't know.*

Q: *Can you tell me what she's doing?*

CB: [Looking at right side of picture—woman at the sink] *Anything* [?]. *I mean, she is a beautiful girl. And this is the same with her. And now its coming there and* [?]. *Now what about here or anything like that . . . what any.*

Q: *Is that a good artist's sketch there?*

CB: *For this?*

Q: *Uh huh.*

CB: *Yeah, sure. Yes, fine. Yes.*

Q: *Anything else?*

CB: *Nothing the* [kísəriz] *the, these are* [dǽvəriz] *and these and this one and these are living. This one's right in and these are . . . uh . . . and that's nothing, that's nothing . . . I can see things like this. You know, this type of thing. I can* [dréəbit], *but so what.*

November 9, 1978 (Interview carried out by Hugh Buckingham)

Q: *Tell me what's happening here.*

CB: [Looking at left side of picture] *You mean* [θrɟ] [?] *all the way around? Well, the* [bíəstiŋ] *of the* [vígəriŋ] *. . . and then there's somethings going up here with this . . .* [ðéə dyɔ́] *going here. And then of course the* [míkəniz] *like here* [íriŋ]. *And this is bring out that is* [?] [θ:] [sɪŋ] *with a . . . one, two, three. Three* [bɔŋ] *in here,* [trévòrz]. [Now shifting to right side] *And then I guess the . . .* [ðɔ:] *this is* [təʔ], *I guess it* [gənz] *on something, but anyway. This* [buš] [dʊʔ] *both* [?] *comes to this one, with both these things. . . . This here, and all this.*

Q: *Yeah, what's happening here?*

CB: *Well, it's just a* [bǽdər] *of* [wɔʔ] [wɔ́lər] *. . . Uh, it's the . . . uh . . . , this* [pɔ́r:bəl] [dírdəl] [pír pír], *you know, there.*

March 15, 1979 (Interview carried out by Hugh Buckingham)

Q: *Tell me everything that's going on.*

CB: *Everything?*

Q: *Yeah. What's happening?*

CB: *You mean from this thing right here?*

Q: *Everything. Right.*

CB: [Looking at left side of picture] *That, and then this one and this one. And this one here that it is this. Then this one. There's one in it. Then he gets in this one. And this one and* [ðǽs] *one. That has to one in here, too. Then he can* [gódin] *with all the thing here, the boy. He gets on this one,* [dɛbədɛbidɛbi] *then this one,*

[dévəl] *one. This one has another one, boy* [pointing to the girl]. *This is a boy, this is a boy. I forget the boy and a boy. This one ever which ever one is right and a boy. Then this one is right here, right here. And . . . nice right in here.*
Q: *So this is where the theft is taking place?*
CB: *Right, right.*
Q: *How about on the other side?*
CB: [Looking at the right side of the picture] *Uh, well, this is the . . . the* [dídɨŋ] *of this. This and this and this and this. These things going in there like that. This is* [sen] *things here. This one here, these two things here. And the other one here, back in this one, this one* [gɪʔ] *look at this one* [looking at the water spilling over].
Q: *Yeah, what's happening there?*
CB: *I can't tell you what that is, but I know what it is, but I don't know where it is. But I don't know what's under. I know it's you couldn't say it's . . . I couldn't say what it is. I couldn't say what that is. This shu—that should be right in here. That's* [béəli] *bad in there. Anyway, this one here, and that, and that's it. This is the getting in here and that's the getting around here, this one and one with this one. And this one, and that's it, isn't it? I don't know what else you'd want.*

June 7, 1979 (Interview carried out by Hugh Buckingham)

CB: [Looking at left side of picture] *Alright, so the* [kæd bæd] *is going up here to see the thing under this thing because of this. This one, this one here, and this one and that's all right. Then he comes to this one. What's she doing up in here? I don't know. I never could see this one, this one. I can see what he's going. Probably say, well alright, I'll do something. And this would be the boy. Boy or boy, boy . . . anyway, it's a boy . . . boy, no. "P", "P" "I" "R" "T" "L" "S"* [spelling aloud]. [Shifting to right side of picture] *And then this one, and the- this one at three. And three of them right in here. And three of them, and then she's* [čænəlz] *to go back at the thing thing like this one.* [lɛdædædædi], *and this one. This and* [dékɔrz] *is* [dækɨŋ] *in this one. And that's—this one, and this one, and that's about it. This one and that one.*
(Describing the Schuell, 1965, yard picture with the kite in the tree, *etc.*)
CB: *Then this one is good. Then, this, this one, one, two, three, four, five, six, seven, this the thing in here. The . . . a thousand ways. This one go* [tu du di du]. *This one goes up in here, like this one. Then this one with the dog, and this one and this one and this one. I don't know what's this, that being right up in this one. Well sure, he's okay. Then he does the same thing, riding on this one. This one does the same things. Why are you doing this one up here? And this one, and this one. Not this one, but this one. And this one that's no good* [nod] *right and that's it.*

APPENDIX 2. SPONTANEOUS SPEECH SAMPLES OF NEOLOGISTIC JARGON.

Patient B.F. suffered a ruptured aneurysm with a resulting large left posterior lesion and neologistic jargon aphasia. For more detailed descriptions of the linguistic and anatomical aspects of this case, see Buckingham and Kertesz (1974, 1976) and Kertesz, Harlock, and Coates (1979, Figure 6, p. 39). In general, see Kertesz and Benson (1970) for an in-depth study of the clinicopathological correlates of neologistic jargon. Patient B.F. was under the care of Dr. Kertesz at St. Joseph's Hospital, London, Ontario, Canada.

August 19, 1970 (Interview carried out by Andrew Kertesz)

Q: *Were you talking about your business?*

A: *Yes, well I don't know that we'd particularly* [míst kə́rDiz ər héktiz] *but we had the* [bérəst]. *They were* [ínvɛntəd kǽstərz wɪs kístək æn nи̌čəz ɪk hǽmpəs fər nékstəs ən térəs] *and so on. And then as I started to doing that with* [mи̌čənə], *this has gone to one or two* [vɛrn we]. [kə́ntðiz ɔr wašʲ] *right into a perfect* [mɔ́čnər] *or customer, this lady would be too lack to reverse, riding right over the* [tawt] . . .

Q: *Where is your business? Which town?*

A: *I think my* [fɔ́rməst əkúšnər] *looks* [éliŋtən]. *I feel good do this all the time, but I don't know anything about special* [ədváyzət]. *But I think I do true to* [tróplis] *people, and go along spent the* [yɛr], *what their troubles are. But, I say it's kind of empty to mark these customers, too. I'm not sure exactly what I'm talking about.*

Q: *I gather you have a hardware store.*

A: [kɔ́ləs] *yes. Yes we would lots of corn hash* [hɛs] *has to* [blǽli] *out the doors.*

Q: *Who's running the store now?*

A.: *I don't know. Yes, the* [bɪk]. *Yes, I would say that the* [mи́k désəs nósəs ər či̯píktərz]. *Of course, I have also missed on the* [kárftər ték]. *Do you know what that is? I've* [tókən] *to* [íŋgəš]. *They have been* [tóst sósɪli]. *They'd have been put to* [mayǽfə] *and made* [pálɪs] *and a* [máyədákəl] *send to you. That is me* [əlɔ́rdədəs]. *That makes* [ənǽkrənə séndə].

Q: *How is your arm coming along?*

A: *To my person, I don't have any much of nothing* [ɔ́fsɛt]. *I know a* [déprəkɔl], *over american person churches such as* [nóDəš] *or* [pénθənəs].

Q: [Showing patient a rubber ball] *What is it?*

A: *Well, no. I guess I don't think* [véli] *too much about that. It's a, it does some . . . a* [bám slébi] *like a* [kúmp skɔ́Dɪŋ mayǽnəməl pítswəh].

Q: *Hold it in your hand. What is it?*

A: *Well, it's a* [pan šep] *of* [šuts] *that* [šep] . . .

Q: [Later on in the interview] *What were you saying?*

A: *I was just wondering what kind of a* [hot mon mə́čɔ́rn] *it is. . . . So,* [ɪmz] *is* [lɔ́rkɪŋ] *with this* [sáDər] *that was sticking him. His company is a* [náDərd slíŋkəŋ] *up out of the pipe* [sìn glís]. *And this is the thing, you know, as I've kidded to you, having* [yéstər] *and* [mɪsdɔ́], *the man right* [əpstéə] *has come down in the main office right in Windsor, and put up with the* [lips]. *And he sticked up a. He like to was talking right along with the* [mérilǽnd]. *He's be stand there all night with the* [mǽnəskǽn].

Q: *The fellow in the next bed, is he from Windsor?*

A: *Yeah, George has gone up a short time. But I mean the thing is no* [səslípər]. *The* [ard tɔ́pəl] *to we* [hæ] *as I said as we've* [kɔ́stəmər mískəstər márkəmər], *just last week.*

Q: *What do you mean?*

A: *Well, when I went down you were in* [blækénət], *and you went in the* [plǽDəsk fent sǽDər] *which was some* [pard]. *You were going to stick at* [si ay e ɛl] *and* [blǽDər] *at north. Good they got with you. Did you recall this?*

Q: *I'm not sure what you mean.*

A: *Well, what I'm trying to tell you is that in this* [sǽDərdi ɛsdísno æn mǽstərpéšən]. *Get a* [smɔlt] *one, and turn it to you, and I hear this on the* [ɔ́čəl plénər] *or the old* [plénər]. *There, an old cleaner. That's something hear,* [síDər pléʊk]. *And connected with this* [sáDər] *might be the* [áčəmənt] *that you were listening about his* [áDəpi]. . . .

Q: [Later on in the interview, showing patient a pipe] *What is this?*

A: *Well, the only thing I can say it again is* [mǽDər] *or* [mɔ́Dər] *fish or* [sádən] *fishin', sewed into the accident to miss in the* [pɔ́rDəlz].

September 29, 1971 (Interview carried out by Elizabeth Pool, psychometrician in Dr. Kertesz's laboratory, and Hugh Buckingham.)

Q: *You look well.*

A.: [æts] *right do, because we* [hǽvən nɛ́Dər hǽdæfən]—

Q: *Have you ever been here before?*

A: *With you? Oh, yes, dear.*

Q: *How many times? Do you remember?*

A: *Well, I don't know. It was quite a number of* [rɪz] *down here that we* [flæš dəm].

Q: *Can you tell me your full name?*

A: *Down here the* [krɪd]? *One of the* [bi skíDɪk fawntən. *But that's it really honest. It's really* [kánfɛsjən kándrəd sol] *and that's what the man had. That's what we* [ɔ́nəs] *to get most to get out to give you. What's happened? Terrible.*

Q: *What's your name? Tell me your name.*

A: *With what?* [θərd šem]?

Q: *Your name.*

A: [se šad jəs barn] *sure, my dear, sure and* [jər šɛlf].

Q: *Where do you live?*

A: *Mine? Mine's right at home in* [kɛl šáDi]—*I know what, unless they kiss me off I owe her something about* [tɔ́ni]. *I must say well* [di] *I'm sorry the* [trídiz] *not right because that's what the* [trɪs] *is right. I know my* [trésəz] *are all right. I know every monk I drew as I love everyone of them. Ever* [ðət ðay wɔ́nəm].

Q: *Can you tell me what kind of work you did?*

A: *Might. What kind?*

Q: *What kind of work did you do before you became ill?*

A: *Oh no. You mean* [wɪš frɛnč mɛ́nči]?

Q: *Did you work?*

A: *Oh, I don't know where it* [rɛ́nt lɪsdísɪt. *It came and* [tɛrd] *it and got it . . .* [čun sɔ́ldə]. *He didn't have* [yuk]. *And why? Well, he didn't seem to know. He didn't know what to do with that dope. That dumb Tony that I had. He said you're going on a* [tɛ́mpo]. *What's a* [jɔ́mpʊdər]? *As* [ænəstrúDəš], *I was still so much. I was always* [lúdən] *like* [tíši]. *That's all I wanted to try* [məs] *the left* [álmə]. *These little* [tréftiz]. *. . . Like my* [šem bʊðz]?

Q: *You got new shoes?*

A: *Oh yeah. Oh no, dear. Do you know that I been wearing* [ðəz] *in* [sɛn yɪr zɪŋg]? *I* [bɛt] *these my* [læs mɪnəsɔ́rDək]. *. . . . They're* [bɔ́rDəfəl].

Q: *Are they?*

A: *They are.*

Q: *They're comfortable.*

A: *I never* [túθ may tós wɪtít ðay tíg] *take them right out and get them to use my* [stɛf] *all over.* [hɛf sɔ́m fər ɔ́m] *. . .*

Q: *Tell me about your sickness. When you were sick.*

A: *Well, I don't know* [sər fə so sərm]. *I mean, I try do. I do. I know that the* [rírDər] *things have got to be my* [pɔ́rDə]. *They've got to be. They've got to* [mi], *by dear. But I don't always a get what I wanted, what I want to do. My* [nits əm nər stɔ́rtən] *with them. But they can* [sɪ klɛ́rɪŋ taym]. *I've get them back* [gi hays]. *I don't know what to do. They don't come here and talk to them. I talk to them, talk to them. What do they* [wóik]? *Well, go and had it. Take it all and take it out. Take it a, take, take, take this out. Goes, goes, goes. You know* [sləš dərstəd], *taste this and make it out. You* [čɪrəməkəm] *doesn't like 'em. And then, as I say,* [lɔ́ tɔ́g]. *I'm sorry. I said you took* [čɪŋk] *down like that. You* [tárt tárDər gədɪŋlər fárnər dəzə čɛŋk fárDər slálɛ]. *And why? 'Cause you going to* [jokəm]. *'Cause you're not going to be* [kókəram kégɪk kwínsɪt], *everything* [ízəm]. *I want the guy come up and tell me* [ðəm]. *I know that the* [wɪmpərz írz ə wənt ðə məmps ə wənt ðə gəmps ə wənt ðə nət ðən haus]. *I like the.* . . . *I don't know how to tell you, this is so* [fέrəŋgi]. *What is* [so nói sə fyέn]. *What did they get down here? How long did you have? Your* [nayf] *I know. Look, look at things now. I look at your notice, and I went, what the devil does this thing? I was a* [dín bó yú:], *didn't you? And I get a* [kópɛ]. *Well, what is that? Oh, that was our* [wíŋkə]. *A* [wíŋəz] *Honey, I didn't mean it. I didn't honest. My kid, kid, I didn't have any was in that* [bánɪks]. *I couldn't say the talk* [swíŋəs]. *But I tell you now I do. I do believe. I've got to believe they got to be* [trɪm] *clothes, haven't they. Have they,* [wínə]? *Because I don't want them. I'm having trouble* [əf] *here, too. What's make them be so* [lǽfəl]?—*Sure we can. We can get at the* [fə́rməs] *and get* [ǽnəs] *and* [skɛt] *with the* [kamps], *and* [kɪt] *on us, and* [skɪt] *it out. We want to make things go for 'em, a* [mɛg skɪŋ fə́nəm] *a* [lɛg skɪn], *for all these fellas.* . . .

Q: *Are you married?*
A: *No, dear. I have a wife, and I've got a* [blast wayf dárli].
Q: *Do you have children?*
A: *My* [lays]? *My life is right here with me.*
Q: *Do you have children?*
A: *She's getting, my wife's* [kráyDi] *out there.*
Q: *She's out there, is she?*
A: *No, she didn't come* [wɪs] *us. She's* [dɔ́rvɪŋ ə́ðənə́ðər krásɪt dézɪn] *but she* [bátwe] *three* [klánəs] *with her.*
Q: *Did you have to come a long way to get here today?*
A: *No we.* . . . *Three miles, about* [θridi mɪlz].
Q: *Thirty miles?*
A: *Yes, it's down about a hundred and some* [ɔr:dərtən] *in* [flɔrn]. *Do you know where* [frέŋən frέŋən ru láynə]?
Q: *No.*
A: *Well, sure you can. You're driving along the, you go on the* [šáDər], *you know the* [šápɛnər].
Q: *Uh huh.*
A: *I don't seem to have any* . . .
Q: *I'm not too good at directions.*
A: *That's really not a whole* [véndəs]. *It's on a* [trɪm]. *We're on a* [trésdən] *most of it coming* [mǽstíl]. *We get* [mod] *of it.*
Q: *Do you live in the country?*
A: *No, just in the. Well, we're doing it now. We used to* [nɪš]. *I used to* [nɪš]. *I used to* [fɪp] *in a* [fɛd bǽDər] *on* [flɛš] *island. I always* [féšəst] *in broad* [íŋglən].

APPENDIX 3. NEOLOGY ON PICTURE
DESCRIPTION AND ON CONFRONTATION NAMING

Patient J.T. suffered from a stroke with damage in the left temporo-parietal region. She was left with a Wernicke's aphasia which, with gradual improvement in comprehension, cleared to a "conduction" aphasia. Throughout the period during which the author worked with her (September 1973 to April 1974), J.T.'s speech showed neology, and she continued to have severe difficulty with accessing nouns. Further details concerning the linguistic aspects of this case may be found in Buckingham, Whitaker, and Whitaker (1979). Patient J.T. was under the care of Dr. Robert Joynt at Strong Memorial Hospital and at Monroe Community Hospital, both in Rochester, New York. The following speech samples include a description of the Boston (Goodglass and Kaplan, 1972) "Cookie Theft" picture, which is immediately followed by the confrontation naming task with Schuell's (1965) picture cards. Note the perserverative carry-overs from the first task to the second.

November 1, 1973 (Interview carried out by Hugh Buckingham)

JT: [Looking at left side of picture] *Well, this is a little girl boy. And that's a little girl, he's a* [trə tráksər] *candy. And, my lights are, oh* [kǽθəl dúnət], [kǽnə dónət]. *And he was up on the* [ráksər], *but it's a wonder he wasn't* [ɔ́fə] *fell* [ɔ́fə] *there.* [Switching to right side of picture] *Now, this is his mother, I imagine. And she's got the* [rɔ́pər] *on. And he* [krǽkər jídzə krǽkə] . . . [krǽksər]. *And,* [ráksɪnəz] *spilling the water . . . running the run all over, running the water. Oh, here's a cup. Here's the, some of the* [frǽŋšəni].
[End of picture description]

1. Chair
   JT: *Well, that's a* [rɔ́:] [ré:] *the* [ræg], *uh, the* [rǽksər] *chair we sit on.*
2. House
   JT: *That's a house, uh,* [ə ræ:] *and a* [fríji] i] *color, and a* [pəró].
3. Hand
   HB: *This.*
   JT: *Rug.*
   HB: *What's that?*
   JT: *Well, a* [krǽkbrɛ̀š] [krǽkbròš].
   HB: *Your hand.*
   JT: *Yeah, the* [fænd].
4. Car
   JT: *That's a* [pérɔ̀rǽks] [pɛ̀rɔ̀ráks] . . . [rag], *uh,* [prédrá:] . . . *evening rock. And, uh, I guess that's the front part, isn't it?*
   HB: *What's that called?*
   JT: *Well, I use I could one . . . a rug. I used to ride a* [ræb] *too when I was younger.*
5. Little girl
   JT: *This is little* [ge]. *She was, uh,* [kráksɪŋ] *with her mother, and she had a . . .* [kɔ́mpiŋ] *in the cup.*
6. Cup of coffee
   JT: *A coffee. I'll have one now if we* [hal].
7. Knife
   JT: *That's a* [rəš]. *Sometimes I get one around here that I can cut a couple* [rəgz]. *There's no rugs around here and nothing cut right. But that's a rug, and I had some nice* [rɔ́kəbz]. *I wish I had one now. Say, how* [wɪ́ši] [ɪdaw], *uh, windy, look how windy. It's really window, isn't it?* [looking out her window].
   HB: *This is a knife.*
   JT: *That's a* [kwíkɔ̀ràp] . . . *the* [kwékrɔ̀g] . . . [krèpɔ̀rɔ́g].
   HB: *Can you say knife? Knife.*
   JT: *Knife. Frank knife. Yeah, a* [ro:], *nice sharper.*
   Gee, I used to [píədə] *nice one, too.*
8. Sheep
   JT: *Oh, that's a gray rugs. A rug. Isn't it?*
   HB: *That's a sheep.*
   JT: [kwiš].
   HB: *A sheep.*
   JT: *A* [kwiš] [kwiš]

HB: *A sheep.*
JT: *Didn't I say* [kwiš]?
HB: *Sheep.*
JT: *Uh,* [kweš], *uh,* [ragz]. *That's wool* [lɔb].

9. Bell

JT: *That's uh, a* [kwɛrn], *before we'll be signing for the* [kwébèl] *to be* [z] *play* [ríŋəl] [ríŋəl] *bell.* [ríŋgə] *bell . . . maybe* [əbə] *they time I'll be able to sign some. I don't know.*

10. Clock

JT: *That's the, uh, time. See my time, uh, too, over there.* (pointing to her clock)
HB: *What's that called? What is that?*
JT: *Yeah, uh, that's a* [kwékræ̀] [prékyè:], *uh, the* [kıˀ] [dàynīrám] [dram] *. . . the* [díθəl] *evening down.*
HB: *Clock.*
JT: *Huh?*
HB: *Clock.*
JT: *The* [braks].
HB: *Clock.*
JT: *The well, play well.*
HB: *Clock.*
JT: *Yeah. Which one is that now?*
HB: *Tick tock, tick tock. Clock.*
JT: [kɛl] *. . .* [pɛl], *my, uh, oh, I know, I get it right.*
HB: *It's a clock.*
JT: *Yeah, it's, uh, three . . . numbers now. 'Bout nine somewheres around in there.*

11. Barn

JT: *Well, that's the . . . looks like a rug . . . or the* [kweb] *. . . the ball. The ball for the man making the fall. And the player,* [plépər] *of the house. And it has the wool on it.*
HB: *Is that a barn?*
JT: *Huh.*
HB: *In the country. Barn. The farmer.*
JT: *That's a* [bɔ́lfèv], *That's the ball, uh,* [ðèčɚbél], *isn't it?*

12. Hammer

JT: *Uh, quaker pass. I used to have one of that, but I wouldn't where that is anymore.* [kwípɚkæ̀ŋɚr] *. . . uh, . . . I got about a* [édəd] *bill.*
HB: *Hammer*
JT: *One, two, three . . . bill* [fayr].
HB: *Hammer.*
JT: [kıl] *hammer . . . kill hammer. Hammer.*

13. Fork

JT: *That's a fork. I just knocked one over.*

14. Leaf

JT: *That's a* [kwel]. *That's a* [kwek]. *That could be a . . .* [fræbɚlǽf], *too. That could be different things, too.*

15. Ladder

JT: [hǽpɚlæ̀čɚr]

16. Umbrella

JT: *That's a* [byɚ klǽk], *rain bell . . . raining the bell. The bell is raining. Is that what I said?*
HB: *Umbrella.*
JT: *Huh?*
HB: *Umbrella.*

JT: *A* [pélɔblò].
HB: *Umbrella.*
JT: *A what?*
HB: *Umbrella.*
JT: *Well, that's a rain* . . . [bɛl] [bɛl] *rainbow* . . . *blue rainbow* . . . *when it's raining, it'll come down to there.*
HB: *Umbrella.*
JT: [ɔbélɔ].
HB: *Umbrella.*
JT: [ɔbélɔ].
HB: *Umbrella.*
JT: *Yeah. What did I say?* . . . *a* [bélɔrènɔ].
17. Rake
JT: *That's* [flakiŋ], *uh, to* [gres] *off of the wall.* [gréswɔl].
18. Calendar
JT: *That's a* [bélɔgɔr] [klak] [édɔ]. Well, it's a little bit late, though. It says eight o'clock. Now it's going on to, uh, [nɔ́rvi] [nárvi] . . .
HB: *November.*
JT: *Yesterday was ninety. No, it's* [vɔrnáyndi] *now. Yeah, see that, uh, what's it say?* [nɔ́rvi] . . . [nóšɔr] [pointing to her calendar].
HB: *November.*
JT: [nóčɔrɔr].
HB: *November.*
JT: *"N" "O"* [spelling] [óvɛri] . . . [ɔvéri] [élɔbè].
19. Sled
JT: *That's a* [kwálɔbebɔr]. *Before they'll be filling* [ðɔ] *we get a lot of snow, they'll be filling up the, uh,* [slébɔd] *for the children to wax.*
20. Horseshoe
JT: *That's a* [kwɔ́rwèk] . . . *play* [kwar] *to play* [wɔlt].

REFERENCES

Alajouanine, Th. Verbal realization in aphasia. *Brain*, 1956, *79*, 1–28.
Aronoff, M. *Word formation in generative grammar.* Cambridge, Mass.: MIT Press, 1976.
Brown, J. W. *Aphasia, apraxia and agnosia: Clinical and theoretical aspects.* Springfield, Ill.: Charles C Thomas, 1972.
Brown, J. W. On the neural organization of language: Thalamic and cortical relationships. *Brain and Language*, 1975, *2*, 18–30.
Brown, J. W. *Mind, brain, and consciousness: The neuropsychology of cognition.* New York: Academic Press, 1977.
Buckingham, H. W. The conduction theory and neologistic jargon. *Language and Speech*, 1977, *20*, 174–184.
Buckingham, H. W. Linguistic aspects of lexical retrieval disturbances in the posterior fluent aphasias. In H. Whitaker & H. A. Whitaker (Eds.), *Studies in neurolinguistics* (Vol. 4). New York: Academic Press, 1979.
Buckingham, H. W. & Kertesz, A. A linguistic analysis of fluent aphasia. *Brain and Language*, 1974, *1*, 43–61.
Buckingham, H. W. & Kertesz, A. *Neologistic jargon aphasia.* Amsterdam: Swets and Zeitlinger, 1976.
Buckingham, H. W., Whitaker, H., & Whitaker, H. A. Alliteration and assonance in neologistic jargon aphasia. *Cortex*, 1978 *14*, 365–380.

Buckingham, H. W., Whitaker, H. & Whitaker, H. A. On linguistic perseveration. In H. Whitaker & H. A. Whitaker (Eds.), *Studies in neurolinguistics* (Vol. 4). New York: Academic Press, 1979.

Butterworth, B. Hesitation and the production of verbal paraphasias and neologisms in jargon aphasia. *Brain and Language*, 1979, *8*, 133–161.

Caplan, D., Keller, L., & Locke, S. Inflection of neologisms in aphasia. *Brain*, 1972, *95*, 169–172.

Fay, D. & Culter, A. Malapropisms and the structure of the mental lexicon. *Linguistic Inquiry*, 1977, *8*, 505–520.

Freud, S. 1901. Slips of the tongue. [Reprinted in R. T. DeGeorge & F. DeGeorge (Eds.), *The structuralists from Marx to Levi-Strauss*. New York: Doubleday, 1972.]

Fromkin, V. The non-anomalous nature of anomalous utterances. *Language*, 1971, *47*, 27–52.

Garrett, M. F. The analysis of sentence production. In G. Bower (Ed.), *The psychology of learning and motivation: Advances in research and theory*. New York: Academic Press, 1975.

Green, E. Phonological and grammatical aspects of jargon in an aphasic patient: A case study. *Language and Speech*, 1969, *12*, 103–118.

Goodglass, H. & Kaplan, E. *The Boston diagnostic aphasia test*. Washington: Lea and Febiger, 1972.

Halle, M. Prolegomena to a theory of word formation. *Linguistic Inquiry*, 1973, *4*, 3–16.

Kertesz, A. & Benson, D. F. Neologistic jargon: A clinicopathological study. *Cortex*, 1970, *6*, 362–386.

Kertesz, A., Harlock, W., & Coates, R. Computer tomographic localization, lesion size, and prognosis in aphasia and nonverbal impairment. *Brain and Language*, 1979, *8*, 34–50.

Kimura, D. The neural basis of language qua gesture. In H. Whitaker & H. A. Whitaker (Eds.), *Studies in neurolinguistics* (Vol. 2). New York: Academic Press, 1976.

Lecours, A. R., & Lhermitte, F. Phonemic paraphasias: Linguistic structures and tentative hypotheses. *Cortex*, 1969, *5*, 193–228.

Lecours, A. R., & Lhermitte, F. Recherches sur le language des aphasiques: 4. Analyse d'un corpus de néologismes; notion de paraphasie monémique. *Encéphale*, 1972, *61*, 295–315.

Lecours, A. R., & Rouillon, F. Neurolinguistic analysis of jargonaphasia and jargonagraphia. In H. Whitaker & H. A. Whitaker (Eds.), *Studies in neurolinguistics* (Vol. 2). New York: Academic Press, 1976.

Lecours, A. R., & Vanier-Clement, M. Schizophasia and jargonaphasia: A comparative description with comments on Chaika's and Fromkin's respective looks at "schizophrenic" language. *Brain and Language*, 1976, *3*, 516–565.

Luria, A. R. *Traumatic aphasia*. The Hague: Mouton, 1970.

Mateer, C., & Kimura, D. Impairment of nonverbal oral movements in aphasia. *Brain and Language*, 1977, *4*, 262–276.

Shattuck-Hufnagel, S., & Klatt, D. The limited use of distinctive features and markedness in speech production: Evidence from speech error data. *Journal of Verbal Learning and Verbal Behavior*, 1979, *18*, 41–55.

Schuell, H. *Differential diagnosis of aphasia with the Minnesota test*. Minneapolis: University of Minnesota Press, 1965.

Vennemann, T. Words and syllables in natural generative grammar. In A. Bruck, R. Fox, & M. LeGaly (Eds.), *Papers from the parasession on natural phonology*. Chicago: Chicago Linguistic Society, 1974.

Weinstein, E. A. & Puig-Antich, J. Jargon and its analogues. *Cortex*, 1974, *10*, 75–83.

Chapter 4

The Anatomy of Jargon

ANDREW KERTESZ

INTRODUCTION

The anatomy of language impairment is in need of reexamination with our new methods of determining the extent and location of cerebral damage. These methods, the radionucleide isotope scan (IS) and computerized tomography (CT), will provide three-dimensional localizing information at the time the patient is examined. Thus, either the various physiological and linguistic changes can be "frozen" in time in relationship to the lesion (or the new added lesion) or the extent of recovery can be measured against any changes in the clinical and linguistic state of the patient. The number of such observations greatly exceeds the number of autopsies in the past, increasing the reliability of localization. These methods have been applied to the fluency–nonfluency dichotomy in aphasia with IS scans (Benson, 1967), to neologistic jargonaphasia with IS scans and autopsy studies (Kertesz & Benson, 1970), to IS localization of lesion in various types of aphasia (Kertesz, Lesk, & McCabe, 1977), CT localization in aphasia (Naeser & Hayward, 1978; Kertesz, Harlock, & Coates, 1979), Broca's aphasia with autopsy and CT (Mohr, Pessin, Finkelstein, Funkenstein, Duncan, & Davis, 1978), Gerstmann syndrome (Kertesz, 1979), and in many other instances, usually reports of individual cases.

63

JARGONAPHASIA

Copyright © 1981 by Academic Press, Inc.
All rights in any form reserved.
ISBN 0-12-137580-3

The striking language output in jargonaphasia has long intrigued clinicians and linguists alike. It is hoped that defining the neural structures involved in cases of jargonaphasia will provide some insight into the complex processes of language, in addition to the practical value of localization in a clinical setting.

In this chapter, I shall review the literature of the localization of lesions in jargonasia, present new material utilizing IS and CT localization, and conclude with a clinicopathological correlation.

REVIEW OF THE LITERATURE

Wernicke had two autopsied cases of sensory aphasia in 1874, one with a softening in the first temporal convolution in addition to generalized atrophy and another with a temporal lobe abscess. He did not distinguish jargonaphasia. Subsequent investigators became interested in the anatomical differences between pure word deafness (acknowledged by everyone to be rarely if ever pure), and sensory aphasia with paraphasias (Wernicke's aphasia). Starr (1889) reviewed 50 cases of sensory aphasia and concluded that there was no constant pathological difference between the cases with or without paraphasia.

Pick (1892), after whom focal atrophy of the brain in senile dementia is named as a separate disease entity, published a case of jargonaphasia with focal atrophy of the left temporal lobe. The distinction of neologistic jargon was not made, and in the protocol, mostly semantic jargon is recorded.

Henschen (1922) tabulated 12 cases with jargonaphasia, in his sixth volume of clinicopathological correlations. Eight cases were considered with unilateral lesions. Two other cases had too short periods of observations or incomplete descriptions. Two cases were considered paradoxical. Mingazzini's case of word deafness and aphasia with a left T3 lesion had a lesion on the opposite side also. Thomas's case was considered paradoxical by Henschen because the anterior portion of T1, and T2 were destroyed. None of these cases had photographs or transcriptions of speech available. It is difficult to draw conclusions as to the validity of the localizations but the eight principal cases all had involvement of the first two temporal gyri (T1 and T2). Gyrus Q (Heschl's gyrus) is mentioned to be involved in most of these cases, and the importance of this area in word deafness is emphasized.

Head (1926) provided localizing information (details of skull wounds) for three cases of syntactical aphasia, two of whom had jargon. In one of them, he was certain that both lips of the sylvian fissure were involved posteriorly.

Neilsen's (1946) review of temporal lobectomies contains a number of Henschen's cases of jargon. Two of his own cases have fluent paraphasic speech. Case 2 with neologisms and jargon ("amnestic aphasia and formulation aphasia") has an illustration showing the extent of the temporal lobe removed, but no mention is made of microscopic sections to detect any involvement of other areas. In his Case 3, the language disturbance appears to be mostly semantic with some neologistic jargon. Although no autopsy is available, the excision for glioma is drawn to show that Broadmann area 37 and the angular gyrus are spared. Neilsen concludes that jargonaphasia (formulation aphasia) is related to lesions in area 37 of the temporal lobe, even though some of his cases (#3) were shown to spare this region and involve others such as the supramarginal gyrus.

The posterior superior temporal and the supramarginal gyrus and the underlying subcortical white matter including the arcuate fasciculus were involved in the autopsied case of a jargonaphasia of Cohn and Neumann (1958). A smaller right-sided lesion was also present, undercutting the posterior frontal region.

Kleist (1962) published anatomical reports of sensory aphasia and these exemplify the difficulties when detailed gross and microscopic descriptions of lesions are accompanied by inconsistent clinical descriptions. Only two of his cases (De and Del) had neologisms and both had similar lesions affecting the transverse gyri, the "regio paratransversalis" in the planum temporale and the posterior third of the first temporal convolutions, and some other areas of the temporal lobes somewhat less consistently. The supramarginal gyrus was not involved in either case. One patient with what Kleist called "sentence deafness" (Seuff) characterized by "digressions and paragrammatisms" had detailed transcription from which he appears to have had semantic jargon with a great deal of irrelevant paragrammatic output but no neologisms. The anatomical description is detailed and the lesion is interesting because the localized contusion in the temporoparietal area was similar to stroke lesions although somewhat more scattered. The first and second temporal and supramarginal convolutions were affected mainly, but the case is complicated by scattered bilateral orbitofrontal and additional right temporal lesions. The distinction between work, sentence, speech, and word sense deafness is poorly defined and at times arbitrary. In some cases, repetition was examined without quantitation to classify them as conduction aphasia; in others, it was not documented. Kleist also concluded that the "same clinical pictures of sensory aphasia" can be brought about by lesions in different situations in relation to the cerebral cortex.

Weinstein, Lyerly, Cole, & Ozer (1966) suggested that bilateral involvement was present in all their cases of jargon. They based their conclusion on the fact that most of their cases had trauma, tumor, or aneurysm.

However, their cases were mostly semantic jargon without much comprehension deficit, with the exception of two cases which showed more neologisms. One of these (Case 17) was caused by a cerebrovasular accident.
Neologistic jargonaphasia was the target of the localization study of
Kertesz and Benson (1970). The patients were chosen because of characteristic copious neologistic jargon from a larger group of fluent aphasics.
Patients with predominantly semantic jargon or mumbling stereotypic, pal-
lilalic speech were specifically excluded. Autopsy findings were given in
five cases and scan and angiographic localization were reported in the
remaining cases. All of the autopsied cases showed a parietotemporal lesion.
The temporal lesion was quite posterior and small in four cases (6,7,9, and
10). One of the autopsied cases also had an IS scan which revealed an uptake
somewhat larger than that apparent on the surface of the brain, at the
posterior end of the sylvian fissure. Both the superior temporal and the
supramarginal gyri were clearly involved but the subcortical lesion was
more extensive as evidenced on the coronal cut of the brain. The IS uptakes
were all in a similar position in the left parietotemporal area. To summarize
this localization, they were drawn on an anatomical template, and overlapped (Figures 4.1 and 4.2). For the clinical and localizing details of these
cases, the original paper should be consulted (Kertesz & Benson, 1970).
From the evidence it was concluded that neologistic jargon appears in
lesions of BOTH the posterior portion of the first temporal gyrus (auditory
association area) and the arcuate fasciculus underlying the supramarginal
gyrus connecting this area with the frontal lobes.
    Another case of neologistic jargon was published with autopsy findings
(Buckingham & Kertesz, 1974). Obstruction of the posterior branches of
the middle cerebral artery resulted in infarction of the left posterior sylvian

NEOLOGISTIC JARGON-
ISOTOPE & AUTOPSY OVERLAP

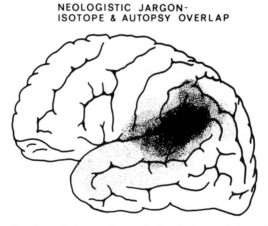

Figure 4.1. Overlap of the tracings of nine lesions of the 1970 study on the
lateral template from Sobotta's atlas.

AUTOPSIED NEOLOGISTIC JARGON

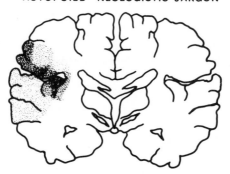

Figure 4.2. Overlap of the tracings of four lesions of the 1970 study where coronal sections were available (all autopsies) and the new Case 10 (R.S.).

region with involvement of the first temporal convolution, the supramarginal gyrus, and the left parietal lobule. Although the patient had bilateral infarctions at autopsy, the right-sided lesion was a fresh one and played no role in the language disturbance. The unilaterality of the lesion responsible for the aphasia was further supported by the isotope scan at the time of onset of the patient's jargonaphasia. More details about this patient (C.M.) were published in our monograph on neologistic jargon (Buckingham & Kertesz, 1976).

Lhermitte, Lecours, Ducarne, & Escourolla (1973) described the autopsy findings in a patient who initially had Wernicke's aphasia with neologistic jargon, but who, in the course of recovery, was noted to have segments of nonfluent, dysarthric, and agrammatic speech coexisting with fluent, meaningless, paragrammatic elements. The pathology showed extensive frontoparietal and temporal infarction, destroying Broca's and Wernicke's area, arcuate fasciculus, inferior parietal lobule, the opercular third of the pre- and postcentral gyri, and some of the supramarginal gyrus. An old infarct on the right was smaller and spared but undercut the homologue of Broca's area. New infarcts on the right side produced global aphasia before the patient died. The slow laborious mode of expression was attributed to the left prerolandic involvement, and possibly to the effect of intensive speech therapy designed to slow down the patient. The authors suggested that the motor control of the fluent, meaningless jargon was assumed by subcortical gray structures.

Thalamic hemorrhage on CT scans has been described as causing intermittent, transient, logorrheic paraphasia resembling delirium (Mohr, Wattes, & Duncan, 1975). The role of the thalamus in language has not been fully clarified although it is generally acknowledged that thalamic structures have an integrative and driving function in relationship to cortical language mechanisms. Temporary damage or dysfunction to the posterior thalamic regions will affect the input to Wernicke's area and also, because of the anatomical proximity to the temporal isthmus and arcuate fasciculus, these structures may be affected by edema, vascular changes, etc. The indirect effect of the loss of thalamic connections, something akin to dia-schisis, could temporarily produce jargon without actually involving the structures that usually cause the syndrome. The temporary and fluctuating nature of jargon in these cases is compatible with these mechanisms.

MATERIAL AND METHODS

This present series of patients were selected because they had well-documented neologistic jargonaphasia and concurrent localizing information. The method of selection utilized our large aphasic population with computerized data base (Kertesz, 1979). We found 18 patients who had fluent neologistic jargon among 62 Wernicke's aphasics in a total population of 420 aphasics. We also found 44 Wernicke's aphasics who had localizing information and reviewed their spontaneous speech for the presence of neologistic jargon. From these two lists, we selected 10 patients whose conversational speech was characteristic of neologistic jargonaphasia. We took agreement about this among three judges as the criteria for admission to the study. Among the 10 with localizing information available, 8 patients had positive isotope scans, 5 had CT scans, and 1 had an autopsy as well as an isotope scan. All these patients had the complete spoken language portion of the Western Aphasia Battery (WAB) (Kertesz & Poole, 1974), and most of them, the written and nonverbal subtests as well. The clinical details concerning age, associated neurological signs, and localizing information are included in Table 4.1. The results of the psychological and language examination are detailed in the following protocols and the test scores are summarized in Table 4.2. The isotope scans were done in the acute state and CT scans both in the acute and chronic stages of the aphasic impairment. The degree of recovery is described in the protocols and in the summary of the salient test results (Table 4.2). The IS and CT images were transferred to lateral, coronal, and oblique templates according to techniques described elsewhere (Kertesz et al., 1977; Kertesz et al., 1979). The most important feature of these techniques is the objective outlining of the lesions by a neuroradiologist or an isotope specialist who does not know the patient but is well versed in anatomy applied to these imaging methods. The CT cuts were transferred to templates drawn after Gonzalez, Grossman, & Palacios (1976) and Shipps, Madeira, & Huntington (1975). Cut 1 represents the lowest, Cut 2 the highest, oblique layer. In the illustrations, Cuts 3, 4, and 5 are used most often as they are through the posterior superior temporal gyrus and the supramarginal gyrus. The lateral templates are after Sobotta and Figge (1963).

TABLE 4.1.

Clinical Summary

Case no.	Initials	Age	Logorrhea[a]	Hemianopsia	Hemiplegia	Isotope scan[b]	Time of isotope scan[c]	CT scan	Time of CT scan
1	J.A.	74	Severe	+	Transient	PTO(high)	11 days	PTO	3 weeks
								PTO	11 months
2	J.D.	57	Severe	−	Mild		−	FT	1 week
								TP	7 weeks
3	B.F.	63	Severe	+	−			PTO	7 years
4	M.H.	67	Mild	−	−	TP(low)	3 weeks	−	−
5	W.P.	75	Moderate	−	−	TPO(low)	10 days	TPO	18 months
6	J.R.	60	Mild	+	−	TPO(low)	14 days	TPO	1 month
7	N.T.	69	Moderate	+	−	TPO	2 days	−	−
8	D.W.	71	Moderate	+	Transient	TP	18 days	−	−
9	V.W.	44	Severe	−	−	TPO	12 days	−	−
10	R.S.	79	Moderate	+	Transient	PT(high)	6 days	Autopsy	2 months

[a] Logorrhea refers to pressure of speech.
[b] PTO = parietotemporo-occipital; TP = temporoparietal, *etc.*, (high) and (low) refer to location on the lateral templates.
[c] Time of scans after onset.

TABLE 4.2.
Aphasia Test Scores on the WAB

Case no.	Initials	Sex	Type	Onset–test interval	AQ[a] (100)	Comprehension (10)	Repetition (10)	Naming (10)	Reading (100)	Writing (100)	Praxis (60)	Calculation (24)	Block Design (9)	Drawing (30)	RCPM[b] (36)
1	J.A.	F	W	2 weeks	23.4	2.7	0	0	2	3	11	0	0	0	—
			W	11 months	19.3	2.35	0	0.3	5	0	7	—	—	—	9
2	J.D.	F	W	9 weeks	22.2	3.6	0	.5	46	9	28	10	3	13	21
			W	5 months	30.7	5.15	2.5	.7	55.5	60	48	24	9	19	17
3	B.F.	M	W	7 weeks	14.0	0	0	0	0	0	0	0	0	0	0
			W	7 years	15.4	.7	0	0	0	0	0	0	0	0	0
			W	9 years	20.7	1.35	0	0	0	0	0	0	0	0	0
4	M.H.	F	W	6 weeks	49.1	3.7	5.4	4.5	80	—	49	10	0	9	10
			W	7 months	61.7	5.45	5.1	5.8	61	18	50	6	3	10	19
5	W.P.	M	W	3 days	24.7	3.25	1.7	0.4	25	15	27	12	8	14	5
			A	3 months	70.3	7.9	7.9	4.4	76	53	—	16	—	—	13
			A	18 months	76.8	7.2	7.2	7.0	95	90	58	24	9	19	26
6	J.R.	F	W	3 weeks	51.6	5.2	6.6	2.0	19	5	43	8	0	5	9
			A	4 months	84.4	9.4	8.0	7.8	86	48	58	20	6	16	24
7	N.T.	M	W	2 weeks	19.3	2.3	.5	0	0	.2	0	0	0	0	0
8	D.W.	F	W	1 month	24.3	2.85	.3	0	0	0	39	0	0	8	6
			W	3 months	38.6	5.9	2.0	.4	24	6	47	0	5	8	8
9	V.W.	M	W	1 month	46.0	4.5	2.7	2.8	52	23	48	10	3	9.5	16
			W	4 months	54.8	5.6	2.5	4.3	42	35	43	20	3	13	9
10	R.S.	M	W	3 years	66.2	6.7	6.1	5.3	59	40	—	24	—	15	19
			W	1 month	42.7	8.7	1.1	2.4	—	—	—	—	—	18	—

[a] AQ = Aphasia Quotient (summary scores) reflects overall severity.
[b] RCPM = Raven's Colored Progressive Matrices.

CASE PRESENTATIONS

Case 1

Mrs. J.A., a 74-year-old woman, developed jargon speech suddenly. She had a right homonymous hemianopsia and a mild right arm paresis and motor neglect on admission. She was alert and cooperative.

Her first test on the WAB, 2 weeks postonset, was characterized by fluent, extended neologistic jargon and severely impaired auditory and reading comprehension. Her writing consisted of neologistic and occasionally correct words. Repetition and naming were severely impaired and the stimuli elicited jargon not much different from her conversational replies. She was apractic even on imitation and with object use. She could not calculate or draw or perform the block design or Raven's Colored Progressive Matrices. She had Wernicke's aphasia with an aphasia quotient (AQ) of 23.4% (a summary score).

An isotope scan, 10 days postonset, shows a wedge-shaped uptake in the parietotemporal area with the center of the lesion at the parietotemporal junction (Figure 4.3). The lesion appears to involve most of the supra-

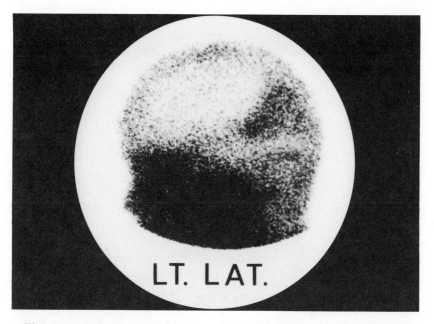

Figure 4.3 Left lateral view of the isotope scan of Case 1 (J.A.). The nose is on the left. The abnormal uptake is a wedge in the posterior temporal and parietal region. Another smaller distinct uptake under the infarct is the transverse sinus (normal).

marginal gyrus and the posterior third of the first temporal gyrus, and extends considerably into the white matter (Figure 4.4).

The CT scan, 3 weeks postonset, shows decreased density with indistinct edges in the left temporoparietal junction (Figure 4.5). The second higher resolution CT scan nearly a year later shows a more distinct outline of the same lesion and a smaller decreased density, higher on the convexity of the right parietal lobe, possibly a small infarct which probably occurred at a different time because it was not seen on the isotope scan (Figures 4.6 and 4.7).

Her comprehension improved at the one year test and the neologisms were less but she still had jargonaphasia. She received only 6 weeks of speech therapy as an outpatient. She now lives alone with help from her family.

SUMMARY

This case of typical persisting neologistic jargonaphasia involves a left posterior temporoparietal infarct. A small right parietal lesion of doubtful significance is present.

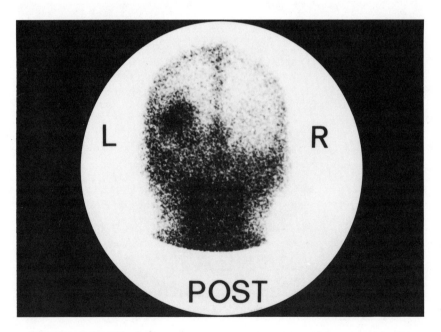

Figure 4.4. Isotope uptake, posterior view of Case 1 (J.A.). Note the sagittal sinus in the midline and the normal "empty" right side.

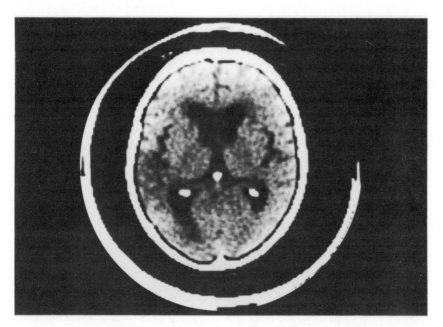

Figure 4.5. The first CT scan of Case 1, 3 weeks poststroke. The lesion in the temporal region is indistinct, the ventricles are large, the zigzag lines bilaterally are the sylvian fissures and the surface of the insula.

MRS. J.A.—TRANSCRIPT OF THE FIRST INTERVIEW, 2 WEEKS POSTSTROKE

E: *How are you today, Mrs. A.?*

JA: *Yes.*

E: *Have I ever tested you before?*

JA: *No, I mean I haven't.*

E: *Can you tell me what your name is?*

JA: *No, I don't I—right I'm right now here.*

E: *What is your address?*

JA: *I cud [kʌd] if I can help these this like you know—to make it. We are seeing for him. That is my father.*

E: *What kind of work did you do before you came into the hospital?*

JA: *Never, now Mista Oyge [ɔɪdʒ] I wanna tell you this happened when happened when he rent. His—his kell [kɛl] come down here and is—he got ren [rɛn] something. It happened. In thesse [ðɪs] Ropiers [ropiɚz] were with him for hi—is friend—like was. And it just happened so I don't know, he did not bring around anything. And he did not pay it. And he roden [rodɛn] all o' these arranjen [ərendʒən] from the pedis [pɛdɪs] on from iss [ɪs] pescid [pɛskɪd]. In these floors now and so. He hasn't had em round here.*

E: *Can you tell me a little bit about why you are in the hospital?*

JA: *No, I don't think I have. . . . No, I haven't.*

E: *Can you tell me what you see going on in the picture?* [A drawing of children flying a kite]

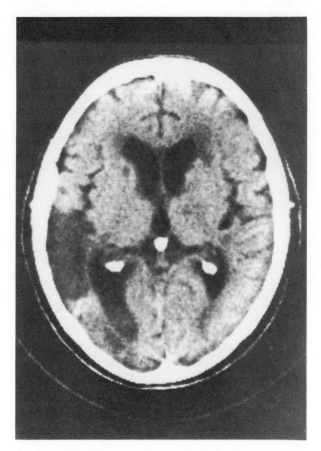

Figure 4.6. The same cut as in Figure 4.5 of Case 1, a year poststroke. The edges of the lesions are more distinct although the lesion remains about the same size.

JA: *No, I can uh take him.—Uh. I haven't read* [rid] *'em anybody to right in there. That's the little girl here.*

E: *Anything else? What do you see over here?*

JA: *No.* [pause] *I really had pays* [pez] *too. Inste van gup.* [ɪnstɛ væn gʌp]. *Here's ee* [i] *little boy being read, too. There he's being there on the ceiling there.*

MRS. J.A.—TRANSCRIPT OF THE SECOND INTERVIEW, A YEAR POSTSTROKE

E: *You were in the hospital about a year ago, weren't you?*

JA: *He was just one und ta dead* [ʌnd tʌdɛd] *You fie* [faɪ] *come over, you know. Showed some things over here.*

E: *What kind of work did you do before you became ill?*

JA: *No, he was all right. I'd ma deadsnot dog* [mɛ dɛdsnɔt dɔg] *mine nahthink* [nɔθɪnk] *or anythink* [ɛniθɪŋk], *no.*

E: *Is your name Brown?*

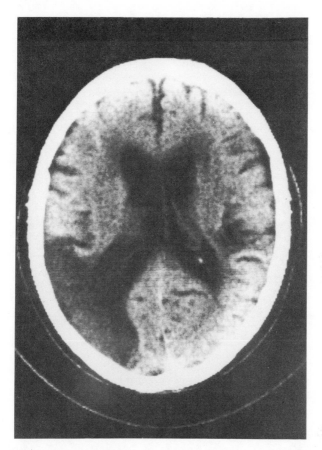

Figure 4.7. A higher parietal cut of Case 1, a year poststroke. The lesion
extends more posteriorly. A small, deep lesion near the right lateral ventricle is
also suspected.

JA: *Oh Misstrus Prang* [mɪstrəs præŋ] *went one wissenyer* [wɪsɛnjɚ] *walking ul* [ʌl]
    thing thing this thing here for thee.

E: *Ok. Just say yes or no. Is your name Brown?*

JA: *Well it is here then let me see I just don't know.*

E: *Is your name A————?*

JA: *Well my fred* [frɛd] *mine is my fredmayuv* [frɛdmeəv]—*of my ed my—my father*
    you know I don't know why what is they doing allike [ɔlaɪk] *this thingses* [θɪŋzəz]
    I could not tell you.

E: *What's happening here?* [Pointing to Schuell's picture of children flying a kite
    around a pond]

JA: *It's just like a—it's a little boy* (pointing to girl) *Fie fie* [faɪ faɪ] *there you know. An*
    fine.

E: *What about here?*

JA: *The ju si dra da thad 'n theuther* [dʒʌ sɪ dræ dʌ æd n̩ ðiʌðɚ]. *Thuts* [ðʌts] *all*
    right. Just don't know. Gees I don't know very much of all this suffs [sʌfs']—*this*

all ray [re-] *I just telling you. I just could not tell you. Because we are air* [eɚ]
eating—my dadme [dædmi-] *is a fathermin* [fɔðɚmɪn] *and he likes to eat and my*
fader [fɔdɚ] *I think everything clean me and I like to clean. Eat my think so I'm*
all right. I just don't know what is wrong.

Case 2

Mrs. J.D., a 57-year-old woman, had a subarachnoid hemorrhage due
to a ruptured left middle cerebral artery aneurysm. Initially she could not
talk at all, but in 24 hours she developed neologistic jargonaphasia and
angiograms showed arterial spasm. Her first CT scan (Figure 4.8), a week
after the hemorrhage, shows the blood in the sylvian fissure and neighboring

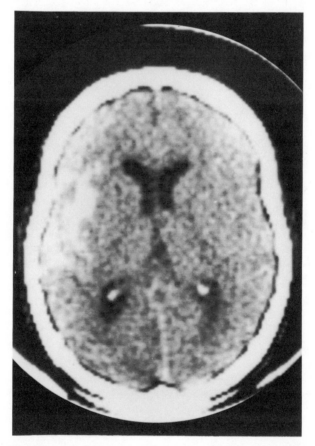

Figure 4.8. CT scan of Case 2 (J.D.), 1 week postonset. Blood in white area
of the left sylvian fissure from a ruptured aneurysm. The lesion producing the
aphasia is not evident yet (see Figure 4.9).

areas. The aneurysm was clipped 3 weeks later. A month after that, a right occipital ventriculoperitoneal shunt was done.

When she was tested on the WAB 2 months after the onset, her spontaneous speech was fluent with neologistic and semantic jargon, with a great deal of pressure of speech. Her comprehension, repetition, and naming were severely impaired. She understood written sentences better, and was able to choose a few correct answers, and match pictures and words. Her writing contained neologistic errors, but copying was much better. She copied drawings, but could not duplicate block designs. Her calculation was relatively good. Her Raven's Colored Progressive Matrices score was only 21. Her AQ was only 22.2% and she fell into Wernicke's category. She was retested 3 months later; her comprehension showed some improvement and her AQ was 30.7%, still in Wernicke's group.

Her CT scan 7 weeks after the onset of her aphasia shows a poorly defined left parietotemporal infarct with a questionable decreased density in the posterior frontal region, above and posterior to the operative exposure (Figure 4.9). The ventricles enlarged since the initial CT.

SUMMARY

This was a case of classical, severe persisting neologistic jargon following an aneurysm rupture and infarct secondary to vasospasm. The relatively small parietotemporal infarct is probably responsible for the jargon, although multiple operations, hydrocephalus, and some other questionable decreased densities complicate the anatomical correlation.

MRS. J.D.—TRANSCRIPT OF SPONTANEOUS SPEECH
2 MONTHS POSTONSET

> E: *How are you feeling today?*
> JD: *Like, What I what I had doing beef-beef* [bif-bif]*?*
> E: *No no. Don't worry about that. How are you feeling?*
> JD: *What—what's been were* [wɜ˞] *me is now is my is my trumi* [trəmi] *right now?*
> E: *Um hum.*
> JD: *Well, I guess—I guess it was little fog* [fɔg] *that—I would—get too much fat on my legs my canul* [kænəl] *itud* [ɪtəd] *the blon* [blɔn] *that I want to, but I din dead* [dɪn dɛd] *I would do it but it's been doing along to do it to—to wah* [wʌ]—*it's too small—like you know. And I—I don't—know—I ca* [kæ]—*I can't seem funny from rothesben* [rɔθəsbən]. *Therbesthen* [ð˞bəsθən] *strange?*
> E: *Um hum.*
> JD: *You know, I can't do that, so I'm trying to get a little small—I'm trying a little— trying to be s-sore* [s:ɔr] *that I am trating* [tretɪŋ] *it you know. And—and that's what it is.*
> E: *Have I ever tested you before?*
> JD: *Well, just that one night from—i* [ɪ]—*was it name Bangurs* [bæŋɚz]*? Her napskin* [nəepskɪn] *came on. And when she came up uh—and I know I guess I was—I was s . . . it was share* [ʃeɚ]. *It was very sho* [ʃo] *that day. And I suppose I was tearid* [terɪd]. *And then first I thought—I thought I was going to be carid* [kerɪd]. *You*

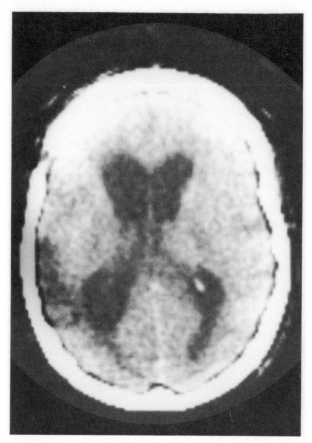

Figure 4.9. CT scan of Case 2, 6 weeks postonset. Relatively small parieto-temporal cortical infarct is seen. The slightly decreased density in the posterior frontal region is near the operative exposure.

know like mascare [məskeɚ]. *But then I said I think maybe I did. Well, it war very cold that morning—you know—and so—I think it needs a little bit more. So then I-I hend* [hɛnd] *back to my own—my carstris* [karstrɪs] *and just—and I got on to a bit* [bɪt] *and—and—I finally got out all right the next thing I was okay. And I think I wanted ta* [tə] *do somie* [sʌmi] *of it but it's just that—you know.*
E: *What's your address?*
JD: *Well I used to did—like it was like—um—oh. . . . It was in—in come flashes—of—I—I did all the mosse beckages* [mos bɛkədʒəz] *for all the meeple* [mipəl] *from like—like the—the—the umpid* [ʌmpɪd]—*the umpid* [ʌmpɪd]—*oh dear—at the—the—at the—the doisy* [dɔɪsi]. *You know—I—I always did—did all the chummings* [tʃʌmɪŋz] *and—and—there—well—the new kessifce* [kɛsɪfəs] *his wade* [wed] *up and I had to make her ovizez* [ɔvɪzəz] *for this does and how the bedzul* [bɛdzəl] *had to do. And tid* [tɪd] *I did the pearitsus* [pɛrɪtsəs] *that came the elsus* [ɛlsəz]. *And I did all that do all the time. But there's—it's just really—a—a dressing 'cause I've done a light levered* [lɛvɚd] *word but they didn't say well I am not kuminus*

[kʌmɪnəs] or [kɔnɪs] *but when the eckzecknel* [ɛkzɛknəl] *come in and the tawked* [tɔkəd] *said, "Well, Jean, I want you to come to do this jessusup* [dʒɛsɪsəp] *and I then I do these worth* [wɝθ] *done you know.*

Case 3

Mr. B.F., a 55-year-old man, became severely aphasic and drowsy, and a large left middle cerebral artery aneurysm was found and clipped. Two days later, he suddenly deteriorated with a right hemiplegia, hemianopsia, and global aphasia. He began to speak in sentences and developed jargonaphasia a few weeks later.

The WAB was given 7 weeks after onset. His spontaneous speech was under pressure and consisted of severe neologistic jargon with occasional normal words. Although his speech was unintelligible most of the time, his inflection and syntactical organization appeared normal. His responses to questions were very inconsistent, mostly inappropriate. Short common phrases were intact, for example, *I don't know what you are talking about.* His comprehension, naming, and repetition were severely impaired. He could not read, write, calculate, or do visuospatial tasks, although his drawings were relatively spared. His AQ was 14.0%. He was seen again in 6 months with practically no improvement in his AQ (17.4%). A year after his stroke, he remained a severe Wernicke's aphasic with copious neologistic jargon. He was subsequently retested 4, 5, 7, and 9 years poststroke, and remained essentially unchanged, with AQs of 15.7%, 19.2%, 15.4%, and 20.7%.

He had an isotope scan 2 months after his surgery for a subarachnoid hemorrhage, and this showed a left frontotemporal uptake, corresponding to the bone flap for the surgery. A CT scan 7 years after the onset shows a large temporoparietal and occipital infarction (Figure 4.10).

Many of his neologisms have been quoted in previous publications (Buckingham & Kertesz, 1976) and transcripts of his 1970 and 1971 interviews appear in Appendix 2 of Hugh Buckingham's chapter in this volume. A brief excerpt of his recent jargon at the time of his 9-year follow-up will be given here.

SUMMARY

This case shows a typical persisting severe neologistic jargon due to a ruptured aneurysm and vasospastic infarct. He has been followed longer than any other case in the literature. His temporoparietal infarct is large and extends occipitally.

MR. B.F.—TRANSCRIPT OF INTERVIEW 9 YEARS AFTER ONSET

E: *How are you today, Mr. F.?*
BF: *Oh fine.*

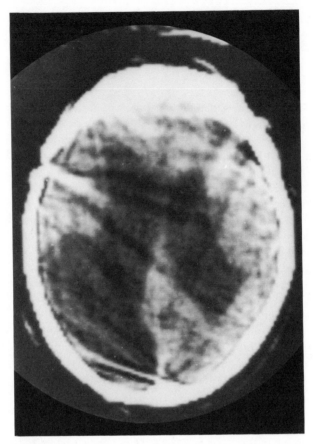

Figure 4.10. CT scan of Case 3 (B.F.), 7 years poststroke. Note the large ventricles in addition to the parietotemporal infarct on the left.

E: *Have you been here before?*
BF: *O a lawva nices gone* [o ʌ lɔv ʌ naɪsəz gɔn].
E: *Have I tested you before?*
BF: *No. Doh yes, uh guh bo ver za.* [ʌ gʊ go vɝzæ].
E: *What is your full name?*
BF: *Umyoon* [əmaɪʊn].
E: *Your name?*
BF: *That's about four minutes from veefums* [vifəmz].
E: *Pardon?*
BF: *Finega solly forse fay fargazus mingslaw* [faɪŋə sɔli fors fe fargæzəz maɪŋzlɔ].
E: *I see. Can you tell me your address?*
BF: *My do myakay* [maɪ du maɪɛke].
E: *Your address.*
BF: *Ya the chumber—eazum* [tʃʌmbɚ—izəm].
E: *What kind of work did you do before you became ill?*
BF: *No don narakinny is all vensus.* [no don neɚəkɪni ɪz ɔl vɛnsəs].
E: *Can you tell me a little bit about why you're here?*

BF: *Right now?*
E: *Um hum.*
BF: *I don't know cuhie zee vaor* [kəi zi vɔor] *I come awang* [əwæŋ]. *So I says you're coming along too. I'll go with you honey.*
E: *I have a picture here. Can you tell me what you see happening in this picture?*
BF: *I guess that there's wha* [wʌ] *doesn't look side a perni* [saɪdə pɚni].
E: *Uh huh.*
BF: *That's froy* [frɔi]. *There's a farber* [farbɚ]. *Fargus, tuckers linegays, colie* [fargəz, tʌkɚz, laɪngez, coli] *e'rything, seegles* [sigəlz].

Case 4

Mrs. M.H., a 67-year-old ambidextrous woman, suddenly became "confused and incoherent" and was admitted with a fluent aphasia. Two weeks prior to that she had focal seizures in her left side and right leg. She has been treated for chronic renal failure with dialysis.

She was tested on the WAB 6 weeks after the onset of her speech disturbance. She had long runs of neologistic jargon with occasionally clear sentences. Her comprehension, repetition, and naming were impaired severely. Her reading comprehension was unexpectedly good (80%), but her writing consisted of jargon words and paraphasias even on copying. Her praxis on command was poor but she imitated well. Her drawing, calculation, block design, and Raven's Colored Progressive Matrices performance were significantly impaired. She only identified half of the nonverbal environmental sounds presented. Her scores were compatible with Wernicke's aphasia and her AQ was 49.1%.

She was tested again 6 months later after receiving speech therapy once weekly. Her speech was fluent and circumlocutory with abundant phonemic paraphasias and impaired comprehension, repetition, and naming. Her AQ was 60.8% and she remained in the Wernicke's category. A year later, she was retested. Her comprehension improved a little but her speech and writing remained paraphasic and paragraphic. She remained in Wernicke's group with an AQ of 64.6%.

An isotope scan, a week after her stroke, showed a moderate size wedge-shaped lesion in the temporoparietal region (Figure 4.11) on the left side.

SUMMARY

This case involved relatively milder aphasia and persisting jargon alternating with clear sentences without pressure of speech. The IS uptake was moderate in size and more temporal than parietal.

MRS. M.H.—TRANSCRIPT OF INTERVIEW 6 WEEKS POSTONSET

E: *How are you today?*
MH: *Eight—eighty 'undred* [ʌndrɛd].

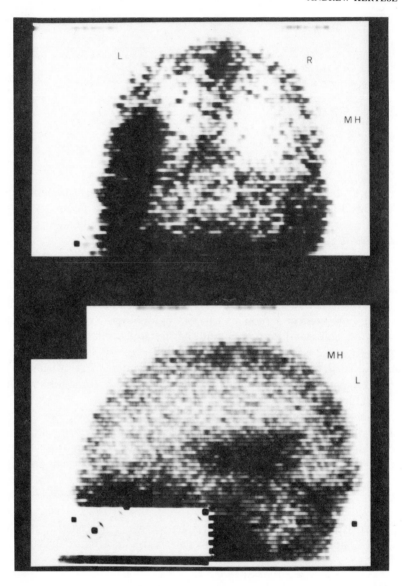

Figure 4.11. Isotope scan of Case 4 (M.H.), 1 week poststroke. Posterior view on the top is slightly rotated. Left lateral view on bottom shows a temporoparietal uptake.

E: *No, how are you feeling?*
MH: *You mean . . .*
E: *How are you feeling?*
MH: *Well I'm fell—fik* [fɪk] *now with a something like that. Uh what is that what it means?*
E: *Um hum. Have I tested you before?*

MH: *I don't think so.*
E: *What is your address?*
MH: *My address? Four-seventy uduft* [ədʌft] *in London.*
E: *Pardon?*
MH: *London ospaposeettech* [ɔspəpɔsititʃ] *. . . four seventy londef* [lʌndɛf]. *London district.*
E: *What kind of work did you do before you became ill?*
MH: *Working?*
E: *Ya, what sort of work?*
MH: *No dear.*
E: *You didn't work?*
MH: *No.*
E: *What seems to be the trouble?*
MH: *With me?*
E: *Um hum.*
MH: *Well I don't know whether it was starting from this marjishin* [mardʒɪʃɪn] [indicating catheter] *started with this thing for staffed* [stæfɛd]. *And it kept so much pretful* [prɛtfʌl] *and worry me and I couldn't sleep for it anywhere I couldn't waesitin* [wesɪtɪn] *and oh it was just terrible.*
E: *When did you come into hospital?*
MH: *In 'ospital?*
E: *Ya.*
MH: *Well I remember callin' in—in the masjesen* [mæsdʒɛsən] *do it one Saturday night, to recorrect right now because I was very sick. Just when.*
E: *I'd like you to look at this picture and tell me what you see going on in the picture.*
MH: *Well, my eyes is not, Julius* [dʒuliəs]. *The little girl and the boy. Trees.*
E: *What else? Anything else?*
MH: *Is that a store there? Shore. Three cutaninse* [kʌtənɪns].
E: *What else?*
MH: *Kye* [kaɪ] *fought was it? . . . and the other.*
E: *What else?*
MH: *Not less I know on.—no.*

Case 5

Mr. W.P., a 75-year-old man, suddenly developed garbled speech without hemiplegia, hemianopsia, or sensory loss. He had had a cardiac pacemaker a year before, and a femoral bypass for peripheral vascular disease.

He was tested on the WAB 3 days poststroke. He exhibited much phonemic jargon in his spontaneous speech, which was devoid of any content. His comprehension was poor. He could point better to real objects, pictures, and colors than to body parts, geometric forms, letters, numbers, or furniture. His repetition and naming were poor. He was severely agraphic and alexic. He performed some written commands even though he read them aloud as jargon. His calculation, drawing, praxis, and block design were moderately impaired, and he could not do Raven's Colored Progressive Matrices. His AQ was 24.7% and he was placed in Wernicke's category. Three months later he showed considerable gains in comprehension and repetition, and, although his speech was paraphasic and circumlocutory, it did not contain as many neologisms. His AQ rose to 70.3%! He had scores compatible with anomic aphasia. His AQ remained the same at 6 months and was 75.8% at 18 months poststroke, the time of his CT scan. An isotope scan 10 days after his infarct showed a posterior parieto-temporo-occipital wedge-shaped lesion (Figure 4.12). His CT scan 18 months later revealed a multilobular infarct or possibly two infarcts in the left hemisphere, a posterior parietotemporal one, which clearly corresponded to the lesion demonstrated on the isotope scan before, and a smaller rounded lesion, which seemed to be separated from the other one, located more anteriorly in the temporal lobe (Figure 4.13). This may have occurred before or after the aphasia-producing stroke but it did not cause any recorded symptoms.

SUMMARY

This case displayed neologistic jargon with less logorrhea. A temporoparietal lesion localized on IS and CT.

MR. W.P.—TRANSCRIPT OF SPONTANEOUS SPEECH
3 DAYS POSTSTROKE

E: *How are you today?*
WP: *It uh . . . caught . . . two . . . joad-joan* [dʒod-dʒon].
E: *Have you been here before?*
WP: *Did I have—when?*
E: *Have you been to this hospital before?*
WP: *Uh . . . yes . . . that-uh . . . uh-two-uh . . . two dot . . . call me.*
E: *What's your full name?*
WP: *How—how did it?*
E: *No, what's your name?*
WP: *Um . . . you . . . you—it pode* [pod] *me. Uh . . . uh . . . that . . . um . . . too hot. Too hime* [haɪm]. *And one . . . more . . . still-got one. Uh—by it uh-um . . . um.*
E: *What is your address?*
WP: *I can't—uh—real act* [ril ækt] *that—um. Top my uh joan.* [tɔp maɪ ʌ dʒon]. *I—I— I could—uh . . . koe a ma-map* [ko ʌ mɪ-mæp] *to—uh . . . the—um . . . uh . . . the uh . . . I can—uh . . . did—uh—did no the un—I only uh—the uh . . . chet* [tʃɛt] *the uh . . . the ome* [om].
E: *Can you tell me what kind of work you did?*
WP: *Uh—well it was a—uh . . . um . . . it was a—um . . . it was a—moe* [mo]. *uh—it was a . . .*
E: *Can you tell me a little about why you're here?*
WP: *Yes—I uh—I uh—hope—the um-uh—my uh—home—uh—my uh—uh—um . . . um . . . his uh his load* [lod]—*the uh . . . the girl . . . is my . . . um . . . um—mine— uh——her—her m-moe* [mo] *too. He—mi-mine* [mə-maɪn] *his—her. Mine—miss. That's uh—his uh—she . . . seemed—my—no—to—my herm* [hɝm].
E: *Tell me a little about what you see going on in this picture.*
WP: *Oh yes I—I can uh see uh—uh—the um . . . ya—well what is this—they* [θe]? *Uh . . . and uh . . . the—um—man—in the uh . . . in the um . . . in the—uh. It—um— it um . . . uh the uh . . . golly I like the darn thing and I can't uh—can't it . . . and the uh—this . . . a—um . . . um. . . . A ma—ma* [ʌ mæ mæ] *. . . golly—it's in here someplace but I can't even—uh—um.*

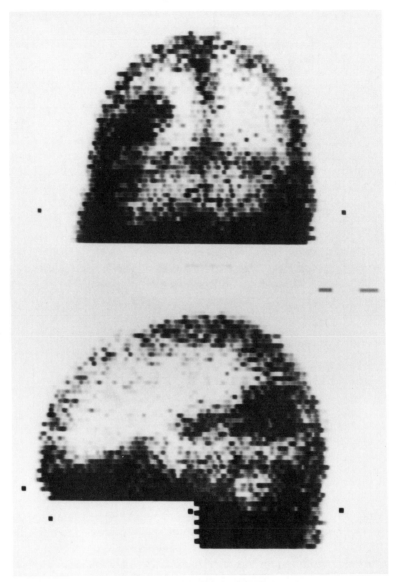

Figure 4.12. Isotope scan of Case 5 (W.P.). Posterior view on top shows the uptake on the left side. The central cross-shaped uptake represents the venous sinuses.

E: *How about over here. Do you see anything going on over here?*
WP: *Oh yes—the—the things with—um. There's the um—um . . . um . . . um . . . ma.*
E: *Tell me what you see happening in this picture.*
WP: *The uh—the little picture. The uh boy with the scoot er site* [skut ɔ˞ saɪt]. *What is it—no—that's neither scoot* [skut] *nor a site* [saɪt]. *Uh—seal* [si]—*uh—uh lobs* [lɔbz]—*uh-uh . . . a glot* [glɔt] *. . . God! The uh tree . . . the uh . . . the uh house*

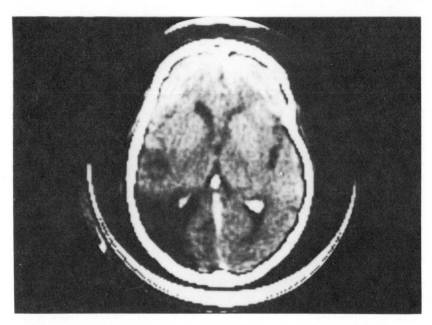

Figure 4.13. CT scan of Case 5 (W.P.), 18 months after the stroke, showing a distinct parietotemporo-occipital lesion corresponding to the isotope uptake in Figure 4.12.

and the . . . flock fell [flɔk fɛl] *(pointing to walkway). Duck . . . and the uh . . . boy up in the uh tree here. A few uh—oh . . . bu-burushes* [bʊ-bʊrəʃəz]—*burushes* [bʊrəʃəz]—*something like that anyway. And uh oh yes a little dog there. And I think they're most of the uh—little syrup* [sɝəp]—*uh—syrup* [sɝəp]—*meaning the spurit* [spɝɪt]—*no it's not spurit* [spɝɪt]. *Dear of dear—dust. . . . Drat it . . . oh ya—that's a—that's another uh grate* [gret].

Case 6

Mrs. J.R., a 60-year-old right-handed woman, was admitted after 5 days of "confusion" at home. She did not seem to recognize her relatives, could not follow conversation, and her speech appeared irrelevant. She had bilateral leg amputation for vascular disease. On examination, she had fluent aphasia and right homonymous hemianopsia.

She was tested 3 weeks poststroke on the WAB. Her speech was very fluent, containing at times semantic, at times neologistic, jargon. Her comprehension, repetition, and naming were impaired moderately; her reading, writing, calculation, and drawing were poor; and her performance on block design and Raven's Colored Progressive Matrices was very poor. Her AQ was 51.6% and she fell into the Wernicke's group. She was retested 3 months later and showed considerably improved comprehension so her scores placed her in the anomic category with an AQ of 84.4%!

Her isotope scan showed a larger posterior temporal and parietal wedge-shaped lesion 4 weeks poststroke (Figures 4.14 and 4.15). Her CT scan also showed a left parietotemporal lesion 1 month after the stroke (Figure 4.16). There is a hint of a vague, smaller, round anterior lesion in the left central operculum.

SUMMARY

This case displayed more moderate neologistic and semantic jargon, milder and recovering aphasia, and a left temporoparietal lesion. The temporoparietal lesion is quite typical but the CT shows a vague questionable central opercular lesion as well.

MRS. J.R.—TRANSCRIPT OF THE CONVERSATIONAL
SPEECH OF THE FIRST INTERVIEW

E: *How are you today, Mrs. R.?*
JR: *I wish my goot* [gʊt] *my had smore* [smɔr] *clothes.*
E: *Have you ever been here before?*
JR: *I haven't got any out pate* [pətɛ] *now, just now.*
E: *Have I ever tested you before?*
JR: *No. Your sit* [sɪt]—*your wife did this morng* [mɔrŋ] *er last night.*
E: *Can you tell me your address?*
JR: *I don't wutch* [wʌtʃ] *uh green out on uh north gren* [grɛn]—*dors* [dors]—*dorth western.*

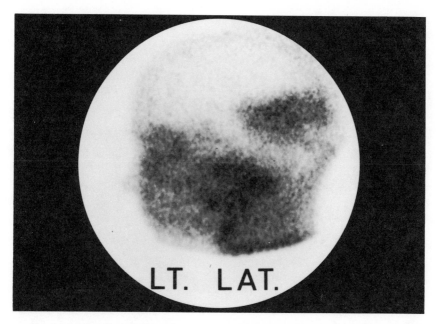

Figure 4.14. The left lateral view of the isotope scan of Case 6 (J.R.), showing a temporoparieto-occipital uptake.

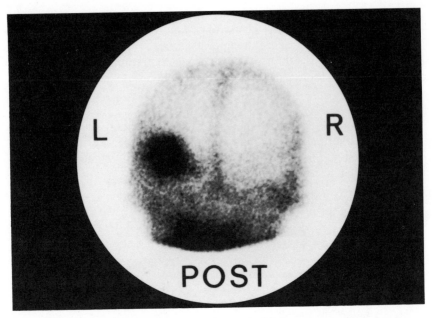

Figure 4.15. The scan uptake of case 6 (J.R.) on a posterior view.

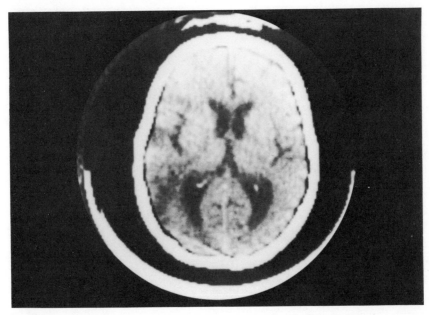

Figure 4.16. CT scan of Case 6 (J.R.), 1 month poststroke shows a left parietotemporal lesion with a mildly decreased density in the left central operculum.

E: *What kind of work did you do before you came into the hospital?*
JR: *I used to workt* [wɜːrkt] *at home emfigus holota* [ɛmfigəs holɔtə] *upper room.*
E: *Can you tell me a little bit about why you're in the hospital?*
JR: *Ya I took this upsie* [ʌpsaɪ] *at Saint Joses stop. inta* [ɪntə] *too weak. And I just droke* [drok] *up dis* [dɪs] *in disperd* [dɪspɪrd].
E: *I'm going to show you a picture now. I want you to tell me everything that you see in this picture. Do you wear glasses?*
JR: *I don't see very much uh. All this is a chi* [tʃɪ]—*child. That like that. Di* [dɪ] *that what you mean?*
E: *Ya, just tell me everything that you see on here.*
JR: *I can't see there. Eza* [ɛzə] *tall tall of them. Ass—is* [æs-ɪz] *that a file—folagren* [fɔləgrɛn]? *A little kid. Dut* [dʌt]—*duck.*

Case 7

Mr. N.T., a 69-year-old right-handed man, was transferred from the Men's Mission because of sudden difficulty with speech. He was initially agitated, probably because of alcohol withdrawal. He was tested on the WAB 2 weeks after his stroke. He produced neologistic jargon, and perseverative stock phrases and comments. His comprehension was severely impaired, and paraphasic responses were obtained on naming and repetition. He could not read and only wrote his name. His praxis was nil; he did not even attempt to imitate the examiner, he just kept talking. He could not do calculation, drawing, or other performance tasks. His AQ was only 19.3% and he fell into Wernicke's category.

The isotope scan showed a large temporoparieto-occipital uptake (Figure 4.17). The temporal lobe is probably infarcted as far as the anterior tip. Unfortunately, he was not available for follow-up or CT scanning.

SUMMARY

This case of milder jargon could not be followed up. The isotope scan shows extensive temporal involvement in addition to the parieto-occipital lesion seen in the other cases.

MR. N.T.—TRANSCRIPT OF CONVERSATIONAL
SPEECH 2 WEEKS POSTSTROKE

E: *Why are you here in the hospital?*
NT: *I wouldn't know it. In fact, I'd like—ed* [ɛd] *her to go—with—rule my hair. Certainly* [sɜːtnli]. *She doesn't need that. Like if I . . . heard her her dreamind* [drimənd]—*she give it to me. That's right. I'm not fooling any* [ɛni] *'bout that. Not true.*
E: *Tell me what you see going on.*
NT: *Do—I beg your pardon.*
E: *Tell me what you see in the picture.*
NT: *Well—uh . . . there's a way—uh—just a wa* [wə]—*wachine* [wəʃin]. *There's a recognize-ed'* [rɛkəgnaɪzɛd'] *here. And uh—well—a little hair and what's the name of the horse's name that? And—probly* [prɔbli]—*his leg made of hairs. And, naturally, his leg. There goes his little mini. Now just a moment.*

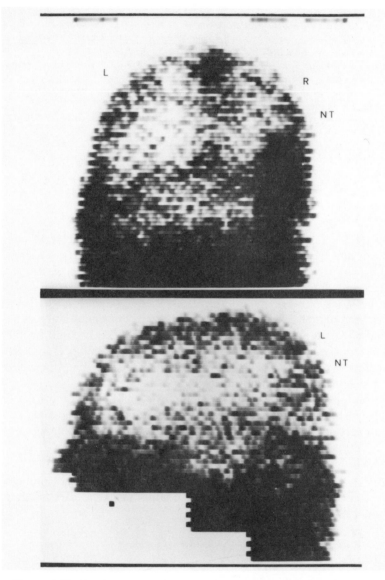

Figure 4.17. Isotope scan of Case 7 (N.T.), 2 days poststroke. The uptake involves the entire temporal lobe and parieto-occipital region as well on the convexity.

E: *What?*

NT: *Now just moment. Now I lead Master Mackenzie—let's see—dravis* [drævɪs] . . . *And what's his name? Up in til 'bout toe sep-tep-tem-ridie* [sɛptɛptɛmridi].

E: *What?*

NT: *Cause they didn't have it.*

E: *What's wrong?*

NT: *Well, I hadn't had her yet but there was a—Janu* [ʒænju]*—January, September and
. . . Tell it was a little glet* [glɛt] *me see. Forget what it wa* [wʌ] *guess. Seldening*
[sɛldənɪŋ] *his selden* [sɛldən]. *That's right.*

Case 8

Mrs. D.W., a 71-year-old woman, developed jargonaphasia and transient right hemiplegia. She had had previous heart attacks and transient
ischemic attacks involving the right arm. Initially, drowsy and mute, she
was later considered globally aphasic.

She was tested 4 weeks poststroke on the WAB. Her spontaneous
speech, although hesitant at times, was fluent with excess output most of
the time. She did not communicate as much with gestures as other patients.
Her comprehension, repetition, and naming were poor. She did not read
or attempt the visual matching task. Writing, drawing, calculation, block
design, and Raven's Colored Progressive Matrices scores were very poor.
Her AQ was only 24.3%. This improved to 38.6% at 3 months postonset
although she continued with neologistic jargon and Wernicke's aphasia. She
would not cooperate at a later attempt to retest her.

An isotope scan 2 weeks poststroke showed an uptake at the central
and temporoparietal region of the left hemisphere (Figure 4.18).

SUMMARY

This case displays typical persisting neologistic jargon with moderate
logorrhea. A temporoparietal lesion probably involves the postcentral gyrus
as well. Her speech comes close to undifferentiated jargon at times.

MRS. D.W.—INTERVIEW 4 WEEKS POSTSTROKE

E: *How are you today, Mrs. W.?*
DW: *I'm just lonely izall* [ɪzɔl].
E: *Are you feeling better than this morning?*
DW: *Not too mels ise* [tu mɛls aɪs] *I don't think.*
E: *Pardon me?*
DW: *I mot* [mɔt] *sum* [sʌm] *sirs* [sɜ·z], *orie* [ori:].
· E: *Uh huh.*
DW: *Es* [ɛs] *my mosk* [mɔsk] *I think.*
E: *Have you ever been here before?*
DW: *No.*
E: *No? What's your name?*
DW: *I'm uh . . .*
E: *Can you tell me your full name?*
DW: *Aybra* [ebrɔ] *for—teelwort* [tilwort] . . . *fie* [faɪ].
E: *Yes? Can you tell me your first name?*
DW: *Ayels* [aɪəls]*—ayels* [aɪəls].
E: *Can you say daisy?*
DW: *Dayvah* [devə]. *Nayvahgilvl* [nevəgɪləl].
E: *Where do you live, Mrs. W?*

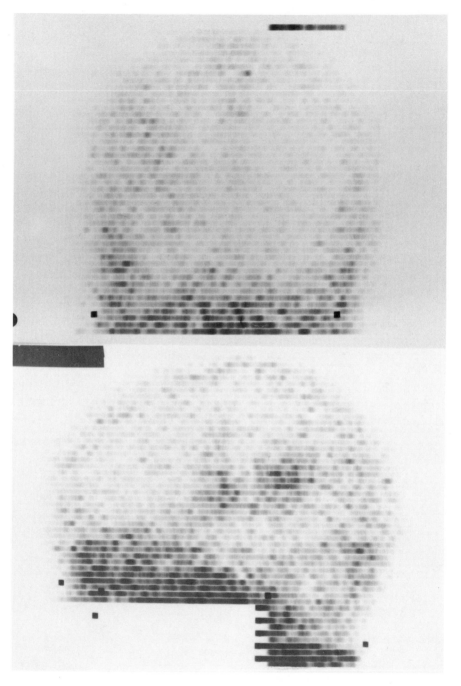

Figure 4.18. Isotope scan of Case 8 (D.W.), 2 weeks poststroke.

DW: *Inosiensus* [ınɔsiɛnsəs].
E: *Where?*
DW: *I don't know. Donoereshesinthe* [donoeəˑʃizınðɛ].
E: *What did you do before you became ill?*
DW: *Shie* [Saı] *think I will.*
E: *Um hum?*
DW: *I was gonna eat there once this afternoon.*
E: *Were you a housewife?*
DW: *Just amoldka* [əmoldkə]. *Lilanareaka* [lıləneəˑəkə].
E: *How old are you, Mrs. W?*
DW: *Fiftynigh* [fıftinaı]. [Patient was 71.]
E: *Fifty-nine?*
DW: *I don* [don]—*I din* [dın] *live that ole* [ol] *Fakonsin.* [fəkɔnsın] *I'm forya* [forjə].
    For all. Owse [aus] *essembalrygirls* [ɛsɛmbælrigɜˑlz].
E: *Look at this picture and tell me what's going on in it?*
DW: *Dahnay* [dɔne]. *Enambalsay* [ɛnəmbɔlse]. *Fack—anadee* [fæk-ænədi]. *Whynow-
    neea* [waınɔniə]. *O!deea* [o:diə]. *Eggerferma gerfriend* [egɜˑfɜˑməgɜˑfrɛnd].
E: *What's he doing?*
DW: *Goin' tagowi* [təgɔı]. *She's got a rabliun* [ræbliən]. *I think I wanta. . . . Oh
    he . . .*
E: *Do you know what this is over here?*
DW: *No. Balky* [bælki]. *I—isetinga* [ısɛtıŋə].
E: *It's all right. You're doing fine.*
DW: *Inever* [ınɛvɜˑ]. *Oh . . . no. I hadinagalji* [hædınəgɔlji]. *Onusbigwaltzes* [ɔnəsb-
    ıgwɔltzıs]. *Oh . . . hungry.*

Case 9

Mr. V.W., a 44-year-old left-handed man, suddenly developed garbled speech. He also stumbled temporarily. Ten years previously, he had a transient attack of right hemiplegia and aphasia and, subsequently, two transient episodes of left-sided weakness and one episode of brief unconsciousness with confusion following but without seizures.

When he was first tested 5 days after the onset of his stroke, he appeared to be agitated and produced a great deal of jargon under considerable pressure, answering with long paragraphs to simple questions. His comprehension was poor, and repetition and naming tasks elicited many jargon words. His reading comprehension was bad, although he could match single words to pictures. His writing was impaired except for copying. He did not do well on the performance tasks. He did better on imitation on the praxis tasks. His AQ was 25.4% in Wernicke's category. He had an IS which showed a large temporoparietal uptake (Figure 4.19). A month later, although his comprehension improved, he still produced a lot of neologisms but more semantic jargon. The AQ was 46% in Wernicke's category. He still had neologistic and semantic jargon at 5 and 12 months poststroke and his AQs were 54.8% and 58.8%. Three years later, his jargon virtually disappeared but he was still a Wernicke's aphasic with an AQ of 66.2%.

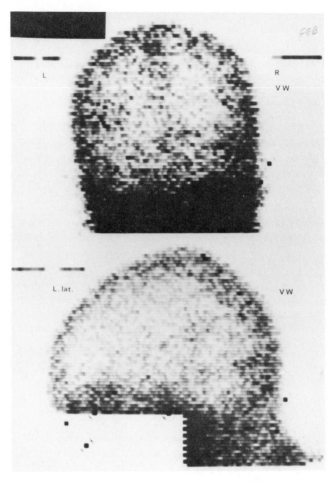

Figure 4.19. Isotope scan of Case 9 (V.W.), 12 days poststroke. A vague uptake.

SUMMARY

This case of typical persisting neologistic jargon was followed frequently. He had a large temporoparieto-occipital lesion.

MR. V.W.—TRANSCRIPT OF HIS FIRST TEST 5 DAYS
AFTER ONSET

E: *What is your full name?*

VW: *Well normally what I'm trying to tell you explainmunie* [ɛksplɛnmәni] *is that ah—well I had a ree* [ri] *thirty ah—thirty-five times ah—ah—lance—lance tu* [læns-læns tu]—*I had a ah—ah—a bat uh tra-va* [trʌ-yʌ] *thirty-fifth. Well anyway, it was the same as ananagerel* [ænænædʒɚʌl] *ment-munautry* [mɛnt-manɔtri] *and you coulda* [kʊdә] *get anything by it—thus. The way it worked was I acted—I couldn't speak. This would be—it was like my voice was confixed* [kәnfɪksɛd] *that I couldn't think what I wanted* [wɔntədəd] *it. But it only lasted my the* [ð:ʌ] *hog—this happened at home and the* [ð:ʌ] *haw—hawstyer* [hɔstjɚ] *come to see me and I couldn't get my skirt out any march out of it and it only lasted about ten minutes and afterwards che* [tʃi] *was the hospital and everything and I walked just like I always did.*

E: *See this picture? Tell me about it. What do you see?*

VW: *Oh there's a hosse* [hos] *there's a vadog* [aivədɔg] *men, and then they have a— on top of a—a stationize* [steʃənaiz] *for wiking* [waikiŋ] *on the time through the— the personger* [pɚsəndʒɚ] *is doing his baz* [bæz] *out atrels* [ætrɛlz]. *And there's a girl down here. She's watching what's going on, and the toshwell* [tɔʃwɛl] *is too. And there's a mailmanks* [melmænks] *over here.*

Case 10

Mr. R.S., a 78-year-old man, was admitted with sudden onset of speech difficulty and transient right arm weakness. He was tested on the WAB a month after his stroke. He showed striking jargonaphasia with pressure of speech and chiefly semantic jargon but at times he lapsed into neologistic jargon as well. His comprehension was poor although he comprehended simple commands and was able to point to furniture in the room quite well. He had difficulty answering questions pertaining to his illness; such questions elicited a torrent of words with little meaning. He showed little concern and no frustration. His naming and repetition were also impaired. On visual field testing, he seemed to have at least a neglect of the right lower quadrant on double simultaneous stimulation.

An isotope scan showed a relatively small left parietal uptake 4 weeks postonset (Figures 4.20 and 4.21). He died with a pulmonary embolism about 2 months after the onset of his stroke. An autopsy shows that the major portion of the infarct is in the parietal lobe, sparing the temporal lobe except a small amount posteriorly (Figure 4.22), and in the depth of the temporal operculum and planum temporale (Figure 4.23). The lesion is deeper than what one would expect from the surface area involved.

SUMMARY

This case was a typical moderately severe neologistic jargonaphasia with predominantly a parietal, and only a minor temporal, involvement. Autopsy–isotope correlation is available. This is probably the minimum lesion producing neologistic jargonaphasia. It is important in defining the role of the inferior parietal structures in the formation of neologisms.

MR. R.S.—INTERVIEW A MONTH AFTER STROKE

E: *How are you today?*

RS: *Well not too bad. I ah—surprise.*

E: *Why? . . . Why are you surprised?*

RS: *Well I ah—I can't ah—my ah—some of the things ya know.*

E: *What do you mean?*

RS: *Ah—I got ah—ah—vistava fankas* [vistəvə fænkəs] *this and—this ah—what I say*

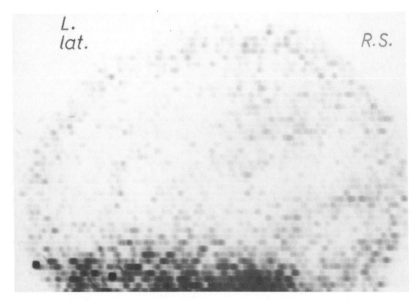

Figure 4.20. Lateral isotope scan of Case 10 (R.S.), 4 weeks poststroke shows an essentially parietal uptake on the left.

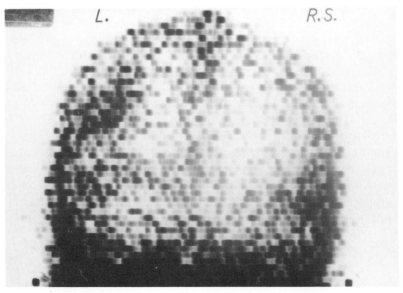

Figure 4.21. Posterior scan of Case 10 (R.S.). A coronal cut of the lesion in Figure 4.20.

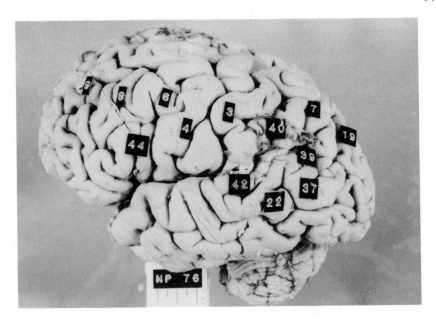

Figure 4.22. The lateral surface of the brain of Case 10 (R.S.), 2 months postonset.

    must ah—fights. It just seems to ah—just goes funny ah—at you—but ah—not that ah—I can't.

E: *You can't say the things you want?*

RS: *I can't I can't do it—nothing—I mean ah—I—I can't ah—I was ah—I used to be able to ah—do everything o' course. But ah—but that I used ta do and what I've a but now muckila* [mʌkələ] *this—this ah—for here—this ah—is ah fodaway* [fɔdəwe].

E: *What did you used to do? What was your occupation?*

RS: *Pardon?*

E: *What was your occupation? What did you used to do?*

RS: *Well ah—I was ah—I was ah in ah with ah—with fisheries ah—that's ah ah fish ah—fish—fish sa* [sæ] *fish ah—ah wat* [wɔt] *fishery ah fishery man—manamus* [mænəməs]*—ah it's called ah ah hollingos* [hɔlɪŋɔs] *is at carry . . . down see I was I was in ah—in the—in the—service there weed* [wid] *ah an ah weeds* [widz] *with you with ah ah—with ah—um—ah buse* [bjuz] *had—that's a ner ner* [nɝnɝ] *puddock* [pʌdək] *all these such things o' course as is that's a caratype* [kerətaɪp] *there and sometimes it can't get—made the difference that ah—my rights—this hand this not bad that is this here I can ah trust this in for another problem.*

Five cases of Wernicke's aphasics with copious fluent *semantic jargon* also had localizing information in addition to several others with diffuse degenerative (Alzheimer's or Pick's) disease. The focal unilateral lesions due to strokes are located in the same region of the brain as those of the previously detailed patients with neologistic jargonaphasia, except that the

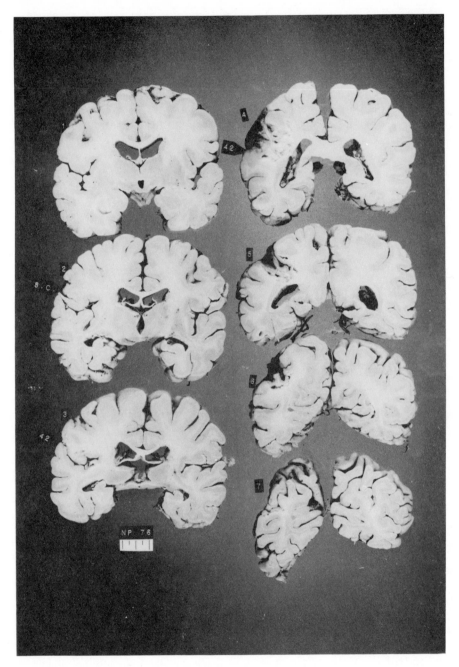

Figure 4.23. Coronal cuts of the brain of Case 10 (R.S.).

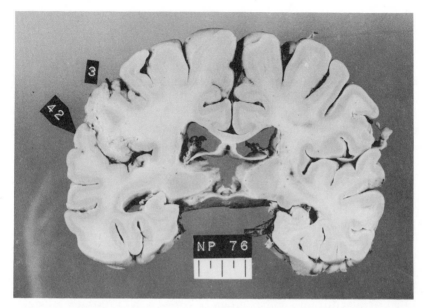

Figure 4.24. Enlargement of Cut 3 through area 42 showing the infarct in the depth of the sylvian fissure involving the parietal and temporal opercula.

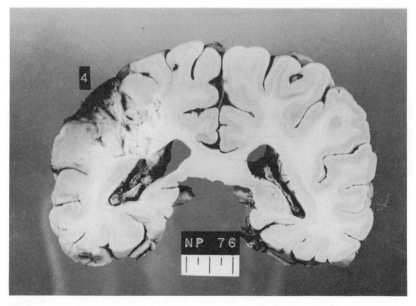

Figure 4.25. Enlargement of Cut 4 through the supramarginal gyrus showing the largest crossection of the infarct.

COLORADO COLLEGE LIBRARY
COLORADO SPRINGS,
COLORADO

lesions are smaller. It also appears that these lesions do not occupy the entire extent of the temporoparietal area at the end of the sylvian fissure, but they appear to be slightly more temporal (inferior and anterior) in contrast to our cases of transcortical sensory aphasia (Kertesz, 1979) with semantic jargon which are clearly more posterior in location. Wernicke's aphasics with semantic jargon are distinguished from transcortical sensory aphasics who may have similar irrelevant speech by their poorer performance on repetition tasks. Patients with semantic jargon have higher language and performance scores than those with neologistic jargon, and they recover considerably better as a rule, provided their deficit is due to a stroke.

THE LOCALIZATION OF LESIONS

The extent of overlap among the cases of neologistic jargon (Figures 4.26–4.30) is considerable, indicating a strong clinicoanatomical correlation. The lateral overlap of the isotope scans (Figure 4.26) is almost identical to that obtained from another group of patients in 1970 (Figure 4.1), confirming the impression that certain structures are regularly affected in the brain when neologistic jargon is produced. The study of these selected patients is a step toward determining what these structures are. The overlap results indicate that the most consistently affected regions are the supramarginal gyrus, the posterior parietal operculum, the inferior parietal lobule, the posterior portion of the first temporal gyrus, the posterior temporal operculum (planum temporale), and the angular gyrus. The involvement of these neighboring structures at the end of the sylvian fissure cannot and

NEOLOGISTIC JARGON - ISOTOPE OVERLAP

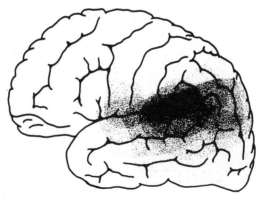

Figure 4.26. The overlap of the isotope traced on the lateral template. Cases 1,4,5,6,7,8,9, and 10 are included.

NEOLOGISTIC JARGON - ISOTOPE OVERLAP

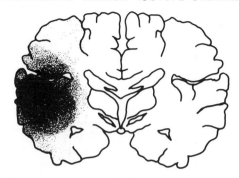

Figure 4.27. The overlap of the posterior (coronal) views of the isotope scans in Figure 4.26.

should not be taken as evidence that destruction of all of them is necessary to produce neologistic jargonaphasia. Because the vascular territories of the brain do not necessarily overlap with functional areas, it is likely that functionally irrelevant or "silent" areas will be also involved in many of these infarcts. In other words, even though the overlap technique allows us to detect which is the area common to all cases with neologistic jargon, the area of the overlap may include structures that do not play a role in the clinical syndrome. The variation between the stroke lesions is limited to some extent by the similarity of the blood supply to the area, involving certain structures. Increasing the number of observations overcomes this limitation to some extent by introducing more variability.

The experience with the overlap technique indicates that the larger the number of cases that are included, the smaller the overlap area becomes

NEOLOGISTIC JARGON CT OVERLAP

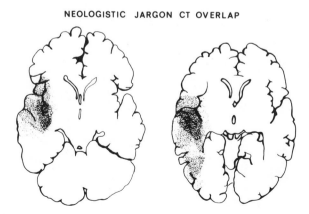

Figure 4.28. The overlap of the CT scans in Cuts 1 and 2 (inferior frontal and temporal region).

ANDREW KERTESZ

NEOLOGISTIC JARGON CT OVERLAP

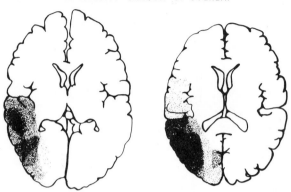

Figure 4.29. The overlap of the CT scans in Cuts 3 and 4 (Broca's and Wernicke's area).

(Kertesz, 1979). If one collects enough cases, sooner or later the overlap may become incomplete. The optimum number of cases depends on the distinctiveness of the clinical syndrome and the variability among the lesions. A persisting sizeable overlap in a reasonable number of cases suggests good correlation between the symptoms and the structures destroyed. On the other hand, too small an overlap or no overlap at all among various cases suggests that the symptoms may be produced by lesions of different structures. It is likely, however, that the destruction of each structure represented in an overlap alone may not reproduce the syndrome, and that a combination of involvement of several or all areas is necessary.

The isotope and CT lesions were practically identical in cases J.A., J.R., and W.P. (Figures 4.3, 4.12, and 4.14). M.H.'s lesion (Figure 14.11) was slightly lower and more anterior than the others, mostly temporal. J.A., M.H., and W.P. had persistent jargon, but J.R. recovered to anomic

NEOLOGISTIC JARGON CT OVERLAP

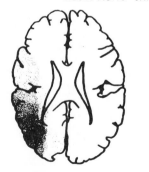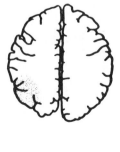

Figure 4.30. The overlap of the CT scans in Cuts 5 and 6 (superior frontal and parietal).

aphasia by 3 months postonset. B.F. (Figure 4.10), N.T. (Figure 4.17), and V.W. (Figure 4.19) had the largest lesions similar in location to those above. B.F. had persistent severe jargon for 9 years, the longest one recorded in the literature so far. N.T. was lost to follow-up, and V.W., by the time of his third-year test, lost most of his jargon.

The persistence of severe neologistic jargonaphasia is related to large lesions involving the temporal, parietal, and occipital lobes. The involvement of three lobes of the brain is at times considered an argument against localization and in favor of the diffuse representation of the functions impaired. However, at times, only the junction of the temporal, parietal, and occipital lobes are involved and this area can be relatively small. From the evidence, it appears that the parietotemporal junction and parietal operculum is the crucial cortical area and the underlying white matter, the arcuate fasciculus, is always involved. The more outlying regions of the occipital, temporal, and parietal lobes appear to be more optional. The use of the terms parietotemporal and temporoparietal by the specialists reading the film was somewhat arbitrary. If the brunt of the lesion was borne by one lobe over the others then that was mentioned first (Table 4.1).

R.S. had a lesion that is of special interest as it is relatively small. It is probably the smallest of the isotope lesions, and, on the lateral surface of the autopsied brain, it appears to be even smaller (Figure 4.22). The most interesting aspect of this lesion was the relative sparing of the temporal lobe. Only the medial aspect of the opercular surface seems to be infarcted in the crossections, but on the lateral surface, the posterior end of the first temporal convolution seems to be also involved. This underlines the importance of obtaining crossections as the surface involvement may suggest a smaller lesion.

If one is to point to one identifiable structure that is invariably destroyed in the lesions causing neologistic jargon, it is the supramarginal gyrus and the posterior parietal operculum, and the underlying white matter, the arcuate portion of the inferior longitudinal fasciculus (the arcuate fasciculus). This is the area involved also in cases of conduction aphasia (Benson, Sheremata, Bouchard, Segarra, Price, & Geschwind, 1973), which is characterized by phonemic paraphasias and phonemic approximation of target words. Occasionally, conduction aphasics have fluent paraphasic speech, at times resembling neologistic jargon. One of the stages in the evolution of language impairment of patients with initial neologistic jargonaphasia may be conduction aphasia when comprehension improves but paraphasias persist. In these cases, the spontaneous speech usually contains less jargon than in those with persisting severe Wernicke's aphasia. Their lesions are also smaller and more anteriorly placed. These cases form a link between Wernicke's aphasia with neologistic jargon and conduction aphasia with severe phonemic paraphasias.

Four of the five autopsied cases in our first series (Kertesz & Benson, 1970) and the most recent autopsied case, R.S., definitely involve the supramarginal gyrus, the parietal operculum, and the underlying arcuate fasciculus, and, only to a minor degree, the temporal lobe. The important coronal cuts of these autopsied cases have been summarized in Figure 4.2 by transferring the lesion outlines on templates and overlapping them. The temporal lobe, on the other hand, does show a major involvement in one of the autopsied cases and in most of the persisting severe jargonaphasia cases, with isotope or CT localization (Figure 4.27). The degree of temporal involvement is likely to play a role in the comprehension deficit of these patients. The question of to what extent it contributes to the jargon formation is of great theoretical interest. The role of temporal lobe auditory association areas in monitoring phonemic, syntactic, and semantic processing and assembly for output will be discussed further.

Green and Howes (1977), reviewing the evidence on the anatomy of conduction aphasia, thought that the cortical area of temporoparietal area acted as a unit. They also stated that partial damage to this area did not necessarily alter the clinical features of conduction aphasia. They felt that variable damage to this unit may result in some differences in behavior such as the presence of ideomotor apraxia in parietal lesions (Benson *et al.*, 1973) or the incidences of neologistic output (they did not say which portion of the unit is responsible) but that "good comprehension, fluent speech and poor repetition recur consistently [p.127]." It is precisely the impairment of comprehension in addition to the amount of neologistic output that separates neologistic jargonaphasics (and Wernicke's aphasics in general) from conduction aphasics. The evidence is strong, exceptions notwithstanding, that impaired comprehension is an important component of the syndrome caused by damage to the temporoparietal junction. That some patients have better comprehension and less jargon (conduction aphasia) may indeed be related to more involvement of the inferior parietal region and the supramarginal gyrus than the temporal lobe, which in turn seems to be involved in severe neologistic jargonaphasia.

The presence or absence of hemianopia indicates involvement of the optic radiation and indirectly the depth and the anteroposterior and vertical location of the lesions. Of the 10 cases, 6 have visual field defects; Case 10, a lower quadrantanopsia indicating higher parietal location. Some more anterior, deeper temporal lesions may also cause field defect as the optic radiation curves forward to a considerable extent.

Three of the cases had a left central lesion in addition to the temporoparietal location of the others. None of these involved Broca's area. Case 2 had an aneurysm repaired in the left frontotemporal region. Case 6 appears to have a questionable vaguely decreased density at the left central (rolandic) operculum on the CT scan but not on the isotope scan, suggesting that this is not clinically relevant. The central uptake in Case 8 is more temporal than rolandic and it probably represents the anterior temporal extension of a temporoparietal infarct. It may account for the occasional hesitation observed in her speech. The significance of these somewhat more anterior lesions is discussed in what follows. Two of the cases (2 and 3) with aneurysms developed considerable hydrocephalus. In Case 2, this has subsided, yet her neologistic jargon persisted. Case 3 still has significant hydrocephalus. This feature does not seem to influence the presence or absence of neologistic jargon.

THE SPECIFICITY OF LOCALIZATION

One of the major problems in determining localization in jargonaphasia is the lack of consensus as to what constitutes "jargon." We defined NEO-LOGISTIC JARGON as very fluent speech, at times under pressure, in which syntactic and prosodic organization is preserved but many words are unrecognizable. We contrasted these cases with those Wernicke's aphasics in whom fluent speech was filled with semantic paraphasias which are recognizably English. This, most authors feel, is different and it may best be termed SEMANTIC JARGON. Pressure of speech characterized neologistic jargon but was not a necessary condition, and it may appear in cases of semantic jargon as well. Unawareness, or anosognosia, for the speech defect is often a prominent feature of both. All of these patients had poor comprehension, repetition, and naming scores, but the neologistic jargon patients were worse than the semantic jargon group.

If one feels that there is a valid clinical and linguistic difference between the two it is then logical to ask the question, Are the lesions specific for the entity of neologistic jargonaphasia? Although lesion localization is similar, lesion size differences seem to be significant: Neologistic jargon is produced by larger lesions. All lesions of severe or persisting neologistic jargonaphasia appeared to involve the posterior end of the first temporal gyrus (T1) and the supramarginal gyrus region. The autopsied case (R.S.) seemed to involve only a very small portion of the posterior end of the temporal operculum, leaving most of the temporal lobe intact. The posterior subcortical portion of the lesion, however, undercut the supposed forward connection of Wernicke's area. T1, and the planum temporale by destroying the arcuate fasciculus. The lesion on the surface was relatively small and this seemed to correlate with the relative mildness of his aphasia.

The less severely affected aphasics with semantic jargon have more posterior lesions (transcortical sensory aphasia) and those with good comprehension but frequent paraphasias (conduction aphasia) have more anteriorly distributed involvement. There are some Wernicke's aphasics who are similar to these categories in their conversatonal speech, but are distinguished by their poor repetition and comprehension. There appears to

ANDREW KERTESZ106

be more scatter in the lesions producing semantic jargon, and the lesions are also smaller.

The confusion involved in labeling the clinical and linguistic phenomena has to be cleared before the localizing information from any study of jargon is interpreted. Unfortunately, since Jackson (1866), recurrent STEREOTYPIC UTTERANCES have, at times been labeled as jargon. Alajouanine (1956) has included these patients under "undifferentiated jargon" in his classification, although the resemblance is only superficial. A few cases where all lexical items uttered were neologistic were published by Lecours and Rouillon (1976) and Brown (1979), who termed these cases PHONEMIC (undifferentiated) jargon. Most of the time, a preserved syntactic framework, often appropriate lexical items, rich phonemic variability, and the preservation of appropriate intonation and stress, easily distinguish true neologistic jargon from the residual utterances of globally aphasic patients or from undifferentiated jargon. Occasionally, mumbling unintelligible relatively fluent speech creates a problem in classification; we misclassified such a patient initially as a global aphasic. These often elderly patients may evolve toward a picture of jargonaphasia with a superimposed articulation problem. We excluded two such patients from this study. One had a large temporal lesion with some frontal and possibly parietal involvement. The distinction between neologistic jargon in Wernicke's aphasia and NEOLOGISMS in the speech of conduction aphasics has been made earlier in the chapter, in discussing the role of supramarginal gyrus and arcuate fasciculus. The term phonemic jargon has been applied in the French literature to conduction aphasia!

The limitation of localization with isotopes and CT scans have been discussed previously (Kertesz, 1979) and need to be considered here also. These methods, on one hand, enabled us to see the extent of localization of lesions at the time of examination; on the other hand, the localization achieved is not as direct as with autopsy. The quality of images can influence localization significantly. In the isotope study, the background radiation count is a physiological variable which changes the contrast and may alter the visible uptake relative to the normal brain tissue even though the scan is performed at an optimum time (10–20 days postonset). Similar problems are encountered with CT images. The acute CT pictures are not as well defined as the chronic ones beyond 3 months. The positioning of the head in the scanner often alters the cut and adjustment has to be made by the radiologist during transfer to the template. Variation in head size, ventricular size, and the shape and direction of the sylvian fissure alters the relationship of lesions to important structures, and this all has to be considered during the process of transfer, which is at best only an approximation of the size and location of the real lesion. Without this process, however, the lesions cannot be overlapped.

We tried to avoid the bias in transferring the images onto structures that are believed to play a role in speech mechanisms by having a neuroradiologist and a nuclear scanning specialist who did not know the clinical condition of the patient but were expert in CT and isotope imaging and anatomy do the tracing. To allow oneself to carry out the tracing would be to let in the possibility of bias through the above-mentioned variables. It is very easy to draw the edges of an isotope image wider or smaller or include another small sulcus or fissure into the CT lesion. Although errors are going to occur during this process, their impact is lessened by unbiased but expert tracing and by using a large enough number of observations in drawing the conclusion.

Isotope scans provide excellent lateral images most of the time although the horizontal CT sections can also be converted to lateral or parasagittal sections by connecting the leading edges, or by a computer. The important difference appears to be that the isotope scans are especially informative in infarcts as they will optimally outline a lesion of any significant size in the 7–28 days poststroke period. On the other hand, CT scans will show the outline of the lesion throughout the chronic period, although at times they are not as distinct in the early acute period as the isotope scan (see Case 5). The combination of the two methods thus provides a more comprehensive method of localization of lesions than either of them alone. The occasional opportunity to see the exact extent of the lesion by autopsy in patients who had one of those imaging procedures, defines the accuracy of the imaging, tracing, and transferring processes. An example of this is R.S., where the isotope image to be viewed in both dimensions corresponds within certain limitations to actual pictures on the surface of the brain. Similar autopsy correlations have been published for CT images (Kinkel & Jacobs, 1976). The continuing improvement in imaging and confirmation with autopsies will refine the method further.

FUNCTIONAL SIGNIFICANCE

The functional significance of the localization of lesions is the most tantalizing, and to some the most important, issue in studying these patients. It has been thought ever since Wernicke (1874) that the disordered auditory monitoring of speech output produces the jargon. Subsequent modifications of and additions to this idea have not entirely clarified this intriguing phenomenon (Geschwind, 1969).

The main theories of the underlying mechanisms are best organized in four groups although there are other variations or combinations. These are not necessarily exclusive, but they are sufficiently distinct to warrant examination in the light of available evidence. Some of the theories are based on anatomical, behavioral, and linguistic data; some are more speculative than others.

1. *Impaired comprehension is associated with disordered auditory monitoring of speech output, or lexical and phonemic assembly.* In favor

of this theory is the overwhelming evidence that severe neologistic jargon-aphasia is invariably associated with severe comprehension deficit. However, when neologisms appear in cases of conduction aphasia with preserved comprehension, this does not account for the production of phonemic errors. Nevertheless, one could argue up to a certain extent that conduction aphasics have mild but significant comprehension deficit, especially those with neologistic paraphasias. The frequent and probably essential involvement of the posterior auditory association areas in the lesions producing neologistic jargon has been one of the most important arguments in favor of the impaired auditory monitoring mechanism. Other unrelated experimental evidence of producing paraphasic speech with delayed auditory feedback also suggests this theory (Lee, 1950).

The degree of anosognosia or unawareness of speech defect which was first emphasized by Alajonanine (1956) is not seen without significant comprehension deficit. There are cases with severe lack of comprehension who do not have jargon or anosognosia. Therefore, comprehension and awareness or auditory monitoring may be dissociated.

The recovery of comprehension closely parallels the recovery from neologistic output disturbance. This in turn suggests the intrinsic relationship between the comprehension deficit and faulty output. However, the dissociation of comprehension deficit from language output is witnessed in other aphasic disturbances as mentioned earlier.

2. *The phonemic selection and assembly is impaired independently; the associated comprehension deficit is not essential for the production of neologistic jargon.* This theory would consider a common mechanism underlying neologistic jargonaphasia and the phonemic paraphasias and phonemic approximations of conduction aphasia. It would also account for the existence of semantic jargon, with impaired lexical selection but an intact phonological process. It would not explain the pressure of speech, anosognosia, and the comprehension deficit seen, unless these are considered just neighborhood signs, peripheral to the issue of phonemic jargon. Somewhat against this consideration is that most patients with neologistic jargonaphasia lose their neologisms first during recovery and their subsequent clinical picture is usually semantic jargon or circumlocutory speech with anomic gaps, rather than conduction aphasia with continuing prominent paraphasias. It is possible, however, that some patients who show recovery in the direction of conduction aphasia have more anterior parietal lesions in front of and involving the supramarginal gyrus, than those others whose recovery is the more usual loss of neologisms but persistent semantic jargon and comprehension deficit.

3. *The primary disorder is anomia or word-finding difficulty (impaired lexical selector) in which the anomic gaps are filled by a disinhibited phonemic selector.* Anomic gaps alone will not account for the severely anomic

patients who do not produce neologisms or for the purely semantic jargon. Why are the anomic gaps filled on one occasion with neologisms and on other occasions with intelligible words? This theory will not explain why cases of undifferentiated jargon replace even the function words with neologisms, whereas in anomia and in neologistic jargon it is the substantive lexical items, especially nouns, that characteristically are affected. The phonemic distortions and neologisms require something else in addition to the word-finding difficulty. It is likely that a two-stage distortion takes place, in which, first, a wrong lexical item is selected for a certain intended semantic and syntactic framework, and, second, the item is rendered an unrecognizable neologism by disturbed phonological selection (Lecours & Lhermitte, 1969; Brown, 1972). The mechanism of disinhibition of the phonemic selector over and above the semantic selector has been invoked (Buckingham & Kertesz, 1976). The disinhibition may or may not be related to the lack of auditory monitoring or comprehension problem. The temporoparietal area, however, is not usually considered inhibitory in the same sense as are, for instance, the frontal lobes. Nevertheless, the more modern evidence of widespread inhibitory and regulatory processes in the cortex challenges this restricted view.

4. *Damage to the contralateral hemisphere interferes with the compensatory mechanisms in dominant temporoparietal area damage.* A higher frequency of bilateral involvement in jargonaphasia has been suggested (Cohn & Neumann, 1958; Lhermittee *et al.,* 1973; Weinstein *et al.,* 1966). The great majority of severe jargonaphasics with strokes have only a unilateral lesion in a stroke population like ours, however, and Cohn and Neumann's theory of bihemispheric interference is not a likely explanation for the production of jargon. Cohn and Neumann assumed that both temporal lobes receive data in parallel. The synchronization of recall and/or the pacemaker function of the other temporal lobe may be lost in cases of scrambled jargon output. The intensity of the jargon would appear to be a function of the degree of interaction of the damaged and relatively intact structures. The bilaterality of lesions may be more frequent in cases with different etiology. This in most series is not controlled by a comparable survey for bilateral lesions in other aphasic types. Bilateral lesions may be found more frequently in autopsied series ("silent" strokes and more severely affected patients who die).

Brown (1977) considered semantic jargon to occur more likely as the result of bilateral lesions and neologistic jargon in lesions of the dominant focal neocortex. It is our clinical experience also that bilateral cortical degenerative disease often gives rise to semantic jargon; however, identical speech disturbance is seen also with focal lesions in the dominant hemisphere.

The anatomical evidence does not allow us to substantiate either hypothesis alone. The disturbance by lesioning the superior temporal and

ANDREW KERTESZ

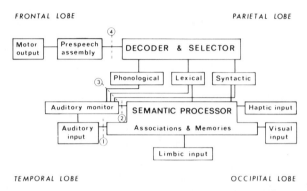

Figure 4.31. A model of function of the temporoparietal language system. The numbered, interrupted lines represent lesions which may correspond to clinical entities (see text).

supramarginal area may indeed affect individuals differently, possibly because of anatomical differences in the lesions so far undetected by our methods or because of individual differences in cerebral organization. A block diagram may be constructed to summarize the clinical and neurolinguistic data that are compatible with various lesions in the temporoparietal junction (Figure 4.31).

Lesions at Location 1 may disconnect auditory input from a semantic processor resulting in "pure word deafness" or verbal auditory agnosia; only few reliable cases have been described in the literature and they are not usually seen in the evolution or recovery of jargonaphasia. This lesion obviously does not lead to the degree of disinhibition necessary for the excessive logorrheic output or anosognosia. Lesions at Location 2 disconnect the auditory monitor from the semantic processor; semantic jargon results from losing control over lexical and syntactical selection mechanisms while retaining phonological mechanisms and repetition. This is often seen in transcortical sensory aphasia. Lesions at Locations 1 and 2 together may result in Wernicke's aphasia with semantic jargon. At Location 3, the lesion will likely produce a complex partial disturbance with excess paraphasic and neologistic speech. A combination of lesions at 1, 2, and 3 will likely produce neologistic jargonaphasia with impaired comprehension, repetition, and loss of auditory monitoring of the selection and prespeech assembly of phonemic, lexical, and syntactical elements of language. Lesions at Location 4 will likely produce conduction aphasia with its propensity for phonenic paraphasias and poor repetition but preserved comprehension.

SUMMARY

A new series of isotope scan and CT localization of lesions in neologistic jargonaphasia and an autopsy correlation is presented. These are contrasted with previous localizations and with lesions causing similar but distinct clinical disturbances.

Neologistic jargonaphasia is produced by lesions of the temporoparietal junction. The temporal lesion can be very small but the supramarginal gyrus and the posterior parietal operculum are always involved.

The lesion size seemed to correlate with the severity of the language disturbance. Persistent neologistic jargon is produced by large lesions; relative sparing of the temporal lobe probably carries a better prognosis. The significance of the anatomical material in the production of this striking linguistic and clinical phenomena is discussed. Neologistic jargon is believed to be the result of disinhibition or the loss of (inner) auditory monitoring of a phonological and lexical selection system of the brain. A direct disturbance of such a decoder and selector mechanism is possible but this less flexible consideration does not account for the variability of the language production and its frequent recovery.

ACKNOWLEDGMENTS

This work was supported by an Ontario Ministry of Health Grant Number PR721. The author is grateful for the ample assistance of Ann Sheppard and Patricia McCabe, and to Sally Beech for secretarial work and the Audiovisual Department of St. Joseph's Hospital for the numerous illustrations.

REFERENCES

Alajouanine, Th. Verbal realization in aphasia. *Brain,* 1956, *79,* 1–28.
Benson, D. F. Fluency in aphasia: Correlation with radioactive scan localization. *Cortex,* 1967, *3,* 373–394.
Benson, D. F., Sheremata, W. A., Bouchard, R., Segarra, J. M., Price, D., & Geschwind, N. Conduction aphasia—A clinicopathological study. *Archives of Neurology,* 1973, *28,* 339–346.
Brown, J. *Aphasia, apraxia and agnosia: Clinical and theoretical aspects.* Springifeld, Ill.: Thomas, 1972.
Brown, J. *Mind, brain and consciousness: The neuropsychology of cognition.* New York: Academic Press, 1977.
Brown, J. Language representation in the brain. In H. Steklis & M. Raleigh (Eds.), *Neurobiology of social communication in primates.* New York: Academic Press, 1979. Pp. 133–195.
Buckingham, H. W., & Kertesz, A. A linguistic analysis of fluent aphasia. *Brain and Language,* 1974, *1,* 43–62.
Buckingham, H. W., & Kertesz, A. *Neologistic jargon aphasia.* Amsterdam: Swets & Zeitlinger, 1976.
Cohn, R., & Neumann, M. Jargon aphasia. *Journal of Nervous and Mental Disease,* 1958, *127,* 381–399.
Geschwind, N. The work and influence of Wernicke. In R. Cohen & M. Wartofsky (Eds.), *Studies in the philosophy of science* (Vol. 4). Dordrecht: Reidel, 1969.
Gonzalez, C. F., Grossman, C. B., & Palacios, E. *Computed brain and orbital tomography: Technique and interpretation.* New York: Wiley, 1976.

Green, E., & Howes, D. The nature of conduction aphasia: A study of anatomic and clinical features and of underlying mechanism. In H. Whitaker & H. A. Whitaker (Eds.), *Studies in neurolinguistics* (Vol. 3). New York: Academic Press, 1977. Pp. 123–156.

Head, H. *Aphasia and kindred disorders of speech.* Cambridge: Cambridge University Press, 1926.

Henschen, S. E. Klinische und Anatomische Beitrage zur Pathologie des Gehirns (Vols. 5–7). Stockholm: Nordiska Bokhandel, 1922.

Jackson, H. Remarks on those cases of disease of the nervous system in which defect of expression is the most striking symptom. *Medical Times Gazette,* 1866.

Kertesz, A. *Aphasia and associated disorders: Taxonomy, localization and recovery.* New York: Grune and Stratton, 1979.

Kertesz, A., & Benson, D. F. Neologistic jargon: A clinicopathological study. *Cortex,* 1970, *6,* 362–386.

Kertesz, A., Harlock, W., & Coates, R. Computer tomographic localization, lesion size and prognosis in aphasia and nonverbal impairment. *Brain and Language,* 1979, *8,* 34–50.

Kertesz, A., Lesk, D., & McCabe, P. Isotope localization of infarcts in aphasia. *Archives of Neurology,* 1977, *34,* 590–601.

Kertesz, A., & Poole, E. The aphasia quotient: The taxonomic approach to measurement of aphasic disability. *Canadian Journal of Neurological Science,* 1974, *1,* 7–16.

Kinkel, W. R., & Jacobs, L. Computerized axial transverse tomography in cerebrovascular disease. *Neurology,* 1976, *26,* 924–930.

Kleist, K. [Sensory aphasia and amusia.] In F. J. Fish & J. B. Stanton: (Eds. and trans.), *The myeloarchitectonic basis.* Oxford: Pergamon, 1962.

Lecours, A., & Lhermitte, F. Phonemic paraphasias: Linguistic structures and tentative hypothesis. *Cortex,* 1969, *5,* 193–228.

Lecours, A. R., & Rouillion, F. Neurolinguistic analysis of jargonaphasia and jargonagraphia. In H. Whitaker & H. A. Whitaker (Eds.), *Studies in neurolinguistics* (Vol. 2). New York: Academic Press, 1976.

Lee, B. S. Effect of delayed speech feedback. *Journal of the Acoustical Society of America,* 1950, *22,* 824–826.

Lhermitte, F., Lecours, A. R., Ducarne, B., & Escourolla, R. Unexpected anatomical findings in a case of fluent jargon aphasia. *Cortex,* 1973, *9,* 436–449.

Mohr, J. P., Pessin, M. S., Finkelstein, S., Funkenstein, H. H., Duncan, G. W., & Davis, K. R. Broca aphasia: Pathologic and clinical aspects. *Neurology,* 1978, *28,* 311–324.

Mohr, J. P., Wattes, W. C., & Duncan, G. W. Thalamic hemorrhage and aphasia. *Brain and Language,* 1975, *2,* 3–18.

Naeser, M. A., & Hayward, R. W. Lesion localization in aphasia with cranial computed tomography and the Boston Diagnostic Aphasia Exam. *Neurology,* 1978, *28,* 545–551.

Nielson, J. M. *Agnosia, apraxia, aphasia.* New York: Hoeber, 1946.

Pick, A. Beitrage zur Lehre von den Störungen der Sprache. *Archiv Fur Psychiatrie und Nervenkranheiten (Berlin),* 1892, *23,* 896–918.

Shipps, F. C., Madeira, J. T., Huntington, H. W. *Atlas of brain anatomy for EMI scans.* Springfield, Ill.: Thomas, 1975.

Sobotta, J., & Figge, F. *Atlas of human anatomy* (Vol. 3, Part 2). New York: Hafner, 1963.

Starr, M. A. The pathology of sensory aphasia, with an analysis of fifty cases in which Broca's centre was not diseased. *Brain,* 1889, *12,* 82–101.

Weinstein, E., Lyerly, O., Cole, M., & Ozer, M. Meaning in jargon aphasia. *Cortex,* 1966, *2,* 166–187.

Wernicke, C. *Der aphasische symptomenkomplex.* Breslau: Cohn & Weigart, 1871. (Reprinted in R. Cohen & M. Wartofsky (Eds.), *Boston Studies on the Philosophy of Science* (Vol. 4). Dordrecht: Reidel, 1969.)

Chapter 5

Gestures and Lexical Processes in Jargonaphasia

BRIAN BUTTERWORTH
JOHN SWALLOW
MALCOLM GRIMSTON

INTRODUCTION

Analysis of Lexical Processes in Jargonaphasia

Although the speech of jargonaphasics sounds grossly abnormal, some cases, at least, seem explicable in terms of a single functional impairment and the speaker's strategic adaptation to it. The detailed study of one such patient, K.C., revealed apparently intact systems in production for syntactic organization, intonation, morphology (both grammatical and derivational), phonology, and phonetics (Butterworth, 1979). K.C.'s control of function words and many very common lexical items also appeared quite normal. An analysis of silent hesitations disclosed a problem specific to lexical processes: In normal speakers, some of these pauses immediately precede words unpredictable in context and are explained as delays caused by searching the lexicon for these words (Beattie & Butterworth, 1979; Butterworth, 1980a; Goldman-Eisler, 1958). In K.C., paraphasias and neologisms were more likely than real words to be preceded by pauses, suggesting, unsurprisingly (Howes, 1964; Newcombe, Oldfield, & Wingfield, 1965), a difficulty in finding less common or less predictable words.[1]

---

[1] Beattie and Butterworth (1979) found that, although word frequency and word predictability in context were normally confounded, some pauses were attributable to predictability independent of frequency.

This finding has, of course, little or nothing to say about why problems in lexical search should lead to neologisms. However, it turned out on closer inspection that types of neologism and pause duration corresponded in a systematic and revealing manner. Neologisms were classified according to their phonological relationship to other words or to other neologisms in the following way:

A. Neologisms phonologically related to a prior word:

(1) . . . *want everything to be so **talk**. I do not yet* /dɔːk/

(2) . . . *I was able to show it to a friend. And then I have er—I have another* /frʌnd/ *or two*

A neologism was counted in this category if it had at least four features in common with the prior word, where "feature" means a phoneme or its position in the syllable. Thus in (1) *talk* (/tɔːk/) is related to /dɔːk/ on four features—two phonemes, /ɔː,k/, in the same syllable positions.

B. Neologisms phonologically related to a following word:

(3) *She has to do things* /wʌmən/ *a **woman** who helps*

(4) *I've been very much* /wɔ́tɪŋ/ *what to do.*

Again the criterion is four features in common between the neologism and the following word.

C. Neologisms phonologically related to a target word:

(5) *I remember the* /dɔ́kumèn/ [target word = *doctor*]

(6) *A* /čərk/ [*chair*]

Again, the four-feature criterion is used.

D. Neologisms phonologically linked to other neologisms:

(7) /bæklənd/ . . . /bændɪks/ . . . /bændɪks/ . . . /zændɪks/ . . . /lændɔks/ . . . /zæprɪks/

(8) /nɔks/ . . . /mɔk/ . . . /ínvɔk/ . . . /wɔ́kʌf/ . . . /vok/

These neologisms typically were interleaved among sequences of real words, and thus differ from classic uninterrupted sequences in *conduite d'approche*.

E. Other neologisms, some possibly related to targets:

(9) *I used to get my* /gɔ́rdərwə̀rd pídlʌm/ [*word order muddled?*]

(10)   . . . *because I'm* /wɔ́trɛd/ *waiting* [taps belly] [*weight watching?*]

others apparently not:

(11)   . . . *even with a* /kwailai/ *return.*

(A transcript of the whole sample can be found as an appendix to Butter-worth, 1979.)

The duration of the pauses immediately preceding neologisms were measured for each of the categories A–E and an average calculated. These data, along with the findings for verbal paraphasias, are summarized in Table 5.1. The interesting feature of these results is that the delays before neologisms phonologically related to real words are shorter than those before neologisms related to other neologisms, and both require longer average delays than wrong (real) words (verbal paraphasias). These differ-ences in delay times indicate that the routes to the productions in the error categories must be, in some respects, at least, different; and, indeed, the times appear to correspond to the amount of phonological information K.C. can retrieve from lexical search. Thus, in verbal paraphasias, complete information is retrieved, but not necessarily from the target word; and, in Category D, apparently no phonological information from the lexicon is retrieved, although information from other neologisms is. This assumes that the speaker is unable to distinguish target and nontarget information.

The explanation offered in Butterworth (1979) revolves around the idea of a strategic adaptation to the functional deficit in the retrieval of phon-

TABLE 5.1.

Mean Silent Delays before Six Types of Error

| | Verbal paraphasias | Error category | | | | |
		A	B	C	D	E
N	35	12	8	21	55	68
Mean delay (sec)	.135	.233	.250	.348	.494	.301
			.295			

t-tests verbal paraphasias versus A + B + C
$\quad$ $t(74) = 1.66, p < .05$ (one-tailed)
$\quad$ A + B + C versus D
$\quad$ $t(94) = 1.85, p < .05$ (one-tailed)
A: Neologisms phonologically related to a prior word
B: Neologisms phonologically related to a following word
C: Neologisms phonologically related to a target word
D: Neologisms not related to a real word
E: Other neologisms

ological information from the lexicon. The speaker uses whatever information is available, augmenting where necessary so that the result will make a complete and regular phoneme string. This augmented string may make a real word by chance, but usually will result in neologisms similar to a real word (sometimes called "phonemic" or "literal" paraphasias). If this strategy fails to retrieve any information, a "device" constructs a phoneme string according to the rules of English phonotactics (but not according to the frequency distribution of phonemes in English). Each running of the device leaves a residue which decays over time, and which can be reused on the next running, hence the sequences of similar neologisms exemplified in Category D. Deploying the device only after the complete failure of lexical retrieval predicts the greater delay before items so generated.

Given that the speaker, K.C., is unable directly to check the appropriateness of his output, this strategy would have the advantage of permitting him to match his output to the gross requirements of the conversational task: English-sounding words and normal or near normal fluency.

This account, however, is unsatisfactory in two important ways. First, it would predict that K.C. would be unable to correct his utterances, as it assumes that he cannot check that a given expression is appropriate to his intended meaning; yet—contrary to theories of jargonaphasia that maintain that patients say the first thing that comes into their heads and are unable to inhibit incorrect output[2]—K.C. certainly does show correction, or, at least, false starts (what I called "high level amendments"):

(12) *I've done one or two things with that—with my brother*

(13) *Then I had to get—I then had to get*

(14) *The /læklʌ/—the general /ɛksli/*

(15) *Then I have a lot of /dɪk/—er /grud/*

These examples all clearly show "correction intonation" and on this basis can be distinguished from apparent changes in the direction of a sentence which do not.

Second, the account given fails to identify the locus of the deficit in the model of lexical selection. We cannot tell whether something is wrong with stored word meanings, with stored word sounds, with the addressing systems for accessing these (the links between meanings and sounds), with the mechanisms of search or, indeed, whether the higher level meaning processes are intact or impaired.

---

[2] Such theories are proposed by, for example, Kinsbourne and Warrington (1963), Pick (1931), and Rochford (1974).

HAND GESTURES AND LEXICAL PROCESSES

Spontaneous speech is characteristically accompanied by bodily movements, most noticeably of the arms and hands. Some of these appear intimately linked with the processes of speech production, being rhythmically timed with the speech, and they often seem to reflect the meaning that the speech expresses. Butterworth and Beattie (1978) called these movements "Speech-Focused Movements" (SFMs) to distinguish them from other movements that may also accompany talk—scratching, twitching, self-touching—but that neither are timed with the speech, nor, in any apparent way, reflect the meaning of what is said.

Previous studies have generally not made this distinction (Dittman, 1972; Freud, 1905); some studies, in a structural analysis, have tried specifically to associate ALL movements with subdivisions of the linguistic structure of the message (Birdwhitsell, 1970; Kendon, 1972). Two main classes of explanations have been offered. First, in the psychoanalytic tradition, movements are held to reveal the speaker's emotional or affective state (e.g., Deutsch, 1947, 1952; Feldman, 1959; Freud, 1905). Second, movements have been considered as constituting an alternative channel of communication—either augmenting the verbal message or substituting for all or part of it (Baxter, Winters, & Hammer, 1969; Mahl, Danet, & Norton, 1959).

Some authors, however, have proposed that movements may be symptomatic of underlying cognitive processes, starting, of course, with Freud (1905, p. 77), but more recently as a way of determining whether deficits in the cognitive processes involved in language are reflected in deficits in gestural performance (Cicone, Wapner, Foldi, Zurif, & Gardner, 1979; Delis, Foldi, Hamby, Gardner, & Zurif, 1979; Goldblum, 1980) or pantomime (Goodglass & Kaplan, 1963).

In our study of normal speakers (Butterworth & Beattie, 1978), we were looking for evidence of links between gestures and specific systems in production. To this end, we further subdivided SFMs into complex nonce movements, which reflect the meaning of what is said (gestures), and those simple repetitive movements which, while speech-timed, do not reflect meaning, although they may serve for emphasis (batonic movements).

Analysis of the location of SFMs with respect to the speech revealed that gestures tended to be associated with lexical items (nouns, verbs, adjectives), whereas batonic movements were associated with all form classes, but especially with demonstratives and *wh-* words (see Table 5.2). Second, the temporal onsets of gestures, but not batonic movements, overwhelmingly occurred in pauses rather than speech, and there was twice as much speech time as pause time in our samples). The mean asynchrony between gesture onset and the onset of the associated word was as follows:

TABLE 5.2.
Percentages of Gestures and Batonic Movements by Syntactic Category[a]

	Gestures (%)	Batonic movements (%)
Noun	26.20	11.05
Verb	16.88	9.15
Adjective	28.61	8.02
Adverb	2.71	4.98
Pronoun	8.73	3.88
Preposition	5.72	2.76
Conjunction	4.82	6.63
Dem. adj.	6.33	22.93
Wh-	—	30.62
Others	—	—
Total	100.00	100.00

[a] Figures adjusted for the number of occurrences of words in each category.

Nouns: 770 msec
Verbs: 661 msec
Adjectives: 664 msec

We concluded that, since a gesture reflects the meaning of a word (or phrase), the meaning must be known in advance of the word onset by at least the duration of the asynchrony. The asynchrony was held to reflect the time taken to search the lexicon given a meaning specification of that word, and the gesture was held to be directly activated by the meaning specification.

A MODEL OF THE LEXICON AND K.C.'S IMPAIRMENT

In a later theoretical paper, these results were collated with others bearing on lexical processes, and derived a model containing two processes and two resources (Butterworth, 1980b). Process 1 formulates the meaning, or semantic, specification, and this can be carried out well in advance of the location of the word in the speech stream. The specification can be treated as an address for an item in the first resource, the "semantic lexicon," which contains a listing of semantic items. Each item, accessible via the semantic address, is associated with an address that can be used by Process 2—a search through Resource 2, the "phonological lexicon." The phonological lexicon contains a listing of the phonological forms of word stems (endings are added by later processes), and retrieving items from it is carried out locally where the word will be needed in output. Lexical hesitations in speech are held to be the result of long searches through this lexicon.

Now, although K.C.'s neologisms tend to follow pauses and to substitute for words typically implicated in lexical pauses[3] in normals (nouns, verbs, adjectives, rather than prepositions, pronouns, *etc.*), a variety of interpretations are still theoretically possible. For example, the formulation of the semantic specification may be impaired, which would create confusion in the rest of the system, thereby slowing down lexical access, particularly where the specification itself is unfamiliar and requires a relatively uncommon word to meet it. In such cases, one would expect lexical pauses and neologisms substituting for uncommon words. One might also expect an overall slowing down of the speech rate—or more pauses—but this does not seem to happen. However, individual patterns vary quite a lot (a standard deviation of 9.4% around a mean 36% of total time normally spent in pausing), and K.C.'s pretraumatic rate may have been much more fluent than his post traumatic rate of 29% pause time.

Alternatively, formulation of semantic specifications may be unimpaired, but items in the semantic lexicon may be damaged, affecting either access or retrieval of the address for the appropriate phonological item.

Both of these possibilities could be eliminated if K.C.'s gestures, which are dependent on the semantics of the system, correspond closely to normal patterns.

ANALYSIS OF K.C.'S GESTURES

The Subject

K.C., a patient under the care of Sir Roger Bannister, at the National Hospital for Nervous Diseases, London, was a 72-year-old retired solicitor with no history of previous neurological disease. He collapsed in his garden; a few minutes later there were signs of slight weakness and a very severe speech disturbance. The weakness rapidly resolved, but the language disturbance persisted; his speech was fluent but full of neologisms and other jargon. There was a suggestion of visual inattention toward the right although this was inconsistent. The right side of the face moved more slowly than the left but otherwise the cranial nerves were normal. In the limbs there was no weakness demonstrable, although the right hand was rather slower and more clumsy than the left. On the sensory side there was no definite abnormality although again there was a suggestion of inattention toward the right. He obeyed some commands, presumably making use of the nonlinguistic information available in the context, but on the whole appeared unable to comprehend speech. Psychological testing could not be carried out in full because of the communication difficulty. He performed,

---

[3] Butterworth (1980a) distinguishes pauses and pause time attributable to lexical selection from pauses attributable to syntactic marking and longer range planning.

however, at the superior level on WAIS Block Design, which is a strong counterindication to any possibility of dementia. He was unable to name objects, or to read or write spontaneously, but he could copy individual letters. Skull x ray and isotope scan were normal. A diagnosis of left hemisphere vascular occlusive lesion was made.

Procedure 1

A videotape recording was made of a conversation and a brief picture-naming session. The whole lasted 24 min. Speech Focused Movements (SFMs)—gestures and batonic movements—were identified independently by two of the authors (J. S. and M. G.), following the procedure described in Butterworth and Beattie (1978), and the onsets of SFMs were located in relation to the words uttered and pauses using the slow motion facility of the VTR. Those portions of the tape where the subject pointed to a picture card and where he was manipulating objects were excluded from the analysis. A total of 795 sec of tape were analyzed.

Results 1

The rate of production of SFMs was assessed; each gesture was classified according to whether the onset occurred in a pause (H) or in speech (S). The results are given in Table 5.3. The delay between the onset of the gesture and the onset of the associated word was measured. As with normals, no gestures started after the associated word. (Neologisms were excluded from this analysis, as the criterial meaning relation between a gesture and a neologism could not be established. Analysis of gestures occurring with neologisms is described in what follows.) The mean delays

TABLE 5.3.
Number and Rate of Production of Speech Focused Movements in K.C. as Compared to Normals[a]

	Gestures H	Gestures S	Batonic movements	Total
K.C.				
Number	53	64	174	291
Rate per 100 sec	6.7	8.1	21.9	36.6
Normals				
Rate per 100 sec	13.7	9.0	16.7	39.4

[a] The data on normal speakers are taken from Butterworth and Beattie, 1978. Gestures are classified according to whether they start in a pause (H) or in speech (S).

TABLE 5.4.

Mean Duration of Delay (in Sec) between Gesture Onsets and Word Onsets, by
Syntactic Category and as Compared to Normals[a]

	Noun	Verb	Adjective
K.C.			
Number	41	40	15
Mean delay	.672	.601	.632
Normals			
Mean delay	.770	.661	.664

[a] The data on normal speakers are taken from Butterworth and Beattie (1978).

for nouns, verbs, and adjectives is given in Table 5.4. The range of delays
was also similar to normal speakers: K.C. 0–2.2 sec, normals 0–2.5 sec.

Discussion 1

K.C. produced roughly the same overall rate of SFMs as normals;
although rather fewer gestures started in pauses, this was still within the
range of individual differences found in the original study (Butterworth
& Beattie, unpublished data). The delays between gesture and word onsets
were also very similar to our normal population. There are no grounds,
therefore, for differentiating K.C.'s gestural performance from normals,
and thus for differentiating his control of lexical semantics.

It was proposed that when lexical search fails to retrieve any phonological information on the target word, a "device" generates a neologism.
That is, control of word output passes temporarily from lexical semantics
to the device. Alternatively, failure to retrieve the information may lead
to a restart of the sentence—a "high level amendment." Again control
passes from the original semantic item, but this time to a new item to go
with the new sentence plan. What happens to the gesture also controlled
by the original semantic item in each eventuality? It should be abandoned
in midcourse. One might further expect that this would be more likely to
occur when the target is a relatively uncommon word. This would be
evidenced by a pause following the gesture onset.

Analysis 2

We reexamined the videotape and selected 13 gestures[4] that seemed
to us complete and 12 that seemed incomplete—for example, where K.C.
started a gesture and then suddenly dropped his hands into a resting po-

[4] For gestures accompanying neologisms, the criterion of meaning relatedness could not,
of course, be used. In these cases, we included SFMs that were complex, not repeated
elsewhere in the tape, and were timed with the speech.

sition. Seven naive subjects—Cambridge undergraduates—were asked to classify these 25 gestures as complete or incomplete. They were not told the distribution, and they were shown a brief extract of another part of the tape to accustom them to K.C.'s hand movements. There was highly significant agreement among judges about both categories. With this validation of our judgment as a basis, we classified all gestures in our sample as complete or incomplete.

Of 104 completed gestures, 77 occurred with real and appropriate words, 24 with verbal paraphasias and Category A–C neologisms, and 3 with Category D neologisms (those bearing no phonological relation to a target or a contextual word). Of the 13 incomplete gestures, 10 occurred with Category D neologisms or high level amendments, and only 1 with a real word and 2 with Category A and C neologisms. The difference in distribution between complete and incomplete gestures is highly significant ($\chi^2 = 54.50$, df 1, $p < .001$).

The onsets of complete and incomplete gestures were classified as to whether they occurred in pauses or in speech. These data are summarized in Table 5.5. There is a significant difference between the distributions ($\chi^2 = 7.45$, df 1, $p < .01$).

Discussion 2

These results suggest that gestures are abandoned when the target word is relatively inaccessible, as can be seen by the predominance of incomplete gestures starting in pauses, which we assumed are delays in lexical search. The incomplete gestures, moreover, accompany behavior symptomatic of total search failure—category D neologisms or high level amendments.

CONCLUSIONS

In this study, we used analyses of gestural behavior to evaluate hypotheses about the intactness of lexical processes in a single case, K.C. We argued that semantic lexical processes could be considered intact if K.C. showed normal gestural behavior. It turned out that his performance was very similar to data from a normal population (Results 1), which thereby

TABLE 5.5.

Completed and Incomplete Gestures Beginning in Pauses (H) and in Speech (S)

	H	S	Total
Completed gestures	42	62	104
Incomplete gestures	11	2	13

indicated that deficits in lexical performance could be located in the process of searching the phonological lexicon.

We further argued that if search failure was the cause of the underlying anomia, then gestures linked to the semantic information controlling the search would be abandoned when search failed. The second analysis showed that incomplete gestures occurred at those points where search failure could be supposed—with neologisms phonologically unrelated to a real word or when K.C. abandons a sentence in midcourse and restarts. Whether search failure results from corruption of the phonological lexicon itself, or of the meaning–sound addressing which guides search, cannot be decided on these data.

This account provides, in addition, an explanation for apparent corrections. Although K.C. may genuinely correct using intact nonlexical routes, in some instances, other false starts may simply reflect another strategic adaptation to search failure.

As in our previous studies (Shallice & Butterworth, 1977; Butterworth, 1979), we have found that investigative tools developed for the study of normal speech production—hesitation and gestural analyses—can be used fruitfully in the identification of intact and impaired functions in aphasia.

ACKNOWLEDGMENTS

We would like to thank Sir Roger Bannister and the Department of Psychology at the National Hospital for Nervous Diseases, Queen Square, London, who allowed us to use their videotape of K.C. to do these analyses, and, in particular, Mr. J. Stevenson, who carried out the psychological testing and supervised the interview.

REFERENCES

Baxter, G. C., Winters, E. P., & Hammer, R. E. Gestural behaviour during a brief interview as a function of cognitive variables. *Journal of Personality and Social Psychology,* 1968, *8,* 303–307.

Beattie, G. W., & Butterworth, B. Contextual probability and word frequency as determinants of pauses and errors in spontaneous speech. *Language and Speech* 1979, *22,* 201–211.

Birdwhitsell, R. L. *Kinesics and context.* London: Penguin Books, 1971.

Butterworth, B. Hesitation and the production of verbal paraphasias and neologisms in jargon aphasia. *Brain and Language,* 1979, *8,* 133–161.

Butterworth, B. Evidence from pauses. In B. Butterworth (Ed.), *Language production* (Vol. 1). London: Academic Press, 1980. (a)

Butterworth, B. Constraints on models of language production. In B. Butterworth (Ed.), *Language production* (Vol. 1). London: Academic Press, 1980. (b)

Butterworth, B., & Beattie, G. W. Gesture and silence as indicators of planning in speech. In R. Campbell & P. T. Smith (Eds.), *Recent advances in the psychology of language: Formal and experimental approaches.* New York: Plenum, 1978.

Cicone, M., Wapner, W., Foldi, N., Zurif, E., & Gardner, H. The relations between gesture and language in aphasic communication. *Brain and Language,* 1979, 324–349.

Delis, D., Foldi, N., Hamby, S., Gardner, H., & Zurif, E. A note on temporal relations between language and gestures. *Brain and Language,* 1979, 350–354.

Deutsch, F. Analysis of postural behaviour. *Psychoanalytic Quarterly,* 1947, *16,* 195–213.

Deutsch, F. Analytic posturology. *Psychoanalytic Quarterly,* 1952, *21,* 196–214.

Dittman, A. T. The body-movement–speech rhythm relationship as a cue to speech encoding. In A. W. Siegman & B. Pope (Eds.), *Studies in dyadic communication.* New York: Pergamon Press, 1972.

Feldman, S. S. *Mannerisms of speech and gestures.* New York: International Universities Press, 1959.

Freud, S. [Fragments of an analysis of a case of hysteria.] In the *Standard Edition of the Complete Works of Sigmund Freud,* (Vol. 7). London: Hogarth, 1953. (Originally published, 1905.)

Goldblum, M. C. Les troubles des gestes d'accompagnement du langage au cours des lesions corticales unilaterales. In H. Hecaen & M. Jeannerod (Eds.), *Du Contrôl moteur a l'organisation du geste.* Paris: Masson et Cie, 1980.

Goldman-Eisler, F. Speech production and predictability of words in context. *Quarterly Journal of Experimental Psychology,* 1958, *10,* 96–106.

Goodglass, H., & Kaplan, E. Disturbance of gesture and pantomime in aphasia. *Brain,* 1963, *86,* 703–720.

Howes, D. Application of the word-frequency concept to aphasia. In A. V. S. de Reuck & M. O'Connor (Eds.), *Disorders of Language.* Baltimore: Williams and Wilkins, 1964.

Kendon, A. Some relations between body motion and speech. In A. W. Siegman & B. Pope (Eds.), *Studies in Dyadic Communication.* New York: Pergamon Press, 1972.

Kinsbourne, M., & Warrington, E. Jargon aphasia. *Neuropsychologia,* 1963, *2,* 27–37.

Mahl, G. F., Danet, B., & Norton, N. *Reflection of major personality characteristics in gestures and body movement.* Paper presented at the Annual Meeting of the American Psychological Association, Cincinnati, Ohio, September 1975.

Newcombe, F. N., Oldfield, R. C., & Wingfield, A. Object-naming by dysphasic patients. *Nature (London),* 1965, *207,* 1217–1218.

Pick, A. (1931). Aphasie. In A. Bethe (Ed.), *Handbuch der normalen und pathologischen Physiologie* 15 (Part 2). Berlin: Springer. (Translated by J. W. Brown as *Aphasia.* Springfield: Thomas, 1973.)

Rochford, G. Are jargon dysphasics dysphasic? *British Journal of Disorders of Communication,* 1974, *9,* 35–44.

Shallice, T., & Butterworth, B. Short-term memory impairment and spontaneous speech. *Neuropsychologia,* 1977, *15,* 729–735.

Chapter 6

Aphasic Jargon and the Speech Acts of Naming and Judging

EUGENE GREEN

APHASIC JARGON AND MEANING

Aphasic jargon by its very nature involves questions having to do with meaning. A typical definition of such jargon, say the one by Kertesz and Benson (1970), presents it as "largely unintelligible speech consisting of a mixture of neologistic, paraphrasic, and inappropriate words." Analyses of jargon, moreover, have identified different grades of meaninglessness— from the absence of comprehensibility in neologistic episodes to the unreliability and ambiguity of paraphasic speech that is marked by misuses of words and by disturbances of syntax (Alajouanine, 1956). Furthermore, the work of Weinstein and his associates (1966) has addressed itself to the circumstances in which patients are likely to produce unintelligible speech, namely, when they are "trying to explain, discuss or rationalize, [when they are responding] to queries about disability and hospitalization, and in situations where the patient's capacities are being tested." The value of these studies is, then, that they have identified contexts in which aphasic jargon is likely to occur and the kinds of linguistic deficits that result in various degrees of unintelligibility.

But to say that aphasic jargon is in some measure unintelligible does not in and of itself describe or explain what the deficits in meaning are.

125

JARGONAPHASIA

Copyright © 1981 by Academic Press, Inc.
All rights in any form reserved.
ISBN 0-12-137580-3

Although the evidence is persuasive that different forms of linguistic breakdown bear upon the degree of meaninglessness in a patient's utterances, no analysis so far has determined what mechanisms underlie deficits in intelligibility. The premise, for example, that the meaninglessness of aphasic jargon is due to poorly formed utterances does not account for inadequacies of these utterances, for the possibility that a patient cannot govern the semantic structures or rules underlying them. What is needed, clearly, is an analysis of the impaired semantic structures. A direct study of failures in intelligibility related to aphasic jargon suggests some awareness, at the very least, of three issues: (*a*) whether the patient understands the examiner's questions and attempts to answer them as accurately as he can; (*b*) whether the questions presented conform to a cogent design; and (*c*) whether the patient can in some situations speak clearly enough—whether his utterances are sufficiently well formed—to enable easy comprehension.

If two of these issues obviously concern the patients' condition and the design of a a test battery, they are nonetheless fundamental to a study of semantics and aphasic jargon. The theory of speech acts, for example, argues that successful communication depends on the speaker's intent to have his listener understand what he is trying to tell him. And characteristically, as clinical reports indicate, most patients whose speech output contains the features of aphasic jargon attempt, despite their impairment, to make themselves understood. The second issue, related to the design of a test battery, also has implications for a semantic theory such as speech act theory. The idea of speech acts is, according to Searle (1969), that of "a rule-governed form of behavior," exemplified by such modes of speech as "making statements, giving commands, asking questions, making promises"; furthermore, "these acts are in general made possible by and are performed in accordance with certain rules for the use of linguistic elements." To apply such a hypothesis, then, to a study of meaning and aphasic jargon involves the design of a test in which the questions are directed at semantic rules governing specific speech acts. The third issue, finally, that which centers on a patient's ability to make himself understood at least in some situations, is fundamental for learning about semantic structures underlying speech, for determining the nature of the change and loss that result from brain damage.

The analysis that follows uses speech act theory to assess the impaired intelligibility of one patient's aphasic jargon.[1] The speech acts under study are those of naming and judging. The purpose of the analysis is to determine

[1] I wish to thank Barbara Z. Heiman for permission to use some of her data and to draw upon the design and some results of her unpublished dissertation *Some linguistic and neurological correlates of aphasia* (University of California, 1972). The very different use of Dr. Heiman's data in this study, however, in no way qualifies the valuable perspectives and discussion in her own work.

through the use of two tests, a matching task and a sorting task, the ability of the patient, whose speech was described clinically as an example of mild aphasic jargon, to name pictures of animals and to judge their relationships to one another. The questions fundamental to the analysis are these:

1. Are there characteristic patterns in the patient's speech that indicate he can use semantic rules in acts of naming and judging?
2. If a patient's responses show some impairment in the use of these semantic rules, what is the nature of the impairment? Is it possible to determine just how semantic rules undergo modification?
3. In which ways, if any, do the patient's responses differ from those of normal subjects?

PROCEDURE

The Subjects

The aphasic subject C.A. was at the time of his examination a 30-year-old left-handed male, a high school graduate, who had within 12 months suffered injury to his brain in two separate automobile accidents. The first injury involved a fracture of the right temporal bone and a subdural hematoma, the second injury a large subdural hematoma on the left side. After the first accident, C.A. had some difficulty in word finding and in auditory comprehension, followed by gradual, complete recovery. After the second accident, he became markedly aphasic with well-articulated but unintelligible speech and a severe disturbance of comprehension. His speech had the features of aphasic jargon. After entering the Aphasia Unit of the BVAH, his speech showed some improvement. His ability to name was quite good; his utterances, for the most part intelligible, were filled with verbal paraphrasia, circumlocution, and cliché. His speech exemplified a mild form of aphasic jargon.

Three non-brain-damaged subjects agreed to serve as controls.

Methods

This study is based on an analysis of two tests: a picture matching test and a battery sorting test.

Test of Matching Pictures: The examiner presented pictures of animals in 14 sets, 3 pictures in each set. The task for the patient was to say which 2 of 3 pictures in a set were more closely related. He was encouraged to identify a generic name for the 2 pictures he matched (e.g., *Can you think of a name to use for these 2 pictures?*)

Test of Sorting Pictures: This test consists of 86 pictures, again of animals, presented seriatim in groups of 10 or 12. The examiner asked the patient to name each animal in turn and to sort groups of 12 pictures into different "piles," depending on which animals were "closer" to one another. After the patient sorted the first 12 cards into piles, he could add to them pictures of animals from groups presented subsequently or rearrange the piles as he saw fit. The examiner administered the picture matching test before the picture sorting test and recorded the entire session.

FORMS OF RESPONSE AND SCORING

Scoring the patient's responses in accordance with a scheme consonant with a theory of speech acts requires some sense of the forms likely to be used in naming and judging. As for the act of naming, the variants are few and straightforward. To name an animal, a subject generally uses the name alone or a simple utterance such as *That is a frog.* A fully articulated expression, something like *I call that a frog,* is rare.

The variants possible for expressing acts of judging, however, are numerous, and Table 6.1 exemplifies some of them. The examples themselves represent some of the utterances likely to be expressed in judging relationships between two animals. The table is arranged into 20 types, from those most formal and detailed to those consisting of deictic pronouns and indefinite nouns.

Type 1, exemplified by the expression *I'd say the eagle goes with the owl because they're birds,* has related to it at least four semantic rules:

1. A rule governing the use of a performative verb of judging—in this instance, *I'd say.*
2. A rule governing the use of specific terms—for example, *eagle* and *owl.*
3. A rule governing the use of a verb of relationship—for example, *go with.*
4. A rule governing the use of a superordinate—for example, *birds.*

The remaining types of utterance in Table 6.1 do not manifest the same degree of structure; they have fewer verbs or substantives or else contain pronominal forms and indefinite nouns. Table 6.1 also assumes that a subject could use even a brief utterance such as Type 20, *This one there,* and still be intelligible, so long as the grouping of pictures was comprehensible to an examiner. The strategy in such an instance would be to imply a judgment primarily by an arrangement of pictures in cogent ways rather than by a full expression of intent.

The purpose of Table 6.2 is to estimate the differences in the explicit

TABLE 6.1.

Semantic Rules and Their Realization in Acts of Judging

1. A performative verb expressing an act of judging
   (e.g., *I judge, I'd say, I believe, I think*)
2. A verb of relationship
   (e.g., *goes with, goes under, belongs to, belongs under*)
3. Members of superordinate classes or specific terms
   (e.g., *eagle, owl*)
4. A superordinate term
   (*birds, avian*)

TYPES
1. *I'd say that the eagle goes with the owl because they're birds.*
2. *I'd say the eagle and the owl go under this species.*
3. *I'd say this one and the owl go with the birds.*
4. *I'd say the eagle goes with the birds.*
5. *I'd say the eagle goes with the owl.*
6. *The eagle and the owl go with the birds.*
7. *I'd say these go with the birds.*
8. *I'd say this goes with the owl.*
9. *The eagle and the owl belong to that species.*
10. *This one goes with the owl under bird.*
11. *I'd say this one goes in that species.*
12. *The eagle goes with the birds.*
13. *The eagle goes with the owl.*
14. *These go with the birds.*
15. *This one goes with the owl.*
16. *The eagle goes in that species.*
17. *The eagle and the owl.*
18. *This one belongs to that species.*
19. *This one goes with that one.*
20. *This one there.*

use of semantic rules among the types of utterance in Table 6.1 (the numbers in the left hand column—1–20—of the two tables correspond to one another). The categories at the top of Table 6.2 refer to the four semantic rules important to the act of judging relationships: rules for performative verbs, for specific terms, for verbs of relationship, for superordinates. The forms that can express these rules may carry different weights: a weight of 1 for a verb or noun that clearly indicates the use of a semantic rule (e.g., *goes with* to indicate a verb of relationship and *eagle* to indicate a specific term); a weight of 1/2 if the form used is deictic or indefinite (e.g., *that* to indicate a specific animal and the word *species* to indicate a particular superordinate). The weights assigned to the types of utterance in the table thus provide an index of how fully expressive each one is of underlying semantic rules.

TABLE 6.2.

Weightings of Linguistic Elements in Utterances Expressing Acts of Judgment

Type	Performative verb of judgment	Specific$_1$	Specific$_2$	Verb of relationship	Superordinate	Weight
1	1	1	1	1	1	5.0
2	1	1	1	1	½	4.5
3	1	½	1	1	1	4.5
4	1	1	—	1	1	4.0
5	1	1	1	1	—	4.0
6	—	1	1	1	1	4.0
7	1	½	—	1	1	3.5
8	1	½	1	1	—	3.5
9	—	1	1	1	½	3.5
10	—	½	1	1	1	3.5
11	1	½	—	1	½	3.0
12	—	1	—	1	1	3.0
13	—	1	1	1	—	3.0
14	—	½	—	1	1	2.5
15	—	½	1	1	—	2.5
16	—	1	—	1	½	2.5
17	—	1	1	—	—	2.0
18	—	½	—	1	½	2.0
19	—	½	½	1	—	2.0
20	—	½	—	—	½	1.0

RESULTS

Picture Matching Test: C.A. had no difficulty in comprehending the instructions of the test and completing it successfully. His ability to name and to judge was quite good. He made, in all, one error in the 14 sets of pictures presented to him.

Picture Sorting Test

1. *Naming.* Of the 86 pictured animals presented to C.A., he named 68 (or 79%) correctly, somewhat less than the average performance of 90% correct for normal subjects. Most of C.A.'s namings were simple phrases, for example, *a fox, a parrot, a cobra,* or short sentences as in *This is a cow* and *Here you have a monkey.* Uncertain about the names of some animals, he said in response to a lizard, *It's the species of an iguana;* shown a gibbon, he said, *This becomes very close to becoming as an orangutan.* Although none of C.A.'s namings are neologistic, a good number are circumlocutory: Referring to two pictures of fish, for example, a trout and a goldfish, he said, *There is no fish except these two, but this is somewhat domesticated but this one isn't.*

2. *Judging.* A transcription of C.A.'s responses during the picture sorting test provides 51 utterances in which he offers some judgment on ways to classify the animals presented to him. Of these 51 utterances, 33 are analogous to response types listed in Table 6.1.

Table 6.3 indicates, in the column to the left, the types of utterance, corresponding to the types appearing in Table 6.1, which C.A. used. The column to the right in Table 6.3 registers the weightings, corresponding to those in Table 6.2, of the utterance types that occur in C.A.'s responses. Thus C.A.'s transcript shows that he had 8 utterances of Type 18 in Table 6.1 *This one belongs to that species,* a type which has a weight of 2.0. At the bottom of Table 6.3 appear examples of C.A.'s utterances.

Most of C.A.'s judgments, as Table 6.3 shows, are expressed in utterances with weightings of 2.5 or 2.0, utterances which by and large contain no more than one content word. Of the 33 utterances included in the table, only 1 (Type 7) has in it a performative verb of judgment. Only 3 utterances—Types 9, 13, and 17—contain two specific names of animals. Four utterances—Types 10 and 12—have a specific name of an animal and a superordinate. The great majority of the utterances, on the other hand,

TABLE 6.3.
Types and Weightings of C.A.'s Utterances Expressing Judgments

Type	Number	Weighting
7	1	3.5
9	1	3.5
10	1	3.5
12	3	3.0
13	1	3.0
14	10	2.5
15	4	2.5
17	1	2.0
18	8	2.0
19	3	2.0

EXAMPLES OF TYPES
7 *We can take this, I think, with birds in general.*
9 *It's a bobcat. This is a lynx. These would be under this vicinity, so to speak.*
10 *They're of a domestic animal. So this of course would be along with cows and all that.*
12 *This being a hen, they go domestic.*
13 *And with the monkey you have the orangutan.*
14 *This is under rodent, as these here.*
14 *What you can do, is take these and this because they all come from the same country.*
15 *This, of course, will go along with the platypus.*
17 *Yeah, possum and a coon.*
18 *They are underneath of the type, species, up to a certain extent, of course.*
19 *This one's like this.*

have one content word and one or more deictic pronouns and indefinite nouns.

Eighteen utterances related to making judgments do not figure in Table 6.3. Of these, 1 is neologistic, 7 have too many omissions to be intelligible, and 10 are ambiguous. The omissions in C.A.'s utterances concern mostly the names of animals or superordinates, as in these two examples:

1. *You could under that type of reason.*
2. *Swan that comes from the United States and I think, we could put it.*

The 10 ambiguous utterances in C.A.'s transcript reveal a difficulty in choosing nouns as superordinates. Here are three examples:

1. *A chipmunk we can say that it comes somewhat under the species of being a chipmunk.* [The same noun is both a specific name and a superordinate.]
2. *So of course this is not being an animal, being a bird, Audubon type, it would have to be under . . . well let's see. Right now we don't have anything under that particular category.* [It is difficult to see whether C.A. is using the word *bird* as a specific name or a superordinate.]
3. *You're running kinda close on space, so I think possibly what we could do is these, all the ones that come here in this, in the United States, could be all under the same category, so to speak.* [In this example, it is hard to see how C.A. is using the name *United States*—as a way to divide the test table into convenient areas, as a superordinate for animals, or both.]

Altogether, C.A. sorted the pictured animals into three large groups, which he called the *United States, Africa,* and the neologistic *two strikes off.* Within these groups, he could identify some animals as more closely related to one another, yet he seemed unwilling to make further subdivisions. His arrangements of the animals differed sharply from the judgments of normal controls, who sorted the pictures into an average of 20 categories.

An analysis of utterances used by normal controls to make judgments is also instructive. Table 6.4 outlines the types, numbers, and weightings of utterances expressed by the three control subjects. As the table plainly shows, the subjects varied considerably in the types and numbers of utterances they used in judging which animals were related. A comparison, furthermore, of Tables 6.4 and 6.2, reveals differences between the control subjects and the patient C.A. in the types and weightings of utterances. Although the number of utterances expressed by the control subjects and C.A. is of no apparent significance (the range is from 29 to 143 utterances), the types used indicate clear distinctions. All three control subjects have instances of Type 6 and Type 16 in their responses (C.A. has none); in

TABLE 6.4.

Types and Weightings of Utterances by Control Subjects

	Subject 1			Subject 2			Subject 3		
	Type	Number	Weighting	Type	Number	Weighting	Type	Number	Weighting
	4	2	4.0	1	1	5.0	1	10	5.0
	6	4	4.0	4	1	4.0	3	2	4.5
	11	1	3.0	5	1	4.0	5	1	4.0
	12	114	3.0	6	5	4.0	6	32	4.0
	14	2	2.5	12	7	3.0	9	6	3.5
	15	1	2.5	14	8	2.5	10	2	3.5
	16	14	2.5	16	2	2.5	16	4	2.5
	17	2	2.0	17	4	2.0			
Total utterances		143			29			57	

contrast C.A. has instances of Types 18 and 19 (one-third of all his responses), but neither of these types occurs in the responses of the control subjects. One-fifth of the normal utterances exemplify Types 1–6; none of C.A.'s responses conforms with any of these types. Type 14 occurs most frequently in C.A.'s responses (nearly one-third of his utterances); it occurs very little in the speech of the normal controls (less than 5%).

The weightings of the utterance types, however, provide the sharpest contrast in the performances of C.A. and the control subjects. Table 6.5 sets the utterances of each subject (C.A. and the normal controls) in ranks according to their weightings: the first rank is for those utterances with weightings from 4.0 to 5.0; the second rank is for those utterances with weightings of 3.0 and 3.5; the third rank is for those utterances with weightings of 1.0 to 2.5. According to Table 6.5, nearly 80% of C.A.'s responses have a weighting of 1.0 to 2.5; the percentage of responses among the control subjects within this third rank is considerably lower. The responses of Subject 2, for example, is just short of 50%. The bulk of utterances for the normal controls falls within the first or second rank (nearly four-fifths of the utterances produced by Subject 3 is in the first rank; four-fifths of the utterances produced by Subject 1 is in the second rank). All the control subjects have responses that fall within the three ranks; C.A. has not a single response in the first rank.

DISCUSSION

The results of the picture sorting task support the findings of C.A.'s clinical report: Although he names well, his speech has a mild component of aphasic jargon. From the point of view of speech act theory, this distinction in performance suggests that in an aphasic patient the ability to control different aspects of semantic structure may vary. The analysis of C.A.'s responses to the picture matching test and the picture sorting test helps to make the nature of this variability clearer.

First, consider the tests in themselves. The picture matching test is

TABLE 6.5.

Weightings of Utterances by Rank

Rank[a]	Subject 1	Subject 2	Subject 3	C.A.
1 (4.0–5.0)	6	8	45	0
2 (3.0–3.5)	115	7	8	7
3 (1.0–2.5)	22	14	4	26

[a] Rank 1 includes Types 1–6; Rank 2 includes Types 7–13; Rank 3 includes Types 14–20 (see Table 6.1).

by design a simpler task than the picture sorting test. In the picture matching test, the aphasic subject works within a narrow context; he has to make a forced choice, to match two of the three animals presented at a time.

The picture sorting test introduces a number of variables. Preliminary testing of normal subjects (data not directly incorporated in this study) suggests that the conditions of an experiment may influence the form of the utterances used to express judgments. For instance, if an examiner presents few items (less than a dozen) and does not record the subject's responses on magnetic tape, the utterances are likely to have low weightings (as in *This goes with that*). Second, subjects vary considerably in their style of response: For example, some subjects are inclined to work silently and need reminding during a test session to express their judgments verbally; other subjects rely primarily on a particular form of response (see Table 6.4, Subject 1). Finally, the test items themselves may have a bearing on the form of response. Suppose the items for comparison were annuals and perennials rather than animals; it is difficult to predict the form of response one might have from normal subjects.

In this study, however, regardless of the particular test items and conditions, and regardless of individual styles of response, the normal controls all produced utterances with greater weightings than C.A. did (see Table 6.5). This result argues that one consequence of C.A.'s aphasic disorder, no matter how fluent he is, is a reduced capacity to employ for a single utterance the array of semantic rules related to making judgments in a picture sorting test. None of C.A.'s responses exhibits the Type 1 expression produced by a control subject in *Tortoise—I'd say it goes also with the frog and the toad, because the're both amphibians*. Moreover, it is likely that normal subjects on demand could articulate their judgments in utterances modeled on Type 1. That C.A. could seems doubtful.

If aphasic disorders are responsible for a diminished capacity to artic-ulate fully those judgments required in a picture sorting test, then it is of interest to determine the nature of the semantic deficits. A comparison of the first three tables reveals that, through the course of C.A.'s responses, he is able, at least once, to articulate each of the four underlying semantic rules governing utterances of judgment. What distinguishes his perform-ance, however, is, first, that he did not in any instance use all the semantic rules for an utterance (as each of the normal controls did), and, second, that in most responses he relied on deictic pronouns and indefinite nouns to give expression to his judgments. Whereas the occurrences of such pronouns and nouns is no greater than 35% in the responses of any control subject, their incidence in C.A.'s responses is more than 84%. Thus C.A.'s deficit is not one of total loss, but one which prevents the full use and the full expression (by means of specific and superordinate terms) in a particular response of the applicable rules.

For the most part, his responses are not likely to include a performative verb, expressing an act of judging; most often they will contain only one specific term (e.g., *hen* or *monkey*); about one-fourth of his responses fail to include a generic term (e.g., *rodent* or *birds*). The responses of the normal controls are in part analogous to C.A.'s: Their utterances contain relatively few instances of performative verbs; and like C.A., their utterances contain in most instances specific terms (it is well to note that normal controls occasionally link more than two specific terms as in *Goat and lamb and cow are farm animals*—a linkage not found in C.A.'s utterances). On the other hand, normal controls make greater use of generic terms (none uses less than 83%, as compared to C.A.'s 76%).

This finding of a reduced incidence of generic terms in C.A.'s responses comports also with his difficulty, as the results show, in distinguishing superordinate terms for animals from the specific names and from locatives. In his effort to sort 86 pictured animals, C.A. often used, in the place of appropriate superordinate terms, specific names (e.g., *chipmunk*), locatives (e.g., *United States*), and the neologistic *two strikes off*. The consequence is that, in sorting pictures of animals, C.A. fails in a number of instances to express clear judgments. The speech act falters.

One explanation for such failure is that the processes requisite for producing superordinates are not altogether the same as those needed for producing specific terms. The very pictures of animals function as visual stimuli to help in the search for their specific names. In the search for superordinate terms, however, these pictures have a different function; they are not stimuli to name but are rather sources for inference. It is one thing to name a picture of a kangaroo or an opossum accurately; it is quite another to recognize the animals pictured and infer that they are marsupials. The subject has to resort to a second order of knowledge, to fix upon the conjunction of features common to both animals, which has associated with it a name of its own. C.A.'s performance reveals that in acts of judging, this search for an appropriate superordinate term is the most demanding, the most vulnerable to brain damage.

This study of C.A.'s performance, then, exemplifies one way to approach semantic aspects of aphasic jargon. The number of speech acts to be investigated is extensive; the test designs for them can vary in scope and complexity. The ways in which semantic rules undergo modification needs to be defined. In sum, the theory of speech acts surely provides one way to examine the ranges of intelligibility in aphasic jargon.

APPENDIX. A SAMPLE OF C.A.'s SPEECH

> E: *Allright, how about these?*
> C.A. *This one? . . . to be quite honest with you I can't say as I . . .*
> E: *I haven't ever seen a real one. How about these? Are any of these in the United States?*

C.A. *No. This one is, yeah. This one is. Now meaning, from the United States, is, um, some of these can be, uh, born in the United States, but they weren't originally, back we would say, oh, about 500 years ago, or something they didn't, uh . . .*

E: *Right.*

C.A. *This is not where they were originally born.*

E: *OK, so these are in the United States. Now let's, let's do Africa up here. These are Africa.*

C.A. *Oh this would not be Africa because this would be under the United States. Um, this would be—no it won't.* (discussing marine animals)

E: *Why don't you just put it down in the corner, because it's just different?*

C.A. *Because then you have to come down under three mile limit, this would be then very controversial as to whether they do. OK . . . this, comes from, usually, Canada, or, uh, or Alaska . . . So, um, of course this is not being an animal, being a bird, Audubon type, it would have to be, um, under . . . well let's see. Right now we don't have uh anything under that particular category.*

E: *Well, there'll be more. OK, we have some more room now, so why don't I give you some more cards?*

C.A. *Hum?*

E: *Unless you want to put everything from Africa together, I mean in one section.*

C.A. *Yeah, OK, Africa will go . . . (sigh) Now this, of course, all goes to my knowledge. Um, it'll be these . . . three, along with two here, and . . . there are certain boars, do come, but, uh, some do, they come from quite a few different parts of the world, so we'll have to leave that be. And, (sigh) . . . I don't know, there may be—I don't know anything about it so it maybe comes from Africas, I can't say so I'll have to put this one, under the one's that's two strikes . . . off. And, to my knowledge I believe that these are the only ones that, uh, come under—*

E: *Where's this?*

C.A. *Well, that one I thought that, I thought that was to be under Africa. OK, yeah— wait a minute . . . I believe that's where, I believe that's where it um, it lives, more so. And here, you have two here from India. The llama, the llama originally came from India, Tibet. Some time ago I spent some time in India, that I do know. Wait a minute. Now . . . camel . . . well, this comes under, this comes from Africa, but this thing comes more of South Africa, of course Africa's a pretty good sized continent, so this one, being under of a different part of the—the continent we have to put that there I believe um . . .*

E: *That's the camel.*

C.A. *Huh?*

E: *I was just saying that that's the camel.*

C.A. *No, it's a dromedary. Wait a minute, um, yeah, that's a camel.*

E: *Yeah, it's got one hump.*

C.A. *Hum?*

E: *It's got one hump. I'm not sure which is which.*

C.A. *Yeah that, no it's a camel. A dromedary is so* (gestures two humps)

E: *It has two humps.*

C.A. *Yeah. Um . . . this one, the only thing I can figure with this is being under this country. There are those of these come from Lord knows where, some of 'em. Um, these two, coming from uh Mexico, there's a lot of 'em in Mexico, as such. . . . They're not a very popular type animal. So Mexico is, in Central America is pretty close to this continent, so we'll have to put this pretty close to it. This, of course, comes from this part o'—this, um, this c-continent, so this one being uh, we'll have to sit and wait and see what else we can find. Maybe something else. These . . . this is speculating on this, I don't know. I believe this may come*

down from, um, the northern hemisphere which could be Alaska which, of course,
being part of the United States so, um, I believe that would be under . . . another
part, that is, that's questionable. . . . . These two, come from—wait a minute, this
is a rather, this one I believe was [kam-bist] to be somewhat of a cartoon.
   E: Which one? Yes.
C.A. Um, these I think come, under, United States. Jarvalena, this one.
   E: Jarvalena?
C.A. Jarvalena. Umhum. OK, lynx also comes from the United States, but the thing
    is we're gonna have to put that I think, I'll have to think about that, I don't know
    what it is. And these, they come from under the United States. Um . . . of course,
    being . . . This is a rodent so it has to be . . . And this, here's these . . . OK, and
    these, being feline, [?] in the United States of their own type. This will come in
    Africa . . . Africa. Yeah, this is come from the Islands, from the islands of . . .
    I didn't see the movie about the iguana so I don't know where they come from.

REFERENCES

Alajouanine, Th. Verbal realisation in aphasia. Brain, 1956, 79, 1–28.
Kertesz, A., & Benson, D. F. Neologistic jargon: A clinicopathological study. Cortex, 1970,
   6, 362–386.
Searle, J. Speech acts. Cambridge: Cambridge University Press, 1969.
Weinstein, E. A., Lyerly, O. G., Cole, M., & Ozer, M. N. Meaning in jargon aphasia. Cortex,
   1966, 2, 166–187.

Chapter 7

Behavioral Aspects of Jargonaphasia

EDWIN A. WEINSTEIN

Although jargon is defined as utterances without meaning, jargon-aphasia cannot be attributed to the breakdown of the phonetic, verbal, and syntactical organization of language. Word distortions and even neologisms (which are promptly corrected) occur in the speech of standard aphasics, and proper English words used in correct grammatical sequence may under certain circumstances constitute jargon. The distinctive feature of jargon is that the patient behaves as if his utterances are meaningful. He does not recognize that his listeners do not understand him or that he has difficulty in understanding them. On the contrary, he acts as if he and his auditors were in close communication. In these respects, jargon is a disturbance in consciousness and social interaction.

This chapter takes up these behavioral aspects as they appear in mood change, and in the phenomena of anosognosia, disorientation, reduplication, nonaphasic misnaming, and confabulation. The language and behavior of jargon subjects are compared to the language and behavior of patients with standard aphasias and of patients with lesions of the right cerebral hemisphere and the limbic-reticular system.

139

Copyright © 1981 by Academic Press, Inc.
All rights in any form reserved.
ISBN 0-12-137580-3

ANOSOGNOSIA (DENIAL OF ILLNESS)

The term anosognosia—literally lack of knowledge of disease—was introduced in 1914 by Babinski to describe the behavior of two patients with left hemiplegia who ignored and denied their paralysis. Cases of anosognosia for right hemisplegia, blindness, deafness, and many other disabilities were subsequently reported. Verbal denial takes various forms: A hemiplegic patient may completely deny that there is anything wrong with him, or he may admit to some impairment and assign it some trivial cause. He may claim that a paralyzed limb belongs to someone else and talk of himself in the third person. He may joke about or caricature his disability, or he may cope with it by evasion or withdrawal. Anosognosia is associated with hemi-inattention in which a patient ignores and does not seem conscious of the affected side of his body and/or circumambient hemispace. The conditions are accompanied by disorientation for place and time and other disturbances of consciousness.

The anosognosic or hemi-inattentive patient, however, clearly has some knowledge of his condition. Even though he may insist he is well, he follows hospital routine, accepts medication, and cooperates in procedures without question or protest. The patient also indicates some awareness in other contexts of language; in humor, delusions, confabulations, and metaphors. For example, a man who ignored his paralyzed left arm referred to it as *yellow and shriveled, like a canary's claw.* Others use epithets like *dummy.* The element of awareness is also indicated by the fact that anosognosic patients do not use such language or express delusions about a part of the body that is not in some fashion disabled (Weinstein & Cole, 1963; Weinstein & Friedland, 1977; Weinstein & Kahn, 1955).

Observers have long noted that patients with jargonaphasia tend to deny their speech defects (Ajuriaguerra & Hécaen, 1960; Allison, 1962; Bay, 1962; Brain, 1961; Goldstein, 1948; Kinsbourne & Warrington, 1963; Weinstein, Lyerly, Cole, & Ozer, 1966; Weisenburg & McBride, 1935). Critchley (1964) referred to the condition as anosognosic aphasia. As in other forms of anosognosia, denial is expressed in a number of ways. When asked if there is anything wrong with his speech, a patient may reply in the negative. Or he may ignore the question and go on with his jargon. The denial may be complete or partial; some patients admit to a disturbance of speech but ascribe it to something relatively innocuous, like poor hearing or the absence of false teeth. The jargon patient, unlike other aphasics, makes no effort to correct himself or to aid the interviewer's understanding. He may act out his denial, as did a university professor who "read" his lecture notes, "corrected" examinations, and "dictated" to his secretary. After producing jargon in reading a paragraph or repeating a spoken passage, the subject frequently insists that he has given a correct rendition. Jargon is commonly associated with denial of other neurological disabilities such as a hemiparesis or visual field defect. If a right homonymous hemianopia is present, it is usually accompanied by visual hemi-inattention. Conversely, subjects with visual hemi-inattention are not aphasic, or if they are, they generally have jargon; less often they show marked verbal stereotypy. Standard aphasics rarely deny aphasia and associated deficits and, although they may have a visual field defect, they do not manifest hemi-inattention (Weinstein & Friedland, 1977).

When the jargon patient is asked if there is anything wrong with his speech and responds in the negative, his answer should not necessarily be attributed to his not understanding the question. Patients with severe receptive difficulties, as in word deafness, may have no jargon, and jargon subjects may have only moderate difficulty in comprehension (Dejerine, 1914). Jargon subjects understand other questions of comparable complexity and can carry out many instructions. Moreover, they recognize "jargon" when it is spoken to them in the form of exotic languages like Bulgarian, Catalan, Estonian, Hindi, or Hungarian; when so addressed, they register nonunderstanding. Polyglots usually respond in the language in which they are approached.

Jargon patients also seek to give the impression of being erudite. They use a greater proportion of low frequency words than do standard aphasics (Howes & Geschwind, 1964) and their speech contains ornate phraseology, pedantic redundancies, and "high sounding" malapropisms. When one patient was asked what was wrong with him, he replied with *Well, it has been suggested that there were certain oddities and restrictions, technically the activities of the student body, so to speak.* Even when speech has improved and the patient no longer has neologisms, he tends to make unusual word choices. For example, one man commented on the *congestion* of his speech, and another recalled having done a lot of *verbal gambling* with words. When tested for ability to generate rhymes, alliterations, synonyms, antonyms, and homonyms, patients produce strings of impressive sounding but inappropriate words. A woman "rhymed" the following: *Ovoid, ovum, spectrum, parallax, quadrangle, trigonometry, algebra.* Some subjects speak officialese (Weinstein & Puig-Antich, 1974).[1] The use of alliterations and assonances and an exaggerated rhythm may impart a poetic quality.

The proportion of jargon to normal speech varies widely. Jargon may be highly selective in that neologisms appear mainly in answer to questions about illness. For example, a woman who said that she had a *fressary of my mouthpiece,* spoke intelligibly about her job, her children, and her boy friend. The longest passages of jargon often appeared when the patient was speaking about his illness and his work. At times, the patient gave a jargon version of a word in talking about his problem, and a correct rendition in

---

[1] Officialese refers to the use of professional, bureaucratic, or technical terminology in a manner devoid of responsive information and designed to obscure referential meaning.

another context. Thus a soldier who had been injured in an accident in Germany misstated that the injury had been caused by a *rood in Koreeja, correc reejus in Koreeda*. Later in the interview he remarked that he had been stationed in northern Korea on a previous tour of duty. Jargon was frequently associated with verbal stereotypy. Many of the perseverated words like *faculties, normal, program,* and *relapse* had to do with the patient's concern about himself. Some patients displayed more jargon in formal interviews than in conversations with their families.

MOOD CHANGES

Most jargon patients are bland, somewhat euphoric, and speak in animated fashion. Some are extremely garrulous, but, on the whole, they do not speak more than left hemiparetics or paraplegics. The great majority do not seem anxious or depressed over their condition. They often display "ludic" behavior—a term introduced by Piaget (1951) to describe the play, imitative, and dramatic aspects of the behavior of young children. A young soldier boasted that he could speak four languages—English, French, Japanese, and Kentuckian—and accosted people in mock Japanese. He insisted that the expression *no unnerstan* was Japanese. Another patient, truly bilingual, corrected my Italian pronunciation. Some patients show paranoid reactions in the manner of the subject who, when I indicated difficulty in understanding him, charged that he was not being listened to because he had not gone to college. As jargon clears in the course of clinical improvement, some patients become depressed.

There is a relationship between the emotional state and the character and completeness of denial. The subjects who denied their aphasia most explicitly were the least demonstrative, and those who admitted to some problem and dramatized it were the most disturbed. A highly agitated woman repeatedly exclaimed *Why is my sandwich turned? Why is my think all messed up? How about my breechiteach* [speech therapy]?" Of the 64 subjects on which this report is based, 8 had episodes classed by staff members as psychotic. The following case is illustrative.

Dr. J., a 60-year-old left-handed dentist, specializing in oral surgery, was brought to the Emergency Room of Mount Sinai Hospital because he had gone "beserk" in his office. He was reported to have spoken in confused fashion and to have not answered questions. His nurse had to restrain him from operating on a patient with the haft of a knife and he refused to cancel his appointments or have a doctor summoned. He had a history of hypertension and myocardial infarction, and 8 years previously had experienced an episode of speech difficulty and left-sided weakness. Neurological examination showed a left homonymous hemianopia, mild sensory loss over his left side, and visuo-constructional difficulties. The first verbatim interview took place 2 days after admission:

DOCTOR: *How are you?*
PATIENT: *I'm fine.*
D: *How long have you been here?*
P: *Two years.*
D: *What is your main trouble?*
P: *It's a rose of another kind which really shouldn't swell as sweet.*
D: *Tell me more about that.*
P: *Well, I have a stroke and I uh what's there to say.*
D: *Tell me about your work.*
P: *I'm close to too much upset is* [sighs] *it's the uh thing that uh what's the use.*
D: *You're a dentist?*
P: *Yes.*
D: *What k kind of dentistry do you do?*
P: *Oh, I occupy belief in surgery, prosthetics, prostadontics, functional jawpedics.*
D: *Do you have any trouble in talking?*
P: *Do you have any trouble in talking? There's the chief of surgery at the Hospital for* [one of the hospitals in which he worked] *and there's attending oral surgery at* xxxxx *functional therapy department.*
D: *But do you have any trouble with your speech?*
P: *Well, I originally conceived of my typical type of situation and every day I have an unusual* xxxx *recurring I feel this way and have no flexibility whatever. I seem to be getting things done but nothing is acting anywhere at the moment.*
D: *Are you married?*
P: *I have two children, one 18 and one 20. My pupil is being confirmed one at Radcliffe and one at Harvard.* [correct]
D: *Do you always say what you want to say?*
P: *I could hesitate more gradually than if I would x-ray it slowly.*
D: *What is the name of the place we are in now?*
P: *Massachusetts Life Insurance Company, North American Hospital Insurance, Liberty Mutual, four forms.*

His behavior was ludic. He recited the alphabet in singsong fashion. When asked for homonyms for the word *fire*, he gave *anguish, excitedness, rampant, disaster, tinkle, tinkle on the icy **arm*** [author's emphasis] *of night, it's the hamburger* [*ambience?*] *of urgency and expectancy.* Asked to give words beginning with the letters *BL* he responded with *bullshit, bulldozer.* Dr. J. said that he had two wives (reduplication, not bigamy) and accused one of them of having an affair with his associate who was trying to steal his business. He demanded that he be seen by Dean Rusk.

DISORIENTATION, REDUPLICATION AND NONAPHASIC MISNAMING

Jargon patients usually express disorientation or reduplication for place and time. Disorientation for place is the misnaming or mislocation of the hospital. In disturbances of consciousness resulting from right hemisphere and limbic system lesions, the patient usually names an actual hospital near his home or work, or, if he names the hospital correctly, he puts it in his own home town, neighborhood, or place of occupation. The name given may be a metaphorical or humorous representation of the patient's feelings as in the case of the woman who said that she was in "Misericordia." This self-referential aspect is emphasized by the fact that the patient usually persists in his misdesignation despite clues, cues, and corrections. For example, an officer hospitalized at Walter Reed after having spent his military career in the artillery at Fort Sill, crossed out the Walter Reed heading on the hospital stationery and substituted "Fort Sill." Disorientation for place can be both an aspect of denial and an assertion of identity (Weinstein & Kahn, 1955). Jargon patients used such designations as *Fireside Hospital, Jewish Israel Arangick,* and a *factory for medical instrumentation.*

In reduplication, the referential and experiential contexts are separated.[2] The patient says that there are two (or more) Walter Reed hospitals. One of these conforms to the fact and the other represents his feelings. Thus the extra hospital may be located in his home town; or it may be a "convalescent place" or a hospital that does not perform operations. Commonly it is a branch or annex. A woman at Mount Sinai thought the building was divided into two parts; one of these was a hospital, the other a shul where the doctors, instead of doing their regular work, davened. Similarly, in reduplication for time, person, and parts of the body, the extra event, person, or bodily member is the vehicle for symbolizing some particular concern of the speaker (Weinstein & Kahn, 1955).

Nonaphasic misnaming is the selective misdesignation of objects connected with the patient's illness or other personal problems. The patient names key rings, buttonholes, and sleeves correctly, but errs on syringes, drinking straws, and thermometers. He does not accept corrections, as does the ordinary aphasic patient, because the names are so personally and experientially meaningful. Responses are selective and may be highly condensed or sophisticated. A man who had just returned from a carotid angiogram which had necessitated painful sticks in his neck described his experience in a single word, *Robespierre* (Weinstein & Kahn, 1952; Weinstein & Keller, 1963). Jargon subjects have a mixture of aphasic and nonaphasic misnaming.

CONFABULATION

Although a confabulation is a false recollection, it is also a metaphorical or allegorical representation of current problems and relationships (Wein-

---

[2] Referential denotative, universal) symbols involve a fixed one-to-one relationship between symbol and referent. Experiential (connotative) symbols are more idiosyncratic; they express and evoke feelings, and meaning is determined more by context. In a referential sense, the American flag signifies sovereignty; in the experiential mode, it represents feelings of patriotism. Siberia is a geographical entity but it connotes exile and desolation.

stein, Kahn, & Malitz, 1956; Weinstein & Lyerly, 1968). For example, an army officer about to be discharged from service because of mental deficits consequent to a brain injury confabulated an account of his activities in "counterintelligence." When paratroopers confabulate after having sustained head injuries in car accidents, they tell stories of having been hurt in parachute drops. The content of a confabulation thus is determined by two factors. One is the nature of the incapacity and the other is a theme that has been an element in a pattern of social relatedness and a source of identity and status. Stories about work and occupation are particularly elaborate and lengthy. Confabulations are not simply distortions of memory; they are important modes of adaptation to stress. They constitute a "problem-solving" language and reinforce a sense of social relatedness.[3]

It is not necessary for a confabulation to be untrue for it to serve adaptive functions. For instance, a woman with a left homonymous hemianopia repeatedly told the true story of how her son had lost his left eye in a hunting accident. Another case was that of a patient who had sustained a crushing head injury. When asked how it had happened, the patient often went into a long rambling account of how on their first date he had taken his [estranged] wife to see the film *Samson and Delilah*.

Jargon patients frequently tell long stories, the content of which can be distinguished if the jargon is not too severe. Like confabulations, these stories often involve work and elements from the patient's personal life. The following was elicited in answer to a request to repeat the phrase *This is a nice day*. The patient responded: *This is a terrific beautiful day. The only reason I say it is a nice day I see all the girls working behind the floor and believe me when I worked for people on Broadway they were glad to work because it is nice to do it in the afternoon. They're being pressed that's all, they're outside. You know how many apartments there are on Broadway and 50th that's 40th. I worked almost 10 years, I never desist anyone that's not advisable for doing this but if your wife wants a new dress I'll help her, darling."* Jargon, like confabulation, is often succeeded by euphemisms, colloquialisms, malapropisms, puns, idiomatic expressions, and other forms of "social language" (Weinstein *et al.*, 1966).

INTERPRETATION OF IDIOMS AND PROVERBS

Although the jargon patient is not usually conscious that he is speaking jargon, the inner knowledge that something is wrong with his speech and thinking is a motivating factor in his behavior. This has been shown in the self-referential features of disorientation, reduplication, and confabulation and this altered use of metaphor is strikingly manifested in interpretations of idioms and proverbs. Many aphasic subjects have difficulty in such

---

[3] The original meaning of confabulation is to talk together.

interpretations. They say that they do not know, simply repeat the item, or give "concrete" answers. The patient with a right hemisphere or limbic system lesion, on the other hand, interprets the great majority of proverbs correctly, but selectively incorporates references to himself and his problems. For example, a colonel with a left homonymous hemianopia interpreted all idioms correctly except those which had to do with vision. His version of *starry-eyed* was *That's when you're waiting for that big star.*

Jargon patients give a mixture of responses, but seldom state they do not know. One subject interpreted *A rolling stone gathers no moss* as *The activity of the stone is to prevent moss,* and rendered *Birds of a feather flock together* as *They have some affinity which causes them to associate.* Other responses are long, circumlocutory, and self-referential. When asked to interpret *swell headed,* a patient replied, *Oh, now that's a big question. Why you can inform on a person by saying well he's swell headed. Could be a lot of things. Sometimes there might not be a point of truth in it. Something he is saying or how he is saying it. Right? It can still make him an honest man not necessarily a big headed one.* More succinctly, a patient interpreted the adage *You can lead a horse to water but you can't make him drink* as *You can lead a horse to water but you can't make him learn.* Dr. J., whose case was cited earlier, interpreted *level headed* as *topsy, I get excited and I really understand what you talk to me and I talk to you.* The most idiosyncratic self-reference was made by a patient who developed a subdural hematoma as a result of a fall on the way home from an extramarital experience. He interpreted *Birds of a feather flock together* as *People with the same dissitudes copulate together.* Standard aphasics used less than half as many self-references, and these were more apt to be comments on performance than incoporations into the body of the interpretation. There was no correlation between the degree of self-reference and the number of correct interpretations (Weinstein *et al.,* 1966).

PREMORBID PERSONALITY FACTORS

Certain character traits were reported more frequently in the background of jargon patients than in the histories of other aphasics. Most were described by relatives and colleagues as having been driving, compulsive people; very conscientious about work, and eager to improve themselves and others. The wife of one patient described him as someone who "always had to be right. He was stubborn and had to gain his own way. Always was a very hard worker, loved his work but people didn't live up to his standards." Another spouse reported of her husband: "very determined, if he got an idea into his head the Angel Gabriel couldn't get it out . . . no matter how badly he felt he got to the office and Mass." A patient's daughter characterized her mother as "very careful and meticulous . . .

kept feelings to herself . . . very dominating type always involved in some project to help people."

Most jargon patients in their previous experience had tended to ignore or rationalize illness. They regarded it as a sign of character weakness or personal failure. Illness and idleness alike seemed to have produced feelings of guilt and social isolation; and they had worked even when not feeling well. Other jargon subjects were described as having been openly frightened, sometimes dramatically so, of illness and medical procedures; and this subgroup had had a higher incidence of serious illness in the past. In hospital, they produced the most agitated behavior. When 20 jargon patients were compared to an equal number of other aphasics, 19 of the jargon patients were reported as having reacted to illness with marked denial or exaggerated fear, whereas only 5 of the standard aphasics were so characterized. The incidence of high work orientation was also significantly greater among the jargon subjects (Weinstein & Lyerly, 1976).

We also looked into the personality background of patients who were so withdrawn and uncooperative that it was difficult to determine in which category of aphasia they fell. They were characterized in a fashion far different from that of the compulsive work-oriented jargon patient. They were less well educated and younger than either the jargon or standard aphasic group, and alcoholism and episodes of violence were prominent behavioral features.

CORRELATIONS OF BEHAVIOR AND BRAIN DYSFUNCTION

Jargonaphasia is an aphasia plus a disturbance of consciousness. The minimal brain pathology is centered in the perisylvian area, but aphasia with jargon can occur with deep-seated frontal lesions (Weinstein *et al.*, 1966); and "logorrheic paraphasia" has been reported after left thalamic hemorrhage (Mohr, Walters, & Duncan, 1975). Jargon patients have more extensive lesions than standard aphasics. This is related to the finding that they are older than Broca's and conduction aphasics. It is common for jargon to occur during the first few days after an ictus and then clear, presumably because of subsidence of edema, while dysnomia and difficulty in repetitions and formation of word categories persist. (Most but not all jargon subjects have repetition disturbances.) Conversely, as neoplasms progress, standard aphasia may be converted to jargon (Cohn & Neumann, 1958). In subdural hematoma, a condition usually associated with disturbances of consciousness and bilateral brain dysfunction, jargon is common whereas standard aphasias are rare.

Jargon may be produced by the intravenous administration of amobarbital sodium to aphasic patients, just as denial and disorientation appear, after the same procedure, in patients with right hemisphere lesions (Weinstein, Kahn, Sugarman, & Linn, 1953). The following report is illustrative. The patient, following the removal of a sphenoid ridge meningioma had a paucity of speech with marked naming and repetition difficulties. An intensely perfectionistic person, she was extremely upset by her speech failures. When in the predrug interview she was asked what her main trouble was, she replied, *My mā uh my mā it's up in here* [pointing to her mouth]. After receiving 450 mgs of sodium amytal to the point of nystagmus and slight drowsiness, she answered the same question with *I just went to see a thalmos or thalmosot and I've looked at the darn thing and I set it up don't forget the glamorous crisis and he looked at her xxx and he said good gosh you must have something behind your, your extrodam.*

COMMENT

Jargonaphasia should be considered in the total context of behavior with regard for the metaphorical, motivational, social, and adaptive aspects of language. It is not only a form of aphasia, but presents the altered interaction of the self in the environment found in patients with right hemisphere and limbic-reticular system pathology. Were the lesions of jargonaphasia to occur on the opposite side of the brain we might have the clinical picture of anosognosia, confabulation, and nonaphasic misnaming. The aphasic patient's attempt to use these adaptive mechanisms, however, makes his language even more incomprehensible. A major aspect of jargon is that it is an attempt to imitate normal—even elegant—speech in order to avoid depression and preserve a sense of identity and social relatedness.

REFERENCES

Ajuriaguerra, J. de, & Hécaen, H. *Le Cortex cerebral.* Paris: Masson et Cie, 1960.
Allison, R. S. *The senile brain: A clinical study.* London: Edward Arnold, 1962.
Bastian, H. C. In T. C. Allbutt (Ed.), *A system of medicine.* London: Macmillan, 1900.
Bay, E. Aphasia and non-verbal disorders of language. *Brain,* 1962, *85,* 411–426.
Brain, R. *Speech disorders.* Washington: Butterworth, 1961.
Cohn, R., & Neumann, M. Jargon aphasia. *Journal of Nervous and Mental Disease,* 1958, *127,* 381–399.
Critchley, M. The neurology of psychotic speech. *British Journal of Psychiatry,* 1964, *110,* 353–364.
Dejerine, J. *Semiologie des affections du system nerveux.* Paris: Masson et Cie, 1914.
Goldstein, K. *Language and language disturbances.* New Gork: Grune and Stratton, 1948.
Howes, D., & Geschwind, N. Quantitative studies of aphasic language. In D. Rioch & E. A. Weinstein (Eds.), *Disorders of communication.* New York and Baltimore: Williams and Wilkins, 1964. Pp. 229–244.
Kinsbourne, M., & Warrington, E. Jargon aphasia. *Neuropsychologia,* 1963 *1,* 27–37.

Mohr, J. P., Watters, W. C., & Duncan, G. W. Thalamic hemorrhage and aphasia. *Brain and Language*, 1975, *2*, 3–17.

Piaget, J. *Play, dreams and imitation in childhood*. New York: W. W. Norton, 1951.

Weinstein, E. A., & Cole, M. Concepts of anosognosia. In L. Halpern (Ed.), *Problems of dynamic neurology*. Department of Nervous Diseases of the Rothschild Hadassah University Hospital and the Hebrew University, Hadassah Medical School, Jerusalem, 1963. Pp. 254–273.

Weinstein, E. A., & Friedland, R. P. Behavioral disorders associated with hemi-inattention. In E. A. Weinstein & R. P. Friedland (Eds.), *Advances in neurology 18*. New York: Raven Press, 1977. Pp. 51–62.

Weinstein, E. A., & Kahn, R. L. Nonaphasic misnaming (paraphasia) in organic brain disease. *AMA Archives of Neurology and Psychiatry*, 1952, *67*, 1–8.

Weinstein, E. A., & Kahn, R. L. *Denial of illness. Symbolic and physiological aspects*. Springfield, Ill.: Charles C. Thomas, 1955.

Weinstein, E. A., Kahn, R. L., & Malitz, S. Confabulations as a social process. *Psychiatry*, 1956, *19*, 348–354.

Weinstein, E. A., Kahn, R. L., Sugarman, L. A., & Linn, L. Diagnostic use of amobarbital sodium ("amytal sodium") in brain disease. *American Journal of Psychiatry*, 1953, *109*, 889–894.

Weinstein, E. A., & Keller, N. J. A. Linguistic patterns of misnaming after brain injury. *Neuropsychologia*, 1963, *1*, 79–90.

Weinstein, E. A., & Lyerly, O. G. Confabulations following brain injury: Its analogs and sequelae. *Archives of General Psychiatry*, 1968, *18*, 348–384.

Weinstein, E. A., & Lyerly, O. G. Personality factors in jargon aphasia. *Cortex*, 1976, *12*, 122–133.

Weinstein, E. A., Lyerly, O. G., Cole, M., & Ozer, M. N. Meaning in jargon aphasia. *Cortex*, 1966, *2*, 165–187.

Weinstein, E. A., & Puig-Antich, J. Jargon and its analogues. *Cortex*, 1974, *10*, 75–83.

Weisenburg, T., & McBride, K. E. *Aphasia*. New York: The Commonwealth Fund, 1935.

Chapter 8

Associative Processes in Semantic Jargon and in Schizophrenic Language

K. ZAIMOV

In studying speech and thought disorders in dementia praecox, Krae-pelin (1913) described some typical "derailments" (*Entgleisungen*) of the associative process according to word meaning and phonetic relationships (*Sinn- und Klangverwandschaft*).

In his classic work on schizophrenia, Bleuler (1911) came to the conclusion that, in the thought of patients with this psychosis, the normal associative paths are "loosened" (*gelockert*), and therefore thought deviates from its normal direction in a characteristic manner.

In a series of works,[1] I tried to show that associative process deviations described by Kraepelin in schizophrenia could be observed not only in this psychosis but also in other schizophrenia-like psychoses, in psychotic (somatically determined) cloudings of consciousness (e.g., in delirium and amentia) and in psychogenic cloudings of consciousness, as well as in normal sleep. Kraepelin (1906) himself, on the basis of self-observations at times of falling asleep or waking, pointed out the striking similarities between associative process "derailments" during sleep and in schizophrenia.

For example, in sleep Kraepelin formed the sentence *Ich sage immer zufällig die Wahrheit* (I say the truth always by chance). On waking, Kraepelin realized

[1] Zaimov (1953, 1959, 1961, 1964, 1969, 1972, 1976a, 1976b, 1977, 1978a, 1979a, 1979b).

151

JARGONAPHASIA

Copyright © 1981 by Academic Press, Inc.
All rights in any form reserved.
ISBN 0-12-137580-3

that in fact he had "thought" *Ich sage immer zuverlässig die Wahrheit* (I say the truth always reliably).

I pointed out that analogous associative process derailments could also be observed in agnosia, aphasia, and apraxia. In aphasia they are particularly distinct in the phenomenon of paraphasia, which is analogous to paragnosia and parapraxia in agnosia and apraxia.

A comparison between certain phenomena of schizophrenic thought and certain elements of aphasia and apraxia symptomatology was also made by Kleist (1914, 1923, 1934).

In my early work, I pointed out that the associative derailments which Kraepelin described in schizophrenia and in sleep thought can also be observed in healthy persons, in slips of the tongue. These speech errors were first systematically studied in relation to their structure by Meringer and Mayer (1895), and they subsequently, became an object of Freud's (1924) well-known interpretations.

In studying associative process derailments in normals and in pathology, I gradually came to the conclusion that behind this "elementary" phenomenon are hidden many rich regularities, and I suggested the term DISINTEGRATIVE DEVIATION of the associative process. For the discovery of regularities in this disintegrative deviation I find slips of the tongue to be especially useful.

In this chapter, I will point out the broad range of states, and syndromes in which the schizophrenic phenomena of disintegrative deviation of the associative process can be observed, and I shall attempt

1. To reveal the pathophysiological (and physiological) basis of this kind of phenomenon, that is, to penetrate its neuropsychology.
2. Using the model of slips of the tongue to delimit the basic types of disintegrative deviation of the associative process and then to look for and analyze this phenomenon in schizophrenic thought and in semantic jargon.

In my early work, I attempted to find the pathophysiological (and physiological) explanation of the associative process deviations in Wedensky's doctrine of parabiosis and in Pavlov's principle of the ultraparadoxical phase. Gradually it became clear that for a fuller understanding of this kind of phenomena one must also take into account Jackson's doctrine of dissolution and Uchtomsky's principle of the dominant.

As is well known, we owe to Jackson (1931–1932) the concept of a systematically hierarchical organization of the nervous system and the related concept of dissolution, a layer-by-layer dropping off of separate functions, with "loss of control" of the higher layers over the lower ones and with the development of negative and positive symptoms in pathological conditions. Jackson's concepts have withstood the test of time, and today they are prerequisites for the analysis of symptom formation in neurology and in psychiatry.

Accordingly, with the help of Jackson's principles we can explain some aspects of disintegrative deviations, since in associative links thought is operating with ontogenetically "old" and "new" layers.

Some elements of Jackson's doctrine—as I have noted earlier (Zaimov, 1949, 1976a)—are subject to criticism. A basic problem, in my opinion, is that Jackson does not assume any intermediate qualitative disturbances of nerve tissue function during its necrotization, the period between its normal state and its "death." According to Jackson, a nervous system layer either exists or totally drops off: "Atrophied nerve tissue," he writes, "is not nerve tissue at all; it is functionally just nothing and can not be the cause of anything positive . . . [Vol. 2, p.46]." In this way the positive symptoms derive from the "activity of a lower level of evolution [Vol. 2, p.46]," from the activity of "healthy nervous arrangements [Vol. 2, p.73]," and from release of control "in non atrophic, in healthy nervous elements [Vol. 2, p. 24]."

Thus, according to Jackson, the separate levels (layers) of the nervous system drop off, and it is assumed that their functional dropping off is an "instantaneous" phenomenon rather than a process within which the layers show complex qualitative changes of neural function. This problem of functional qualitative changes of nerve cells in pathological conditions has been investigated by Wedensky (1901), who developed the concept of parabiosis (i.e., of the functional state of the neuron "between life and death").

Wedensky's concept is based on experiments with neuromuscular preparations of the sciatic nerve and musculus gastrocnemius of frogs. He exposed (Figure 8.1) part of the peripheral nerve to the action of cocaine and observed its subsequent excitability and conductivity. Electrical currents of different strengths were applied above the point of intoxication, and the strength of muscle contraction was measured. During the process of intoxication, the conductivity of the nerve showed characteristic changes. These changes were divided by Wedensky into three stages. In the first stage, called the PROVISORY STAGE, the muscle responds equally to strong and weak currents. In the next, PARADOXICAL STAGE, strength of muscle contraction is greater in response to weak currents than in response to strong ones. Finally, a stage of COMPLETE INHIBITION of the conductivity of the nerve ensues. Depending on the degree of intoxication, normal conductivity of the nerve can be restored; if this is done the stages appear in reverse order. If, however, the intoxication progresses, the nerve is necrotized.

From Wedensky's experiments it becomes clear that necrotization of a nerve exposed to intoxication is a complicated process in which the nerve tissue, before its necrotization, passes through qualitatively different functional states (phases).

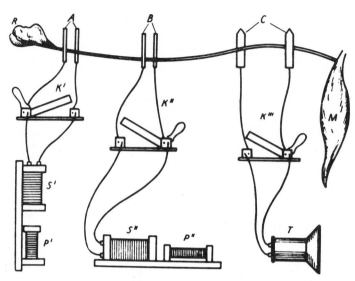

Figure 8.1. Wedensky's experiments were performed on a neuromuscular prep-
aration (sciatic nerve–gastrocnemius muscle) of a frog. In these experiments one
region of the nerve is submitted to intoxication, and electrical stimulation is applied
to the nerve above this region (or in the region itself). Using a pair of electrodes
as a telephone receiver, one "listens" to the nerve impulses going to the muscle.
Changes in these signals in the course of the experiment lead Wedensky to conclude
that the "death" of the nerve is not a momentary phenomenon but rather a process.
R—portion of the vertebral column with the outgoing sciatic nerve; M—gastrocnemius muscle; A—electrodes on the nerve above the region of intoxication (parabiotization); B—electrodes on the region of parabiosis (the hatched region of the
nerve); C—electrodes of the telephone receiver (T); P'S' and P"S"—induction devices; K', K" and K'''—circuit breakers (from Wedensky 1901, p. 323).

In his first experiments, Wedensky established the parabiotic stages
by examining the influence of cocaine on the nerve. Later, he repeated the
experiments with chloral hydrate, phenol, ether, chloroform, chloralose,
carbonic acid, and salts of heavy metals. The results were identical. The
stages were the same as those he saw with galvanic current (Figure 8.2)
and with mechanical lesions. Analysis of these facts led Wedensky to conclude that the observed phenomena are the result of a universal reaction
in the nerve.

   In his experiments with conditioned reflexes in animals, both in pathological conditions and in normal sleep, Pavlov (1949, 1951) found analogous
characteristics in his so-called HYPNOTIC PHASES. The EQUALIZING PHASE,
corresponding to the Wedensky's provisory stage, is characterized by
equalization of the effect (the amount of saliva) of strong and weak stimuli.
In Pavlov's PARADOXICAL PHASE, as in Wedensky's paradoxical stage, there
is less response to strong stimuli than there is to weak ones.

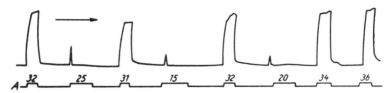

Figure 8.2. Myographic registration in Wedensky's experiments of paradoxical phase by means of parabiotization of the nerve by direct current. The figures below indicate the distance of the elements of the inductive device. These figures are inversely proportional to the strength of the current (from Wedensky 1901, p. 342).

In addition to Wedensky's three stages, Pavlov found a fourth stage, the so-called ULTRAPARADOXICAL PHASE. In this stage, the sign of the stimulus changes: Normally positive stimuli become negative; normally negative stimuli become positive. I will explain the principle of the ultraparadoxical phase with an example (Figure 8.3). In an experiment with a dog, a positive conditioned reflex is produced to metronome set at 100 strokes per min. After sufficient pairings of this metronome stroke frequency with unconditioned reinforcement (giving food), the reflex is established and the appearance of the stimulus is followed by a salivary reaction. Once the reflex is established at 100 strokes, if another frequency, say 150 strokes, is tried, the salivary reaction is also seen. This phenomenon is called STIMULUS GENERALIZATION. It is due to the fact that, with the initial metronome frequency (100) in effect, the process of excitation spreads from the fundamental stimulus, and, simultaneously with the establishment of the primary conditioned reflex, other, "unexpected" connections are also established, including the 150 metronome frequency.

Stimulus generalization can easily be extinguished. To do so, the experimenter simply does not reinforce responses to 150 strokes per minute.

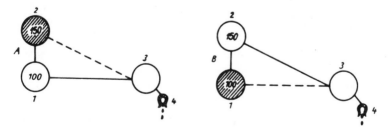

Figure 8.3. Schematic representation of Pavlov's ultraparadoxical phase. 1—brain structure corresponding to metronome frequency of 100 strokes per min; 2—brain structure corresponding to the frequency 150; 3—brain structure of the salivary gland; 4—salivary gland. A—correct relation; B—relations of the ultraparadoxical phase.

In this way the reinforced 100 frequency remains a positive stimulus, and the nonreinforced 150 frequency becomes a negative stimulus. Thus the two stimuli are differentiated and the negative stimulus is called a DIFFERENTIATION.

Pavlov termed this pair of stimuli an ASSOCIATED PAIR, as, between the two brain "points" (structures) of the pair, corresponding to the two stimuli in the nervous system, there exist relations of reciprocal induction. That is to say, when the positive stimulus structure has reached the state of excitation, the other structure is inhibited. In this case, on the level of the conditioned reflexes one observes relations analogous to the reciprocal inhibition.

In pathological conditions, as well as in the transitional state between waking and sleeping, one observes the ultraparadoxical phase in the associated pairs. This phase leads to the inversion of the signs of the stimuli: The positive stimulus becomes negative, and the negative becomes positive. Thus, the ultraparadoxical phase makes it possible to observe a "negative" of the animal's normal reactions, elaborated in the process of its adaptation to the experimental conditions. In our example, during the ultraparadoxical phase, salivation occurs in response to the normally negative stimulus of 150 strokes rather than in response to the positive stimulus of 100 strokes. This principle of the ultraparadoxical phase is a basic pathological (and physiological) mechanism which can explain a great part of the phenomena of the associative process disintegrative deviations in schizophrenia, in jargonaphasia, and elsewhere.

A third factor of relevance is Uchtomsky's (1966) concept of the DOMINANT. Uchtomsky developed the concept of the dominant in 1923, defining it as an area (or a constellation of "points") of higher excitability which has a temporary dominance over reflex arcs acting together with it. The dominant focus attracts the subdominant excitations of the other areas of the nervous system and "feeds" itself at their expense, inhibiting the activity of the reflex arcs that are not included in its structure.

During electric stimulation of the cortical motor area of cats, Uchtomsky by chance observed the following phenomenon. When stimulation was applied to an animal that had a full rectum, the immediate response was not the expected movement of the limb, but rather an act of defecation. With continued stimulation, the defecation was completed and only then did the expected limb movement occur. Uchtomsky concluded that stimuli coming from the full rectum created a sort of a barrier to the natural diffusion of the excitation from the electric stimulation of the motor area, deviating it toward the dominant. In support of these initial observations, Uchtomsky later accumulated a rich body of experimental findings.

The principle of the dominant shows that if the nervous system is engaged by an activity (or a tendency toward an activity), and a competing tendency toward an activity arises, then the impulses of the weaker activity automatically deviate toward the stronger, biologically more important activity. This deviation occurs not only in the elementary and "rigid" paths of nonconditioned reflex activities, which Uchtomsky initially investigated, but also—and to an even greater extent—in the associative process paths.

In order to explain the phenomenon of the associative process disintegrative deviation in schizophrenia and in jargonaphasia, I shall first examine slips of the tongue. The question that naturally arises is whether conclusions concerning pathological states may be based on a normal phenomenon. In this regard, it should be noted that in formulating the laws of dissolution, Jackson demonstrated that the boundary between the normal and pathological, between the functional and the organic, cannot be strictly drawn. For example, he noted that "sleep is a normal dissolution; the dream is analogous to our positive element [Vol. 2, p. 25]." Similarly, it is difficult to draw the boundary between certain pathological illusions and the illusions of healthy persons in a state of temporary relaxation of "object consciousness," which is "a temporary normal dissolution [Vol. 2, p. 25]." In studying the laws of parabiosis (and, more concretely, the phenomena of parabiosis in the neuromuscular synapsis in a continuous muscle tetanization through frequent and strong electric stimuli of the nerve, without any intervention upon the synapsis itself), Wedensky (1901) draws analogous conclusions with regard to "physiological parabiosis" (p. 395).[2] I have already pointed out that Pavlov observed his hypnotic phases in the normal sleep of the animals as well as in pathological states. Moreover, Uchtomsky views the dominant as a principle of both the normal and the pathological.

Thus some aspects of the associative process in schizophrenia and in semantic jargon may be explained in the following way. When the speech areas of the brain are affected by some morbid process (vascular, toxic, *etc.*), the phenomena of parabiosis takes place; as Wedensky's experiments showed, parabiosis is the universal reaction of nerve cells to damage. In the development of thought and speech, each word (its corresponding structure or constellation of structures in the brain respectively) has been associated and differentiated from a number of other words. In parabiosis, according to the principle of the ultraparadoxical phase, the word structures[3] begin nonelectively to be replaced by their differentiations (e.g., on the basis of semantic or phonetic relationships). On the basis of parabiosis, phenomena of dissolution arise as the "old"—and inhibited as inadequate— associative paths and connections are also differentiations of the "new"

---

[2] Instead of "physiological parabiosis," I prefer to speak of parabiosis-like states of the normal.

[3] Because of space limitations, I purposely disregard the fact that each word is associatively related not only to other words (on the level of the second signal system) but also to the corresponding images (on the level of the first signal system). An in-depth analysis of thought disorders must take this duality of associative relationships into account.

ones. On the other hand, "dominant" deviations are also facilitated because, as Uchtomsky's studies show, the phenomena of parabiosis and the dominant can be closely related.

What is observed in speech functions affected by morbid processes can be "modeled" in healthy persons under certain circumstances, for example, in states of stress or fatigue, upon falling asleep or waking, in sleep, in slips of the tongue, etc.

My self-observations concerning slips of the tongue (1979a, 1979b) comprise a total of 137 slips (during the period of February 1975–March 1978). Of these, 102 (74.55%) are verbal and 35 (25.55%) are phonetic. Here I shall give only examples of verbal slips, which may be subdivided into four types: non-dissolutive, dissolutive, dominant, and mixed.[4]

1. NONDISSOLUTIVE verbal slips of the tongue are based on meaning relationships and are an expression of the ultraparadoxical phase mechanism. (They accounted for 26.47% of the total number of verbal observed slips.)

Late at night I am watching television. I want to say "Let's switch off the TV set," but instead I say "Let's switch off the radio."

The words *television* and *radio* are constantly associated in our daily experience. In a sentence spoken in the parabiosis-like state of normal evening fatigue, instead of the correct word *TV set,* according to the principle of the replacement of the ultraparadoxical phase differentiations, the word *radio* slips out.

The most common nondissolutive slips employ the three classic types of associations—analogy, contiguity and, contrast.[5]

2. DISSOLUTIVE verbal slips of the tongue (accounting for 10.78% of the verbal slips) are an expression of Jackson's "loss of control" mechanism.

When, while in a state of fatigue, I am asked where I live, I reply with my old address "Mizia 25" and not "Assen Zlatarov 3" where I live at present.

In fatigue new associative connections are inhibited and instead old ones reemerge.

This category of slips includes the replacement of words on the basis of phonetic similarities (7.84% of verbal slips)—for example, the use of *Pechkata e zapazena* (The stove is reserved) instead of *Pechkata e zapalena*

[4] Elsewhere, each of the four types of slips is further differentiated into a number of varieties which will not be discussed here.

[5] For the sake of brevity, I shall combine verbal replacements by analogy, contiguity, and contrast under the rubric of replacement by meaning relationship (Kraepelin's *Sinnverwandschaft*). Clearly, replacement by contiguity and, particularly, by contrast (i.e., *dead* instead of *alive*) can only with great reservations be treated as "analogous."

(The stove is kindled)—since the phonetic associations are of a "lower type."[6]

3. The third type of slips are dominant verbal slips of the tongue (accounting for 4.90% of the verbal slips).

Having just finished writing a lengthy and difficult manuscript, I worry that some of the pages may have been lost. In this anxious state, I go in the bathroom to take a shower and relax, but there I find some shirts that have been washed. I ask "When are you going to take the complete text [instead of "the washed shirts"] from the bathroom?"

These dominant slips of the tongue were first mentioned tentatively by Meringer (1900). They were subsequently discussed by Freud (1924), who viewed them as expressions of deep personality attitudes. Thus, to Freud goes the credit for introducing these kinds of slips as a problem of psychology and psychopathology, although in this connection I should add that I do not accept the psychoanalytic interpretations in which such slips are viewed as always revealing repressed sexual psychotraumas.

4. Verbal slips of the tongue of mixed type (48.04% of the verbal slips) are slips of the tongue in which nondissolutive, dissolutive, and dominant elements are combined.

I am attending a gathering to celebrate the beginning of construction of a new building for the Institute of Pediatrics. In my greeting, instead of saying "I congratulate you on the future Institute of Pediatrics," I say "I congratulate you on the future Institute of Psychiatry."

This slip is dominant because it reveals my basic professional attitude of a psychiatrist. But it is also dissolutive because the words *pediatrics* and *psychiatry* (in Bulgarian *pediatria* and *psihiatria*) have a marked phonetic relationship. In addition, the slip also contains a nondissolutive link by analogy as the words both refer to branches of the medical profession. Thus the slip is a dominant–nondissolutive–dissolutive one.

The slips also include neologisms (6.86%) agrammatic word forms (2.19%), which will not be analyzed in detail here.

Having delineated these basic types of "deviations" of the associative process as they occur in normals, we shall analyze a case of thought

---

[6] Associations on the basis of phonetic similarities are observed as a regular stage in the development of child's thought, who gradually abandons phonetic analogies to make way for associations based on the meaning. The regular rhythmic disinhibition of these associations in poetry, where they occur in conjunction with emotionally charged meaning relationships, is part of the mechanism by which rhyme in poetry gives particular pleasure (Zaimov, 1963a).

dissociation in schizophrenia (on the basis of excerpts from the tape-recorded speech of patient S.S.).[7]

Q: *How are you?*
A: *The devil* [*pointing at a reproduction of Vincent van Gogh's self-portrait as he evidently identifies the painter's image with that of the devil*]. *. . . How did Alexander look at Caesar in order and Napoleon to look towards Caesar. That was a mistake, the North Pole, the South Pole. . . . You are a criminal! What are you doing here? What is this—is it a bathroom?* [looking at the white tile walls of the consulting room]. *. . . A shower, a shower, water—not fire. I am not nervous! I am not a genius! Neither am I a real martyr! Jesus Christ . . . Kirka* [a proper name] *is a witch. Alexander said one should not always be silent. . . . Not Alexander—Spartacus was the bad man. . . . Alexander is Caesar's star. . . . I will not tell. . . . I will not tell. . . . Nazim Hikmet . . . Alexander ten letters . . .* [the Bulgarian spelling of the name of Alexander consists really of ten letters]. *Ten, not nine . . .* [in Bulgarian, *desset, ne devet*] *. . . not Virgin Mary* [in Bulgarian, *ne Deva Maria*] *. . . not virgin . . .* [in Bulgarian, *ne devstven*].

This monologue, taped at the time of the patient's admission for treatment, remained completely incomprehensible to us until the patient recovered from his psychotic attack. At that time, a detailed conversation took place in which he was asked to explain each word and phrase from the tape. It then became clear that before the onset of the psychosis the patient had been in contact with a sort of occult group in which the questions of transmigration had been often discussed. The patient became convinced that he had received the spirit of Alexander the Great, which had previously transmigrated into Caesar and Napoleon. Thus the appearance of these names in the thought dissociation is an expression of a corresponding dominant deviation of the associative process.[8] The associative flow also contains the dominant delusions that the psychiatrist is his enemy and that his acquaintance Kirka has become a witch. Other deviations of the associative process are due to an intensification of passive attention. One element of the setting, Van Gogh's self-portrait is interpreted as a devil; another element—the white tile walls—leads him to incorrectly interpret the setting as a bathroom. We interpret this intensification of passive attention as a dissolutive release from control of the "orientation reflex" which, gaining dominance in this way, accounts for the dissolutive-dominant "intrusions" in the associative flow.

This tape also contains inadequate associations by contrast (e.g., *the North Pole, the South Pole*), dissolutive associative deviations by phonetic

[7] Taken from Zaimov 1979b.
[8] In another study (Zaimov & Kisselintcheva, 1967), we showed the presence of dominant intrusions in the thought of patients with manic-depressive psychosis as well.

relationship [*nyama da kaza* ("I will not tell") . . . *Nazim Hikmet* . . .
Alexander desset bukvi . . . desset, ne devet . . . ne deva . . . ne devstven
. . . ("Alexander ten letters . . . ten, not none . . . not Virgin Mary . . .
not virgin")] *etc.*

This comparative analysis of the slips of the tongue and of thought
dissociation in schizophrenia provides a basis for analyzing the phenomena
of deviations of the associative flow in semantic jargon.

Consider the following excerpts from the tape-recorded speech of A.B.,[9]
a 67 year-old man, who, after a thrombosis, had sensory aphasia and semantic jargon in which "both reference and context are involved [Brown,
1977, p. 33]."

Q: *How are you?*
A: *I will not. . . . They said they would put this but they would not. Those
over there are ill people. . . . They say I am the ill one. . . .*
Q: *How is your sleep?*
A: *We cannot sleep. . . . They say I am ill. . . . How am I ill after I am not
ill. . . . We cannot thrive here. They are good to me. . . . Intenigent*
[instead of "intelligent"] *people. Those are laughing at me. Ill people.
If they take this out of me they will make me die.*
Q: *Have you an appetite?*
A: *I do not feel like eating, I do not. . . . I have seen those that are looking
at me; they are laughing at me. They will take here a thread, will they
not? They will tapat* [neologism] *. . . will they not* [pointing at the vein
in his arm]. *They are young people, they have ill legs, I have not. I do
not understand them. You were not here, we cannot write any more.*

In this text one is impressed by the marked inertness of the nervous
processes with a great number of perseverations. The anxious experience
of an illness becomes quite apparent since the word *ill* makes seven dominant intrusions in the associative flow. In addition, the word *thrive* (in
Bulgarian, *vireem*) in the sentence *We cannot thrive here* appears as a
nondissolutive–dissolutive replacement, by the ultraparadoxical phase
mechanism, of the word *live* (in Bulgarian, *jiveem*). A probable expression
of such a replacement is the word *thread* in the sentence *They will take
a thread here, will they not?* spoken while pointing to a vein from which
blood has been taken by a syringe (replacement via the contiguity association *needle–thread*).

In this record of colloquial speech taped a week after the attack, the
greater part of the mechanisms of disintegrative deviations in the associative
flow remained incomprehensible, and the slow recovery process did not
allow additional questioning, as in the case of schizophrenia. It is obvious
that in the "free association" of the colloquial speech a great number of

[9] This case is described in detail in Zaimov (1965, pp.82–92).

intermediate links of the associative process dropped off, not reaching expressive speech and thus remaining beyond our analysis.[10]

In contrast to the situation in colloquial speech, associative deviations were considerably more comprehensible when the patient was required to designate certain objects, as here it was possible to compare an answer to a known target. The following are some examples of patient's paraphasias in object naming:

Pen ——→ *Pencil*
Pencil ——→ *Ink*
Key ——→ *This is an iron pencil, filed, an iron stick.*
Small cup ——→ *This is brandy, bottle, small cup for brandy.*
Nail (in Bulgarian, *pirron*) ——→ *Pillin* [neologism] . . . *nail, sharply to hammer it, pillon* [neologism], *pillo* [neologism], *file* [in Bulgarian *pila*].

In these paraphasias one can identify some of the mechanisms of associative disintegration that have already been described, with replacements on the basis of meaning relationships (e.g., pen → *pencil*, pencil → *ink*) and by phonetic analogy (e.g., nail → *file*—in Bulgarian, *pirron* → *pila*), as well as a number of perseverative paraphasias. In some cases, the replacements by meaning relationships "organize" themselves in circumlocutions (for example key → *This is . . . an iron stick*).

However, not all cases of the deviations in the associative flow were so readily explicable. Some responses given during this same test remained incomprehensible, for example:

Glove ——→ *This . . . a sort of such a thing . . . When there are lots of housemaids to keep warm, for a plate, for a small cup.*
Handbag ——→ *I do not know it, I have already forgotten them. It is too much, it is five days.*

This patient was followed for a 5-month period. At certain intervals, he was asked to name certain objects, which were always presented in the same order. This made it possible to see the way in which the associative process deviations gradually approached the correct answer. In the following example, the object shown the patient was a bottle of medicine.

24 March 1956 ——→ *We smoke*
25 March 1956 ——→ *Fountain*

---

[10] No doubt many associative relations would become comprehensible if we were familiar with the patient's whole life and daily experiences; this, however, remains an unattainable ideal of every thought and speech pathology study.

27 March 1956 ⟶ *Glass*
30 March 1956 ⟶ *Medicine*
9 April   1956 ⟶ *Tumbler*
10 April 1956 ⟶ *Jug*
16 May   1956 ⟶ *Bottle of water*
7 June   1956 ⟶ *Bottle*
2 July   1956 ⟶ *Bottle*
6 August 1956 ⟶ *Bottle*

This series of paraphasias provides a semantic index of the depth of the associative process parabiotic disintegration and of its reintegration in which the answers gradually become adequate. The first paraphasia (bottle → we smoke—in Bulgarian, *shishe* → *pushim*) involves only a distant phonetic relationship, with a single shared syllable, *shi*. The association is comprehensible only because the object provides a basis for analysis; without the presence of the object itself, to assume such a relationship would be extremely hypothetical and risky. This explains why in "free association" in colloquial speech a great number of associative relations remain incomprehensible.

The chronological series of paraphasias corresponds to the clinical experience, which shows that in the recovery of an aphasia with paraphasias, the latter become increasingly comprehensible and semantically closer to the correct response. It also corresponds to clinical observations in schizophrenia. Here associative deviations may initially be with minor semantic deviations; as the disorder progresses, such semantically based associations gradually disappear and are replaced by an abundance of phonetic associations. These observations on disintegration and reintegration of the associative process lead to the question of the relationship between parabiosis and dissolution.

According to Jackson, dissolution occurs only when a reaction (or a functional tendency) which is inhibited in phylogenesis or ontogenesis is released as a result of a morbid process. This is the case with phonetic associations, which are characteristic of a certain stage in the development of the child's thought but are subsequently inhibited as being ill-suited to the mature logical thought. That is why I classify verbal replacements based on phonetic relationship as dissolutive.

In contrast, meaning associations are necessary in logical thought; thus replacements on the basis of meaning are defined as nondissolutive. Nonetheless, there is an element of dissolution in the progressive deviation in semantic differentiations, which starts with the nearer (finer) relationships and extends to those that are more remote, given that, in the development of speech and thought, first the meaning differentiations formed are initially rough and then progressively finer. For this reason, I will assume that the semantically related replacements, although nondissolutive in respect to semantic structure,[11] nonetheless contain a dissolutive element (or a dissolutive "coefficient"), in that the tendency toward incorrect designation of the objects has existed at a certain stage of child language development and has gradually been overcome.

Thus, although parabiosis and dissolution are distinct concepts, they are closely interrelated in pathology.

Of interest in this respect is the manic–depressive psychosis. To explain the pathological dissociation of the "gay" and the "sad" element in this psychosis through Jackson's concept of dissolution, we would have to assume either that the gay element develops in phylogenesis before the sad element, which subsequently builds itself upon the gay element and inhibits it, or the reverse, namely that the sad element existed prior to the gay one. Obviously both those possibilities are unacceptable. Similar arguments could be made in respect to catatonic excitement and stupor in schizophrenia: In this case, it would be paradoxical to hold that the chaotic hyperkinesis phylogenetically preceded, and then was inhibited by, the stupor, or vice versa.

Clearly, we must assume that in addition to the contrary functional forces between evolutionary layers of the nervous system, there exist similar forces within the layers themselves—and they are proved by the existence of reciprocal inhibition (Bell & Bell 1826; Weber & Weber 1846; Sherrington 1893a, 1893b; Wedensky 1897; Sherrington 1906). Accordingly, the phases of the manic-depressive psychosis are an expression of the development of an alternating parabiotic process. In the manic phase this process seizes that half of the reciprocally organized functional system which directs (mobilizes) the negative emotions with a positive induction (in accordance with Pavlov's concept of inductive regularities in the associated pair) of its reciprocal partner—the subsystem directing the positive emotions. In the depressive phase, the parabiotic process development seizes the other element of this functional system. Mutatis mutandis the same correlations must be assumed in the catatonic excitement and stupor, where reciprocal elements regulate (activate or inhibit) the general motility (Zaimov, 1949, 1978b).

I will assume an analogous "horizontal" arrangement of the elements of an associated (reciprocal) pair in the paraphasia *chair → table*. However, in the development of semantic relations in speech and thought, this pair is also included in a complex hierarchical organization of a semantic system. Thus the moment of its disintegration in the parabiotizing of this system

---

[11] For example, we cannot define the paraphasia chair → *table* as dissolutive since the two words are assimilated in principle at the same time in ontogenesis and this meaning relation is continuously used in logical thought. Still less can we define as dissolutive the paraphasia of another patient with sensory aphasia who, on being shown a pen, designates it as a *utensil,* that is, by a word undoubtedly assimilated later in speech ontogenesis and from another semantic sequence (a general concept). With respect to the semantic system, this paraphasia could be even called "antidissolutive."

in aphasia by the ultraparadoxical phase is determined by its "vertical" aspect—its place in this hierarchical organization.

The idea that the terms parabiosis and dissolution should not be equated receives additional support from the fact that the phenomena of dissolution can exist without phenomena of parabiosis. For example, a total section of the spinal cord can take place where, after the shock parabiotic period, the dissolutive automatism of the bladder comes into play.

Following Kraepelin,[12] who showed the great phenomenological relationship between schizophrenic and sleep thought, and following Kleist, who showed the relationship of some clinical phenomena in schizophrenia[13] to the organically determined syndromes of aphasia and apraxia, I have long maintained (Zaimov, 1953, 1959) that in respect to symptomatology there exists an indisputable phenomenological analogy between organic and functional disorders of the nervous system. As has been shown, one can go even further, using slips of the tongue as a model for studying associative deviations in schizophrenia and semantic jargon.

In this connection, as has been pointed out, the question arises as to whether one can draw such important conclusions for pathology on the basis of normal behavior, that is, whether fundamental qualitative differences do not exist between the normal and the pathological. To the already cited views of Jackson concerning "normal dissolution" and Wedensky concerning "normal parabiosis," I should like to add the following. In comparing the patterns of disintegration in paraphasia and in slips of the tongue, one cannot ignore the crucial difference between the state of the healthy person and that of the ill one. This difference, however, lies not in the isolated manifestations, but in the overall state of being —in that totality of behavioral phenomena and their quantitatively qualitative characteristics, which Aristotle and Hegel referred to with the philosophical concept of "measure" (Lossev, 1964). For example, in the healthy person, the substitution of the word *chair* by the word *table,* although structurally identical to the same paraphasia in semantic jargon, represents an isolated phenomenon in a background of an adequate associative process, whereas, in a marked semantic jargon, paraphasia is the rule and the adequate answer the exception. Thus, in respect to that phenomenon, the two states have an entirely different functional measure. Moreover, semantic jargon is characterized by a great number of verbal perseverations; this is entirely alien to normal speech, in which, however, perseverative verbal slips do occasionally occur. Again this reveals the fundamental quantitative-qualitative difference between the verbal behavior of the healthy person and that of the aphasic with semantic jargon.

[12] A number of correlations between the phenomena of the mental illness and sleep can be found in the literature before Kraepelin.

[13] In my opinion, schizophrenia is an organically determined psychosis with a long functional stage and must be clearly delimited from schizophrenia-like psychogenic psychoses.

These correlations of some phenomena of normal and pathological behavior, and of functional and organic pathological states, are directed mainly toward deviations of thought, speech, praxis, and gnosis, as well as toward memory disorders (Zaimov, 1963b; Zaimov, 1971; Zaimov & Kisselintcheva, 1966).

In a series of studies summarized in two monographs (1972, 1977), Brown pays particular attention to symptom formation in organic and functional states. His studies, which are based on a large body of clinical and experimental data, deal with problems of integration and of functional and organic disintegration of language, action, perception, thought and memory, affect, consciousness, volition, and creativity. From the point of view of the problems discussed in this chapter, I should like to note that Brown arrives at some interesting correlations between paralogical thought in schizophrenia and paralogical turns of speech in semantic jargon.

CONCLUSIONS

1. In comparing the disintegration of the associative process in semantic jargon and in schizophrenia, it is possible to find elements that are phenomenologically similar, or even identical. Such elements include the associative deviations based on meaning and phonetic relationships, as first described by Kraepelin. To them may be added associative deviations with intrusions of dominant personality attitudes, persevering deviations, deviations by "loss of control" of passive attention, *etc.* For these types of disintegrative phenomena I proposed the term disintegrative deviation of the associative process.[14]

2. The slips of the tongue of healthy persons can be used as a model for studying these phenomena.

3. In a pathophysiological framework, deviations in the associative flow in schizophrenia and in semantic jargon can be interpreted on the basis of Jackson's concept of dissolution, Wedensky's doctrine of parabiosis, Pavlov's doctrine of phase states, and Uchtomsky's concept of the dominant.

REFERENCES

Bell, J., & Bell, C. *The anatomy and physiology of the human body* (Vol. 3) (6th ed.). London: Longman, Rees, 1826.
Bleuler, E. *Dementia praecox oder Gruppe der Schizophrenien.* Leipzig and Wien: Deutike, 1911.

[14] A more detailed description of the pathways of the disintegrative deviation can be found in Zaimov (1979a, 1979b).

Brown, J. W. *Aphasia, apraxia and agnosia: Clinical and theoretical aspects.* Springfield, Ill.: Charles C Thomas, 1972.

Brown, J. W. *Mind, brain and consciousness: The neuropsychology of cognition.* New York: Academic Press, 1977.

Freud, S. *Zur Psychopathologie des Alltagsleben.* Gesammelte Schriften, Internationaler psychoanalytischer Verlag, Leipzig, Bd. 4, S. 1–310. 1924.

Jackson, J. H. *Selected writings* (2 vols.). (J. Taylor, Ed.). London: Hodder and Stoughton, 1931–1932.

Kleist, K. Aphasie und Geisteskrankheiten. *Münch. med. Wschr.,* 1914, *61,* 8–12.

Kleist, K. Wesen und Lokalisation der Paralogie. *Zbl. f.d.ges. Neurol, Psychiat.,* 1923, *33,* 82–83.

Kleist, K. *Gehirnpathologie.* Leipzig: Barth, 1934.

Kraepelin, E. Über Sprachstörungen im Traume. In *Psychologische Arbeiten* (E. Kraepelin, Herausg.), Bd 5, SS. 1–104. Wilhelm Engelmann, Leipzig. 1906.

Kraepelin, E. (1913), Psychiatrie. Achte Aufl., Bd 3, Teil 2. Barth, Leipzig.

Lossev, A. (1964), [Measure]. In *Philosophical encyclopedia* (Vol. 3). Moscow: Soviet Encyclopedia Publishing House. Pp. 389–394. (In Russian.)

Meringer, R. (1900). Wie man sich versprechen kann. Neue freie Presse, 23 August (zit. nach S. Freud, 1924, S. 67).

Meringer, R., & Mayer, C. *Versprechen und Verlesen: Eine psychologischlinguistische Studie.* Stuttgart: Göschensche Verlagshandlung, 1895.

Pavlov, I. P. [*Lectures on the functioning of the great hemispheres of the brain.*] Moscow: Academy of Sciences of the Soviet Union Publishing House, 1949. (In Russian.)

Pavlov, I. P. [Twenty-year experience of objective research into the higher nervous activity (the behavior) of animals. Moscow: Medgiz., 1951. (In Russian.)

Sherrington, C. Note on the knee-jerk and the correlation of action of antagonistic muscles. *Proceedings of the Royal Society,* 1893, *52,* 556–564. (a)

Sherrington, C. Further experimental note on the correlation of action of antagonistic muscles. *Proceedings of the Royal Society,* 1893, *53,* 407–420. (b)

Sherrington, C. *The integrative action of the nervous system.* New Haven: Yale University Press, 1906.

Uchtomsky, A. A. [The dominant.] Moscow: Nauka Publishing House, 1966. (In Russian.)

Weber, E., & Weber, E. H. (1846). Expériences qui prouvent que les nerfs vagues, stimulés par l'appareil de rotation galvano-magnétique, peuvent retarder et même arrêter le mouvement du coeur. *Archives générales de médecine.* Journal complémentaire des sciences médicales. 4e série, vol. suppl. de l'année 1946. Archives d'anatomie générale et de physiologie. Paris, p. 12–13.

Wedensky, N. E. [On the reciprocal relation between the psychomotor centres.] In K. M. Bikov (Ed.), [I. *I. M. Setshenov, I. P. Pavlov, N. E. Wedensky: Physiology of the nervous system*] (Vol. 3). Moscow: Medgiz., 1952. Pp. 181–189. (In Russian; previously published in 1897, also in Russian.)

Wedensky, N. E. [Excitation, inhibition and narcosis.] In K. M. Bikov (Ed.), [*I. M. Setshenov, I. P. Pavlov, N. E. Wedensky: Physiology of the nervous system*] (Vol. 2). Pp. 314–412. Moscow: Medgiz., 1952. (In Russian; previously published in 1901, also in Russian.)

Zaimov, K. [Analytical notes on the doctrine of J. H. Jackson.] *Annals of Medicine, Neurology and Psychiatry,* 1949, *1,* 77–88. (In Bulgarian.)

Zaimov, K. Die Rolle der Phasenzustände bei der Zerfahrenheit und Inkohärenz des Denkens bei Psychosen. *Deutsch. Gesundheitswes.,* (Faltbeilage), 1957, *12,* 213–236. (Previously published in Bulgarian, 1953.)

Zaimov, K. Über die Pathophysiologie der Agnosien, Aphasien, Apraxien und der Zerfahrenheit des Denkens bei der Schizophrenie. Fischer, Iena, 1965. (Originally written in Bulgarian as a dissertation in 1959.)

Zaimov, K. [An attempt to transfer the inductive relations of the ultraparadoxical phase to the differentiations of the motor analyzer of the cerebral cortex (the parabiosis as general pathophysiological basis of aphasia, apraxia, agnosia and of the dissociation of thought in schizophrenia).] *Korsakov's J., 1961, 61,* 1204–1209. (In Russian.)

Zaimov, K. [On the physiological and psychological basis of the rhyme.] *Annals of the University of Sofia, Philosophical–Historical Faculty,* 1963, *57,* 179–192. (In Bulgarian.) (a)

Zaimov, K. [*Clinical phenomenology and pathophysiology of some disturbances of the memory.*] Sofia: Medizina i Fizkultura Publishing House, 1963. (In Bulgarian.) (b)

Zaimov, K. [Investigation of the errors of speech in experimental alcoholic intoxication.] *Nevrol., psihiatr., nevrohirurg, 1964, 3,* 455–465. (In Bulgarian.)

Zaimov, K. Die Sprachstörungen als Kriterium der Bewusstseinstrübungen. *Psychiat., Neurol. med. Psychol.,* 1969, *21,* 218–225.

Zaimov, K. *Psychopathologie.* Sofia: Nauka i Izkustvo Publishing House, 1971. (In Bulgarian.)

Zaimov, K. Parabiosis and dissolution. *Nevrol., psihiatr. nevrohirurg,* 1972, *11,* 299–301. (In Bulgarian.)

Zaimov, K. Pathophysiological analysis of the verbal paraphasia. *Nevrol., psihiatr. i nevrohirurg, 1976, 15,* 9–14. (In Bulgarian.) (a)

Zaimov, K. The verbal slips of the tongue as model for investigation of the dissociation of thought in schizophrenia. *Nevrol., psihiatr. i nevrohirurg, 1976, 15,* 387–391. (In Bulgarian.) (b)

Zaimov, K. On the dominant verbal errors (according to data of self-analysis). *Nevrol., psihiatr. i nevrohirurg, (1977), 16,* 330–337. (In Bulgarian.)

Zaimov, K. [On the treacherous role of the slips of the tongue.] *Nevrol. psihiatr. i nevrohirurg, (1978), 17,* 77–81. (In Bulgarian.) (a)

Zaimov, K. [The antagonistic (or counteracting) synergism as principle of the functional organization of the nervous system in normal and in pathological conditions.] *Nevrol., psihiatr. i nevrohirurg, (1978), 17,* 221–224 (In Bulgarian.) (b)

Zaimov, K. [On the mechanism of occurrence and the structure of the conversational slips of the tongue (according to self-analysis data).] *Nevrol., psihiatr. i nevrohirurg, (1979), 18,* 3–12 (In Bulgarian.) (a)

Zaimov, K. Von der Paraphasie, durch das Versprechen, zu der Zerfahrenheit des Denkens bei der Schizophrenie. *Psychiatr. Neurol. med. Psychol, 1979, 31,* 148–156. (b)

Zaimov, K., & Kisselintcheva V. [Some observations on the memory functions in students during examinations.] *Nevrol., psihiatr. i nevrohirurg, (1966), 5,* 135–138. (In Bulgarian.)

Zaimov, K., & Kisselintcheva V. Au sujet de troubles de la pensée dans la psychose maniaco-dépressive. *Ann. méd.-psychol,* 1967, *125/1,* 357–375.

Zaimov, K., and Rainov V. [Dissociation of speech in schizophrenia and incoherence of speech in patients with clouding of consciousness.] *Nevrol., psihiatr. i nevrohirurg, (1976), 15,* 206–208. (In Bulgarian.) (a)

Zaimov, K., & Rainov, V. Dissolutive und nichtdissolutive Elemente in den phonetischen Störungen von Aphasie-Kranken. *Psychiat. Neurol. med. Psychol., (1976), 28,* 553–558. (b)

Chapter 9

Case Reports of Semantic Jargon

JASON W. BROWN

Semantic jargon is characterized by the production of fluent, well-articulated, but semantically anomalous utterances with no more than occasional phonemic or neologistic errors. The jargon may be continuous or interspersed with runs of normal, intelligible speech. Semantic errors are typically distant in meaning from their presumed targets, and differ in this way from the paraphasic errors of, say, the anomic, where the category of the target is often respected.

Paraphasias in which compound words are formed (e.g., *featherhair*) are quite common, and recall descriptions of schizophasic language and sleep speech. Verbal errors in which there is a sound relation (e.g., *pear* for *hair*) are uncommon, in my experience occurring more in association with phonemic than semantic disorders. Semantic jargon is frequently seen in dementia, especially in posterior dementias such as Alzheimer's disease. When there is reasonably good repetition, this may lead to a diagnosis of transcortical sensory aphasia.

The following cases are included to give the reader some feeling for this unusual type of aphasia, and to indicate the frequent relationship of the disorder to bilateral temporal lobe pathology.

169

JARGONAPHASIA

Copyright © 1981 by Academic Press, Inc.
All rights in any form reserved.
ISBN 0-12-137580-3

CASE 1

This 72-year-old man fell down a flight of stairs and sustained a left temporoparietal skull fracture and hematoma. There was initial confusion and jargon. Otherwise, the neurological examination was normal. The patient was well educated, and spoke French and German as second languages (L2s). There were several left-sided seizures shortly after the injury, indicating right hemisphere involvement. The EEG showed bilateral posterior slow activity. The CT scan (Figure 9.1) showed a vascular lesion in the RIGHT temporal lobe (incorrectly cited as LEFT in Brown, 1979).

Speech was fluent and well-articulated, with semantic and some neologistic jargon:

And I say, this is wrong, I'm going out and doing things and getting ukeleles taken every time and I think I'm doing wrong because I'm supposed to take

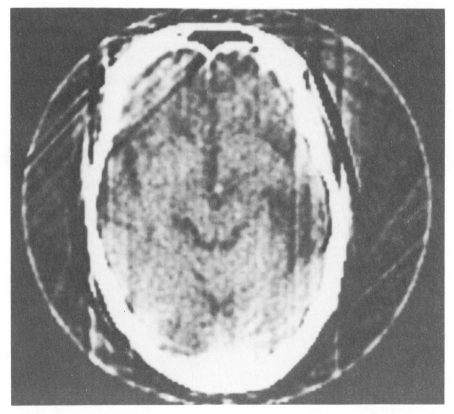

Figure 9.1. A lesion in the right temporal lobe (CT scan). There is clinical evidence of bilateral involvement.

everything from the top so that we do four flashes of four volumes before we get down low. . . . Face of everything. This guy has got to this thing, this thing made out in order to slash immediately to all of the windpails. . . . This is going right over me from there, That's up to is 5 station stuff from manatime, and with that put it all in and build it all up so it will all be spent with him conversing his condessing. Condessing his treatment of this for he has got to spend this thing. [Examiner holds up handkerchief: What is that?] Well this is a lady's line, and this is not longer what he wants. He is now leaving their mellonpush. Which is spelled "U" something or other which also commence the fact that they're gonna finish the end of that letter which is spelled in their stalegame and opens up here and runs across what "M", it wasn't "M", it's "A" and "M" is the interval title and it is spelled out with all of this.

Naming was at times correct or with semantic paraphasia: *thumb*—"envelope"; *ear*—"a pair of a shoe"; *pipe*—"smokin mob"; *ashtray*—"mouse looker-atter"; *cup*—"takes a stairtime"; *elbow*—"taking it together you can get bad pressure with it." Similarly, on word and sound repetition there were either correct performances or semantic jargon; for example, *sh*—"a mud layer singer gets a normal rate." He pointed to 50% of single objects and carried out simple commands. No French or German language or jargon was produced. Comprehension could not be assessed in these languages though he reacted when addressed in a foreign tongue.

CASE 2

This 69-year-old Italian–English-speaking woman was seen in January 1979 with the sudden onset of incoherent speech. There was a previous right embolic stroke with left hemiplegia, which did not affect her speech. The CT scan (Figure 9.2) showed a large old right temporal infarct and a recent infarct in the left posterior temporal region, confirmed by nuclear medicine scan.

Spontaneous speech consisted of fluent, relatively grammatical, well-articulated semantic jargon with frequent neologisms, and occasional correct sentences:

I just stayed there to park with me you know. I stayed park with this . . . and there he's gonna go to wash, uh, washbraisin . . . where he's gonna burn his house. He bought his house down there. A house, a eagle house for the farm. I forgot to ask you . . . where they buy a farm, where they buy orangefarm . . . my father the brother he bought the house there and he eats [piænt], they call it [piænt] whether they call the [bɪ] farm [briænts] and is bred, the [frijrlčaz] he eats in his sleeves.

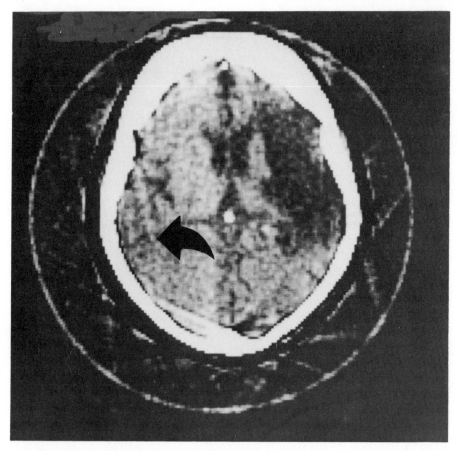

Figure 9.2. Old right temporal lesion. There is a recent CVA (indicated by the arrow) in the left posterior temporal area (CT scan).

Namings and descriptions were occasionally correct, but more often consisted of semantic errors or compounds; *coffee*—"the spoon doesn't taste right"; *glove*—"bread, you can wear bread"; *key*—"kittycar, key, tail, key." Examples of compounds are "floorpark," "flybrown," "featherhair," or "the woman was salespaper here." Single words and short concrete phrases were often repeated well with jargon on longer material; *pry the tin lid off*—"pray the din [weyf] help from." She could point to some single objects and followed simple commands. No Italian (L1) jargon or normal Italian speech was heard.

CASE 3

This 70-year-old man was seen in January 1979. The CT scan (Figure 9.3) showed bilateral temporoparietal lesions. The patient was born in Berlin

and had been in the United States for 30 years. He was fluent in English
(L2), and spoke French and Spanish (L3s). Speech was fluent and well-
articulated. On initial questioning in English it was not apparent that he
was aphasic. However, over several minutes, with fatigue, English conversation gradually changed into jargon, beginning with circumlocution:
"Well sir, I would say that you want me to name these [keys] and that is
a very simple matter for me to do . . . a ring of potatoes." To the *color
of a lemon,* he responded with, "Well a citrone that would be greenish if
it was a young citrone." This sort of vaguely acceptable English utterance
then deteriorated through a brief phase of semantically anomalous English
to a mixed French–Spanish semantic jargon. He could not be induced to
speak, repeat, or respond to German, nor was jargon heard in this language.
There were no phonological or neologistic errors. Repetition and reading

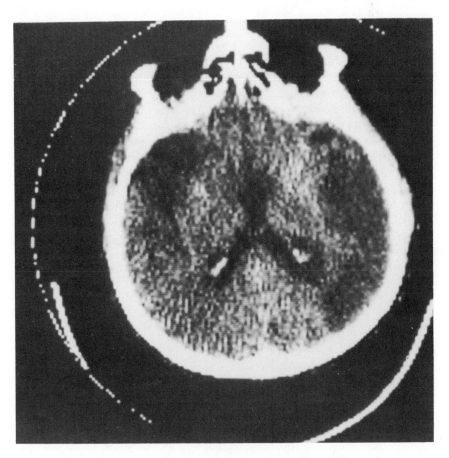

Figure 9.3. Bilateral temporoparietal lesions (CT scan).

aloud were good in English, with verbal transformation and language mixing in French and Spanish. Comprehension was fair in English, poor in French and Spanish, with semantic paraphasia on naming.

CASE 4

This 74-year-old accountant developed a fluent jargonaphasia after several years of progressive confusion and language change. The patient spoke three languages: German (L1), English (L2), and French (L3). An EEG was diffusely abnormal. The CT scan showed diffuse atrophy. A diagnosis of Alzheimer's disease was made.

Spontaneous speech consisted of fluent, well-articulated jargon:

Perhaps there was a possibility that I reach, reach a photograph for someone who teaches a photograph of some sort. I may have been asked for it and I would have assumed my own vantage of yes or no.

Semantic jargon was present in English, German, and French; it was most severe on object naming, and more pronounced in French (L3) than in the other languages. There were infrequent phonemic errors, rare neologisms. The jargon was increased on story recall and proverb interpretation, as in his response to the meaning of a *chip on one's shoulder:* "It is principle to vote a certain item." Performance was variable as to language preference. At times, there was marked language mixing, especially of French and English, less commonly with German. Rarely, languages were mixed within individual lexical items, as in "geswelled." Frequently he would respond in German when addressed in English, and vice versa, at times spontaneously translating from one language to another. He could also translate on request across all three languages.

Naming was at times normal, or with semantic paraphasias. The same was true of repetition, for example, *the spy fled to Greece*—"the spy is glad to a degree." On comprehension, he could point to single objects and carry out simple commands.

COMMENT ON CASES

Four patients are described with semantic jargon, all with bilateral lesions, polyglots ranging in age from 69 to 74 years. Characteristically, the dense semantic jargon was accompanied by confusion, impaired verbal memory, modest comprehension ability (i.e., not severe impairment as in neologistic jargon), and fairly good repetition with frequent verbal transformations. No clear patterns were discerned in the bilingual jargon. In some cases, jargon appeared more severe in the secondary languages, but these patients could not be induced to speak the mother tongue (Cases 2 and 3). Conceivably, L1 would have been even more unintelligible (see below). In another case (Case 1), the jargon was present only in L1, and the patient could not be induced to speak the secondary languages. However, there is reason to question his premorbid fluency in these languages. Case 4 was of particular interest in that semantic jargon was present in all three languages tested—most severe in L3—and spontaneous translations across all three languages—at times correct, at other times in jargon—often characterized his response to questions, commands, or repetition requests given in one language. These cases raise the question of whether semantic jargon is more common in older patients and in bilinguals.

As was noted, in the bilingual patient, semantic jargon may involve L2 more than L1, at least if there is moderate fluency in L2 to begin with. This may not be true of neologistic jargon, which, perhaps by virtue of the phonemic disorder, might involve the L1 preferentially. I recall a 70-year-old woman with neologistic jargon in Norwegian (L1), even though, for over 50 years, she had not spoken this language having relied instead on flawless unaccented English (L2). Of course, the critical case would be one with neologistic jargon in L1, and semantic jargon in L2. To my knowledge, such a case has not yet been reported. However, there may be an analogous situation in the dissociation between oral and written expression reported in some jargonaphasics.

These cases of semantic jargon did not show a striking difference between spoken and written expression, other than that written language was often more defective. Yet, for neologistic jargon, the ability to correctly name objects in writing with neologisms on oral naming has been described. Such a dissociation was also present in our case of phonemic jargon (Chapter 10, this volume) and it occurs in some cases of phonemic (conduction) aphasia. Conceivably, this reflects direct access in writing to the semantic representation in spite of the "overlying" phonological deficit. In fact, the presence of this dissociation might indicate whether the jargon is purely phonological or combined with a semantic disorder.[1]

The spontaneous translations of Case 4 raise the question of a correspondence in semantic jargon across languages WITHIN a single conceptual domain. This patient, given a question in English, might respond in German with a jargon translation linked semantically to the stimulus material. In this respect, I am reminded of a German–English jargonaphasic who in

---

[1] In the play *Wings*, the author, Kopit, allows us to hear neologistic jargon in the speech of a stroke victim, and semantic jargon in INNER speech. Though presumably a device to make the mental life of the subject more accessible to the audience, this does raise a theoretical question as to whether these two forms of jargon may cooccur depending on the level of phonological realization; that is, semantic jargon occurs mentally, but, because of disturbed phonological processing, jargon becomes neologistic in overt speech.

English had the predilection word *money*, and in German, the word *gelting*. Such cases indicate that errors in semantic jargon are not lexically determined, but reflect meaning relationships. Similar findings might also be expected in bilingual amnestic patients, where retrieval problems should be related to the meaning content of the stimulus and not the specific language in which it was acquired.

Finally, these cases also illustrate the fact that semantic jargon is primarily associated with bilateral lesions, probably involving basal or mesial temporal lobe structures. This localization is reinforced by the obvious clinical relationships to the Korsakoff syndrome (Brown, 1979). Cases with acute toxic or other confusional states where there is a confabulatory picture may also show semantic jargon. In jargonaphasia secondary to bilateral focal lesions, there is generally, if not always, an accompanying confusional state. Semantic jargon, confusion, and the Korsakoff syndrome (confabulatory amnesia) are closely interwoven deficits; perhaps they are intrinsically bound up together. This helps us also to understand the meaning of "confusion," it reflects incomplete semantic realization, both in lexical development and in object formation.

REFERENCE

Brown, J. W. Language representation in the brain. In H. Steklis & M. Raleigh (Eds.), *Neurobiology of social communication in primates*. New York: Academic Press, 1979.

Chapter 10

Phonemic Jargon: A Case Report

ELLEN PERECMAN
JASON W. BROWN

INTRODUCTION

Linguistic investigations of aphasia indicate that language breakdown occurs in an orderly and systematic fashion and that it follows principles assumed to underlie the organization of normal language. One such principle is that the organization of the sound system is independent of the organization of the meaning system and that a linguistic meaning is expressed, quite arbitrarily, through a sequence of sounds which are in themselves meaningless. It is therefore of interest that, among the ways in which language may be disturbed by brain injury, there exists a condition in which sequences of phonetic units remain meaningless elements, evoking no semantic content at all.

Perhaps the earliest case report describing such a language disturbance was that published by Jonathan Osborne in 1833. Osborne's patient was a 26-year-old university scholar who was proficient in French, Italian, and German. The man apparently suffered a stroke which left him with speech that "caused him to be treated as a foreigner." Osborne characterized his patient's "imperfection" as a "loss of recollection of the mode of using the vocal apparatus so as to pronounce [words] [p. 158]." He describes the jargon only by saying that it consisted of a variety of syllables. Other symptoms included (*a*) excellent comprehension for oral as well as written language; (*b*) good writing; (*c*) intact ability to perform arithmetic calculations; and (*d*) repetition confined to certain monosyllables, with an inability to repeat sounds corresponding to the letters *k, q, u, v, w, x,* and usually *i*. When asked to read the sentence *It shall be in the power of the College to examine or not examine any licentiate, previously to his admission to a fellowship, as they shall think fit*, he produced the following: *An the be what in the temother of the trothotodoo to majorum or that emidrate ein einkrastrai mestreit to ketra totombreidei to ra fromtreido asthat kekritest*. Several days later he read the same passage as *Be mather be in the kondreit of the compestret to samtreis amtreit emtreido am temtreido mestreiterso to his eftreido tun bried rederiso of deid daf drit des trest*. The patient appeared to be aware of his impairment and evidence in the case report indicates normal affect. Osborne also reported the progress of the patient's recovery. At 6 months following the onset of the disturbance, the patient read the original test sentence as follows: *It may be in the power of the college to evhavine or not, ariatin any licentiate seviously to his amission to a spolowship, as they shall think fit*. Finally, after one year, Osborne reports the patient to have improved almost totally.

A patient described by Browne (cited in Bateman, 1890) produced incessant jargon consisting of sequences such as *kalluios, tallulios, kaskos, tellulios, karoka, keka*, and appeared surprised that she was not understood.

Alajouanine (1956) introduced the term UNDIFFERENTIATED JARGON to designate a form of aphasic jargon described as consisting of meaningless strings of speech sounds not clearly segmentable into work-like groupings. As an example of this form, he gave the following brief excerpt: *sanénequéduacquitescapi*. Subsequently, Alajouanine and Lhermitte (1964) emphasized other clinical aspects, including the tendency to stereotypy and perseveration, oral apraxia, and the involvement of repetition and reading aloud. Oral and written comprehension were said to be preserved.

Cénac (1925) described a form of jargon in which he observed long stretches of neologism, including only the phonemes of the standard language in phonologically acceptable sequences. He referred to this disturbance as GLOSSOLALIA.[1] The neologistic units in glossolalia were observed to bear structural resemblance to one another and to other utterances of the patient. A predilection for certain segments or sequences was also indicated.

There are some anecdotal references to cases with totally phonemic jargon (LeCours & Rouillon, 1976; Wepman & Jones, 1964). However,

---

[1] More recently, Cénac's term glossolalia has been revived by LeCours and colleagues to refer to a variety of phonemically deviant forms of jargon, including that of aphasics, schizophrenics, and persons said to be in charismatic states. The use of a single term to refer to phenomena of such diverse origins is presumably intended to capture a structural similarity among them.

descriptions are lacking, presumably because the disorder is so rare. The study of K.S. presented here is a thorough investigation of a form of jargon consisting entirely of semantically vacuous phoneme strings. This patient differs from those described by Osborne and Alajouanine in that he demonstrates severe deficits in oral and written comprehension and shows no evidence of oral apraxia. The jargon to be described is characterized by distinct articulation of a diversity of phones corresponding to the phonemes of languages spoken by the patient, English and German. The term PHONEMIC JARGON[2] is preferred over the term undifferentiated jargon, as phonemes are indeed differentiated in the jargon. The term glossolalia was judged inappropriate insofar as its use has not been restricted to aphasic jargon.

LINGUISTIC ANALYSIS OF PHONEMIC JARGON

Phonemic jargonaphasia presents a situation in which the meaning-bearing function of speech sounds has been lost. This form of jargonaphasia, therefore, provides the opportunity to study the sound structure that emerges from a linguistic network in which there is no systematic correspondence between sounds and meanings. This sound structure may reveal properties at the foundation of the phonemic level of the speech production system for intact expressive language, properties that under normal conditions are obscured by the demand to achieve meaningfulness.

Phonological investigations of aphasia have adopted from linguistic theory a descriptive framework in which the phonological aspect of language is represented at two levels of organization: the phonemic level, at which the phonological representation of the language act is encoded, and the phonetic level, at which the motor plans for the execution of the language act are organized. Phonological disturbances have been attributed to level-specific deficits.

Phonetic-level disturbances are characteristic of nonfluent anterior aphasias; phonemic-level disturbances are observed in fluent posterior aphasias. Evidence of motor speech impairment in anterior aphasia (i.e., difficulty in initiating speech, impaired prosody, effortfulness, and paralysis or weakness of speech musculature) suggests that in anterior aphasia what appear to be phonemic errors may be due to neuromuscular incoordination, whereas the effortlessness of speech in fluent aphasia indicates a disorder of mental representation.

[2] Note that the term phonemic jargon has been used by the French school in referring to cases of phonemic (conduction) aphasia. However, this term is inappropriate since the phonemic paraphasias that mark the speech of a phonemic (conduction) aphasic usually do not render his speech uninterpretable, and the speech should therefore not be considered jargon.

The present case study assumes that phonemic jargon reflects a dysfunction, not in the ability to evoke phonetic units, but rather in the ability to evoke those units with reference to their phonemic significance in a linguistic message. Phonemic jargon is not considered to be a disturbance at the level of execution. The study addresses the following questions:

1. Given a dissociation between sound and meaning, what will be the phonological properties of speech?
2. Will those properties be fixed or will they change depending upon whether the aphasic is engaged in a dialogue, producing a lengthy uninterrupted episode of jargon, or reading from written text?
3. Will longitudinal observations provide evidence of recovery toward meaningful speech?

CASE REPORT

K.S. is a 74-year-old male carpenter who, in October 1976, suffered a cerebrovascular accident (CVA) resulting in aphasia. The patient was born in Germany and lived there until he was 20-years-old. He spoke a Bavarian dialect at home and Standard German in school. At age 20, he moved to Argentina, where, over a period of several years, he learned to speak Spanish. He then came to the United States, where he has been living for more than 50 years. His command of English is said to have been excellent, though he spoke with a heavy German accent.

At the time of his stroke, K.S. showed mild left-sided weakness and EEG revealed slowing over the left temporal lobe. He was subsequently evaluated by a neurologist at 2 months poststroke, at which time he was found to be neurologically normal except for the aphasia. A CT scan, obtained in March 1977, demonstrated two discrete lesions (Figure 10.1A). One lesion, which appears as two in the section shown in Figure 10.1A, involves the left temporoparietal region; the other involves the temporoparietal region of the right hemisphere. Mild ventricular dilation was noted. After reviewing the CT scan findings, an effort was made to obtain information on a prior CVA, as it was considered unlikely that both lesions were incurred simultaneously. However, no such history could be obtained. Evidently, this was his first known hospitalization.

K.S. appears to be right-handed as judged from the preferential use of that hand and dexterity in writing. On examination he was alert and very cooperative. Indeed, he was eager to participate in testing. He obeyed normal speaker–listener conventions, responding when addressed, and remaining quiet and attentive when he observed others speaking.

CONVERSATIONAL SPEECH was, on the whole, clearly articulated, consisting of fluent, voluble jargon produced with an apparent logorrhea. He did not seem to be aware that his utterances were jargon, but from time

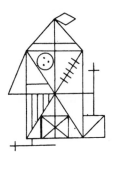

THE QUICK BROWN FOX JUMPS OVER THE LATY DOG

The QUICK BROWN Fox JcumPR the
LAZYDOG

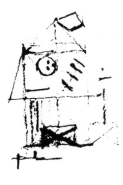

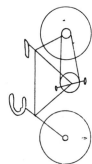

Figure 10.1B. Example of drawing and copying. Note the transliteration in written copy.

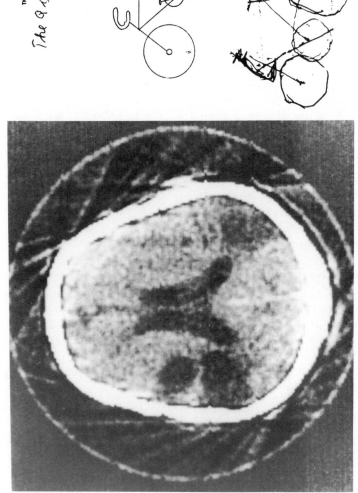

Figure 10.1A. CT scan demonstrating K.S.'s lesions.

to time evidenced frustration, suggesting that he was aware of a failure to communicate. Active gesture occurred both as an accompaniment to speech and as a substitute for it. Prosody and intonation were quite normal.

COMPREHENSION was severely impaired, initially suggesting cortical deafness. It was difficult to distract him with loud noise, or by calling his name from out of sight. Occasionally he followed simple whole-body commands such as *Stand up,* even when the command was whispered from behind him. There was no response to other body, limb, or facial commands, though the examiner noted a difference in K.S.'s response depending upon whether he was addressed in the form of a statement, a command, or a question. Jargon spoken by the examiner was rejected. At times, K.S.'s jargon would incorporate segments from words spoken by the examiner. He was unable to point to objects named, either when the object was placed before him or when it was somewhere else in the room. However, if the object was given a functional context, by means of a pantomimed demonstration of its use, he was sometimes able to point to the target object correctly.

Over several months, comprehension improved to the point where he was able to indicate many single objects named aloud, and even to answer *yes* and *no* to very simple questions. It was apparent that K.S.'s performance on a task was more likely to be successful once a behavioral or psychological set for that particular task had been established.

Audiometric testing indicated a mild hearing loss with normal pure tone thresholds.

K.S. demonstrated no REPETITION upon request, although, as mentioned earlier, words or portions of words produced by the examiner were occasionally detected in his jargon output.

NAMING was jargonized and only rarely could the target word be discerned in his utterance. There was considerable augmentation, with the response including many more syllables than the target in fact included. Perseveration was noted.

READING COMPREHENSION was possible to a limited extent. Though unable to follow simple written commands, K.S. was able to match many written words with correct objects or line drawings of those objects. Performance on this task was better in English than in German. When the written words ENGLISH, GERMAN, FRENCH were displayed before him, and he was asked to match a written or spoken word to the word indicating the language in which the item was presented, he was unable to do so. Over a period of several weeks, he was able to complete simple written phrases with a word selected from a choice card, where the choices included nouns, verbs, and functors. Semantic category information appeared to be intact. When shown the word *tool,* he pointed to a picture of a hammer, pliers, *etc.*; in response to the word *fruit,* he pointed to an apple, banana, *etc.*

WRITING was poor and jargonized for spontaneous productions, but copying was excellent. He showed an ability to transliterate (Figure 10.1B) correctly matching words written in block letters with the same words written in script. In addition, he could write numbers from 1 to 10. In contrast to the apparent lack of awareness for the content of his speech, he was often frustrated by the difficulty in written expression, suggesting an intact regulatory mechanism functioning through some form of either visual or kinesthetic feedback.

LIMB PRAXIS was difficult to evaluate. Some actions were imitated successfully, including eye closure, lifting the hand, and standing up. He was able to match body parts from the examiner to himself, but finger identification on a matching test was poor.

Drawing ability was fairly good (Figure 10.1B). Little perseveration was observed in action and drawing, with such behavior more apparent in writing. There was no evidence of neglect. Line bisection was normal.

Simple WRITTEN CALCULATIONS could not be performed.

METHOD OF INVESTIGATION

Tape-recorded sessions with the patient over a period extending from 4 to 30 months after onset of aphasia were phonetically transcribed (see Table 10.1). Based on these transcriptions, the phonetic content of conversational jargon and reading was analyzed. Conversational samples at 5 and 8 months postonset are from conversations between the patient and a speech therapist during therapy sessions at Goldwater Memorial Hospital. A conversational sample at 30 months post-onset is from a dialogue between the patient and this investigator which took place in the patient's apartment. Reading was sampled at the single word level and in short passages of English and German prose. The English passage is the story "The Hare and the Tortoise," taken from Luria's aphasia battery; the German passage is the introduction to Carnap's *Logische Syntaxe*. The two passages were read at both 4 and 30 months post-onset. The period from 4 to 8 months post-onset will be referred to as Time 1; 30 months post-onset will be referred to as Time 2. A second English text, an adapted excerpt from Chomsky's *Reflections on Language*, was included at Time 2.

As there are no identifiable targets in K.S.'s jargon, the descriptive framework judged to be most appropriate was an analysis in terms of the relative frequency distribution of the phonetic content of the jargon and in terms of the sequential properties of pairs of phonemes. Although any unit of analysis larger than the phoneme will be arbitrary, such a unit has been defined in order to permit determination of properties of the frequency distribution for particular positions within an articulatory sequence. These units are defined over sequences of phones occurring between subjectively

TABLE 10.1A

K.S.'s Consonant Inventory

	Front		Central		Back				
	Bilabial	Labio-dental	Dental/-alveolar	Alveo-palatal	Palatal	Velar	Uvular	Pharyngeal	Glottal
Stop	p b		t d			k g			ʔ
Nasal	m		n			ŋ			
			θ ð	č ǰ					
Fricative		f v				x		h	
			s z	š ž					
Liquid			l r				R		
Glide	w				y				

TABLE 10.1B.

K.S.'s Vowel Inventory

	Front		Central	Back	
	Unrounded	Rounded		Unrounded	Rounded
High	i	ü			u
	ɪ			ʊ	
	e	ø			o
Mid			ə		
	ɛ			Λ	ɔ
Low	æ		a		

determined pauses. The criterion used for marking boundaries between such units was lengthened pause duration and/or lengthened voicing or aspiration in voiced and voiceless stop consonants, respectively. These units are in no way intended to suggest a relation to actual target words, which may or may not in some sense exist for K.S. Rather, they are intended to suggest a relation to segments that may be regarded as single units of production at some level in the organization of articulation.

Samples of conversational jargon and of jargon produced in readings of the English and German passages mentioned earlier, were compared with one another and with various normative data. The frequency distributions of consonants and vowels were analyzed separately. The glides /h/, /y/, and /w/ were treated as consonants. Two consonants that are nonphonemic in both German and English were included in the analyses. Glottal stops were noted out of interest in the use of glottal articulation; the uvular /R/ is distinguished from the alveopalatal /r/ in view of the important role of place features in characterizing the jargon.

Normative data were obtained from several sources. The English language norms were taken from Roberts (1965) and Denes (1963); German norms were taken from Kučera and Monroe (1968). Data were also collected from a normal 70-year-old native German speaker whose language history is similar to that of K.S. in several respects: Both speakers grew up in the Bavarian region of Germany; both have been living in the United States for at least 40 years; and, for both speakers, the pronunciation of English is known to be (or to have been, in K.S.'s case) marked by a heavy German accent. These similarities were believed to justify the decision to base predicted phoneme frequency distributions for K.S. on the distributional properties of this normal speaker's phoneme inventory in the various contexts.

PRESENTATION OF DATA

The data are presented in two parts. The first part describes properties of a sample containing the longest uninterrupted episodes of spontaneous jargon. This sample, referred to as the MONOLOGUE sample, is contrasted with a sample of jargon extracted from a dialogue between the patient and a normal speaker. The second part presents data on reading jargon. This is followed by a comparison of jargon produced in the reading mode with jargon produced spontaneously in conversation.

Spontaneous Jargon

Although K.S. will be shown to produce virtually every phoneme of standard English and German, it will become equally apparent that the frequency distribution of those phonemes in his jargon is not exactly proportional to the pattern found in normal speakers. Indeed, in the case of the monologue sample, the distribution departs quite dramatically from the norm.

Figures 10.2 and 10.3 illustrate the relationship between the consonant distribution in the monologue sample and the typical distributions in normal English and German. K.S. produces [m] and [b] with markedly greater frequency than normal; and [r], [s], [f], and [p] are also found in relatively higher proportions in his jargon. Note, furthermore, that [ð], [y], [h], and [k] occur in much lower proportions than normal, and that [t], [d], and [n] fall somewhat below the normal proportions.

With regard to vowels (Figures 10.4 and 10.5), [i], [a], and [e] are most frequent in the monologue sample. Moreover, the diphthong [ai] is the most common vowel sequence. The graph in Figure 10.5 must be interpreted with caution. The vowel [e] appears there to be very common in K.S.'s jargon. But note that, because the data source for German norms includes [ə] as an allophone of /e/, it was necessary that the [e] in this graph represent a category that collapses [e] and [ə] for K.S. as well. In relation to both

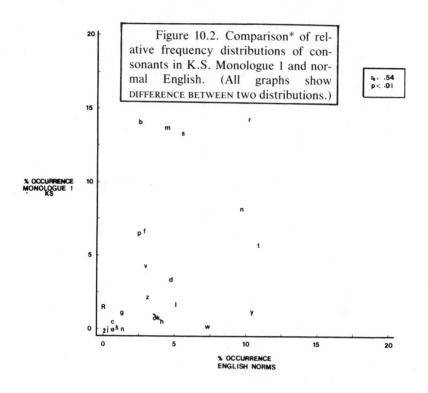

Figure 10.2. Comparison* of relative frequency distributions of consonants in K.S. Monologue 1 and normal English. (All graphs show DIFFERENCE BETWEEN two distributions.)

$r_s = .54$
$p < .01$

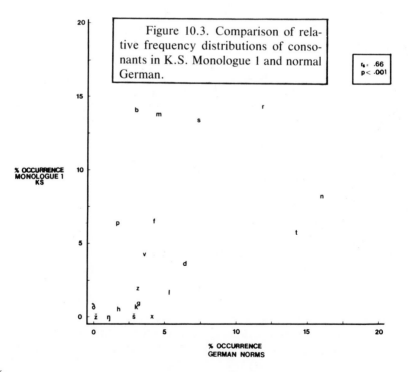

Figure 10.3. Comparison of relative frequency distributions of consonants in K.S. Monologue 1 and normal German.

$r_s = .66$
$p < .001$

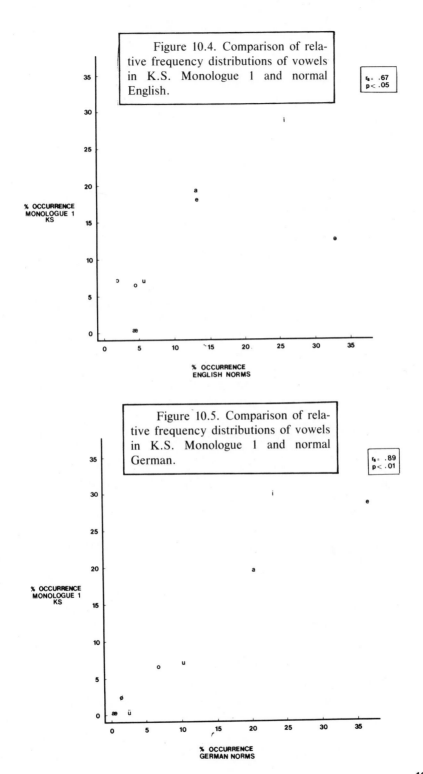

Figure 10.4. Comparison of relative frequency distributions of vowels in K.S. Monologue 1 and normal English.

$r_s = .67$
$p < .05$

% OCCURRENCE
MONOLOGUE 1
KS

% OCCURRENCE
ENGLISH NORMS

Figure 10.5. Comparison of relative frequency distributions of vowels in K.S. Monologue 1 and normal German.

$r_s = .89$
$p < .01$

% OCCURRENCE
MONOLOGUE 1
KS

% OCCURRENCE
GERMAN NORMS

English and German, [i] occurs in the jargon with a higher than normal frequency. The relative frequency of [a] is consistent with German, but greater than the expected frequency for English. In addition, the frequencies of [o] and [ɔ] exceed the English norms; the frequencies of [ə] and [æ] are lower than English norms.

The pattern of phoneme distribution in the monologue sample is also observed in a second spontaneous jargon sample, produced in the context of a dialogue with a normal speaker. Figure 10.6 displays the relation between the monologue and dialogue samples. The distributions are nearly identical. In both cases, the consonant distributions indicate a preference for [r] and [s], whereas glides [y,w,h] and velars [k,g] are noticeably rare. The vowel distributions in these samples are given in Figure 10.7. In both monologue and dialogue jargon there is a preference for [i] and [a].

THE MONOLOGUE SAMPLE

In the case report, it was pointed out that K.S. often included in his jargon sequences of sounds resembling words spoken to him by his examiners. Presumably, the monologue sample, representing the longest uninterrupted episode of jargon, is least likely to have incorporated repetitions of speech addressed to him or, in general, to have been influenced by linguistic stimuli in his environment. It was therefore predicted that this sample would differ significantly from other samples of jargon, in which linguistic context was immediately present. Recall that all samples of jargon other than the monologue sample were produced either in conversation with a normal speaker or in response to written words.

The monologue sample was found to be significantly correlated with all other samples of K.S.'s speech on a Spearman Rank Order Correlation Test. Nonetheless, the monologue sample is the only sample of K.S.'s jargon that was found to deviate from a normal English consonant distribution to a significantly greater extent than did the sample from the normal control speaker on a test of the significance of the difference between rank order correlation coefficients ($z = 2.158$). This result taken together with the fact that the monologue sample is the only sample to have been produced in the absence of an immediate linguistic context, may suggest that the distinct quality of the monologue sample is attributable to the absence of an immediate linguistic context and that it is this sample that reveals properties intrinsic to the jargon. What then are these properties, and is there evidence of them in other jargon samples?

Articulatory Parameters

Characterizing the monologue sample in terms of articulatory parameters, we find the most common place of articulation for consonants to be labial (relative frequency = 45.20%). Velars occur least often, with a frequency of 1.9%. Dental/alveolar consonants account for 35.04% of the

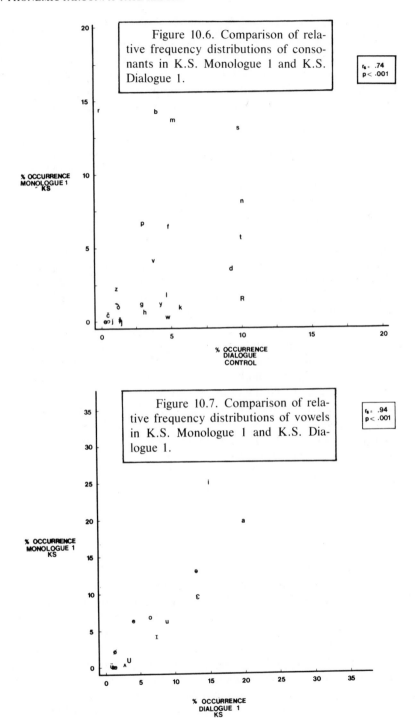

Figure 10.6. Comparison of relative frequency distributions of consonants in K.S. Monologue 1 and K.S. Dialogue 1.

Figure 10.7. Comparison of relative frequency distributions of vowels in K.S. Monologue 1 and K.S. Dialogue 1.

consonants; alveopalatals, 15.07%; uvulars, 1.56%; and other, 1.23%. The most common stop is labial; the most common fricative is dental/alveolar. Nasals occur more often in the labial place of articulation than in the dental. With respect to voicing features, labials are more commonly voiced and labiodentals, voiceless. Dental/alveolar consonants tend to be voiceless. Among the relatively few velars, there is a preference for the voiced member.

In standard English, dental/alveolars, occurring with a relative frequency of 63.58% by far outnumber labials (22.11%) and velars (14.31%). The reduced frequency of dental/alveolars in K.S. may reflect the fact that in English, the dental/alveolar class includes the liquid /r/, while for K.S. that phoneme is an alveo-palatal or less frequently uvular. As in K.S. the stop manner is most common among labials. In contrast to K.S., who prefers labial nasals, the dental/alveolar nasal is more common in normal English. The predominance of voiced over voiceless labial phonemes is not characteristic of normal English, while the predominance of voiceless over voiced dental/alveolars is. It is typical of speakers of southern German dialects to produce all stops and fricatives as voiceless (Moulton, 1967).

In the articulation of vowels, the position of the tongue in the oral cavity varies along two dimensions: front to back and high to low. In terms of the front to back dimension, front vowels [i, ü, e, ø, ε, æ], occurring with a relative frequency of 42.96%, are preferred over central vowels [ɪ,ə], which account for 17.31%, and back vowels [ʊ, ʌ, a, u, o, ɔ], with a relative frequency of 39.72%. From the point of view of tongue height, high vowels [i, ü, ɪ, ʊ, u] produced with a relative frequency of 36.36% are less frequent than mid vowels [e, ε, ø, ə, ʌ, ɔ, o], with a frequency of 43.85%, but are preferred over low vowels [æ, a] at 19.80%. On a two-dimensional plane, the most common vowels are the high front [i] at 24.91%, the low back [a] at 19.43%.

In normal English, front vowels are most frequent at 43.11%, followed by central vowels at 32.73%, and back vowels at 24.15%.

Consonant Clusters

The frequency distribution of consonant combinations was analyzed for each of three positions within the word-like units of K.S.'s jargon: unit initial, intervocalic, and unit final. For each position, different combinations were found to predominate. Recall that the unit over which a position is defined is a sequence bounded by an increase in relative pause duration.

The most frequent initial clusters are [br] (36%; 9 occurrences), [vw] (20%; 5), and [pr] (12%; 3). In normal English, only [pr] is relatively frequent in this position. Among intervocalic clusters, [br] is by far the most frequent (13%), with [ts] next most frequent (8%). The four most common final clusters are [ts] (46%; 25), [ps] (11%; 6), [ns] (11%; 6) and [sč] (9%; 5). Of 3-consonant clusters, [sts] is most frequent.

Thus, across positions, the most common consonant combinations in K.S.'s monologue jargon sample are [br] and [ts]. The cluster [br] alone accounts for 13% of the 2-consonant clusters and 11% of the total. Among 2-consonant clusters in normal English, [br] occurs with a relative frequency of .44% and [ts] with a relative frequency of .67%. Of the total inventory of consonant clusters in normal English, .37% are [br] and .56% are [ts]. Thus we may conclude that K.S.'s monologue jargon reflects a more skewed distribution of consonant clusters than is found in normal English, where the most common cluster, [nt], represents only 5.33% of all clusters across positions within a word.

Summary

Of all jargon samples analyzed in the present study, the longest episode of jargon, referred to as the monologue sample, shows the most extreme departure from the normal phoneme frequency distribution for English and German consonants. This sample is characterized by a marked preference for [r], [s], [m], and [b], in that order. In the case of vowels, the high proportions of [i] and [a] are not incompatible with the general pattern of the distribution of normal English and German. Yet, the diminished frequency of [ə] and the absence of the characteristically English [æ] suggests a German vowel system.

In terms of phonemic features, it appears that the most frequently produced phonemes in this sample, across both consonants and vowels, are those articulated in the front of the oral cavity, with phoneme frequencies decreasing as articulation moves toward the back. Thus, labials [m, b, p] tend to be more common than dental/alveolars [t, n, d], and dental/alveolars more common than velars [k, g]. With respect to vowels, front vowels [i, ü, e, ø, ɛ, æ] are more common than central [ɪ, ə] and back [ʊ, ʌ, a, u, o, ɔ] vowels.

Across initial, intervocal, and final positions defined over an interpausal sequence, the most common consonant combinations are [br] and [ts]. Due to the very high frequency of these combinations, the jargon reflects a more skewed consonant cluster distribution than is found in normal English.

Reading Jargon

Having compared the phoneme frequency distribution found in spontaneously produced jargon with that found in normal English and German, it is of interest to determine whether the distribution in the jargon is a fixed property of jargon production in K.S., or whether it can be manipulated by asking the patient to read written words.

SINGLE-WORD READING

Individual English words, letters, and numbers, printed on 8″ × 10″ index cards, were presented to the patient one at a time. The target items are given in order of presentation in Appendix 3A. Phonemically transcribed responses to each stimulus card are displayed in Appendix 3B, where target words and letters are listed alphabetically and target numbers appear in an ordered list. The column labeled "Reference Number of Related Items" indicates numbers of those items listed in Appendix 3A by order of presentation, that are phonologically or morphologically related to the target word on a given trial. This cross-index demonstrates the lack of correspondence found between responses to, for example, minimally contrastive pairs of words, in terms of both number of syllables and identity of phonemes.

It seems reasonable to assume that if K.S.'s jargon responses can be shown to be phonemically related to target items, such relationships will be most convincingly demonstrated by cases in which it is clear that the appearance of a phone in a jargon response cannot be attributed to the high probability of occurrence of that phone in the jargon generally. Given the low frequency of occurrence of velar consonants in K.S.'s jargon across samples in this investigation, we shall consider the distribution of velar consonants in K.S.'s responses to target words that contain velars as representative of the degree to which the jargon response is phonemically related to the target.

The proportion of instances in which K.S.'s response to a velar-initial target word includes a velar consonant in some position in his utterance, is .304 (7 out of 23 occurrences). When the target word includes a velar in any position, the proportion of instances in which K.S.'s response includes a velar is .286 (20/70). On the other hand, in target words that do not in fact include a velar consonant, K.S. produces a velar with a relative frequency equal to .277 (18/66). Thus, the likelihood of producing a velar consonant in response to a given target word appears to be independent of the presence or absence of a velar consonant in that target. As a result, one can argue that there is no systematic correspondence between the presence of a given phone in a target and the presence of that phone in K.S.'s response to that target.

Upon each presentation, the patient took the stimulus card in his hand and, often using his index finger to guide him across the card, uttered a lengthy sequence of sounds, regardless of the syllabic length of the target. Following each response, the patient would pause, hand the investigator the card he had just read and reach for the next stimulus card. Thus, although the structure of the patient's verbal response was manifestly independent of the actual target, his behavior indicated that he believed himself to be completing the task appropriately.

One particular characteristic of his responses is noteworthy. Frequently, after producing a sequence of syllables at a normal intensity level, the patient's voice began to trail off into a faint whisper, indicating a failure to regulate, in this case, to "turn off," his vocal machinery, as suggested by the notion of pressured speech often associated with jargon production.

In view of the lack of correspondence between stimulus and response, one might wonder whether the patient's behavior was in fact stimulus bound, or whether it was entirely independent of the particular stimulus. A halting verbal response to the target letter Q, as well as a nonverbal response that did not conform to the stereotypic pattern of behavior characterizing the preceding and subsequent responses, suggested that the stimulus items might be presenting different levels of difficulty for the patient. In addition, on many occasions, K.S. was able to correctly point to the referent of a word on a stimulus card, for example, CHIN, BED, indicating that the semantic structure underlying these written words was available to him. These observations motivated the construction of a second reading task, as it was not clear whether K.S. would have responded in his typical fashion to a graphemic sequence that had no semantic content.

This second task was designed to investigate the extent to which K.S.'s responses to words were stimulus bound. In essence, this task was a lexical decision task. The target items to be read included, not only English and German words, but also Hebrew words, representing a language presumably unfamiliar to him, and pronounceable nonsense words. Items presented in this task are listed in Appendix 3C.

K.S. responded to the English and German words in the stereotypic pattern of behavior described earlier. He indicated rejection of the Hebrew and nonsense words by spending much time examining the cards with a puzzled expression on his face, as opposed to responding immediately as he did for English and German words. Moreover, in response to these nonwords, he tended to shake his head, turn his palms upward in resignation, and on several occasions uttered *no*. This behavior suggests that K.S. can recognize the difference between a word and a nonword, and thus that the jargon he produced in response to a target item is indeed to some extent determined by the lexical properties of the target item.

CONNECTED-PROSE READING

The stereotypic quality of K.S.'s jargon is obvious in the consistency between the distribution of phones in his spontaneous speech and the distribution of phones in his reading of written text. Indeed, no apparent relation was found between the single words presented to K.S. in the single-word reading task and his responses to those target words. Yet, in the overall pattern of jargon elicited in response to short texts of connected prose, there is evidence to suggest an element of context dependence in jargon production. In particular, the striking similarity between the samples of jargon produced in reading the same passage twice suggests that the phoneme distribution in his jargon is not fixed, but rather may be responsive to the actual content of the text being read.

The practically diagonal difference curve in Figure 10.8 suggests that K.S.'s jargon may be to some extent text specific. This curve shows the difference between consonants in two jargon readings of the same text on the same day. The near identity of phoneme distributions contrasts with the greater difference between readings of the different texts on the same day (Figure 10.9).

Figures 10.10 and 10.11 illustrate this difference for vowels. Although vowel distributions tend to be quite consistent across texts, the difference between readings of the same text is still smaller, especially with respect to the relative frequency of [i].

To precisely what extent does the specific phonemic content of a text impose constraints on the content of K.S.'s jargon? Figures 10.12 and 10.13 plot the jargon produced in the reading of English and German passages against readings of those same passages by the control speaker. K.S.'s jargon differs from the expected curve as a result of the higher proportion of those consonants typically preferred in his jargon across all samples. Similarly, those consonants that tend to occur rarely in all samples account for the negative deviation from the expected.

For vowels, the only major difference between K.S. and the control for readings in both languages (Figures 10.14 and 10.15) is K.S.'s lower proportion of [ə]. In the English reading, K.S. produces higher than expected proportions of [i], [ɛ], and [a], and lower than expected proportions of [ʌ] and [ə]. In reading German, K.S.'s vowels are more consistent with the control distribution, but perhaps this is only because the distribution of vowels produced by the control is similar to that of the monologue sample.

We may conclude from this comparison with the control reader that the identity between the respective phonemic contents of the two readings of the same text does not stem from specific phonemic constraints within the text. On the contrary, these graphs illustrate the extent to which it is the stereotypic pattern alone that predetermines the quality and content of K.S.'s jargon reading.

In order to determine more conclusively whether specific phonemic content plays a role in constraining K.S.'s jargon production, he was asked to read an English passage edited to include only one instance of the consonant [b], which had earlier been found to predominate in the jargon. The jargon reading, however, included no fewer [b]s than were produced in reading an unweighted passage in which 11 [b]s were actually present.

There appears, then, to be no evidence that the text imposed specific phonemic constraints. There is, however, evidence of a reading mode in jargon production. Let us reconsider Figures 10.9, 10.12, and 10.13. As we have seen, the reading jargon reflects reduced proportions of consonants [m] and [b], which were preferred in the spontaneously produced monologue jargon, and increased proportions of consonants common in normal English, namely [t] and [d]. In these respects, the reading jargon differs less from normal English than does the monologue jargon. In other words, in the

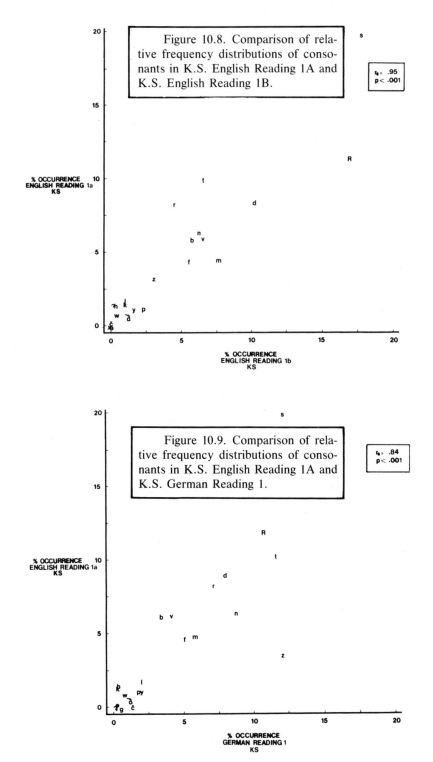

Figure 10.8. Comparison of relative frequency distributions of consonants in K.S. English Reading 1A and K.S. English Reading 1B.

Figure 10.9. Comparison of relative frequency distributions of consonants in K.S. English Reading 1A and K.S. German Reading 1.

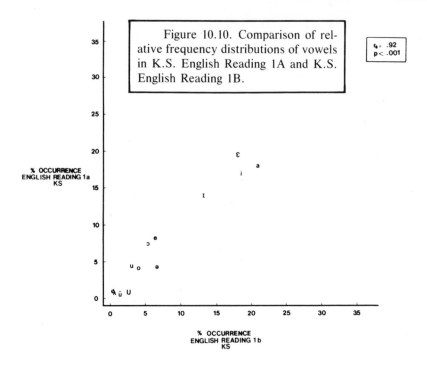

Figure 10.10. Comparison of relative frequency distributions of vowels in K.S. English Reading 1A and K.S. English Reading 1B.

$r_s = .92$
$p < .001$

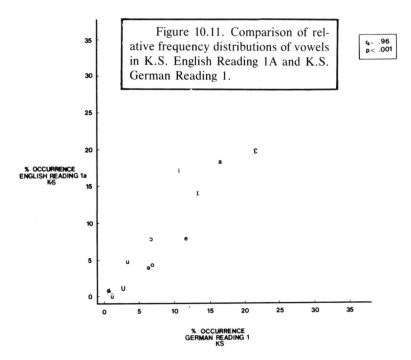

Figure 10.11. Comparison of relative frequency distributions of vowels in K.S. English Reading 1A and K.S. German Reading 1.

$r_s = .96$
$p < .001$

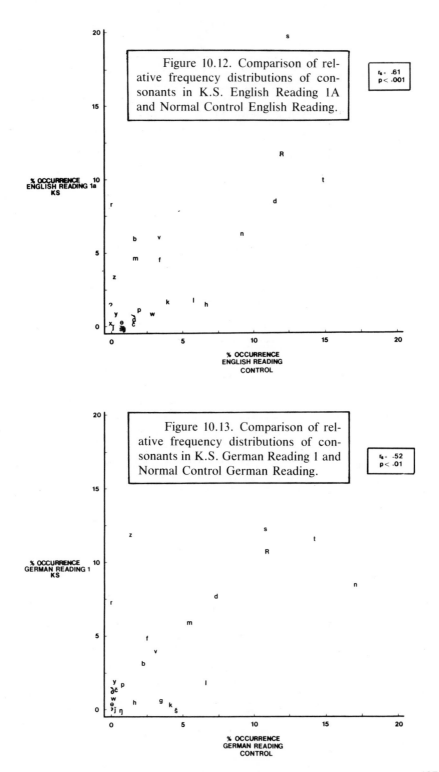

Figure 10.12. Comparison of relative frequency distributions of consonants in K.S. English Reading 1A and Normal Control English Reading.

$r_a = .61$
$p < .001$

% OCCURRENCE
ENGLISH READING 1a
KS

% OCCURRENCE
ENGLISH READING
CONTROL

Figure 10.13. Comparison of relative frequency distributions of consonants in K.S. German Reading 1 and Normal Control German Reading.

$r_a = .52$
$p < .01$

% OCCURRENCE
GERMAN READING 1
KS

% OCCURRENCE
GERMAN READING
CONTROL

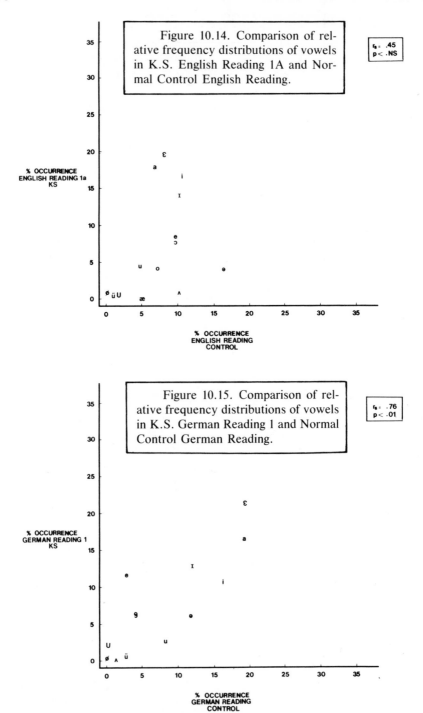

Figure 10.14. Comparison of relative frequency distributions of vowels in K.S. English Reading 1A and Normal Control English Reading.

$r_s = .45$
$p < .NS$

Figure 10.15. Comparison of relative frequency distributions of vowels in K.S. German Reading 1 and Normal Control German Reading.

$r_s = .76$
$p < .01$

presence of a text, K.S.'s jargon patterns more closely with a normal English phoneme distribution.

Figure 10.16 shows the difference between consonant distribution in the normal control speaker's conversational speech and K.S.'s dialogue jargon. Figure 10.17 compares consonant distribution in the control's conversational speech and K.S.'s monologue jargon. The vowel content of the conversational jargon is represented in Figure 10.18, where it is compared with vowels in the control's spontaneous speech. Major departures from the expected distribution consist in much higher proportions of [a] and [ɔ], and lower proportions of [ɪ] and [ʌ].

Possible evidence of conversational constraints is presented in Figure 10.19. Here two samples of jargon produced in the context of dialogues with normal speakers (and obtained 2 years apart) are shown to be more similar to each other in phoneme distribution than either one is to the monologue sample (see Figures 10.20 and 10.6). The fact that the jargon produced in dialogue with a normal speaker has a less deviant phoneme distribution suggests either specific but not consistent influence of the auditory linguistic context of the conversation, or nonspecific psychological effects induced by the conversational situation, for example, by the requirement that participants in a dialogue attend to one another.

SUMMARY

Reading jargon does not appear to reflect specific phonemic content in a written text. Rather, the jargon seems to be predetermined by a stereotypic pattern of production. There are, however, indications that jargon production is sensitive to the presence of normal language context. Visually, a written text provides constraints on reading jargon; auditorily, the normal speech of a partner in conversation may constrain spontaneous jargon.

Segmental Properties of Jargon

The phoneme distributions for jargon produced in reading passages of connected prose are displayed in Figure 10.9. The preference for [r] and [s], as well as the paucity of [y], [w], [h], [k], [ð] and [g], are compatible with the pattern observed in spontaneous jargon.

The vowel distributions in these samples are given in Figure 10.11. Although the reading jargon is consistent with the monologue jargon in its high proportion of [a], it does not show a consistently high proportion of [i], demonstrating, in fact, a strong preference for [ε].

Figures 10.9 and 10.11 in effect summarize the findings with regard to internal consistency of K.S.'s jargon. Figure 10.9 indicates that all jargon samples are consistent with the monologue sample in terms of relative proportions between consonants. Of the most common consonants, only

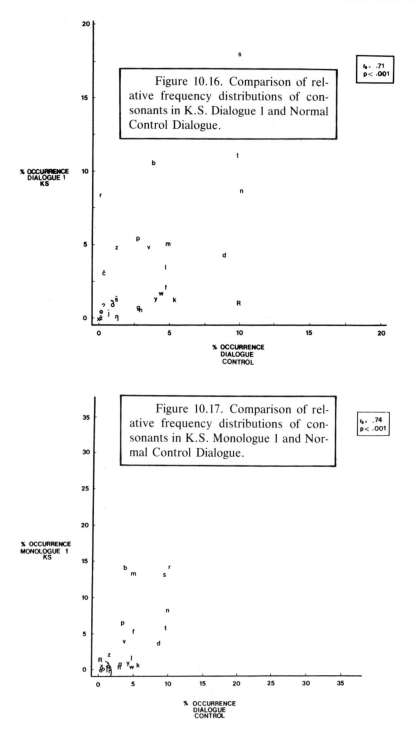

Figure 10.16. Comparison of relative frequency distributions of consonants in K.S. Dialogue 1 and Normal Control Dialogue.

Figure 10.17. Comparison of relative frequency distributions of consonants in K.S. Monologue 1 and Normal Control Dialogue.

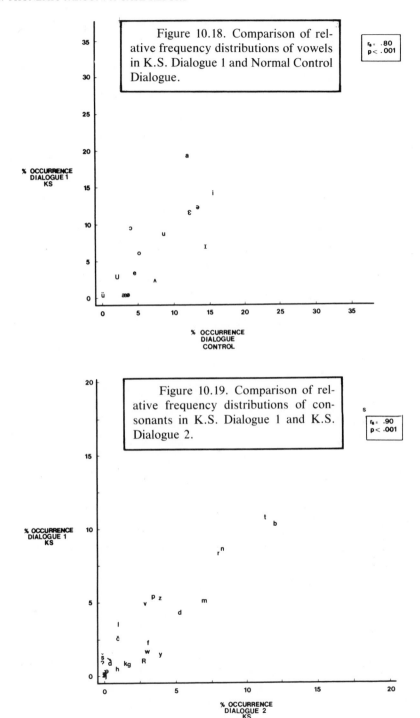

Figure 10.18. Comparison of relative frequency distributions of vowels in K.S. Dialogue 1 and Normal Control Dialogue.

Figure 10.19. Comparison of relative frequency distributions of consonants in K.S. Dialogue 1 and K.S. Dialogue 2.

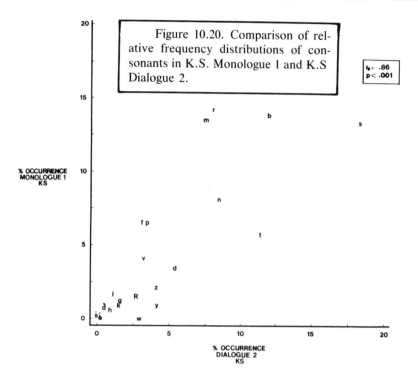

Figure 10.20. Comparison of relative frequency distributions of consonants in K.S. Monologue 1 and K.S Dialogue 2.

$r_s = .86$
$p < .001$

[r][3] and [s] are consistently highest in frequency. The high correlation among jargon samples is indicated by the high levels of significance found for consonants on Spearman Rank Order Correlation Tests. The internal consistency of the jargon is furthermore confirmed by the fact that, whereas the difference between the values of correlation coefficients for samples from the normal control approaches significance ($t = 1.896$), the difference between correlation coefficient values for samples from K.S. is quite minimal ($t = .294$).

Figure 10.11 illustrates the most salient property of K.S.'s vowel distribution, which is the sustained and pronounced preference for [a]. The higher consistency within reading and within spontaneous speech than across the two modes is striking.

The following patterns emerge across samples: For consonants, all samples of K.S.'s jargon indicate consistently high proportions of [r] and [s] and consistently low proportions of [y], [w], [h], [k], [ð], and [g]. In terms of vowels, [a] is found to predominate in all samples, while there is

---

[3] An alveopalatal [r] and a uvular [R] are found to be in almost complementary distribution across reading and spontaneous speech: The uvular is most common in samples of reading; the alveopalatal, in spontaneous speech. These phonetic variants are theoretically in free variation in Standard German although native speakers tend to produce the uvular variant almost exclusively (Moulton, 1962).

a consistently low frequency of occurrence for the rounded front vowels [ü, ø], the central vowels [ɪ, ə,] and the low front [æ]. In all samples the diphthong [ai] is the most common vowel combination.

CONSONANTS: VOWEL RATIO

The proportion of consonants to vowels in the jargon tends to be compatible with a normal German distribution. In German, consonants outnumber vowels by about 1.6:1 (61%:39%); in English, the ratio is about 1.8:1 (64%:36%). In all jargon sampled there is a slight shift away from the normal ratios. The shift is most extreme in the monologue jargon, which consists of 1.1 consonants to every vowel (53%:47%).

Sequential Properties of Jargon

Both in conversation and in reading, K.S. produces fluent and clearly articulated jargon. A distinct reading style is characterized by very deliberate pronunciation and great concentration on performance, often reinforced by the use of his index finger to guide him through the text. The deliberate quality is expressed in his tendency to release stop consonants and aspirate those that are voiceless. This tendency suggests the Standard German practice of nearly always releasing and aspirating final stops. In fact, the authoritative grammar of German pronunciation, *Siebs*, prescribes strong aspiration for initial and medial positions as well.

The rhythmic pattern of K.S.'s reading is often iambic, for example, *opay' edis' bedens'*. His intonation, defined over interpausal units, is characterized by a flat contour which falls prepausally. These properties of his reading speech are in striking contrast to his conversational speech in which rhythmic structure is more variable and intonation fluctuates, often producing a singsong quality. Note that a similar contrast between reading and conversational speech is found in normal speakers.

A greater than normal flow of speech is characteristic of his jargon in general. In conversation this is simply an impression, but the impression is confirmed by studies of jargon reading, where he is found to produce approximately twice the number of syllables (measured in CVC units) produced by the control reading the same texts.

The ratio of single consonants to consonant clusters is 1.95 for conversational jargon and 1.83 for reading jargon. A normal English speaker typically produces 2.59 single consonants for every consonant cluster.

Transitional properties of diphone sequences were determined for the dialogue sample at Time 1 and the English reading sample at Time 1a. Vowel clusters and consonant clusters, as well as consonant–vowel clusters (CV) and vowel–consonant clusters (VC) were included in the analysis. Vowel and consonant clusters were analyzed in terms of place of articulation; consonant clusters were also analyzed in terms of manner of articulation and voicing features. Appendix 5 contains matrices that present the data on phone pairs in terms of these features. In each matrix, the property in question for the first member of a pair is given in the rows; the property for the second member is given in the columns. Each box contains the actual frequencies of occurrence of diphone sequences in these samples. The Øs in effect indicate pause boundaries between units of jargon production. The box in a matrix corresponding to Ø followed by Ø indicates a relatively long pause between units.

Let us consider first the properties of the Dialogue Time 1 sample as represented in these matrices. The data suggest that units of production most often both begin and end on consonants and these consonants most often have a central point of articulation. With respect to clusters, it appears that the most common vowel sequences are low back vowels followed by high front vowels. In consonant clusters, the most common transition for place of articulation seems to be to a central consonant, a sequence of two central consonants being the most common. In terms of manner, stops are most commonly followed by fricatives and liquids. Affricate sequences constitute the only instances in which manner remains unchanged across a sequence of two phones. For the most part, the voicing property of the first consonant is maintained across the sequence, except in the case of voiced fricatives, which are followed by voiceless stops. Regarding CV sequences, place of articulation tends to move backward, with most pairs consisting of central consonants followed by back vowels. In VC sequences, the most common transition is from a back vowel to a central consonant.

Turning to the reading jargon, one finds that, as in the dialogue sample, both the initial and final phones in a unit of production are most often consonants. As in the dialogue jargon, vowel clusters most often consist of a low back vowel followed by a high front vowel, and consonant clusters tend to have a central consonant as their second segment, with the most common CC sequence consisting of two central consonants. As for manner of articulation, it is most often the case that consonant sequences consist of a stop followed by a fricative. In general, the voicing feature remains constant across the members of a CC pair. Thus, the most common consonant sequence is a voiceless stop followed by a voiceless fricative.

Consonant–vowel sequences most often consist of central consonants followed by front vowels. In the typical vowel–consonant sequence, a front vowel is followed by a central consonant. In general, for all three places of articulation of the vowel, the consonant is central.

A sequential pattern found to recur in spontaneous jargon samples takes the form /b (r) V (DENTAL C) $\frac{s}{z}$/ where V is a vowel, C is a consonant, and parentheses indicate phones that occur optionally. Forms that appear to be variations of this pattern may be accounted for as resulting from processes of epenthesis, metathesis, or diphthongization operating on the basic string. Thus, the addition of an epenthetic [ə] separating the [br] cluster in the basic form will yield the observed unit of production [bəras]. Metathesis in the / ...rV..../ portion of the string will produce the observed sequence [bɛrz]. Finally, diphthongization will derive forms with diphthongs in the vowel nucleus, such as [biɛs].

Most of the stereotyped sequences occur in the monologue sample; of those found in the dialogue sample, most occur as variants of this stereotyped form. One might therefore argue that the sequential properties of the monologue sample are more constrained than those of the dialogue sample. That is, the appearance of these variants in the dialogue sample may indicate that the jargon produced in this sample manifests a less rigidly structured sequence and that the mechanism operating in the production of the monologue jargon to induce a highly stereotyped output is weaker or less effective in the dialogue jargon.

Regarding the difference between these spontaneous samples in terms of sequential properties, it is of interest that they differ with respect to the feature of phones repeated in contiguous perseverations. In the monologue sample, labiodental fricatives are most commonly perseverated, whereas in the dialogue sample such perseverations are most common on dental stops.

K.S.'s tendency to produce open juncture between CVC units (that is, to terminate each unified articulatory gesture with a consonant phone, as in *fot-an-bed-ist,* rather than with a vowel, as in *fo-tan-be-dist*) appears to violate the rules of both English and German pronunciation. In English, a consonant or consonant sequence that begins a word is grouped with the following vowel if the preceding vowel is long or unstressed. In German, according to Schulz and Griesbach (1960) "a single consonant or the last of a sequence of consonants is grouped with the following vowel [p.11]."

In consonant sequences of English words, place usually remains constant across the sequence while manner changes. The affricate sequences in K.S.'s dialogue jargon thus contribute a nonEnglish quality to his speech. However, the sequential properties of consonants in K.S.'s dialogue sample are similar to standard English in that, for both, the most frequent initial consonant is centrally articulated.

K.S.'s tendency to produce the fricative [s] followed by a stop is characteristic of English, but not of German, in which the sequence [š] plus stop is more common. (Indeed, K.S. produces several such affricate plus stop sequences as well.) Similarly, the occurrence of [sl, sn, sm] sequences in the jargon reflects English rather than German. There is yet another way in which K.S.'s jargon differs from Standard German speech: Whereas most native German speakers use the uvular [R] exclusively, or at least in the environment preceding a vowel, for K.S., the alveopalatal variant is more common in conversational speech in general and, specifically, in

the environment preceding a vowel. Consistent, however, with German phonology is the presence of affricate plus stop sequences, and the relative
absence of final voiced stops in K.S.'s jargon.

Longitudinal Aspects

We turn now to the longitudinal aspects of the investigation and to the
question of recovery. Does the sound pattern of K.S.'s jargon, as measured
by phoneme frequency distribution, change over a 2-year period? If so,
does the change reflect recovery toward the distribution characteristic of
normal speech?

Figure 10.19 illustrates the similarity between the conversational jargon
produced at Time 1, which is 5 months post-onset, and the conversational
jargon produced at Time 2, 30 months post-onset.

In Figures 10.21 and 10.22, the curve represents the difference between
the distributions of consonants in passages read at Time 1 and again at
Time 2. For both the English and German passages, the frequency of
occurrence of [b] increases over time, as the frequency of occurrence of
[r] and [m] diminishes. In addition, [s] occurs more frequently in the German
reading at Time 2. Notice that for both passages there is a large increase
at Time 2 in the proportions of [t], [n], and, to a lesser extent, [g]. These
consonants accounted for much of the negative deviation from the expected
distribution at Time 1.

Thus, in contrast to the conversational jargon at Time 2, which reflects
the production bias for consonants established at Time 1, the reading jargon
at Time 2 is compatible with a shift toward a normal distribution.

Regarding the change in the vowel distribution over time, Figures 10.23,
10.24, and 10.25 show that, across readings and conversational speech,
there is a significant increase in the relative frequency of [i] and a less
marked increase in the frequency of [a] and [o]. Furthermore, there tends
to be an increase in the occurrence of the diphthong [ai]. For the reading
samples alone, [ə] increases as the proportions of [ɪ] and [ɛ] decrease. It
appears, then, that the direction of change in the vowel distribution reflects
the production bias found in the monologue sample.

A pattern reflecting higher Spearman rank order correlations among
samples within Time 2 than among samples within Time 1, indicates that
K.S.'s jargon is more homogeneous at Time 2. Table 10.2 presents the
correlation coefficients. The table displays the following results:

1. Higher correlations obtain between readings of different texts at
Time 2 than between readings of the same text across Times 1 and 2, where
the difference between the r's is significant at the .01 level, ($z = 4.076$).

2. Higher correlations obtain between conversational speech and each
of the readings at Time 2 than between conversational speech and each of
the readings at Time 1.

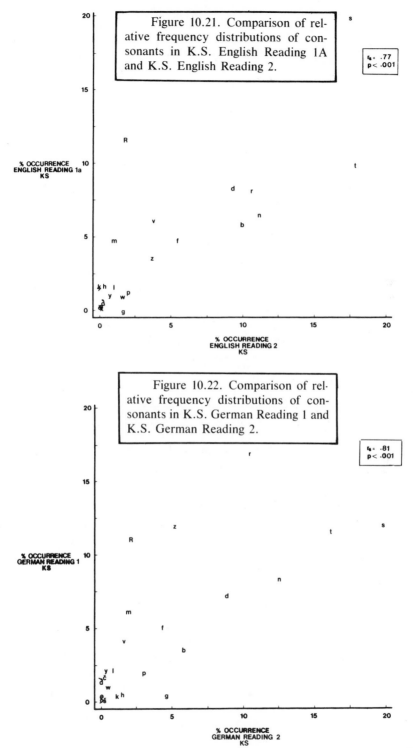

Figure 10.21. Comparison of relative frequency distributions of consonants in K.S. English Reading 1A and K.S. English Reading 2.

$r_s = .77$
$p < .001$

% OCCURRENCE
ENGLISH READING 1a
KS

% OCCURRENCE
ENGLISH READING 2
KS

Figure 10.22. Comparison of relative frequency distributions of consonants in K.S. German Reading 1 and K.S. German Reading 2.

$r_s = .81$
$p < .001$

% OCCURRENCE
GERMAN READING 1
KS

% OCCURRENCE
GERMAN READING 2
KS

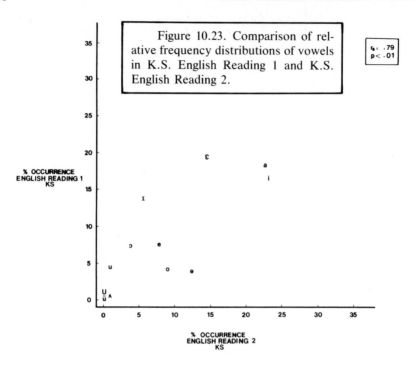

Figure 10.23. Comparison of relative frequency distributions of vowels in K.S. English Reading 1 and K.S. English Reading 2.

$r_s = .79$
$p < .01$

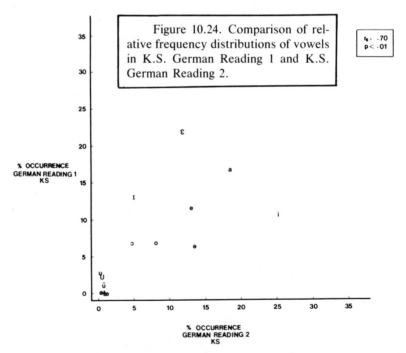

Figure 10.24. Comparison of relative frequency distributions of vowels in K.S. German Reading 1 and K.S. German Reading 2.

$r_s = .70$
$p < .01$

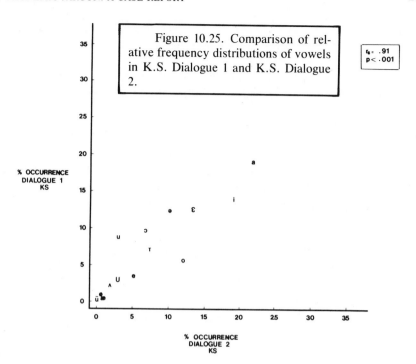

Figure 10.25. Comparison of relative frequency distributions of vowels in K.S. Dialogue 1 and K.S. Dialogue 2.

$r_s = .91$
$p < .001$

3. Across Times 1 and 2, conversational speech samples are more highly correlated than any two reading samples.

Together, these results suggest that the influence of a written text on the quality of K.S.'s jargon increased over time.

With respect to C:V ratio, there appears to be no major change over time. The dialogue samples at Times 1 and 2 both consist of 59% consonants

TABLE 10.2.

Correlations among Samples of K.S.'s Jargon[a]

	GR1	GR2	ER1	ER2	D1	D2
GR1		.81[b]	.84	.86	.79	.78
GR2	.70**		.79	.91	.79	.82
ER1	.96***	.67*		.77	.74	.79
ER2	.78**	.90***	.79**		.84	.82
D1	.79***	.71**	.87***	.84***		.90
D2	.85***	.83***	.85***	.91***	.91***	

[a] Values for consonants above diagonal. Values for vowels below diagonal.
[b] All consonant correlations $p < .001$.
* $p < .05$.
** $p < .01$.
*** $p < .001$.

and 41% vowels. The mean ratio in the reading jargon also remains relatively unchanged, with 59% consonants:41% vowels at Time 1 and 58% consonants:42% vowels at Time 2.

Finally, the longitudinal analysis indicates the tendency toward augmentation found in K.S.'s jargon at both Time 1 and Time 2 (see Table 10.3).

SUMMARY

In conclusion, there is no evidence of recovery. What we do observe is evidence that the jargon is more homogeneous across samples obtained at 30 months post-onset (Time 2) than across samples obtained at 5 months postonset (Time 1). There is no indication that the homogeneity stems from an across-the-board enhancement of the production bias found at Time 1. The important change over time is not in the content of the jargon, but rather in the context-sensitivity of the jargon production. At Time 2, the jargon is apparently more sensitive to the presence of orthographic context, insofar as reading jargon at Time 2 is observed to deviate more than at Time 1 from the monologue sample's distribution and conversational jargon is observed to deviate less.

SUMMARY OF RESULTS

The results of the present investigation may be summarized as follows:

1. K.S. produces virtually all of the sounds of normal English and German.

2. Although overall the frequency distribution of sounds in his jargon is significantly correlated with the distribution found for normal speakers, in terms of individual phonemes the two distributions differ, largely because of a greater than expected proportion of labials in the jargon.

3. Across samples, the jargon is characterized by a stereotypic, repetitious quality attributable to the consistent preference for /r/ and /s/ among consonants and /a/ among vowels.

TABLE 10.3.
Length of Reading Samples in Syllables

Text	K.S.	Normal control	Ratio K.S./control
German Reading 1	396	275	1.44
German Reading 2	394	—	
English Reading 1	259	147	1.76
English Reading 2	247	—	

4. Units of production tend to be initiated and terminated by central consonants. In vowel clusters, there is a transition from low back to high front. For consonant clusters the sequence is typically a centrally articulated stop followed by a centrally articulated fricative. Manner tends to change across consonant clusters, while voicing remains the same. Thus the most common consonant cluster is a voiceless stop followed by a voiceless fricative. In CV clusters, central consonants are followed by back vowels; in VC clusters, back vowels are followed by central consonants.

5. The jargon elicited on reading tasks essentially conforms to the pattern found in spontaneously produced jargon, indicating a single stereotyped mode of production.

6. Over a period of $\frac{1}{2}$ years, the fixed distributional properties of the jargon do not change. Indeed, there is an appearance of greater homogeneity of the jargon at Time 2, in that the phoneme frequency distributions of samples obtained at the end of the $2\frac{1}{2}$ year period are more similar to one another than are samples obtained at the beginning of that period.

DISCUSSION

Evidence that different aspects of language can be affected to varying degrees depending (among other factors) on the region of the left hemisphere that is damaged, indicates a relationship between the organization of language and the organization of the brain with respect to language. Symptoms of jargonaphasia may provide evidence for the psychological reality of levels of linguistic description insofar as errors may reflect either semantic or phonologically related substitutions. Moreover, aphasic jargon may involve the perseveration[4] of units ranging from single phones to whole words.

Changes in predominantly one or another aspect of language behavior suggest at least some degree of functional independence among the neural mechanisms underlying these aspects of language capacity. In phonemic jargon as seen in K.S., the predominant change in language behavior is that sounds of language are no longer used in a way that conveys linguistic meaning, indicating the extent to which the phonic aspect of language may function autonomously. This is not to say that there may not be meaningful intentions underlying the jargon, but whether or not such intentions exist, they cannot be realized in sound according to any known linguistic system.

How does this change in language behavior manifest itself? First of all, although the overall distribution of sounds in the jargon correlates significantly with the overall distribution in the normal language, the particular order of preference with regard to specific phonemes is consistently

---

[4] In the present usage, this term refers to abnormal persistence and excessive recurrence.

different from normal. The four most common consonants in English are /t, y, r, n/, in that order. K.S., on the other hand, tends to produce /r, s, m, b/ more than any other consonants. Furthermore, in K.S.'s jargon, labials as a class consistently occur in greater than normal proportions; in the sample representing the longest stretches of uninterrupted spontaneous jargon, the proportion of labials is considerably greater than normal. This apparent bias toward labials is reduced, however, when jargon is produced in the presence of normal linguistic context.

How shall we characterize the language behavior in phonemic jargon-aphasia? Since one cannot speak of a phonological system in phonemic jargon, neither can one speak of a phonological disturbance in the sense of violations of phonological rules. But, if the function of the phonological component of language is to map sound configurations onto meanings, it is arguable that what is at issue is a phonological disturbance, where that phonological disturbance consists in an inability to assign linguistic values to phones and therefore a failure to select and sequence phonetic units in a linguistically meaningful way.[5]

It was indicated earlier that, in the reading and the conversation samples, the distribution of phonemes in the jargon is more compatible with the distribution found in normal language, as the dental/alveolar place of articulation becomes predominant. This suggests that the presence of linguistic context may provide K.S. with occasional lexical targets, thus "anchoring" the jargon in a normal phoneme distribution. This anchoring context has the effect of constraining the production bias manifest in the absence of linguistic context. An enhancement of the correlation between K.S.'s distribution and a distribution typical in normals would then be explained by the incorporation into the jargon of some of the phones present in the context. Presumably, phonemes are incorporated into the jargon only sporadically, as the distribution curves for the reading samples did not match those for a normal control reader. Such sporadic behavior is not unusual in aphasia, where there is commonly great variability in performance from one moment to the next. The mechanism underlying the sporadic behavior is not clear. But, because dental/alveolars are common in normal speech, they are likely candidates for inclusion in the jargon. Similarly, because labials are relatively uncommon in normal speech but very common in the jargon, it is likely that they will be replaced when other phonemes are incorporated into the jargon.

The bias toward /r/ and /s/ may be related to the relatively high fre-

---

[5] If phonemic jargonaphasia is a problem in the assignment of phonetic or phonemic values to segments and THEREFORE a problem in the selection and sequencing of units, this property might distinguish phonemic jargonaphasia from phonemic (conduction) aphasia. For, in phonemic (conduction) aphasia, the assignment of phonemic values may be unstable, but the capacity for self-correction indicates that the phonemic value of sounds is preserved and the problem may be simply in selection and sequencing.

quency of those consonants in normal speakers of English and German, as they are among the four most common consonants in these languages: /r/ ranks third in German and second in English; /s/ ranks fourth in both German and English.

Indeed, other investigators of jargon have also found a predisposition toward /r/ and /s/. Green (1969) described a stereotypic sequence recurring in the speech of H.P., which always included the consonant /r/. LeCours and Lhermitte (1972) divide their patient's neologisms into three classes, each of which is characterized by a stereotypic sequence of phonemes. In all three classes, /r, s, b, m/ always occur in one position or another. Finally, the phoneme frequency distribution of a corpus of neologisms from Buckingham and Kertesz (1976) also shows a preference for /r/ and /s/.

The preference for /m/ and /b/, however, has no explanation in terms of occurrence in normal language, given that /m/ ranks seventh in German and eighth in English and /b/ ranks fourteenth in German and fifteenth in English. Perhaps the greater than expected frequencies of these labial consonants is interpretable with reference to Jakobson's implicational hierarchy of phonemic structure (Jakobson, 1939). This hierarchy constitutes Jakobson's theory of a universal phonemic system. Jakobson observed that a child's earliest meaningful utterance consists of a labial stop consonant followed by a vowel and that the opposition between labials and dentals becomes stable in the child's phonology before other oppositions. He noted also that, with respect to the phonemic inventories of the languages of the world, the opposition between labial and dental stops is rarely lacking, whereas other place oppositions are optional. The universality of the labial–dental opposition qualifies this distinction as linguistically fundamental. The priority of labials in the acquisition of speech may be seen to establish that class as a foundation for later phonological development. Thus, the predominance of labials in K.S. may reflect their fundamental role in language.

Although this may be a plausible interpretation of the high frequency of labials in the jargon, relative to the proportion of labials in normal speech, it cannot explain the presence of /r/ and /s/, which do not have the high priority of labial stops in the implicational hierarchy. Still, although one might prefer to find a single explanation for why jargon is what it is, it may in fact be the case that some form of the "nature–nurture" question is as relevant to the study of aphasic jargon as it is to the study of language development. Thus one observes in the jargon a preference for a class of sounds which provides a foundation for phonological development and for the phonemic systems of the languages of the world, and for which the articulators happen to be the most visible and manipulable. In this regard, the jargon may be reflecting the salience of labials in perception and production. On the other hand, the high proportions of /r/ and /s/ in the jargon may indicate that frequent exposure to sounds in the environment also influences the content of the jargon. In sum, the quality of the jargon may be a product of both linguistic (and perhaps biological) priority (nature) and experience or environmental cultivation (nurture).

CHILD LANGUAGE AND JARGON

The question of a relationship between the child who is acquiring the sounds of his language and the aphasic with a deterioration of the phonological aspect of his language was raised by Jakobson (1939) and Goldstein (1948) who referred to a phenomenon of phonemic "regression" in aphasia. Jakobson formalized this speculation in a hypothesis which predicted that the likelihood of preservation of phonemic categories in the dissolution of language observed in aphasic speech would mirror a universal order of acquisition of phonemic categories by children learning language. That universal order of acquisition is defined by an implicational hierarchy in which the development of certain sounds presupposes the prior development of others. It forms part of the basis of markedness theory, which provides for a notion of naturalness in generative phonology.

A strict interpretation of Jakobson's regression hypothesis, however, requires that the acquisition of phonology be regarded as the acquisition of phonemic categories. For a child to have "acquired" a phonemic category is for him to manifest systematic behavior with respect to the use of the distinctive features defining that category. Thus, the order of preservation of phoneme categories in aphasia predicted by Jakobson must be based on the systematic use of phonemic contrast by the child, and not simply the appearance of a phoneme in the child's inventory. Accordingly, the predictions of the "regression hypothesis" apply to aphasic speech in which there are identifiable target words and where the systematicity of the substitutions can be evaluated. Because K.S.'s jargon does not contain identifiable targets, strictly speaking it does not provide a testing ground for the "regression hypothesis." Nevertheless, it is of interest whether K.S. is more likely to produce phonemes from the less marked categories, which tend to appear early in the acquisition of language.

A preponderance of stop consonants as opposed to fricatives and nasals is predicted as a consequence of the fundamental contrast between stop consonants and vowels. However, K.S.'s jargon tends to reflect just the opposite behavior, consisting of a higher proportion of fricatives than nasals than stops. Indeed, the fricative /s/ and the liquid /r/ are most common in his jargon, yet they are most often found to remain unstable throughout language development (Ingram, 1976; Leopold, 1953).

The jargon does conform to the predictions of the regression hypothesis in several other respects: Front-articulated consonants (ANTERIOR and CORONAL in the Chomsky–Halle distinctive feature system) are more common than back consonants; the most common fricative in the jargon, /s/, has the lowest markedness value for fricatives; the most common vowel phoneme in the jargon is the unmarked /a/. The other vowel commonly observed in the jargon, /i/, also has a low markedness value. These two vowels together with /u/ constitute an optimal minimal vowel system (Chomsky & Halle, 1968). Note that the /u/, which is a high, back vowel, is rather uncommon in the jargon. But, as Chomsky and Halle make no judgment as to whether back or nonback is less marked for nonlow vowels, one might interpret this to indicate a functional equivalence between the front and back high vowels, /i/ and /u/. Thus /u/ can be regarded as superfluous in the presence of /i/ in the jargon.

With respect to markedness values for phonemes in particular positions within a sequence, the high frequency of /b/ in initial position in the jargon is compatible with the suggestion of Chen (1973) that labials are unmarked in syllable-initial position.

Thus, although the phonemic regression hypothesis, broadly interpreted, does not predict the content of K.S.'s jargon, from the point of view of markedness theory the jargon reflects a natural—that is, phonetically plausible—sound inventory. Indeed, the phones that predominate in K.S.'s monologue sample provide an optimal minimum phonemic inventory.[6] With the exception of the class of glides, this subset includes consonants representing each manner of articulation. Stop consonants are represented by /b/, fricatives by /s/, nasals by /m/, and liquids by /r/. With respect to place of articulation, /b/ and /m/ represent labials, while /r/ and /s/ are dental or alveolar. Only the back region of the oral cavity does not appear to be well-represented in the jargon. However, if we shift our perspective from articulatory to acoustic parameters, the gap in this inventory of sounds disappears: Given that labials and velars are acoustically similar, that is, grave and compact (Jakobson, Fant, & Halle, 1952), the absence of velars may be interpreted as a minimization of redundancy within the inventory.

The principle of maximal phonemic contrast is central to Jakobson's theory of language development and dissolution (1939, p. 14). It is therefore of interest that where a more highly marked segment appears in place of a less marked segment, the more highly marked segment provides for greater phonemic contrast within the inventory. Thus, the optimal contrast achieved between a voiced labial stop /b/ and a voiceless dental fricative /s/ explains the lower relative frequency of the expected less marked labial /p/. Note that /b/ and /s/ differ on every parameter—voicing, place of articulation,

---

[6] Strictly speaking, as K.S.'s jargon conveys no meaning, it has no phonemic content, and one cannot speak of phonemes. However, in order to provide a framework for analyzing the jargon, phonemic values have been assigned to sounds in the jargon on the basis of Standard English and German phonemics.

and manner of articulation—whereas the predicted preference for /p/ would have presented less of a contrast. The high frequency of dental/alveolars, represented by /r/ and /s/, might furthermore explain the lower frequency of the expected dental nasal /n/, which would have contributed a lower markedness value than the /m/, which appears more frequently. Optimal vowel contrast is provided by K.S.'s most common vowels, a maximally open /a/ and a maximally close /i/. This tendency toward maximum contrast among sounds, reflects the preservation of a basic principle of the organization of a phonology.

K.S.'s tendency to maintain the same place of articulation in a consonant cluster is consistent with the pattern of behavior in consonant assimilations of children learning language. Vihman (1968) analyzed these consonant assimilations and found that, although in most cases assimilations involve changes in both place and manner features (39%), when only one of those features was assimilated it was more likely to be place (35%) than manner (27%).

In spite of the apparent structural similarities that have been observed between jargon production and the production of sounds in early child language, it is not obvious that the same underlying mechanism will account for both language behaviors. For, it is difficult to imagine that what constitutes a deteriorated language function in an aphasic and a developing language function in a child are attributable to the same neurodynamic events. If they are not, what can be the theoretical implications of a surface similarity that only masks an essential difference in mechanism?

RELATIONSHIP OF PHONEMIC JARGON TO OTHER JARGONS IN FLUENT APHASIA

The phonemic diversity of phonemic jargon stands in contrast to the restricted inventory of sounds found in the jargon stereotypies that form the residual utterances of motor or global aphasics. In such patients, whose aphasias are associated with large perisylvian lesions, the jargon appears as a vestige of fluency in the presence of an otherwise profound motor speech impairment. These utterances usually consist in the repetition of a single CV syllable such as *titi*, but may include a limited extent of phonemic variation with repetition of several CV sequences. These cases may be transitional to others where there is a still richer flow of CV strings consisting of all of the phonemes of the speaker's language (Brown, 1979). Conceivably there is a kind of expansion within the limits of the residual utterance leading to a phonemic jargon of the type described by Peuser and Temp (Chapter 11, this volume). Such cases may be similar to the description of jargon with apraxia by Alajouanine and Lhermitte (1964), where comprehension was said to be relatively well preserved and there was severe oral apraxia. However, it is questionable that a relation exists between the jargon stereotypies of motor and global aphasics and the form of jargon observed in the present case. Of more immediate interest is the relationship between phonemic jargon and the other fluent jargons.

One possibility is that phonemic jargon is a type of deteriorated neologistic jargon. It is generally held that neologisms conform to the phonological constraints of the speaker's language, that is, patients rarely produce consonant clusters not found in their native language, or clusters in initial position that are restricted to final position in the native language. Alliteration and assonance are characteristic of neologistic jargon. The neologisms often incorporate standard morphemes of the language, such as plural markers for nouns and tense markers for verbs. Moreover, as function words are usually intact in neologistic jargon, it is often possible to establish that in most cases neologisms take the place of nouns.[7]

Certain structural relationships between phonemic jargon and neologistic jargon are apparent. Both forms of jargon respect the phonological constraints of standard language. They also share the properties of alliteration and assonance.[8] The most obvious difference between the two jargons is that in neologistic jargon there is a preferential disturbance of nouns, whereas in phonemic jargon all grammatical categories are equally affected. This difference may simply reflect the greater severity of phonemic jargon. Indeed, it is difficult to establish whether or not grammatical morphemes are preserved in phonemic jargon in view of its entirely unintelligible quality.

An order of preference for phonemes that is distinct from the normal pattern may be characteristic of phonemic jargon. Wepman and Jones (1964) provide a brief description of a jargonaphasic with "a profusion of phonemically disorganized combinations." They noted that "although this patient uses a complete phonemic roster, his phoneme distribution appears to be considerably (and statistically) different from that of a matched normal speaker [p. 195]." The statistical treatment applied was not indicated.

Butterworth (1977) found that, as in the present case, and in a case reported by Wepman and Jones (1964), the neologisms produced by his patient did not reflect normal phoneme frequencies. Butterworth compared the frequency of occurrence of the initial phonemes in a corpus of neologisms with their frequency in forms representing other error types and in standard content words. He found that, relative to standard English phoneme frequencies, the mean frequency values for phonemes in neologisms were much lower than for phonemes in other lexical categories. He

[7] The majority of speech errors in normals occur on nouns (Browman, 1978).

[8] It is of interest that semantic jargon as well is characterized by rhyming and other phonological relationships among verbal paraphasias. Kreindler, Calavrezo, and Mihailescu (1971) describe a semantic jargonaphasic in whom "the criterion for selection of [verbal paraphasias and neologisms] was not the semantic one but exclusively the criterion of auditory similarity determined by the rhyme [p.221]."

concluded that the source of neologisms is not the same as the source for other errors.

LeCours and Lhermitte (1972) also found no overall correspondence between the phoneme distribution in neologisms of their patient and phoneme frequencies in French. The neologisms that LeCours and Lhermitte analyzed were composed of nonstandard combinations of standard morphemes.

These findings are compatible with studies indicating the apparent preservation of distributional properties in aphasic speech, only when either (a) neologisms are not included in the analysis (Blumstein, 1973); or (b) the distributional properties are determined over a heterogeneous group of aphasic patients, in which case any differences among aphasia types will have been obscured (Mihailescu, Voinescu, & Fradis, 1967).

If neologistic and phonemic jargon are distinct from other forms of aphasic speech, that distinction may point to a common source of error in both jargons. Evidence of a combined phonological and semantic deficit in neologistic jargon, where phonemic errors occur on incorrectly selected lexical items, is consistent with the finding that neologistic jargon requires a large lesion of posterior T1 and T2 (Henschen, 1922; Kertesz, this volume). In other words, the lesion involves Wernicke's area proper (posterior T1), lesion of which produces phonemic aphasia, PLUS involvement of surrounding temporoparietal "integration" cortex, lesion of which leads to semantic disorders (Brown, 1979). Figures 10.26 and 10.27 illustrate the proposed correlations between lesion sites and types of disorders.

However, evidence that the semantic code is to some extent preserved in K.S. suggests that phonemic jargon may be a severe form of phonemic (conduction) aphasia, in which relatively good comprehension for spoken and written language, along with the ability to self-correct, indicate access to semantic as well as phonological information.

Phonemic (conduction) aphasia is associated with lesions of the posterior superior temporal convolution (T1) (Brown, 1972; Green & Howes, 1977). A study by Damassio (1979) of five cases confirms the relation to

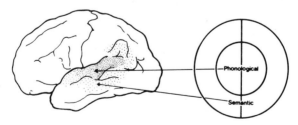

Figure 10.26. Phonological errors occur with lesions of T1; semantic errors occur with lesions of surrounding neocortex.

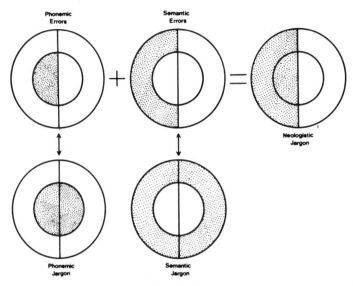

Figure 10.27. Schema of the probable lesion site in unilateral and bilateral phonemic and semantic disorders (refer to Figure 10.26).

left posterior T1. No cases of exclusively subcortical lesions have been reported, controverting the classical arcuate fasciculus model of this disorder. Indeed, there is a report (Puusepp, 1937) of a case of surgical section of the arcuate fasciculus without aphasia.

There is evidence that the relative mildness of the sound errors that occur in the speech of the phonemic aphasic reflect the contribution of the right hemisphere. Kleist (1962) argued in a case of phonemic (conduction) aphasia for moderate right hemisphere language capacity. Benson *et al.* (1973) exploited this theory to explain a case of phonemic aphasia with preservation of the arcuate fasciculus. Brown (1979), Kinsbourne (1971), and Hamanaka *et al.* (1976) demonstrated right hemisphere language with Wada testing in cases of phonemic aphasia. The conclusion from these studies is that both hemispheres can to a variable extent support phonological processing. A left temporal lesion produces either a phonemic aphasia or a jargonaphasia, depending on the extent of right hemisphere language. A bilateral lesion of posterior T1 might obviate right hemisphere compensation and thus lead to a profound phonological deficit.

This anatomical relationship between phonemic (conduction) aphasia and phonemic jargon is also linguistically motivated. If phonemic jargon is conceived of as a failure of semantic content to achieve phonological realization, one might suggest that it reflects a phonological form that is independent of semantic information.

Thus, a unilateral left temporal lesion leads to phonemic errors in correct lexical targets, the symptom of phonemic aphasia. The limited nature of this disturbance is explained by the persisting capacity in the intact left or in the right hemisphere. With bilateral lesions, the capacity to interpret the phonological code is severely reduced; the deficit erodes into the function words and the production of phonemes is no longer responsive to semantic–lexical intentions. The difference between unilateral and bilateral disruption at the phonological level is a difference between phonemic errors linked to lexical targets and phonemic errors independent of lexical control. This hypothesis predicts recovery of phonemic jargon into phonemic (conduction) aphasia.

BILINGUALISM AND
PHONEMIC JARGON

The rarity of the language disorder observed in K.S., together with the fact that K.S. was bilingual, offers an interesting speculation in light of a comment by Leopold (1953) regarding the acquisition of language in a bilingual environment. Remarking on the influence that a bilingual environment may have had on the development of his child's language, he wrote

> The most striking effect of bilingualism was a noticeable looseness of the link between the phonetic word and its meaning . . . [the child] heard the same thing constantly designated by two different phonetic forms. This separation of word and meaning . . . favors content over form . . .

Indeed, Leopold's observation is all the more striking in view of Schvachkin's (1973) suggestion that, at an early stage of language acquisition in the monolingual child, the sounds of language serve to carry meaning directly, and that it is only later that meaning becomes differentiated from sound as an entity independent of the sound configuration which conveys that meaning. In other words, whereas for the monolingual child, the sound is the meaning of the word, for the bilingual child, and indeed, for the bilingual adult, the meaning of a word is less likely to be firmly associated with a particular sound configuration.

Thus, K.S. may have been more predisposed to the loss of the meaning-bearing function of sounds by virtue of his bilingualism, insofar as bilingualism may foster an attitude toward language that emphasizes content over form. The hypothesis that phonemic jargon is more likely to be found in bilinguals may offer an interesting line of investigation.

APPENDIX 1. RELATIVE FREQUENCIES OF PHONEMES

*Key to Abbreviations

Eng N = English Norms

Ger N = German Norms

KSM1 = KS Monologue Time 1

KSD1 = KS Dialogue Time 1

KSD2 = KS Dialogue Time 2

CD = Control Dialogue

KSER1a = KS English Reading
       Time 1a

KSER1b = KS English Reading
       Time 1b

KSER2 = KS English Reading
       Time 2

CER = Control English
     Reading

KSSupER2 = KS Supplementary
      English Reading
      Time 2

KSGR1 = KS German Reading
     Time 1

KSGR2 = KS German Reading
     Time 2

CGR = Control German
     Reading

**Total for consonants and vowels combined

222

Relative Frequencies of Consonant Phonemes

	Eng N* n=66,534	Ger N** n=105,174	KSM1 n=908	KSD1 n=1256	KSD2 n=879	CD n=983	KSER1a n=409	KSER1b n=369	KSER2 n=288	CER *n=234	KS Sup ER2 n=537	KSGR1 n=641	KSGR2 n=588	CGR n=480
t	10.87	14.16	5.84	11.15	11.26	9.78	10.02	6.50	17.71	14.96	17.50	11.70	15.82	14.17
y	10.60	-	1.10	1.51	3.98	4.04	.99	1.63	.69	.43	.19	2.03	.34	.42
r	10.30	12.02	14.10	8.20	7.85	-	8.31	4.34	10.42	-	8.01	7.18	10.20	-
n	9.84	16.08	8.15	8.44	8.19	9.99	6.36	6.50	11.11	8.97	12.48	8.58	12.41	16.87
w	7.07	-	.22	1.59	2.84	4.57	.73	.54	1.74	2.99	1.67	.78	.51	.21
s	6.11	7.36	13.33	18.15	18.32	9.67	19.80	17.89	18.40	12.39	18.99	12.32	19.73	11.04
l	5.18	5.59	1.65	3.34	1.14	4.78	1.71	1.08	1.04	5.98	.19	2.03	1.02	6.67
d	4.76	6.58	3.41	4.22	5.57	8.82	8.56	10.30	9.03	11.54	6.70	7.64	8.67	7.29
h	4.11	1.80	.55	.56	1.02	3.08	1.47	.54	.35	6.84	4.28	.47	1.53	1.67
m	4.09	4.53	13.66	5.09	7.17	4.99	4.64	7.59	1.04	1.71	2.61	6.08	1.87	5.63
k	3.83	3.07	.66	1.03	1.48	5.63	1.47	1.08	-	3.85	.74	.31	1.19	4.17
ð	3.51	-	.66	.87	.57	1.17	.49	1.35	.35	1.71	.37	1.25	-	-
z	3.14	2.91	2.20	5.25	3.87	1.17	3.42	2.98	3.47	.43	3.91	12.01	5.10	1.25
v	2.94	3.34	4.07	4.70	2.84	3.51	6.11	6.50	3.82	3.42	1.86	3.90	1.70	3.12

Relative Frequencies of Consonant Phonemes

	Eng N[*] n=66,534	Ger N[**] n=105,174	KSM1 n=908	KSD1 n=1256	KSD2 n=879	CD n=983	KSER1a n=409	KSER1b n=369	KSER2 n=288	CER n=234	KS Sup ER2 n=537	KSGR1 n=641	KSGR2 n=588	CGR n=480
f	2.66	3.91	6.50	1.91	2.96	4.89	4.64	5.69	5.55	3.42	3.91	4.99	4.08	2.50
b	2.55	2.79	13.88	10.59	11.94	3.72	6.11	5.96	9.72	1.71	3.35	3.43	5.78	2.29
p	2.52	1.64	6.50	5.49	3.30	2.97	1.22	2.44	2.08	2.14	3.16	1.87	2.89	.83
ŋ	1.44	1.09	–	.08	–	1.27	–	–	–	.85	–	–	–	.63
g	1.36	3.19	1.21	.80	1.59	2.66	–	–	1.74	.85	5.21	.62	4.76	3.46
š	1.12	2.76	.11	1.27	–	1.27	–	–	–	.85	–	–	.17	4.56
č	.72		.55	3.02	1.14	.53	.24	–	–	1.71	–	1.40	.17	.42
θ	.66		–	.32	.23	.21	.24	–	–	.85	–	.31	–	–
ǰ	.56		.11	.32	.11	.85	–	–	–	.43	–	.16	–	.21
ž	.05	.02	–	.08	–	–	–	–	–	–	–	–	–	–
x		4.25	–	.08	–	–	.24	–	–	–	–	–	–	–
R			1.54	1.11	2.62	9.99	11.73	16.81	1.74	11.96	4.84	10.86	2.04	10.83
ʔ			–	.80	–	.42	1.47	.27	–	–	–	.16	–	–

223

Relative Frequencies of Vowel Phonemes

	Eng N** n=66,534	Ger N** n=105,174	KSM1 n=803	KSD1 n=864	KSD2 n=617	CD n=713	KSER1a n=278	KSER1b n=266	KSER2 n=228	CER n=158	KS SupER2 n=377	KSGR1 n=414	KSGR2 n=413	CGR n=296
i	25.73	23.29	24.91	13.19	18.96	15.29	16.55	18.80	23.68	10.76	19.89	10.87	25.18	16.22
e	13.11	36.98	6.23	3.47	4.86	4.21	7.91	6.77	7.89	9.49	8.22	11.35	12.83	2.03
ε			9.09	12.49	12.64	11.50	19.78	17.67	14.03	8.22	16.71	21.98	11.62	19.26
ü		2.02	.12	.35	-	-	.36	1.13	-	.63	-	.72	.24	2.36
I			4.48	7.05	6.97	13.74	14.03	13.16	5.26	10.13	3.98	13.28	4.84	11.82
ø		.89	2.24	.69	.16	2.66	.72	-	.44	-	-	.24	.24	-
æ	4.27		.37	.58	.52	2.52	-	-	-	5.06	-	-	.48	-
ə	32.73		12.83	12.37	9.89	12.76	3.96	6.77	12.28	16.45	9.81	6.28	13.32	11.49
a	12.83	20.52	19.43	19.65	21.88	11.42	18.34	21.05	23.25	6.96	21.72	16.42	18.16	19.26
u	5.28	9.83	5.98	8.67	2.43	8.55	4.68	2.63	.44	4.43	-	2.90	-	8.44
ʊ			.87	2.66	2.11	1.40	1.08	2.25	-	1.26	-	2.17	.24	-
o	4.26	6.47	6.35	6.13	11.83	4.77	4.32	3.76	8.77	6.96	13.79	6.76	7.99	4.05
ɔ	1.78		6.60	9.71	6.64	3.37	7.55	5.64	3.51	9.49	5.30	6.76	4.36	4.05
ʌ			.50	2.08	1.13	7.29	.72	.37	.44	10.13	.53	.24	.48	1.01

APPENDIX 2. PHONETIC TRANSCRIPTIONS OF SPONTANEOUS JARGON*

KS Monologue Time 1

[u ɛt vʊni æ piuvwʔvwɛnhi ɛspidə ɛtsəbafɔʁfɔʁ ɔʁɪlik bɔts
bimɛnziɔvəmitsʊhaɹa// aɹu aino pɔ ʌʔʌɹ imɪpəɹ pɹits fɛʁ-
ɛbɹisəmʊpɹi ɹɛdəmɔfipɹitsi avwɔmamibeɹ fatbamasbibɹɔsp-
ailə etəmezpɔmvɹemhia// bʌɹaimʊdɛvəbiastuduautəgeɹn ak-
sɪdeɹvidautʃɛʁ// anɛpɛpɛpɛɹasɪpi adonɛnimimɛɔtbɪlʊz fɔ-
pɹima mibi ʊ amasfə əmafɪbianəlidasbɛɹɛtsbiu// vwʊlbin
ɛn ðeðeðebapfaʁbafəbiɛ demeəfəbasfəbispəɹetəɹɔfbəbia fɔ-
mababispɹɪn// map maɹafəpɹanəɹi mʊabiɬɸɛsənədə ɛbimivin-
iviæɹspɪnifumiəobvimai ɛbidzɔmiɹʊsfɔmivwɔ bamɹɪbjɛspi-
mes fɔaməbɹɛnibɹambos fənandi// mɪɹ as pəlemvasibenʊ ma-
ɔsbəɹɛniasibimjɛnzəs bəɹui fotəeɹofibi ameɹi veɹstioba-
abmatəob [· · · · · · ·ː · ·ʃ˙ɹuɹumatsəmɛəmɛəmɛəɹ igoaɹ ɛgigapomi-
paɹəpɹeni ainipimɪrus imjɛtɔpimybibɪn fɔmai ɛspɹimɔsp-
ɪnəɹe adɛpɹimɔsɪmi mɛɹibos mɛnivɹʌimvid idaras penəɹi
ɛnfəɹi vispəɹiasəɹa ɔɹimjɛsa bɛni amasibɛnmɸv aməbɹis-
unʌ no// kabidɹoseə ɛdɹinɔʃtɪstɹavats majubɹaspon//
aimɔs tʊɹiðɪstəɹadɪs djuju pɛmɹasbɛni japaispi (laughs)
ebjɛɹsəbɪlibo apɹomas bəwima fiətsimɔɹovgauzveɹsə lɛf-
əbɪnɹifə emif apamɪsts ufbimɔfɹenatbrisko// nobibahɛs-
jɛɹis mumɪs fɔɹupi biɛsmɪsge nopɸsekɔntɛstajəbɹisbemɸ-
pɹadvɛzə bɹomi [· · · · · · · · ·] madɹomo enenedebɛɹiɹi aɹo-
bʊlzmifɔɹamaizəs mi ins [· · · · · · · · ·] baitabaibabjɔpɔndꙅ-
eədzeəbisbitat mastəɹobəɹizən nailə zofəmfəvəɹestəɹən

---

* Please note that for reasons of clarity of representation in the transcriptions, the following equivalences obtain between phonetic symbols used in the text and graphs and those used in the transcriptions:

R = ʁ	y = ɹ	
r = ɹ	ž = ȝ	
š = ʃ	j = dȝ	
č = iʃ	ü = y	

*this indicates interruption by a second speaker

```
+ɔimɔsbamɔvɪbɔmʋɔɹaspɔm// mabivɹisbiebmbɪs fɔfəmigobau-
sbeəmás əmi bɵɹimaspóʻəmibɹaspɹoninaɹənɵfɹidɛsviginiɛsbə-
ɹiniæs beɹaɵeɹɔ ɹobeʁausmeʁhebomiʁsafɛʁzibɹɛtsmalɹu
beaɹmusbemaɹbɹuzdɪnbɹɪstʃ anɛfəfɔetsɪbɹizɵf ɵf fɛʁtifɹɔm
aitimuvəvɪʁs afənbɹidz mai mai mai ɔfɛd famɔsi bɹami
ibəbetɵŋ ebɹɛsbɔmɵviasɪbɹɔmɵsən miemɹʋs// +uðəbeʁzən
ovɛʁsbimɵsbenəɹofəbatsio opɹɵmɔspɹu bat hɵɹbamisbɹans
[ ,........ ] ɹubis deəfiɹɔpf maɹemɹɛspəvɵ fɛʁbɹu nopits
no [laughs] geəsɛndigamsiɔ apaɹa aɹɛvamɵts bɔpəɹu bɵfə-
ɹifia atɛsobəɹaspanɪɹo dofɛɹã baɹe misti astʃuli naits//
abɹansigoɹadɪ [ ........] imb apfəbetʃə izɪbantʃəlibi en
eəɹifɛns ɹibɛnsfomatbəɹi obəɹɔpabi ʒivəmatsəpɔvɹɔts
[ ........] ɹubaizmifibɹɪsmiamofai famiɵstuma apvibɔsə-
ɹupinaso napmi noma [laughs] stikvo vwo obumastiɹɹɛbmi
ɛəmuzfia]
```

Excerpt from
KS Dialogue Time 1

Therapist: May

KS: [ɛt man dɹa]

T: May, it's May 2nd, May 2nd

KS: [...adɪbe da ðadz ɹas]

T: nineteen seventy

KS: [...bɹɛts...]

T: seventy-seven. How are you Mr. S—? How are you?

KS: [liɹə bɹo vwaɹɛ]

T: hm?

KS: [lɛvɪ vi faviə fawzɪs...]

T: Fine? You're fine? Are you fine? How are you feeling?
      Fine? Are you feeling fine? Mr. S— are you...

KS: [ja ija ija]

T: Yes?

KS: [dedefotatəsists]

T: How was the weekend?

KS: [o sɛm nəʁists]

T: The same?

KS: [nɔnɛmabis nɔnɔnema [inaudible] nɔ// ad ɛɹɛbidɔ ɔtʃɛn
      daɹ aɹemɪz nɔdɔz]

T: You were writing?

KS: [ja]

T: and reading?

KS: [no ðɹi na nɹiɛvovomdʒivudʒɔmviðɔʃ// wɔʁiðu faɹɛpaɹiz
      fʌɹə tuɹə// nabisabibɔsɔbɹasəbwɔvə vɛɹvistəbɹusts]

T: Writing in the books. Good.

KS: [m̩ hm̩]

T: Good. OK. Today we're just gonna do some simple words.
      I'm gonna show you the same ones again. Pencil, jacket,
      belt and check book.

KS: .(grunting sounds as if his mind had wandered)

T: Mr. S—

KS: [balzɛ balzɛ bʊlzɛn svɛʃtʃ]

T: Mr. S— point to the pencil, pencil.

KS: [vɛstə bɹiz mɔs tosts]

T: Point to the pencil.

KS: [bloblɛstsəbɹovɪts tsuɹblɪsts]

T: Right, um hm. Point to the belt. Mr. S—

KS: [bvɛ fas]

T: Mr. S— point to the belt

KS: [əbɛlɪzvwɛɪnsʋats]

T: Point to the suit jacket.

KS: [ʃutʃ]

T: Good

KS: [ja]

T: Suit

KS: [ja]

T: Point to the check book.

KS: [ʃɛtʃuləbuləbultubɹɛps]

T: Good. You're hearing better.

KS: [daə peʌpɹʋs]

T: Are you hearing me better?

KS: [ja baɹɛɹibus ...]

T: You're hearing it better. OK. Where's the pencil again, <u>pencil</u>.

KS: [atɪpɹɔs pɹinfwis]

T: Show me where is the <u>check book</u> (writing)

KS: [dɔmə tʃvʊmʃvɪts]

T: Show me

KS: [nɔ]

T: Show me where the <u>check book</u> is.

KS: [nɔbɔbɪtʃ]

T: What?

KS: [no]

T: Why?

KS: [ɹuvɹə geməbitsʊtsʊs]

T: um hm

KS: [anubɹubɹɛtubɹɔsubɹɪstsudzaists]

T: You don't have a <u>check book</u>?

KS: [noɹɛnpəvɹɛm bɹivjɛtats]

T: Oh

KS: [nodaʔ no aʔaʔ dɛdzɛnɛbɛsvɔs// ɛndvɔɹablvɔɹabasbɹə// ɔlfəmisɪbasɪbisəbʊsts]

T: Here, match this.

KS: [nabists abʊsts]

T: <u>Match</u> it

KS: [o mɛsmidzɔz ambizɛbɹasdzɛz [sing-song quality] bidʒɛsp
     ɔtʃɛsbvɛnsbɛdzasbeaɹɛsts// øɪnzos tʃatʃatʃɔtʃits sid
     ok tazekatsnɔts]

T: <u>suit jacket</u>

KS: [savik ɛta stɔtɹɔʃtʃ vifʃtʃ]

T: suit <u>jac</u>ket

KS: [øtʃətɛms atʃamtʃitɔdidz ɹɔfts]

T: Do you have a suit jacket?

KS: [θaɪsvɔts]

T: Hm. Do you have one?

KS: [ja waɹɪʔɪʔinəkɔkləvɛnɪtspɪts vʊtsdwɪʃ//   vyɹebusvɛt-
     bʊlsbɛsts]

T: check book

KS: [nɔ]

T: Check book. You don't have one?

KS: [no]

T: OK, alright. Mr. S— I'm gonna say "two" and I want you
      to point to "two" alright?

KS: [əvwats]

T: Point to "two" OK? Listen and point to "two

KS: [bodotɹotɛnɛtʃɛnɛtʃɹotɹuɪnst]

T: Point to the suit jacket and the pencil

KS: [ətsbɹɔnə əf hafdzʌns ʌtsdʌsəs]

T: First point to the suit jacket and then to the pencil.
Where is the s̲uit jacket?

KS: [səgasəbis]

T: Then the pe̲n̲c̲i̲l̲

KS: [dɛtsəpɔləpɛzbʊs]

T: OK, I'm gonna point to, I want, I'm gonna say "two"
and then you point. OK? Point to the belt.

KS: [æləpəlups]

T: "Two." Listen for the "two."

KS: [aməmɪdzʊɪs]

T: Yeah.

KS: [unintelligible]

T: I didn't say anything (KS continues talking) Listen,
listen.

KS: [naw]

Excerpt From
KS Dialogue Time 2

EP: Your name is K— S—

KS: [jɛs]

EP: So tell me your name.

KS: [ad wad hʌŋ mabisəbo]

EP: Tell me your name, your name. No tell me, tell me
    your name.

KS: [ʌ eʁgigoskɛtɹodɛstistɛtistiɹst eɹkopist eɹstistiɹs eɹ-
    ɛsbɔgɪsbadizpəfo wɔs wɔs]

EP: No, no, no, just sit and tell me some — no sit down,
    sit down, sit down (taps seat) it's ok. Um (to J)
    should

KS: [ɹainduɹbaɹist beʁtist eʁtmistɪʁstɔmʁiəsdiʊsts]

EP: um hm

KS: [ɹa]

EP: um hm. What else.

KS: [somɛd nobʁɛm datistɛʁdistodɛgɹɛsɹɛs]

EP: um hm. What did you do today. Tell me what you did
    today.
KS: [batmɔ]

EP: Did you go outside today?

KS: [ɛʔ]

EP: Did you go outside today.

KS: [abɹufədu]

EP: You went outside.

KS: [ɹa]

EP: It's a pretty day? Did you think it was a nice day
    today?

KS: [tuðe*]

EP: Today, right.

KS: [ai* vɛnt* fɔɹ* a* vəlɔwzpoldʒizəzɛzjətsjɛ]

EP: Oh

KS: [ja]

EP: Oh. Do you take walks around the building (making a circle with hand)

KS: [ja fɔn toham jɛ]

EP: Oh I see, back and forth.

KS: [ai dɪdajaibɪst// ai bɹofɪs] [inaudible]...[holds up four fingers]

EP: Sit. No why don't you sit down.

KS: [inaudible]

EP: Sit. Why don't you sit down, sit.

KS: [inaudible]

EP: What's the matter are you worried about the time?

KS: [dɔzənmæɹ ə*mizʊm]

EP: Doesn't matter. Ok, ok. What time do you eat dinner usually?

KS: [o ʌvəɹɛnzəðidədidədistʃ vɛnivɛhomʌbijɛstɛs// jɛ]

EP: Maybe we will

KS: [kɛmɪbajiʌsəs]

     * indicates   word

EP: Yeah

KS: [oke]

EP: OK

KS: [abɹustfiap e ɪnusʁaisʒ[inaudible]

EP: Yes, both of us.

KS: [ɟa bo*]

EP: Um hm. We'll have dinner with you.

KS: [ɟa]

EP: OK good. Do you want to read. Do you want to read. (to J) Should we read some things or I'm gonna ask you to read some things. OK?

KS: [ɹumɪdnadɪs vwat]

       [ks reads text]

EP: OK. What's the matter?

KS: [numa ai bɛd hiə]

EP: Oh you want to eat now. Can we wait a little while.

KS: [əm fɔm]

EP: Can we wait a little while. In a little while

KS: [naw naw naw]

EP: Now?

KS: [abibibɛpfɪlðɛdəʁdɛstəvifə abɹuz fɔt mɛnɪg aibobaisɪsə]

EP: Can you sit down just for a second. Sit down for a
     minute. Can you sit. Five minutes. A little while.

KS: [ja ja ja ja ja]

EP: OK?

KS: [ja]

EP: OK. Can you tell me what this word is? What is this
     word?

KS: [gopnajʊz jɛ ðis bopɛtanist fɛstɛnθos]

EP: OK can we try another one or? Can you read this one.
     Follow along with your finger like this.

     [ks reads text]

EP: OK finished good. OK now there's going to be one more.

JB: Ask him what this was about?

EP: OK. Can you tell me what this was about?

KS: [æʔ]

EP: Can you tell me the story again.

     [ks picks up page of text]

EP: Don't read it, just tell me about it. Tell me who was
     in the story. Who?

KS: [mə ba vəm]

EP: No just tell me. Sit, sit please. Mr.S— please sit.
     Sit down.

     [ks goes to bookcase]

EP: What are you getting. Are you looking for a book. Are
     you looking for a particular book.

KS: [inaudible]

EP: OK what is this. What is this? What is this?

KS: [bɛs fa va fɹom ðɪsɛθfɹɔd bɛn// bɛsbɪ ɹis biəs]

EP: Is this the same kind of story? Did you read this?
     Have you read this book? Have you read this?

KS: [ɹa]

EP: Yes. What was it about?

KS: [ɹa fɔl gɹoma// ɛt a fɔʁb ist bɹod ist pɛʁd iəs diəst]

EP: umhm

KS: [gɹop ɹane bof// ɹo bo pat// bid eʁs bes viəs]

     [ks reads text]

EP: Good. What was this about.

KS: [kɔt ɔt vɔt mɔz mɪzmɛzivi][pointing to neck]

EP: Tell me what this was about. What was this about.

KS: [ɹɛ no bat a vat]

EP: What did he write about.

KS: [ai ino bɛs ɛs ɛ][begins to read text again]

EP: Tell me just tell me in your own words. Tell me. What
     is this about.

KS: [ʌm no no not nɔt həbɹlə ɛs pad bɪs [points to his
     temple or eye] obɹabɛsɛ bɹɛbɹofɛɹmaws eɪs ɔn bot bɪs-
     tan estə baɹiə [gets book from bookshelf and reads]

si ɛf ai sɛn os// si ib abɹofa amtbasɛbɹosɪbimz Jɛ
[reads] ol vais best inbus gɹos ginz fot ain ist god
ɛn iɐ// os vai// o eɐb ai bot ɛn ist ⊐

APPENDIX 3. SINGLE-WORD READING TASKS

Appendix 3A. Reading Task 1: Order of Presentation of Target Words, Numbers, and Letters

1.	start	24.	ask	47.	deer
2.	serve	25.	sense	48.	ball
3.	slab	26.	guard	49.	lake
4.	lark	27.	dart	50.	catch
5.	skirt	28.	whisper	51.	jab
6.	tower	29.	pluck	52.	gin
7.	dip	30.	bank	53.	shirt
8.	bag	31.	crab	54.	miss
9.	melt	32.	fence	55.	zip
10.	try	33.	nerve	56.	bathe
11.	flea	34.	card	57.	gather
12.	blow	35.	snail	58.	thank
13.	arm	36.	drum	59.	give
14.	belt	37.	truck	60.	laugh
15.	glue	38.	farm	61.	avoid
16.	throw	39.	lamp	62.	suffer
17.	survey	40.	buck	63.	feed
18.	fry	41.	cry	64.	zeal
19.	task	42.	sew	65.	lathe
20.	cow	43.	wake	66.	thing
21.	frenzy	44.	hear	67.	graph

22. snake	45. fall	68. fate
23. sulfer	46. live	69. sing

70. beg	97. embark	122. 1	148. G
71. linger	98. rag	123. 6	149. V
72. go	99. flee		
73. kiss	100. convey	124. M	
74. heed	101. jersey	125. S	
75. week	102. whimper	126. U	
76. hate	103. cart	127. H	
77. do	104. camp	128. W	
78. take	105. latch	129. F	
79. come	106. chin	130. P	
80. make	107. sip	131. Z	
81. buy	108. void	132. A	
82. pick	109. seal	133. C	
83. leg	110. lather	134. E	
84. back	111. need	135. J	
85. finger	112. pan	136. R	
86. pickel	113. tail	137. N	
87. car	114. cap	138. K	
88. bed		139. Q	
89. cat		140. Y	
90. nail	115. 2	141. X	
91. gum	116. 7	142. T	
92. cab	117. 4	143. L	
93. man	118. 9	144. B	
94. pie	119. 5	145. O	
95. weak	120. 8	146. D	
96. observe	121. 3	147. I	

Appendix 3B. Reading Task 1: Single Words, Numbers and Letters—Target Items and Corresponding Jargon Responses

Item # by Ord. of Presntn.	Target	Ref. No.*	Phonetic Transcription of Jargon Response
13	arm	38	[o ɹaigiʏniʏts]
24	ask	19	[axʍaɹɪsdzjəʃtʃ]
61	avoid	108	[oʍ ɛzɛnzdzɛʁist sogʏanestainᵻiʏs]
84	back	8	[obaineθiʏs ogʏanesdiʏs]
8	bag	84, 98	[vɔʔfɪns vɔd zijés]
48	ball	45	[hoʍ ausesbesɔsbəsdiəs oʍaudzisᵻbandzospazbɪ]
30	bank	58	[omaɹ imõadediʏsts ɑɹaitanstsɛstsᵻiʏs]
56	bathe	65	[ọdaidɛsdzɛniʏsts odʏataniɹst]
88	bed	70	[ọtainiʏst otavlistvazdʒiʃ]
70	beg	83	[eɡɹaniʏsksotaʍamiʏz]
14	belt	9	[deɹɪtait itsk samasjɛ]
12	blow	72	[ɹɑɹaid iʏs]
40	brick	82	[álæbotaindɛsdiɹs ogɐɹɑɹdensdasᵻdiʏs]
81	buy	94	[obʏainizbɛts baspǿbisbis]
92	cab	3.51,89,114	[ofbainiʏs fɔtabizbɔdɛʏz]
104	camp	39	[oʍanɪsbaniʏsotangɹɛnstɛljiʏs sɔmiɹ]
87	can	93	[apfainiʏst sotainiʏst sotanijəsts]
114	cap	89,92	[ᵻsopainəmiʏzəbaizəvɛ]
34	card	26,103	[ɹɹopaɹɹʊmpfansdiʏsbasdijəzbǿlviᵻjəlziʏvəlpa]

* Reference number of related items refers to item number in list by order or presentation given in Appendix 1A.

103	cart	1,27,34	[soɯaniʁstsoɯaniʁsts]
89	cat	92,114	[ofatiniʁstsotainiʁsbɪdə iʁs]
50	catch	105	[otautestsanists otaidɔspaizdʁs- tzospeʁʃɪ]
106	chin	52	[etainebiʁs ostanestainiʁs estan- besətsan]
79	come	91	[opainesdiʁtsoɯaidensbeʁəbeʁəs- bisbeseʁ]
100	convey	17	[aɯabanɛsdiʁseʔanbɛsbaniəs]
20	cow	6	[owauɡam iəzkeʁs iʁtʃ]
31	crab	51,92	[oweɡʁaivbisvəsbʌsvijəs]
41	cry	18	[tseʃɪst aits diʃɪsts]
27	dart	1	[tapiʁðɛʁst ɪsts]
47	deer	44	[ydanesdiʁs ɔɡʁandests]
7	dip	55,107	[sibəl aid ists]
77	do	15	[odais kodiʃ]
36	drum	79,91	[ɯatanistɔdiʁsviʁsfɑɹaitamzɪst- iʁsts]
97	embark	4	[ofɹadenstsɛniəs sopanɔispanɛsbʁ- ɛʁeiʁzeə]
45	fall	48	[oɯaɯidinz ɛsdiʁsts fɑɯauzɛsts]
38	farm	13	[oɯainstespainiʁsdześiʁs ovɯau- dzainzdzijəsts vosasdinsdasdeʁs]
68	fate	76	[odʁaineistainiʁs sotatɔnaidiʁ- ɪst]
63	feed	74	[apidenijəs otaindɛskaniʁstsʊs iʁdə]
32	fence	25	[ɹopɛdenstseɹ izsopaidzɛstseʁsva- dɪspiəspɪbɛsbə diəzɪ]
85	finger	71	[ovaiɡɛstaniəst sotaindɛnɪbiʁs]
11	flea	99	[wɔtanɛʁvɔɹobaitinzsviʁs tsɛʁs paspimispiʁts]

99	flee	11	[tʃʊbainiʁsbainəɹiz sebaunɛsdiʁs sopaniʁ ɪst]
21	frenzy	101	[obɯamis pizəsopəspanəspɪsdʒɛnsiʁsts]
18	fry	41,81,94	[fawavɹainists fotaɹijəsbɛsbists]
57	gather	110	[ofɹɔdainiʁs otanɛdiʁs totanɛdiʁs ostandɛstsaɹiʁs]
52	gin	51,106	[ejɪdin ists sɛijəns]
59	give	46	[kipadinzdziɹiɹz sobɯaidɛniʁst sobɯamespandɛspɛzbijə]
15	glue	77	[fɹibɯoteəsbɛtsvɛsbɪsʊsveʁtsvensvɪɹtsive]
72	go	12,16,42	[ogɹɛmpf[whisper]...ists]
67	graph	60	[obɯabɛnsainiʁs odʁabɛnsbiʁists]
26	guard	34	[ogadanθazdijəθiʁsts sobɯanbɯasijəsus]
91	gum	79	[ɔmɛɹis fobadibaniʁs]
76	hate	68	[obajədɛsdeɹists odɹaigɛtainiʁzt otanistɔdbiʁz]
44	hear	47	[napədɛdziʁsts...]
74	heed	111	[ogɹainijəsts otanists otaniʁs]
51	jab	31,52,92	[ətanijeziʁsts otʁaidɛnzistsʃ]
101	jersey	21	[tsɔibɛniʁzaniəz tebanɛsvaniəs]
73	kiss	54	[sobɯɛnzijəsdiʁs...]
49	lake	22,43,78,80	[obɯaudɪstsɛʁiʃ otautɛstsaniʁ]
39	lamp	104	[ɹobadenɛdiʁsbɪts]
4	lark	97	[o gaidiʁiz...]
105	latch	50	[sa tɹanɛsbaniʁs ɔstandɪskaniʁs sapanisvadə]
65	lathe	56	[ɔdʁaldɛsdzainijəs ɔsdʁangɛdiʁs obʁandɛs]

110	lather	57	[tsoɪstanɪsbanediʁsɔstaɪndɪspan- iʁst]
60	laugh	67	[samodɛspanedizbɛ tsopanzdɛzbed- zdiʁdzbə tsopadzpɛspɛpɛɹəbizəz- bɛ]
83	leg	70	[obʁaɪnɪsts ̱vbʁaɪnɪsboniəsbɪtspə]
71	linger	85	[o daɪnɛsdzɛniʁs sotaɪdɛstaniəs·· ̤. sopaɪkɛstsadiɛs...]
46	live	59	[odʁaunsɛspaɹɪsdiʁspiʁzbɪs]
80	make	22,43,49,78	[obaɪðɛsdaɪneiʁs dʌn...pɪdiʁz]
93	man	87,112	[owainiʁsfotainiʁs]
9	melt	14	[mɔdɹɪntseɹəsts]
54	miss	73	[napɔtiʁzviɹəs]
90	nail	113	[ɑɹaɪnesdiʁs]
111	need	74	[owgɹanustsɔgɹanizɪʁs sostanlʁist]
33	nerve	2	[ɑɹaɪdansdɛsdɪsts...]
96	observe	2	[topvɔdɛnɔniʁs sofbanefbaniʁs]
112	pan	87,93	[obainiʁsgɛsbainiʁst]
82	pick	40,86	[obɯaɪesbanəvizfə opanezpɪzviʁzb- ɪdiʁ]
86	pickel	82	[seems to him the short- short-long stress pattern]
94	pie	81	[taibiʁ is tsaib ɛniʁzists]
29	pluck	137	[ɹotaɪtsdɛtsdɛɹiəsdɹɛtsəs obɯat- amdɪtsəsfɔɹ]
98	rag	8	[ɑɹaɪdiʁts sɛganɔs sambaneliʁse- zəm]
109	seal	64	[bɪʔɛʁlʁsbaɹəbizbə sopazdɪsbɛðe- diɪbe]
25	sense	32	[ɑɹabɯəmsʌnsɔɪsiʌsɯəsvɔvɹə]
2	serve	17,33,96	[fo veʁzɪ]

42	sew	12,16,72	[ə gɹaʁzdeɹɪsdiʁs dotandɛniʁ...]
53	shirt	5	[odʁanzdɛstain iɹəztsets ɔdaisdzɪztaizdiɹəztɹɛzts]
69	sing	66	[i ɛnediʁs odanediʁs]
107	sip	7,55	[sepamiʁs sopaniʁsviʁs sopainiʁst sopɛbiʁsɛ]
5	skirt	53	[wʌzɪs fɔθɛɾɹainzists ɔdɹedzvists]
3	slab	92	[amɹɛ fɛɹewinuf]
35	snail	90	[natɔtsdɛʁtsdiɹətsts opasɪspɹɔs]
22	snake	43,49,78,80	[ɔɹalganiɹəstsɛʁtsvɪdə oɕɹaɪdanɛdiʁs oɕɹaɪdɛsts ɭɹəɪsts]
1	start	27	[fataɹə ʦaistsitsʌstsɔɹitʃt]
62	suffer	23	[sopadɛniʁstsopanɛspaniʁsps]
23	sulfer	62	[ɔɹabanɛziʁzdzɪsəsas...]
17	survey	2,100	[o ɹaikanizdɹɛziɹəsts soðɛtansɛstsosbistɹəs]
113	tail	90	[ogainiʁstaineɹ izodɹainɛstiʁsts ostainiʁstaniʁs]
78	take	43,49,80	[obanis topaidɛnsbɛsbiʁspɛsɪbiʁs]
19	**task**	24	[ob aiz dainzdɪs vusdɛʁsts]
58	thank	30	[oawamaidɛziʁz sopaiðɛspaniəzpəspazəspiəzə]
66	thing	69	[ibanɪsvaniəs obanɪsbandists]
16	throw	12,42,72	[dɹebotain ditsøststʃ]
6	tower	20	[ɪɔbadbeziɹtseʁmsɪms]

37	truck	29	[ɔɹadawsdɛnsdiɹst odɹadauskaniɹs oskandʌspəsvists]
10	try	18,81,94	(klopainəmiɹzaɹəstsastʃam]
108	void	61	[owainiɹsostanɪstàiniɹs]
43	wake	49,78,80	[obɹaðɛstsaɹoiɹsts ogɹadøstsaniɹ...]
95	weak	75	[bɹlbɛɹsts səpanlɹsp sɹlpɛnlɹos]
75	week	95	[op opɹal obɹaigesiəs ɔfaɪnsdɛs-ban[groping]... iɹəsɛsaspoisvɛf]
102	whimper	28	[ɔbɹimgɛtstaniəs sɛtanɪsbaniɹbəs]
28	whisper	102	[gɹobalð insdazdiɹəztsiəzviɹa obaðisvɛdzɛnɛɹists]
64	zeal	109	[obɹezbainiɹzbizeɹ obanzdɛniɹs]
55	zip	7,107	[segaɹdiɹzdiɹzts sòdaitaniɹɪsts]
122	'1'		[tobainiɹsts]
115	'2'		[kɔpuis]
121	'3'		[obɹainɹst sopaniɹspəs]
117	'4'		[ofɹafdzɪneɹtsitslɹts]
119	'5'		[opainiɹsts]
123	'6'		[fopainiɹsts sopaddaɹɪs]
116	'7'		[waiɹts †sapiɹɛsts ofbɹanztsanziɹst]
120	'8'		[tsapiɹɛsts ofbɹanztsanziɹst]
118	'9'		[odanotainist sotɛɹniɹspʌmiɹs]
132	A		[apiniɹs]
144	B		[obitsomɪɹpofɔmiɹzbaziɹz]
133	C		[dɔɹist sɔpainiɹst]
146	D		[op govɛtsanspɛɹəiɹəspɛsəvɹɛɹs spɪdɛɹ]

134   E   [ɔpainispaniʌst]

129   F   [gʁobaɹɘmɪɘzbosblʌsblʁ]

148   G   [sebɛɹɛmɛɹ soguɛns somaʁis somɛʁ-
                    baas kɔmɘɹazə]

127   H   [mɔɹɘʌns ɛsbaniʁz]

147   I   [iʁdotsiʁbɹos fiʁbozɘhɛʁzə]

135   J   [tsamist sobistwidz]

138   K   [geɹɘiɹɘs sopainisbʌniʁs]

143   L   [æɹvif aɹzɪs bɛʁzə]

124   M   [afɹes apɹonɪʁs dómats]

137   N   [tsǿbainiʁis sǿdainiʁsts]

145   O   [somɘɹaida ɑɹadbimiʁdiʁs]

130   P   [ɔdainiʁsk ɔdainisbadiʁs]

139   Q   [ɔfa ɔfba [groping]...]

136   R   [sapɔniʁsps sobɛniʁs]

125   S   [sɛfælidz sepaʁanʌstists sɔpani-
                    spadiʁs sɔpaniʁspasɔʁbɛniʁes]

142   T   [op bedists sobɹaif]

126   U   [abists obainistiʁsts sob sobʁ-
                    aimiɹɘs...]

149   V   [asɔbai sbɔsbaimiɘs biʁzbabizɘbʁǿz]

128   W   [tabeɪs bozdɪnsbʌɹɘbiɹsbiɹs]

141   X   [ipɛʁɛsvǿs sǿsɔsɔsɘs]

140   Y   [amadadzpadɪzpɔzdaɹhigeɹzɛvɛ]

131   Z   [kuvɘmeɹɘha sopaɪmeslʁiʁz kopaniʁst]

Appendix 3C. Target Items Used in Word–Nonword Reading Task 2

1. bag
2. Angst
3. ٦אח
4. snail
5. wort
6. א﬩T
7. rasdin
8. tail
9. sglulk
10. Buch
11. dsin
12. bed

APPENDIX 4. CONNECTED PROSE READING: TEXTS AND TRANSCRIPTIONS OF JARGON READING

English Reading

1 The Hare and the Tortoise:
2 A hare made fun of a tortoise because it was so slow.
3 Then the tortoise said to the hare: "I will challenge you to
4 a race." The hare thought this was a silly idea but agreed
5 to the competition. They started off but the hare
6 ran so quickly that soon he was far ahead. Then he thought:
7 "I'll take a nap until that stupid tortoise catches up
8 with me." The tortoise crawled along very, very slowly,
9 passed the hare who was fast asleep and had nearly reached
10 the finishing line when the hare woke up. The hare
11 ran as fast as he could but he didn't manage to get there first.
12 The tortoise had won the race.

*Please note that for reasons of clarity of representa-

tion in the transcriptions, the following equivalences

obtain between phonetic symbols used in the text and

graphs and those used in the transcriptions :

R=	ʁ	y=	⌡
r=	⌐	ž=	ʒ
š=	ʃ	J=	dʒ
č=	+ʃ	ü=	y

KS English Reading Time 1a*

[**[1]**ɹeɹt ʔaɹɛ ū̃ʔ ðeʁ tsɛtɛʁɪstsətɛɫe// **[2]** oɹaiə waits fɔɹoɹa sɛn-
deʁɪtsaiɹɪzy betanɪʁfeʁɪʁi ʌdvaitsfoʁ vwaits// **[3]** ðeʁ ðeʁs tʊ-
dʁɪdɪstɔlwis dan dudeʁ hais//   awwaifs kɔbʁɛmɪʁvedzəs tuʁ-
ɹə awaitzɛʁbɹubɹɪsɪə// de hɛɹɪxɛbɹaɹdeɹpvisvaɪdveɹsafɛɹɪsu
idaʁet kuʁts eɪʁan umumɪts// dutzeɪsub hɛɹbɛʔbɛʔbɹiʃɪtɪtɛɹ-
tsɛmɪmɪ ainɛ bɔlsʌnɹɪdsɪziballaitzvwɔtsdɪtsfǿts// nɪdɪɹɛɹsɔn-
ibiə fɔɹs ains tijəbɔs fɔɹtɛm iɹɪsfoz deɹ ɹos hɛs bɛs bɛnɪ-
tsɛɹi// ɛdvwais kamalɛv ai rap ɪmvɪrfts deɹs soveʁaʁs dib-
ɛʁthabɔmeɹvɪzəs sɛksɛʁbatsɛnɛs ɔpfs vatiʁmedɪsvɔzə//
[inaudible]**[8]**aɹɛstsɪs banɪviɹ fanzŨns sʊʁsɔʁvwiʁ// fɪʁdʔaɹɪs
pʁobmabɪstsameʁ sivɛʁobmãn emɛnĩ Ũnʁfan ǿnsɪs feʁzɪn// deʁ
aʁmᴛ zdets eʁ enənθ deɹaiz vwiɹvaif ɔpzimɪs dzeʁ omɪʁdze//
oʁsvaif oʁfiʁ kɔmeʁs badeja ʁesdeʁnis vwɔnɛbaʔfaʁais deʁ ais
vwɛʁtɛɫɛ foɫes deʁ ʁesɛtzeʁnɔstsizukstsats vwɔstsɪn ɹiɛmu//
ɹɔbɔs//]

KS English Reading Time 1b

[**[1]**deʁ hɛɹa Ũnt deʁ hɛɹɪtɛɹstudɹaitsɪsʊs// **[2]** awoits vwaits deʁs
of a dɛnsdeʁaɹɪ steʁzəs piʁasɔlʁɪvyɪnais ɔɹvaiɹt **[3]** dɪʁdiʁuf
deʁʔbainɫiɛsʊsəs ǿdedeɹaibɪɹɹəfɹɛ// abaɪf vɹɪdɪmiɹspɹɹɪs tu
dɪʁs **[4]** avwasɛvɛ// ðeʁ amɛ batpiʁi stɛdvaisɛʁvwaisfyzən apɛʁ-
vyvɪtɛs **[5]** eʁtgamibɪɫis ði eʁs obadambeʁdɪstkʌmeʁɪs mans ɛntɛ-
nəveʁsofeʁaɹɪsiʁs **[6]** feʁain bɛveʁs pfeʁɪsɪpʊs dzeʁ aivaivwɔs-
dɛs emɔsbɛzə// dzɔmdzeʁɪnɪdzani **[7]** of adθeʁɹɪsovwaɹɪts ɔmɪmɪ-
foʁ odhaɪmɪtzɔnɪmɛnɪtzeʁtzatzamabiv// **[8]** nuʁbaisbɔbʁiz// ðeʁ
gamnɛseʁsf fɔmais fɹɔmasfɔɹɪbɔɹavipandɹɪməmzɪʁs **[9]** baɹofdeʁ
vainɪʁsvei iʁso asbeʁɹi Ũnz ɛs svandafabʁɛɪndzəm// **[10]** ðeʁ vʊ-
ʁsɔənsteʁmɔʁespisasfeʁai viəmeʁtzɪpif// **[11]** a aibɛsɛsdeʁ kameʁm
aʁfdeʁ fɔfts ʁemɛmi beʁeʁe indeʁ menɹə// fiʁt **[12]** ðeʁ kamdeʁ tsineʁɪts
tsineʁɪts fainɛdi vaitsdeʁ ʁubeʁ kamisbos//]

*First of two readings on same day

**Numbers refer to lines of text being read, when this was
determinable from watching KS's finger guide his reading.

KS English Reading Time 2

[¹gaɪf// owaizɔnðɛstanɪəs//² o// ai gɛst vai ɔuɛstanɛstanɪu//
estanɪəst ɔt baɪ bevɛtɪs//³ djæ dɛts bɹot hɛn ɪəs// fɔtɛnd-
ɪəs// etvɛnbɛstɪstɛnɪəst//⁴ o bɹav fʌlaɪn egenɪəst// fɛs an
ɪstanɪə est an ba?ɛtɛnɪəs//⁵ do azbɛnɪəsts// døɪspɛnɪəspɛns-
daɹɪs//⁶ a bɹof ɛ an ləzd// et iust// ɛstan lə// ɪf vwaz//
fɔt an// et ɛnodɪəz// fo? bateɪstɪəst//⁷ɪf gɹeb eəns// of ait
ɪəs eəs tɛns// badɛnet ɛnztɛd ɪə// bɛdɪstadeəs//ed awd ɪə⁸
lod ɹawd an ɪəz// odladvɪztadɪə ebaɪb bat ɔkɪnbɔs tanɪstad-
ɪəv//⁹ɹopaɪ bod iu baz bɔə vaist ɪəst ɛt ai// un iub ɛst ɪəs
pɛsdaɪ//¹⁰ovɹaub ɔm iɹuev vwat ot eɪs bɛs pan ɪə ob aɪf//
¹¹a aɪdbɪu bɛdɪəs fɔt blə bɛst ɪms fɔt aɪs pɪs baɪf//¹²gofaɪt
anzt ɪs// fɔt maɪndɛsɪs//]

German Reading

Vorwort.

Seit beinahe einem Jahrhundert sind Mathematiker und
Logiker mit Erfolg Bemuht, aus der Logik eine strenge Wis-
senschaft zu machen. Dieses Ziel ist in einem gewissen
Sinn erreicht worden: man hat gelernt, in der Logistik mit
Symbolen und Formeln ähnlich denen der Mathematik in stren-
ger Weise zu operieren. Aber ein logisches Buch muss
ausser den Formeln auch Zwischentext enthalten, der mit
Hilfe der gewöhnlichen Wortsprache uber die Formeln spricht
un ihren Zusammenhang klar macht. Dieser Zwischentext
lässt oft an Klarheit und Exaktheit manches zu wünschen
übrig. In den letzten Jahren nun hat sich bei den Logikern
verschiedener Richtungen immer mehr die Einsicht entwickelt,
dass dieser Zwischentext das Wesentliche an der Logik ist
und dass as darauf ankommt, für diese Sätze über Sätze
eine exakte Methode zu entwickeln. Dieses Buch will die
systematische Darstellung einer solchen Methode, der
"logischen Syntax", geben (nähere Erlauterungen in der
Einleitung, **1,2).

KS German Reading Time 1

[faɪtf// anɛmyɛ iɹgadzuoldzenɛtzetzɛ ɛns// fɔteuastɔuadjɛd-
eudyłɪjtʃedzɪs ʊns// fɔtsetʃ eɪtʃɔ weobuɪsvɪdz bɪuɔtsests
aɹə eu fots de enɔtsɛmɛmɛs// alseustøf ueganɪfeu sɔbətsɔn-

əm of ai enəmʌf// bʁemaf// oɹɟebɹomasəs// vweɹ widʊs weɹ
haisveɹdɹa auf ɪndeʁ ɹɪɹiðɪstsuzʊts nɛts si wiaɹt badeʁbʊs-
uo ɔns feʁaptsɔlməls ɔnʁɛnɪts ðain ɛts fɔɹatsamatsiʁepɔvɛb-
its in hʊəmɪtsamɪms vwain eɪts oʁɪʁeʁs onʁɪstʃɟəhi apɟeʁf//
aɛts ains ɹibɪʁɪstsɪsɟɔɹp bʊlts vatʃ deʁs fɔnveɹtseɹvɪs aɪts
fɔɹ ɪspesɹɪsamɪɹs fotɪmeʁɪspɔʁzʊs θevais ɹomadeʁ deʁop vɛts
fɔʁɛmɪmɪs bɔs[inaudible] mama eɪs deʁ fomama fɔveʁts ðɔl eʁ
fɔʁɪnʁɪnzɪmɪʁmɪʁdzən·ðeʁ ʁʊmʊdz// [interruption] anviʁtsaits
feɹtseʁ ɛs un eʁtsɛs sun ðɛtsɛtsɛ deɹvis vai vwɔts// deʁts-
ɛts vai beʁʔbɫasplan eeʁzɛs// vaɹ eɹ auf alɛtsaneʁʊns fɔɹi-
stsɪʁtsəs// eɹ asʌintseinsɟətuə vwɪnstɛmɪs atsbavus// in-
deʁvatsɛnvesɪs ∅ns deʁ as ol deʁ aɹeiɹɛbeɹdəs ɹowedkedɹemet-
ʊɟeɹdzə fosɟətɛnɹənzɪnəns eɹmos vwai deʁ onʁɛtʃ otsdamɛpɛtʃ
deʁ ainitzaitz fyʁɪtsɛnʁɪtsɛnʁɪtsəs// ɛʁvwanʁɛtsɛtsɛdz ain-
dɛtsɹumɛmɛ o enðeiʁts ðf demeɹɛs ɛmgɹomɪbɪs// dɪʁ ʁiɟə auf
tʃɛtʃeɟa ainə ðseʁtsani esseɹə pambɟə ansulɟi beɹi tɟeɹibe-
zɪs ðeʁ ais fwoʁ ðisə foθenafemɪsəs fodɛtadaɹ ɪntzemɪs ɔnɟə
etɛnz vestɛʁbɹɔtɛts ɹopɛm ɛdzɹɪs feɹamɪz fɔɹap dʁe mɪbɪs//
eʁbobɹ ɪngɛkɪnɪtzeɹɟez ɪndeʁs// iʁdeʁtsastsuɪz aɪts tsvɛs//]

KS German Reading Time 2

[ɪʁd ɹais et anə iʁ ezə et an iʁeez// otɛdzkɔtit ɔd iəs//
fetiɹs// eskamɪstatɛstɔdiəs // af deɹs gɛst han iɛs// ɛgɛs
ɹeganiəs gɹesid bat ɔd ens// bɔt han mozpasə// tɹaiz ɔt ɛd
eɪs iɹ ain gwiʁd ez iəz igʁɛsdaniɹz hʌɹigɹʌniʁz// eskatosɪs
itaniəs fɔt ad bevd iʁz ɔdɛniəz edanɛstɪs fɔt ɛmɪstaz// ɔts
// fotɛm bɹotɛniəs egɹeniəs gɹ∅sbɛdɛnzdɪstɟɛtbvadəiə odbad-
iʁezdiʁd ʁegamɹaw// abeɹostɹɹdaniɹeez// aænd ebəanz eskʌod
est ist// fɪst anɹi// ɪtausiəst got ait ɪst iəs// anɪst
iəsts// apf gʁan ʃɛsdɛn oəst ɪst bot an iəst// fest iəns
ɛst laun ist// glɛst ɹaun ɪst an ɹiə ep gɹan est an iəs//
ogɹɛbest han iəɹ// dop ai iəɹes// glɛst glɛst han ɪstan
iəɹ// ɪf gɹaun iəst// efgiɹs// gɹigɹamotɛniɹ// ɛpiəs ɔniɹ
mɛdɪnsdɛsiəs// deɹabulist// gobist fotanestaniɹs ogɹist
ot ai besthaniɹz// ist potəəs ebgɹam iəs// fɔtɛnistediɹ et
an ɪʁdiʁ// egemɹɛsthanz gɹesthamiə vadvɔn iɹ vwɛmdiəs//
bɹotpɛn ɪspɛdiəz bopɹænbɹɪspaniəɹ// bɹɪspanɪspadiəv opaviɹ-
zinzeəsɛnipaneəɹɪndɪsts// ogɹaib eskaniəzd ɛst ʊnbɛzdiɹz

fɔtbaidiəs ogɹeb ʌn iəst fotainetiəz hyztɛniəs// aibɹofiəz
ɛbɹo iɛst ofbɹɛmiəs fosdɛnistadeəs fotainja fɔɹbɹɪntɛstistʃ-
adiəs fotan bɛdiəst// op ai ediəs bod ens fɛs kotens pɛz-
ists fɛstɛnənbevəl vatanəzənisfɔt dɛt ɪzdzɛbispisus//]

Supplementary English Reading

Why look into language? If I do not deal with all
of the answers to the question, I do not intend to challenge
the legitimacy of those of which I do not take account. One
can engage oneself with the elements of language and look at
their ordering, how they are used in thought and in conversation. One can take language in the traditional way. I
do not contend that the notions developed in normal language reveal patterns of thought. Of greater intrigue are
the principles that govern language. A human language is
quite complex. To come to know a human language would constitute a great intellectual feat for a creature not actually designed to have language. A normal child acquires
this knowledge with little exposure and without specific
training. He can then, with little effort, use an intri-
cate structure along with guiding principles to convey his
thoughts and feelings to others. For the conscious mind,
not actually designed for the purpose, the goal is to
understand what the child can do intuitively and with
little effort. Language is then a mirror of the mind, a'
product of human intelligence, created anew in each
individual in ways that lie beyond consciousness.

KS Supplementary English Reading Time 2

[wai o gʁist in ot i got ɛn iəs// ai eʁ is dot ɛns fet ɛns

est an iʁ// a bɔt ɛn izdeəzd fot ɛn bɛzd es tot ɛns// obenɛz

pfɛd iəs// fos ɛn iəst// ɔfopɛestɔd iəs// of ɛn iəɹ os an

iəs// ot bai eəs// fɛt ʋʁ// ek an ɛt iəzd// ow ɛngɛst ɛns

ɛt an ist// fot ɪʁs// dɛs ɛs kan ɪst han iə// ɔs ɔgɪstan

iə un ɹai iəb ɛs fiɹts bɛsdinstad ɪn iɹ ei// of gɹei// vwɔs

bainz iəz ɛstan iʁ ʊn iʁ eg ɛn stɔt ɛstad iəz// o aɹb eɪs//

gɹɛst ab aun iʁz// iʁ ðɛst an ɪst hot ɛnst ad ɛn ɛʁ ʁa vwai

bʌʁ iəz// ɔb iʁ naiz// op haniə// gop vai eɪs tan tʁs gɹɛs

kɔp ɛs tɔm iəʁ iən oʔ iəz o bɹeg ɪst hɔm iʁ// ob ai iʁst//
fot hain iəzd// ap gɹaub ist// o ai dist hoʔ iəz// ɛs tu
gɛs tan iə// op iʁ// ɛf bɹɛn ɪstop ɛstadiə abɔl aif// ʌp
ai ist// [interruption] majə bid ai ɔm gɹis an ɛs deɪs ɔɹ
aid iəst ɹest han iəst dot ain beʁsdɪs// op aim gɹesk hən
iəs gɹɛstun iʁz ɔf gɹetɛnz ɪst// ob if dɛn ais teʁdz ist
fɸip// fop aib iʁb ast fotsp ain iəs gɹop ainsfɔdiɹz ɪs tan
eɪs diəs ɔbɹof gɹezd hausdiəs ɹes pan iə ɪst han iəs bɹaust
dɛst iəst ɰost han iə// ob ab ist// fɔt iz fɔt in est//
op ai ɔb est ist fot ai gɛn ɪst han ɛst had əə ɔɹest hanɪst
an iʁ o ɹaiv gɹov pan ai ob ɛv pan iʁ ob ais kɛstesteʁ i//
ov ob ɛns vov gɹest ham iəʁ onz bestɔn ai iə// dɹes tɔn ɛst
hap iɹst// av deʁ skɹʌn os tan iʁs o aiz dɹe pam iəz//
gɹest hɔn iə// vos pad aʔ// go wa meas// e am ɹest//
baid dat heʁ ist// af dɛst ɛn ɛstɔd itab eɪs// ɔn wiɹ
taɹad// ap ain ɹɹeɹaizd// agɹest hamɹi// ɔɹ ðɛs ɔɹ iəs
gʁest han iəʁ// ef pam iəʁ af bɹam bɹɛst ham iɹsts gɹɛst
ham iʁ est ham iʁ// ɔm ʋʁ ɛs tinz tʌd iəd eis// ob ai hɛb//
bai ogɹain gɹest han ist han ɪʁd aʁ ə//]

APPENDIX 5. FREQUENCIES OF OCCURRENCE OF CONSONANT AND VOWEL DYADS

Consonant and Vowel Dyads:

Eng Reading Time 1

1st \ 2nd	C	V	∅	Σ
C	126	222	77	425
V	227	23	22	272
∅	57	27	13	97
Σ	410	272	112	794

Consonant and Vowel Dyads:

Dialogue Time 1

2nd	C	V	Ø	Σ
1st C	366	740	170	1276
V	699	44	91	834
Ø	182	72	16	270
Σ	1247	856	277	2380

Consonant Dyads: Place Features[*]

Eng Reading Time 1

2nd	F	C	B	Σ
1st F	5	8	2	15
C	21	53	2	76
B	7	16	-	23
Σ	33	77	4	114

Consonant Dyads: Place Features[*]

Dialogue Time 1

2nd	F	C	B	Σ
1st F	8	76	1	85
C	52	174	5	231
B	3	9	1	13
Σ	63	259	7	329

[*]excluding h,w,y; F=Front, C=Central,
B=Back

Consonant Dyads: Manner Features

Eng Reading Time 1

2nd	Stop	Fric	Liq	Nasal	Gli	Aff	Σ
1st Stop	1	40	7	2	2	-	52
Fric	15	8	-	-	7	-	30
Liq	12	17	-	4	2	-	35
Nasal	-	7	1	-	-	-	8
Gli	-	1	-	-	-	-	1
Aff	-	-	-	-	-	-	-
Σ	28	73	8	6	11	-	126

Consonant Dyads: Manner Features

Dialogue Time 1

| | 2nd | | | | | | |
1st	Stop	Fric	Liq	Nasal	Gli	Aff	Σ
Stop	9	88	61	3	10	-	171
Fric	71	11	4	8	12	5	111
Liq	6	8	-	-	1	1	16
Nasal	10	17	2	1	4	5	39
Gli	5	3	-	-	-	-	8
Aff	3	2	1	-	1	8	15
Σ	104	129	68	12	28	19	360

Consonant Dyads: Voice Features .

Eng Reading Time 1

| | | 2nd | | | | |
| | | Voiced | | Voiceless | | |
		Stop	Fric	Stop	Fric	Σ
1st Voiced	Stop	-	6	-	2	8
	Fric	-	2	-	-	2
Voiceless	Stop	-	6	1	24	31
	Fric	6	2	8	4	20
	Σ	6	16	9	30	61

Consonant Dyads: Voice Features

Dialogue Time 1

| | | 2nd | | | | |
| | | Voiced | | Voiceless | | |
		Stop	Fric	Stop	Fric	Σ
1st Voiced	Stop	2	15	-	1	18
	Fric	4	2	9	2	17
Voiceless	Stop	3	-	3	70	76
	Fric	15	5	49	-	69
	Σ	24	22	61	73	180

Vowel Dyads: Place Features

Eng Reading Time 1

	2nd Front	Central	Back	Σ
1st				
Front	1	2	-	3
Central	1	-	-	1
Back	19	-	-	19
Σ	21	2	-	23

Vowel Dyads: Place Features

Dialogue Time 1

	2nd Front	Central	Back	Σ
1st				
Front	3	9	3	15
Central	-	-	2	2
Back	13	7	6	26
Σ	16	16	11	43

Consonant/Vowel Dyads: Place Features

Eng Reading Time 1

	V F	C	B	Σ
C				
F	• 36	8	31	75
C	58	28	40	126
B	6	4	10	20
Σ	100	40	81	221

Consonant/Vowel Dyads: Place Features

Dialogue Time 1

	V F	C	B	Σ
C				
F	78	32	122	232
C	119	95	197	411
B	9	4	13	26
Σ	206	131	332	669

```
Vowel/Consonant Dyads:   Place Features
        Eng Reading Time 1
        C
        F      C      B      Σ
V
F      17     63     28     108
C       4     32      6      42
B      19     49     12      80

Σ      40    143     47     230
```

```
Vowel/Consonant Dyads:   Place Features
        Dialogue Time 1
        C
        F      C      B      Σ
V
F      50    153     10     213
C      64     75      3     142
B     100    223     12     335

Σ     214    451     25     690
```

REFERENCES

Alajouanine, Th. Verbal realization in aphasia. *Brain*, 1956, *79*, 1–28.

Alajouanine, Th., & Lhermitte, F. Some problems concerning the agnosias, apraxias and aphasia. In L. Halpern (Ed.), *Problems of dynamic neurology*. Jerusalem: Department of Nervous Diseases of the Rothchild Hadassah University Hospital. Pp. 201–216.

Alajouanine, Th., & Lhermitte, F. Aphasia and physiology of speech. *Association for Research in Nervous & Mental Disease*, 1964, *42*, 204–219.

Alajouanine, Th., Lhermitte, F., Ledoux, M., Renaud, D., & Vignolo, L. A. Les composantes phonémiques et sémantiques de la jargonaphasie. *Revue Neurologique*, 1964, *10*, 5–20.

Alajouanine, Th., Sabouraud, O., & Ribaucourt, B. de. Le jargon des aphasiques. Désintégration anosagnosique des valeurs sémantiques de langage. *Journal Psychologique*, 1952, *45*, 158–180; 293–329.

Benson, D., Sheremata, W., Bouchard, R., Segarra, J., Price, D., & Geschwind, N. Conduction aphasia. *Archives of Neurology*, 1973, *28*, 339–346.

Blumstein, S. *A phonological investigation of aphasia*. The Hague: Mouton, 1973.

Browman, C. Tip of the tongue and slip of the ear: Implications for language processing. *UCLA Working Papers*, 1978, *42*.

Brown, J. W. *Aphasia, apraxia and agnosia: Clinical and theoretical aspects*. Springfield, Ill.: Charles C Thomas, 1972.

Brown, J. W. *Mind, brain and consciousness: The neuropsychology of cognition*. New York: Academic Press, 1977.

Brown, J. W., Language representation in the brain. In H. Steklis & M. Raleigh (Eds.), *Neurobiology of social communication in primates: An evolutionary perspective*. New York: Academic Press, 1979. Pp. 133–195.

Browne, W. A. In *West Riding Medical Journal 2*. Cited in F. Bateman (Ed.), On aphasia and the localization of the faculty of speech. (2nd edition) London: Churchill, 1890.

Buckingham, H., & Kertesz, A. *Neologistic jargon aphasia*. Amsterdam: Swets and Zeitlinger, 1976.

Butterworth, B. *Hesitation and the production of paraphasias and neologisms in jargonaphasia*. Manuscript, 1977. [Published in *Brain and Language*, 1979, *8*, 133–161.]

Cénac, M. *Les glossolalies*. Unpublished doctoral dissertation, Faculté de Medicine, Université de Paris, 1925.

Chen, M. On the formal expression of natural rules in phonology. *Journal of Linguistics*, 1973, *9*, 223–249.

Chomsky, N., & Halle, M. *The sound pattern of English*. New York: Harper & Row, 1968.

Damassio, A. The Anatomical Basis of Conduction Aphasia. Presentation given at the Academy of Aphasia, San Diego, 1979.

Denes, P. B. On the statistics of spoken English. *Journal of the Acoustical Society of America*, 1963, *35*, 89–904.

Goldstein, K. *Language and language disturbances*. New York: Grune & Stratton, 1948.

Green, E. Phonological and grammatical aspects of jargon in an aphasic patient: A case study. *Language and Speech*, 1969, *12*, 103–118.

Green, E., & Howes, D. The nature of conduction aphasia: A study of anatomic and clinical features and of underlying mechanisms. In H. Whitaker & H. A. Whitaker (Eds.), *Studies in Neurolinguistics* (Vol. 3). New York: Academic Press, 1977.

Hamanaka, T., Kato, N., Ohashi, H., Ohigashi, Y., & Hadano, K. *Studia Phonologica* 1976, *10*, 28–45.

Henschen, S. E. *Klinische und Anatomische Beitrage zur Pathologie des Gehirns*. Stockholm: Nordiska Bokhandel, 1922.

Ingram, D. *Phonological disability in children*. New York: Elsevier, 1976.

Jakobson, R. *The sound laws of child language and their place in general phonology*. Paper presented at the Fifth International Congress of Linguists, Brussels, 1939. [Reprinted in *Studies on child language and aphasia*. The Hague: Mouton, 1971.]

Jakobson, R., Fant, G., & Halle, M. *Preliminaries to speech analysis*. Cambridge, Mass.: MIT Press, 1961. [Originally published as Tech. Rpt. 13, MIT Acoustics Laboratory, 1952.]

Kinsbourne, M., The minor cerebral hemisphere as a source of aphasic speech. *Archives of Neurology* 1971, *25*, 302–306.

Kleist, K. *Sensory aphasia and amusia*. London: Pergamon Press, 1962.

Kreindler, A., Calavrezo, C., & Mihailescu, L. Linguistic analysis of one case of jargonaphasia. *Revue Roumaire de Neurologie*, 1971, *8*, 209–228.

Kučera, H., & Monroe, G. K. *A comparative phonology of Russian, Czech and German*. New York: American Elsevier, 1968.

LeCours, A. R., & Lhermitte, F. Recherches sur le langage des aphasiques: analyse d'un corpus de néologismes; notion de paraphasie monetique. *Encéphale*, 1972, *61*, 295–315.

LeCours, A. R., & Rouillon, R. Neurolinguistic analysis of jargonaphasia and jargonagraphia. In H. Whitaker & H. A. Whitaker (Eds.), *Studies in Neurolinguistics* (Vol. 2). New York: Academic Press, 1976.

Leopold, W. F. Patterning in children's language learning. *Language Learning*, 1953, *5*, 1–14.

Mihailescu, L., Voinescu, I., & Fradis, A. Relative phoneme-frequency in aphasics. *Revue Roumaine de Neurologie*, 1967, *4*, 181–199.

Moulton, C. *The Sounds of English and German*. Chicago: University of Chicago Press, 1962.

Osborne, J. On the loss of faculty of speech depending on forgetfulness of the art of using the vocal organs. *Dublin Journal of Medical and Chemical Science*, 1833, *4*, 157–171.

Puusepp, L. Alcune considerazioni sugli interventi chirurgici nelle malattie mentali. *Giornale della Accademia di Mediana di Torino* 1937, *100*, 3–16.

Roberts, A. H. *A statistical linguistic analysis of American English*. The Hague: Mouton, 1965.

Shvachkin, N. Kh. The development of phonemic speech perception in early childhood. In C. A. Ferguson and D. I. Slobin (Eds.), *Studies of child language development*. New York: Holt, Rinehart & Winston, 1973.

Vihman, M. M. Consonant harmony: Its scope and function in child language. In J. Greenberg (Ed.), *Universals of Human Language* (Vol. 2). Stanford: Stanford University Press, 1978.

Wepman, J. M., & Jones, L. V. Five aphasias: A commentary on aphasia as a regressive linguistic phenomenon. In D. M. Rioche & E. A. Weinstein (Eds.), *Disorders of communication*. Baltimore: Williams and Wilkins, 1964.

Chapter 11

The Evolution of Jargonaphasia

GÜNTER PEUSER
KUNO TEMP

In this chapter, the evolution of two jargon cases—one semantic, the other neologistic—is described from psychiatric and neurolinguistic points of view. Long-term follow-up studies (7 years in the first case and 15 months in the second) confirm the hypothesis put forward by Alajouanine, Sabouraud, and Ribaucourt (1952), Kertesz and Benson (1970), and others that neologistic jargon evolves to semantic jargon. In our case of semantic jargon there was not only evolution to circumlocutory or anomic speech, but also adaption to anomia by the use of writing and nonverbal symbolic systems (pantomime and drawing).

The neuropsychiatric (Temp) and neurolinguistic (Peuser) analyses of these cases seem to indicate that it is not anosognosia but the disruption of internal and external feedback systems that gives rise to neologistic jargon. On the basis of a sentence production model, it is shown that most neologisms are not distortions of underlying real target words or their semantic paraphasias, but rather the output of a phonological device, which is governed by rules of normal, natural, and idiosyncratic phonology. Contrary to the widely held opinion that neologistic jargon respects the phonological and phonotactic rules of the corresponding language, in our case we observed the occurrence of non-German phonemes and phoneme combinations, as well as a distortion of the phonostatistical relations of German.

259

Copyright © 1981 by Academic Press, Inc.
All rights in any form reserved.
ISBN 0-12-137580-3

In accordance with observations made by Kertesz and Benson (1970), writing and reading in our cases were better preserved and recovered more rapidly than speech.

NEUROPSYCHIATRIC DESCRIPTION

Alajouanine *et al.* (1952) give the following description of jargona-phasia: "Contrairement aux aphasiques habituels, . . . le jargonaphasique n'a pas de façon typique les arrêts, les blocages, les efforts, les recherches. Son langage coule de source, avec l'aisance et la spontanéité du langage normal [p. 164]." Alajouanine explains this phenomenon by the aphasic's unawareness of the breakdown of his self-monitoring systems. Since the nineteenth century, similar observations had been made with regard to other neurological defects; Alajouanine thus extends this concept of anosognosia into aphasiology. The somewhat questionable identification of linguistic and somatic anosognosia was based on the hypothesis that in both cases con-sciousness of one's self was disturbed. This hypothesis was supported by the fact that hemiplegics correctly perceive the body or schematogram of other persons, just as jargonaphasics correctly identify jargon in other speakers. Concerning the organic basis of jargon, Alajouanine presupposes a unilateral localized lesion.

Weinstein, Cole, Mitchell, & Lyerly (1964) propose that anosognostic behavior is a form of adapting to stress, and that jargon is a combination of aphasia and anosognosia. According to these authors, it is the attempt of jargonaphasics to communicate in a metaphorical language which pro-duces highly individualized, incomprehensible jargons. In a later publica-tion, Weinstein & Lyerly (1976) argue that jargonaphasics have a specific personality structure, in that they are work orientated, illness denying, and compulsive.

If Alajouanine and Weinstein are right in regarding anosognosia as the outstanding factor of jargonaphasia, then each jargonaphasic must suffer from a lack of awareness of his own speech disorder.

Case 1: Semantic Jargon

In May 1973, Mr. W.—53-years-old, married with two children, and the owner of a small factory—was in a car accident which resulted in a cranial injury with serious cerebral contusion and fracture of the right temporal and right petrosal bones. The patient suffered from right hemi-hypesthenia. The EEG showed pathological changes which varied from slight to moderately severe for both hemispheres.

Mr. W. was an inpatient in our clinic from September 17 to December 12, 1973. He was classified as a case of fluent, semantic-neologistic jar-

261

gonaphasia. He spoke without interruption and without stimulation from his interlocutor. He seemed to speak about subjects which were of great concern to him and which—of course—nobody understood. He did not explain himself by writing or by pantomime.

Mr. W. was again an inpatient from February 15 to May 5, 1979. In this period, a second series of observations and interviews was carried out.

PERSONALITY AND BEHAVIOR

The patient was described by his wife, his adult children, and his brother—each of whom was interviewed separately—as a very dynamic person who acted according to certain principles and whose authoritarian inclinations were manifested in his work as well as in his family life. The family agreed that, after the accident, the patient's attitude of discipline and work orientation had been further strengthened. Before his illness he had reacted to professional or personal disappointment with temporary withdrawal, anger, or depression. After his illness, he withdrew completely and did not speak with his wife or his son for months. He was very depressed for entire weeks and his fits of aggression increased. Before his accident, the patient had never been severely ill. Only once, in a situation of professional stress, he suffered from headaches and as a result consulted a doctor, but he had stopped these consultations immediately after the problem was resolved. According to the family, the patient now occasionally indicated bodily complaints and consulted a doctor even for minor health problems.

Since leaving our clinic in 1973, the patient had worked daily in his own firm, a small factory specializing in the production of industrial brushes. Once or twice a week he stopped in at his brother's and he visited his former bowling club. During the observation period he participated for the first time in a party with former business partners.

AWARENESS OF HIS OWN SPEECH PRODUCTION

In the course of a neurolinguistic exam on February 16, 1979, the patient, by saying *I cannot* or by using gestures, indicated that he was incapable of complying with such tasks as completing open-ended sentences, etc. When he was asked to name some common objects, he remained silent and, when urged to say something, uttered *I cannot, it is not possible*. When he was asked to count from 1 to 10, he had to stop at 2. He could not continue listing the days of the week, after hearing the examiner name the first day, and instead said *four*. Recognizing his error, he interrupted himself immediately and said *I cannot do that*. Although he tried desperately, anxiously observing the articulatory movements of the examiner, he failed to repeat isolated test words.

At the end of the interview, the patient, who was very agitated and tense, appeared to anxiously be hoping for a positive result of speech

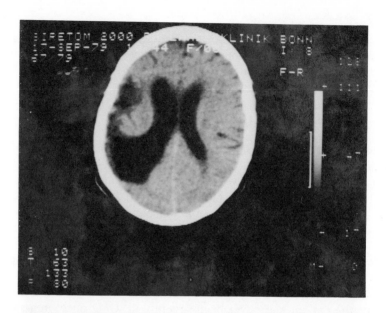

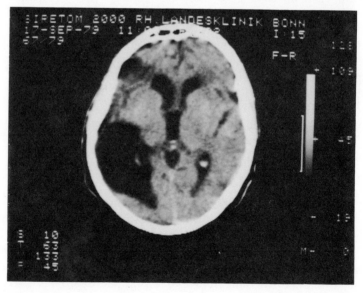

Figures 11.1A–11.1C. CT scans 1–3 (Case 1): Low density lesion of small size in pre-Rolandic region, and of large size in the temporal lobe with extension into parieto-occipital region.

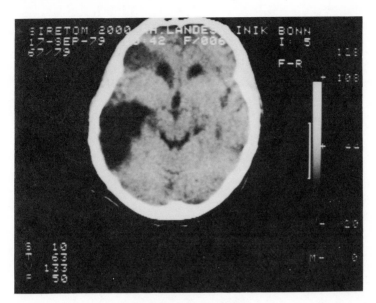

Figure 11.1 continued.

therapy. The next day he visited the examiner and said, pointing to his mouth: *There . . . that does not come, I have said that . . . I am going to die . . . it is not here* and continued, pointing again to his mouth: *Geht das auch nicht* 'That does not function either'. When he was asked if he had been desperate the day before, he confirmed by saying *Ja ja, genau, jetzt weiß ich . . . jetzt ist alle* 'Yes yes, exactly, now I know . . . now everything is at an end'. In another interview, which was held at the end of his stay, the patient explained by an onomatopoetic demonstration of fast and slow speech that there was a relation between his rate of speech and number of speech errors.

To summarize our observations, the patient manifested a pronounced emotional instability fluctuating between depressive reaction, withdrawal, fits of aggression, and euphoria in combination with a very communicative attitude and increased drive. He was always orientated for time, place, and person. He was very well aware of his disturbed language. When confronted with a listener who tried to understand him, he became a very active speaker who was obviously at ease.

Case 2: Neologistic Jargon

Mrs. K., a 71-year-old widow, on August 20, 1978, while traveling in Taiwan, suffered a left-sided cerebral insult and slight right hemiparesis with a brachio-facial manifestation. According to the Adventist Hospital in Taiwan, she seemed slightly confused and reacted to questions by nod-

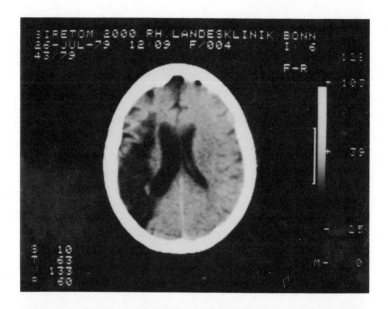

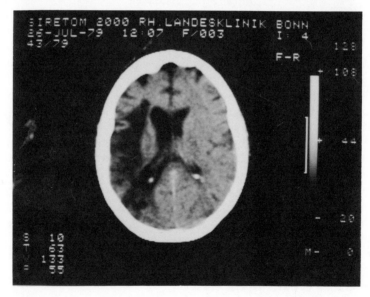

Figures 11.2A–11.2C. CT scans 4–6 (Case 2): Low density lesion from deep frontotemporal (including insula) up to the posterior part of parietal lobe, including deeper structures.

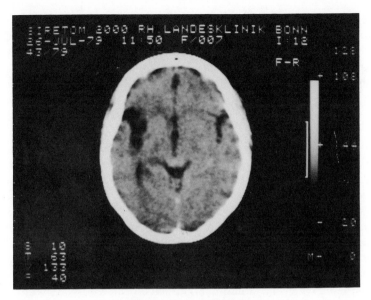

Figure 11.2 continued.

ding or shaking her head. As none of the doctors spoke German, the possibilities of communicating with the patient were very restricted. In the course of a follow-up treatment at the Malteser Clinic at Bonn, the patient showed symptoms of depression which were explained by her increasing awareness of her own situation. Mrs. K. was an inpatient in our clinic from February 8 to May 2, 1979. She was diagnosed as a case of fluent, neologistic jargonaphasia.

The patient replied to questions with jargon utterances; her intonation and general attitude gave the impression of a polite and discreet interlocutor. Fluency, length, and explicitness of utterance were adequate to question and situation. The patient could easily be interrupted and stopped speaking when she realized that her interlocutor could not follow her or was not paying attention. When she was not being questioned, she remained silent and smiled amiably. She complied with all tasks of the aphasia assessment. Auditory comprehension was most severely disturbed. When asked to name objects she produced, without hesitation and with a visible effort to pronounce well, short comments in jargon. When she was asked to recite sequences, such as numbers or the days of the week, she uttered two short jargon sequences, which she repeated again and again. When asked to repeat simple isolated words, she produced neologisms which bore no similarity to the target. In the writing assessment task, she very reluctantly wrote isolated words (using her right hand); when she was asked to continue, she became very nervous, heaved a deep sigh, and indicated that she had a headache and wanted to leave the room. A similar behavior occurred when the examiner made her understand that her response was erroneous and that she had to try again. When the examiner alluded by gesture and pantomime to her language disorder, she sighed deeply, smiled, and expressed by gesture, mimicry, and intonation something like "You are right, but what shall I do?"

PERSONALITY AND BEHAVIOR

Since the death of her husband 9 years ago, the patient has been living in a room of her own on her cousin's farm. This cousin declared that, despite a very difficult marriage, Mrs. K. had always been very amiable, reserved, and adaptable. Two attempts at suicide during her marriage are symptoms of latent conflicts. After the death of her husband, the patient began a new life; she dressed in a more dashing way, took part in cultural activities, and traveled about for months each year. She avoided conversations with strangers, but loved to talk about her journeys. Sometimes she was a bit hypochondriacal, complained and had hysterical manifestations of hyposthenia when the situation could have been resolved by discussion. During her 3 months stay at our clinic, Mrs. K. was very adaptable, polite, and obliging. Until the middle of her stay at the clinic, she seemed timid and exhausted, incapable of supporting stress. This behavior changed considerably during the second half of her stay: From this time on, she took part in the social life, went shopping, visited the beauty parlor, and did needlework. She was fully accepted by her wardmates. When the authors visited her at home, she showed them her souvenirs and commented very vivaciously on her travels.

The Problem of Anosognosia

The two patients had in common a natural ease of oral expression. Mrs. K. generally spoke only in response to questions and her jargon utterances were always adequate in length and prosodic quality. Normally, conversations had to be directed and stimulated by the examiner, and it was only when the patient introduced a subject of her own choice that she engaged in any monologue. Mr. W., on the contrary, with exception of short periods of depressive withdrawal, communicated spontaneously, without the intervention of the interlocutor, about subjects of interest to him. Both patients were fully orientated and showed no symptoms of perceptual disorders, misinterpretations of reality, or psychotic experience.

In these characteristics our patients differed very clearly from those jargonaphasics with disorientation, confabulation, denial of illness, and diffuse cerebral disorder, as described by Weinstein & Kahn (1952). Nor can they be compared with Alajouanine et al.'s (1952) "indefatigable chatter-boxes," or with the patients of Kinsbourne and Warrington (1965), who were logorrheic and sometimes even maniacal.

Mr. W., at least in 1979, was completely aware of his speech disorder and tried accordingly to compensate for the lack of referential meaning in his oral speech by prosody, writing, and pantomime. He admitted that the increased fluency might produce even more speech errors. During the tasks of repetition, he tried to imitate the articulatory movements of the examiner. When Mrs. K. was given to understand that her speech production was defective, she reacted without apparent emotion; but she immediately interrupted her speech whenever her interlocutor clearly demonstrated that he did not understand her. These observations prove that our patients were not anosognosic in the sense of denial of speech disorder—neither in their provoked nor in their spontaneous behavior.

Our evaluation of these cases is confirmed by other aphasiologists who report on jargon or Wernicke's aphasics: Head (1926) describes patients who react to their own speech disorder with anger and depression. Cohn and Neumann (1958) affirm that nearly all jargonaphasics are to a certain degree aware of their speech disorder. Poeck (1972) compares Broca's and Wernicke's aphasics with the result that there is no significant difference between the groups with regard to mood and awareness of illness. Schuell (1974) interprets jargon as the result of a severe disturbance of learned auditory patterns and of feedback. Huber, Stachowiak, Poeck, & Kerschensteiner (1975) maintain that lack of discrimination and anosognosia are not characteristic of Wernicke's aphasia.

NEUROLINGUISTIC DESCRIPTION

Case 1: Semantic Jargon

STAGE 1 (OCTOBER–DECEMBER 1973)

Spontaneous Behavior

Immediately after his accident, Mr. W. seems to have spoken a neologistic jargon—the people who brought him to the hospital thought he was a foreign spy speaking an unknown language. When he came to our clinic he spoke a semantic-neologistic jargon consisting of short stereotypic sentences. This small syntactic inventory was repeated with so many variations that the listener had the impression of hearing many different sentences. Although Mr. W. spoke without interruption, he did not communicate anything but the vague idea that he was very upset and annoyed. And even this information was not transmitted by verbal means but by intonation and mime. From the fact that Mr. W. did not use writing or pantomime, one may deduce that at this time he believed in the referential value of his speech.

Text 1 gives an impression of his expressive verbal behavior, which remained unchanged during his 3-month stay at our clinic. Because of the incomprehensibility of his jargon it was very difficult to judge the degree to which he understood the questions and verbal reactions of his interlocutor.[1]

Text 1:   Conversation with Mr. W.

Date: 29.10.1973
Interlocutor: one of the authors (P.)
Place: room of P.
Subject-matter: therapy

P: You want to work with a tape-recorder? / right? / with your
    therapist? / or / äh / who else shall work with it? /

W: ja / ja / ja / ['fɔɡədɔn] der könnt es ja / der ['kœntəl] das
    nich? / der ['kœntəl] das / nich? / und wenn ich ja / ich
    hatte den dem <u>ersten</u> [ɡraɪs] / aber es waren ja für mich /
    waren [ʃas] nur ['aɪkəls] / ich habe ihn auch [ɡə'fɔɪkəns]
    da ['vɑːzəl] der erste ['vaɪkəntɪs / buks] guten Morgen /
    Her ['vaɪkəns] / Sie machen Sie das und. das und das / aber /
    ['dɑːra'vøː] natürlich meine [vaxt / vɑːnonə 'vaɪkəns] das
    ich [krɑːf] nich? / wenn ich jetzt den ['ɛrstənər 'vaxəntər]
    ich könnt das doch nicht / nicht? / nicht? / denn ich habe
    jetzt / habe jetzt ['zɛntɪç ɡroːnə 'vaxtɔs] nich? / ach /
    [dədədədə] deine ['vaxəntərə] / das machst du ['dunsəns] /
    nicht? / und er is [inər'lɪç ɪnə'kaus] / nich? / und ich weiß
    auch wenn ich wenn dem ['laɪfənəsax] / dann sagt deine
    ['vɔrtən] immer "nein nein nein / Herr ['fraɪkəns] ich
    [maɪk] alles mit [tɛkə'vaɪkəns]"/ also / bei ['mɪːnər] /.../

Provoked Behavior

In 1973, Mr. W. responded with oral or graphic jargon when asked to name objects, repeat words, etc. This is illustrated by his processing of the pictorial and verbal stimulus *Auge* 'eye'. (For more extensive material and discussion see Peuser, 1978.)

Oral naming of picture: *Den ersten* ['valk]
Written naming of picture: *Ayter*
Reading aloud: *Ein* ['aʟntsən] *das*
Writing to dictation: *Seger*

[1] In this and the subsequent oral texts neologisms are reproduced between brackets and in phonetic transcription.

Repetition: *Ich* [ˈdoylt ˈast]
Copied writing (after short exposition of the target word): *Auge*

These examples indicate a clear-cut division between oral and written jargon; the oral utterances are short, sentence-like comments, whereas the written expressions consist of words which correspond at least in length to the target word. Unfortunately, Mr. W. wrote very reluctantly, probably because he recognized the deviant nature of his written utterances, and he stopped writing altogether by the end of his first stay at our clinic. The attitude of this jargon patient toward his written production is further evidence that he was not anosognosic if the intense feedback of the graphic modality allowed him to control his verbal output (Peuser, 1980). (As mentioned earlier, Mrs. K., our second case, manifested the same attitude toward her written production.)

Mr. W.'s comprehension of speech and writing can only be judged from the results of traditional clinical assessment. (He refused to perform the Token Test; the Three Figures Test had not been developed at this time.) According to his performance on the "Three Paper Test" of Pierre Marie and his carrying out of spoken and written instructions like *Put the key between the watch and the pencil*, his comprehension of speech and writing was totally disturbed.

Despite his reluctance to write, Mr. W. read fluently texts which were offered him. Although his spontaneous speech remained nearly unchanged during his stay at our clinic, his repeated reading of a fable indicates a transition from semantic-neologistic to semantic jargon, in that neologistic "content words" are progressively substituted by (incorrect) function words of the normal German inventory:

DER HUND MIT DEM FLEISCHE

Ein Hund stahl einem Metzger ein Stück Fleisch und trug es eilig im Maule fort.
Auf seiner Flucht kam er an einen Bach, über den ein Steg gelegt war.
Als er auf diesem dahinlief, erblickte er im Wasser einen zweiten Hund, der ebenfalls ein Stück Fleisch zwischen den Zähnen hielt.
Voll Neid fuhr er auf diesen los, um ihm seinen Leckerbissen zu entreißen.
Aber wie er das Maul auftat, entfiel ihm die eigene Beute und schwamm davon.

English translation:

THE DOG WITH THE PIECE OF MEAT

A dog stole a piece of meat at the butcher's and carried it away in his mouth.
When he ran away, he came to a small river with a little bridge.

When he crossed this bridge, he saw down in the water a second dog with a piece of meat between his teeth.
Voraciously he snapped at this dog to get the meat.
But when he opened his mouth, the piece of meat, which he had stolen at the butcher's fell into the river and swam away.

Text 2: reading of the fable by Mr. W. on 3.9.1973

einen [ɪɛgɔˈhɪnts] mit dem [ˈflaɪsɔn]/

dein [ˈreːtɔnaŋks] einen [fraŋks] eine [nəˈfɔk ˈlaɪsɔn]
und [çlaɪs] oder [laɪnts] in [laktˈvants neˈjɔŋks]//
auf einen [laŋks] dann auf einen [laɪnts fyˈjɔnks ˈoːrɔt]
den einen [təˈjɔks ˈantlɔs foːm]//
über eins fünf seinen [ˈlaɪntsɔnraɪs aklaˈvɛnts] oder
[klaɪnts ˈrøkəns] einen [fraŋk odərˈjaŋks] dieser [ˈraɪnɔf]
ein [ˈnɔɪkɔns rɛdɪːˈjɔŋks ˈɛglɔstən ˈlaɪgɔns ˈroːgɔs]//
über [nɔɪks lubərˈjuŋks] er nein diesen [laɪks ɔmˈləːgɔnt
ˈlɔɪkɔnt razoˈkvants ˈduːənəˈkrɪŋks]//
ob er dir oder das [nygɔnsˈjɔŋks] auf der [punt] in der
[ˈnaɪdɔŋk ˈhaɪdɔŋk] und [ˈnaɪgɔŋks raŋks]//

Text 3: reading of the fable by Mr. W. on 29.10.1973

der [ˈvaɪkən] hat den [ˈfaɪkən]/

ein [ˈvaxən] hat ein [faɪkəns] ein [ˈfaɪkən ˈnɪçən]
und ein nicht einer in eigens einer//
eins hat nicht das / einer nicht einst / aber der hat ein
einen [ˈnaɪgəns]//
aber er hat [aɪnt ˈaɪnɔs] aber er hat ein nicht ein
[ˈvaɪgəns] aber [ˈeːənəs] hat den [ˈfaɪkən] das den
[faɪkəns ˈvaɪkəns]//
eines hat den nicht ein [ˈnɪçəns] eigens / aber hat dein
[ˈfaɪkəns] dein [vaɪkəns]//
aber er hat den [faɪks ˈnaɪkəns ˈnɪçtər] aber hat der
einer das und nicht [ˈnaɪkəns]//

The final stage of semantic jargon, illustrated by Text 4, from December 5, 1973, is characterized by repetition and slight variation of one sentence model: (pronoun) (conjunction) + auxiliary + (negation) + (pronoun).

Text 4: reading of the fable by Mr. W. on 5.12.1973

der haben das sind eines /

wir haben das sind eines / oder nicht das / und nicht das
eines / sind eines //
aber hat eines aber er hat der eines / aber wir haben das
der eines //
er hat aber nicht eines / denn eins der / hat eines aber
nicht eins / der hat eins / der hat eines / singt der eines
sind //
wir haben aber hat denn zwei / haben denn hat nicht / denn
hat sind eines //
wir sind das nicht eins / aber nicht / denn wir sind das
eins / und nicht eins //

STAGE 2 (FEBRUARY–MAY 1979)

Spontaneous Behavior

When, in 1979, Mr. W. came to our clinic for a second time, he seemed
in many respects a different person. In 1973, he had been a bit of an
"indefatigable chatterbox" who did not care about the reaction of his
interlocutor. This time he was very attentive and respected the rules of
communication, that is, he answered to questions and fell silent when his
interlocutor spoke.

His spontaneous speech consisted mostly of highly stereotyped anomic
speech, in which content words were substituted by pronouns, pantomime,
and, occasionally, by neologisms like ['vaɪnəs], ['vaɪkəns], [(v, d, m)
'axtɔs]. These neologisms had already occurred in both spontaneous speech
and reading in 1973, which shows that as early as half a year after the
accident his jargon had become partially lexicalized. (Stereotyped neologisms are mentioned by Green, 1969 and Buckingham and Kertesz, 1976.)

Table 11.1 shows that in the course of 6 years the quantity of his lexical
inventory remained the same whereas its composition underwent some
significant changes, namely, the reduction of function words and the augmentation of content words. (The prevalence of verbs seems to be a characteristic trait of Wernicke's aphasics; see Fradis & Leischner, 1979.) The
referential value of this inventory is very poor. It includes the names of
his children and three contrasting pairs of adjectives and adverbs, for example, *schön* 'nice' refers to positive circumstances, the "contrary" *tot*
'dead' stands for a wide range of negative circumstances, sadness, anger,

TABLE 11.1.

Semantic Jargon: Comparison of the Lexical Inventory 1973/1979 (in %).

	1973 N = 86	1979 N = 85
Adverbs	41.9	37.6
Verbs	16.3	23.5
Pronouns	15.1	15.3
Conjunctions	9.3	7.1
Prepositions	7.0	2.4
Adjectives	5.8	4.7
Nouns	4.7	9.4

bankruptcy *etc.* Quantative and temporal relations are expressed by the adverbial pairs *nichts–alles* 'nothing–everything' and *früher-jetzt* 'in the past-now'. If he nevertheless successfully commented on many different topics, this was achieved by his very expressive intonation, gesture, mimicry, pantomime, onomatopoetic sounds, and by graphic means (writing and drawing).

These different techniques of communication are illustrated by Text 5: This text demonstrates that the referential function is fulfilled mainly by gesture and pantomime. The spoken text only conveys the semantic dis-

```
Text 5:  Conversation with Mr. W.


Date:            18.3.1979
Interlocutor:    one of the authors (P.)
Place:           room of P.
Subject-matter:  Mr. W.'s predilection for listening to music


P:  Our music therapist told me/that you love music/
W:  Ich hab noch eines / also ich hab / Mensch! ich bin (tapping
    his left temple with his left index) ich war / hätt ich
    mal ['vaxtɔs] hätt ich noch / Thomas! / meine Thomas! / wenn
    wären der ['vaxtɔs] und wo ich der ['vaxtɔs] auch /
    (pointing with both indexes to P.) da hab ich mindestens
    einen das / (indicating with both hands a pile of records)
    ich hab ich habe nur zwei hier / (pointing to the music
    room)
P:  Hm /
W:  Kann ich das? / (taking paper and pencil and writing)
    "Beethoven" (showing the paper to P.) bin ich gut der
    ['vaikəns]? bin ich gut das oder der ['vainəs]?/
```

P: Ah that's good!/

W: Ist das gut?/

P: (reading aloud) "Beethoven"/

W: War ich tot war ich tot hier? also tot oder war gut hier?/

P: That is quite good / yes / easy to be read /

W: Da wäre ich <u>hier</u> / ich hatte (tapping his left temple with
     his left index) da war ich war <u>Thomas</u> / waren wir ja
     (pointing towards the window) raus hier nicht?/ (pointing
     with his right hand to the table) und da habe <u>ich</u>! <u>meine</u>
     (pointing to the paper with the name of Beethoven) wo <u>ich</u>
     war (pointing with his right hand to his breast) minde-
     stens einen das (indicating with both hands a big pile of
     records) ich habe <u>alles</u> <u>alles</u> hier / (confirming gesture
     with both hands)

P: So many records?/

W: Ja! und hier (pointing to the music room) hier / da haben
     wir noch eine / (showing thumb and index of his left hand)
     aber wenn diese / ich mach den nur / wenn immer alle raus
     hier / (gesture with his left hand of pushing somebody out
     of the room) dann für mich hier (pointing with his right
     hand to his breast) dann lieb ich auch einen <u>das</u> hier /
     (gesture of shutting a door)

P: You shut the door?/

W: Ja (putting both hands together before his breast and
     indicating satisfaction) hab ich <u>nur</u> zwei (showing thumb
     and index of his left hand) aber glaubst du Mami /nur der
     [vax] glaubst du Mami? wenn <u>das</u> hier (confirming gesture
     with his left index) und habe <u>einen</u> [max] meistens / ich
     bin meine ich bin tot hier (pointing with both indexes
     to his eyes, indicating tears) ich (pointing with his
     right hand to his breast) da bin ich dann weiß ich genau
     "vertaif" (euphemistic distortion of "devil") Mensch! /
     (beating with his right fist his left palm) dann kommt
     dann bin ich tot! (indicating tears with both indexes)
     dann da bin ich nur ['maxtɔs] da bin ich tot dann der
     [vaɪ...] wenn das so da bin ich tot!/

P: When you are listening to music /

W: Ja /

tinction of correct (*gut*) and incorrect (*tot*) and a state of mind (*dann bin ich tot*); the referential details of this report are expressed by pantomime (i.e., that he owns a lot of records, that he prefers to retire to the music room shutting out other people). Pantomime serves to disambiguate spoken language; thus, the ambiguity of the adjective *tot* is eliminated by the gestural indication of tears. There are only a few idiosyncratic gestures without pantomimic value (e.g., pointing with both indexes to his interlocutor). The name of his favorite composer was communicated by graphic means. This typifies the communicative function of writing for this patient, who very often wrote down names of persons and places, dates and numbers, occasionally complementing his written communication with little drawings (machines, *etc.*).

The systematic substitution of content words by pantomime and neologism proves that Mr.W. is suffering from severe anomia. The very simple, stereotypic, and fragmentary sentences disguise another defect, which occasionally surfaces in the form of violations of word order or false numeric congruence between subject and predicate: Sentences like *Wenn wären der* ['vaxtɔs] instead of *Wenn der* ['vaxtɔs] *wäre* are symptomatic of an underlying dysgrammatism (to avoid the terms agrammatism—used for the telegraphic speech of Broca's aphasics—and paragrammatism—used for the distorted syntax of Wernicke's aphasics characterized by anacoluthons, repetition of clichés, and frequent substitution). Although the characteristics of Mr.W.'s spoken syntax to some extent correspond to the paragrammatic style of Wernicke's aphasia, the intentional shift of referential meaning from language to pantomime permits Mr. W. to avoid the copious stream of paragrammatic, fragmentary, and stereotypic sentence that is so typical of Wernicke's aphasia.

In conclusion, over the course of 7 years, this patient was able, without therapeutic intervention, to build up an efficient communication system, based on some 80 words (most of them function words) and the use of nonverbal symbolic systems. He may serve as an admirable example of the spontaneous healing capacity of the human brain which Monakow and Mourgue (1928) termed "syneidisis."

Provoked Behavior

During his second stay at our clinic, Mr. W. was very cooperative, so that a number of tests could be carried out. Figure 11.3 is based on his performance on 30 phonemes/graphemes and 20 pictures/words of the basic vocabulary. The most striking feature of his lexical performance is the discrepancy between speech and writing: Whereas his oral performance—with the exception of repetition—is very bad, his graphic performance is relatively good. The fact that he repeated well on 50% of the items shows a positive change in auditory comprehension as well as in his command of articulation.

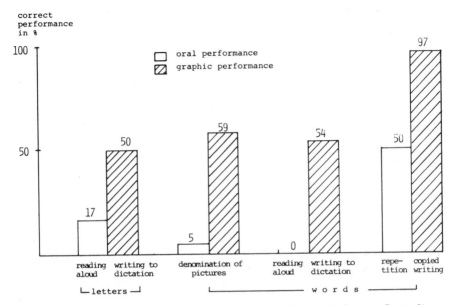

Figure 11.3. Profile of expressive performance: Semantic jargon (Stage 2).

His receptive performance (Figure 11.4) indicates his good capacity for recognizing characteristic sounds (doorbell, car, *etc.*), discriminating phonemic and graphemic minimal pairs (*Tanne–Kanne*), showing the picture corresponding to the stimulus of a spoken or written word, and recognizing grammatically deviant sentences like *Two boys is sitting in the room* (a complete listing of the sentences by which 7 grammatical categories are tested is given in Peuser, 1978). But when he was confronted with the syntactic stimuli of the Token Test or the Three Figures Test (DFT), a dramatical breakdown of his auditory comprehension could be observed. The Three Figures Test (see Peuser 1976, 1978, and Peuser & Schriefers (1980) is a multiple-choice procedure with 20 stimulus sentences, exemplifying active, passive, affirmative, and negative constructions. Mr. W.'s score of 12 incorrect answers (out of 20) on the DFT indicated a comprehension deficit corresponding to that of severe Wernicke's aphasia.

A comparison of these findings with the results of the clinical assessment in 1973 showed that Mr. W.'s language comprehension had improved considerably. The same holds true for his language comprehension in everyday situations. This improved comprehension went hand-in-hand with an ameliorated capacity for monitoring and judging the effect of his own speech. In addition to his development of nonverbal communication systems such as gesture and pantomime, there was other evidence of Mr. W.'s increased capacity for self-monitoring: He refused to read aloud the fable of the voracious dog, which he had so willingly read in 1973.

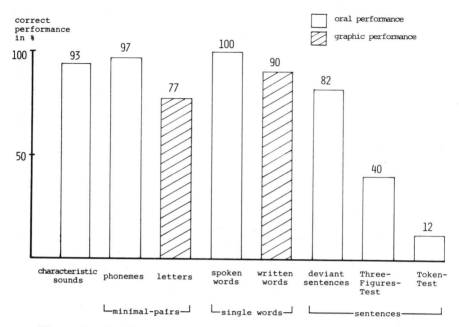

Figure 11.4. Profile of receptive performance: Semantic jargon (Stage 2).

Case 2: Neologistic Jargon

STAGE 1 (FEBRUARY–MAY 1979)

As mentioned earlier, Mrs. K. stayed at our clinic for 3 months. Because she felt very comfortable on her cousin's farm, she did not want to become an inpatient of our clinic again. Information on the evolution of her jargon therefore had to be obtained from the therapist who visited her twice a week and by several visits to her home in 1980. Unfortunately, this restricted testing to the most basic procedures.

Spontaneous Behavior

Although her language comprehension in test situations was nearly as poor as that of Mr. W. (see Figure 11.6), Mrs. K. seemed to grasp the meaning of simple questions about her former life and her actual situation at the clinic. Without expressing anything by mime or gesture, she answered with *yes* or *no* followed by a soft and rapidly spoken stream of neologistic utterances, embedded in what appeared to be normal intonation contours. As stated earlier, her attitude as a speaker was reactive, that is to say, she never initiated conversation but she reacted to the questions or statements of her interlocutor. In her answers she often mixed up *yes* and *no* (a great part of the 3 months therapy was therefore dedicated to teaching her the

correct use of these affirmative and negative particles). To avoid conflicts
with her conversation partners, she had developed an undifferentiated intonation, floating between negation and affirmation.

```
Text 6:   Conversation with Mrs. K.


Date:             13.2.1979
Interlocutor:     one of the authors (P.)
Place:            room of P.
Subject-matter:   biographical data


P:   You are coming from Cologne?/

K:   Ja /

P:   You have been working at the traffic office?/

K:   (hesitating) ja aber so ['vɪzəvɔzəvɔzə'vovɪsovɪzəvɪzə] ja /

P:   But now you are a pensioner?/

K:   Ja /

P:   How long have you been ill?/

K:   Ach / ['içɪçɛtsəvə'voɪimfɪzə'ɪzvɛji'vɔnta]/

P:   Hm /

K:   ['ɛ:hɛ:nvɔzə'voɪjamɑ]/

P:   It happened in 1978?/

K:   Hm?/

P:   In 1978 / that is to say last year?/
```

K: $['ɔdərsitii'mɔdɪɔki^{1}zɛtjɑn]$ des $[gɪgəvɔn'de:səɑ \ 'mɔdɪ$
$'fʊltevɔvɔrɑ]$ und des $['vɔlvəɪm've:ən \ 'mʊg^{2}'əvɪɪ'zɑptə$
$fɑlezəvɑɪ \ 'ɑ:gləvovɑ'dɪ \ 'ɔbəsə'so:vlodvɑd'vɪ:gɑlɑp'te:vɑr]/$

```
P:   Hm /

K:   (low and expressing by her intonation something like "that
     is all I can tell you about it") ['jɑsɑlts'vɔvəltsvɔnə]//
```

Provoked Behavior

The profile of Mrs. K.'s expressive performance, which was assessed
by means of a small inventory of 30 phonemes/graphemes and of 20 pictures/
words, shows a very poor oral and a much better graphic performance,
that is, the same clear-cut division between speech and writing as in Case 1.

Receptive performance was assessed by the same means used in Case
1: characteristic sounds, phonemic and graphemic minimal pairs, spoken
and written words, grammatically deviant sentences, and the instructions
of the Three Figures Test and the Token Test. In all these tests, Mrs. K.'s
performance was as bad or even worse than that of Mr. W. Her scores on

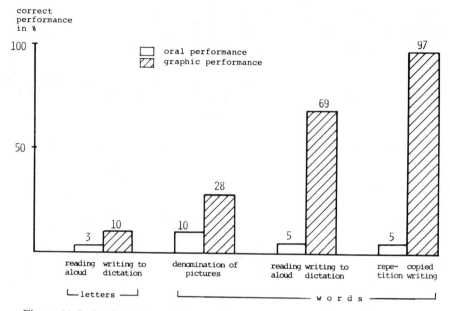

Figure 11.5. Profile of expressive performance: Neologistic jargon (Stage 1).

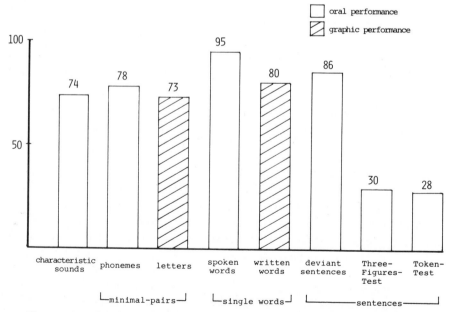

Figure 11.6. Profile of receptive performance: Neologistic jargon (Stage 1).

the Three Figures Test and the Token Test were on the level of global aphasia.

When asked to read the fable of the voracious dog, she eagerly, although with some effort, produced a neologistic word-for-word version of the original text: Although there is a tendency to employ real function words in Text 7, this tendency is not markedly increased in Text 8.

Text 7:   reading of the fable by Mrs. K. on 14.2.1979

[ˈdɛgegən gɛˈvɛvejb̩ ˈgəvɛrdan]

[ˈhɪntliːə geːz glɔɪˈzɔbɪar ˈvɪvəgeːə goːˈzɛzɪɔ ɛrˈgɛveːə
ʊntəˈgeːvɪs ˈeːr ˈgɛdu] und [ˈgɛgləvʊʃt ˈsoːvaɪvaɪ//
ˈnɪsəgəgˈɛlɪvɪeɪ beːzˈvɔseːˈsɛl ˈgɪk] er [geːavˈlɛvlər
ˈvoɪvaɪə ˈʊbɪˈabar ˈdɛgəger ˈavɛleɪ ˈgɛgəval//
ˈɛldeˈanəlaŋ gɪːpt baɪˈdɛlɪu uˈlɛbɪjer ˈolɛvər hʊntəvaɪˈŋevər
hʊɪ zeː gɪˈleːɔ ˈgɛvɪla ʊˈŋeːjɔbaˈvɛrɪ ˈgɪlˈleːjə doɪ
ˈaldəgeːə goɪ goɪ gɪˈlerɪət ˈalde ɪˈlɛf vɛlˈdɪk lɔ//
sɪkdəˈder ˈdeːgjar ˈdɪˈɛr dəˈvɛleɑ ˈvuvaɪə voɪɛlˈdeɪ duˈɛbear
ˈdeɛbərˈdal] der [dəˈɛgəval unˈdɛgəval//
vɪːr ɛ ˈgɛɛːdoˈɛlɪjar eːrˈdɛvəːr ˈduːvar ˈvaɪ ˈeːgɛvətɔ-
ˈʀɪːjɔ ʊlˈɛvələr] er [ˈgɛgəveːjɔˈbɪləver ˈvɛzɪːjɔ]//

Text 8:   reading of the fable by Mrs. K. on 25.4.1979

[ˈɪʟgəˈboːs ˈseːtʟ malˈmiːəvaltsʟ]

[saɪˈgɛgɪl ˈoːˈsaɪ] meine [ˈbɛtəˈgeːə] ein [ˈbɪkəveːr]
mir [ˈbuːsəvaɔ voɪˈmɪvɔldɪ dɛˈlɛlgəval oˈlagəlɪːtsə-
ˈvavʊltsəva//
ˈʊŋkə ˈgɛlea ˈmaɪk ˈvoː ɛsˈkɪːr aldeɑˈvaɪ ˈovəzəaˈlaɪt-
kəbɪːr kɛkəˈvantsiːjɔ//
ˈdoːone ˈoːgəˈgrɪːs gɛgvaltsɪˈmɪːjɔ ˈsoːvɛlɪgərɪnˈfɪndɪlɪgər
oːlɪgəˈvalɪgər gɛvaˈgaltɪvɪːr ˈoː ˈvɪkgvəgɪːr soːˈkɯɛlvə
sɛˈkɪgvɪvɪːjɔ ˈoːgəˈvɛltvɪdɪgjo ˈvoːɛmpasəˈvɪː//
ˈɪɪːgoːlɪləˈglɪːjəvɪzɪ ˈdoː ɔbɔdeːˈvɛvɛlɪgvʊl ˈbatgeː-
ˈmagɪgɪˈvɛzɪ gaɪgɪˈvɛlɪavagɔ] und [ˈdɪtkvə bagˈmeːə//
ˈbal ˈeːts gɛːgəˈvaltigˈvɪːr ˈglaɪgəvəzɪ ˈoː ˈvɛvegeva-
ˈsɪːgvərə ˈbagevɛˈsvɪːggə ˈkoːvadu baˈvatɪgɔ]//

STAGE 2 (JUNE 1980)

After an interval of 14 months, Mrs. K. was visited by the authors in her home. On this occasion a conversation and a reading of the fable were recorded and some basic data of her expressive and receptive performance were obtained.

Spontaneous Behavior

The most striking impression was that her attitude as an interlocutor had changed. Mrs. K. was—perhaps due to the familiar surroundings—a much more active communication partner who, in addition to answering questions, asked some of her own, thus giving her interlocutor some bad moments, for these neologistic questions were completely incomprehensible. The assurance of her attitude and intonation showed that she believed her speech was meaningful.

Her utterances consisted mostly of neologistic jargon, but this time interspersed, not only with correct articles and adverbs, but also with exclamations like *How nice* or *Where did I put it* (when looking for an object). As Text 9 shows, she could not judge the correctness of her reading, for she spontaneously took up a newspaper to demonstrate that she was able to read certain texts. For the rest, the quality and tempo of her soft spoken neologistic jargon had not changed.

Text 9:   Conversation with Mrs. K.

Date: 16.6.1980
Interlocutor: one of the authors (P.)
Place: room of P.
Subject-matter: reading

P: How is your reading?/ do you look sometimes into the
    newspaper? /

K: Ja / soso gewiß / das ist [gəgə'vaksənə 'vetsɪ (incomprehensible)
    ma'vɛntɪ 'mandɪ 'hervɔltɪ] aber ähm ['tundəgɔvusɪ makə'dandə
    'hoegə 'ho:valə 'lal 'he:rvɔldɪ 'ho:'he:rvɔldɪ/(pointing to
    the left and to the right)

P: That is to say / you can read a little bit? /

K: (fetching a picture newspaper) ['tɔlədɪ 'pakəleɪs] nicht? /
    (opening the newspaper) ['ɪt sasəsɪŋe'matsegəban vu:'vɔlta
    fa'faɪn] dann die / aber die ['handə 'kɪəgɔrdən] na na / das war
    aber fein! / (showing the captions) das ins ['gø] aber bitte
    ['kɛmeɪ] ja ja ja /

P: The small letters? /
K: Ja [ˈɪsvɔdɪgɔhoˈgogəso] aber die [ˈmɑːnɪgə] die [ˈgifissɔf-
     ˈɔrdən] /
P: The small letters are still a bit difficult for you /
K: Jaja / jaja (looking into the paper and reading aloud) da da!
     "[ˈgɪːlə ˈvoːdəvavasɪ] aber dir [ˈbaldɪr] dich all [ˈfy ˈɪts]
     dir [ˈmaldɪçj bis [ˈkalə]"[1] //

[1]Originaltext:
"Sie sind, mit Verlaub, höchst seltsam für einen
Kindergeburtstag." (Frau im Spiegel)

Provoked Behavior

On our visits to her home, we did not have enough time to repeat all
the tests we had applied in the clinic. Figure 11.7 summarizes the results
of the administration of our standard 20 pictures/words, the sample of
deviant sentences, and the 20 instructions of the Three Figures Test. Although the 20 pictures and words had not been part of her domestic speech
therapy, a transfer from this training to the nontrained 20 pictures/words
is evident, particularly in repetition, reading aloud, and written denomi-

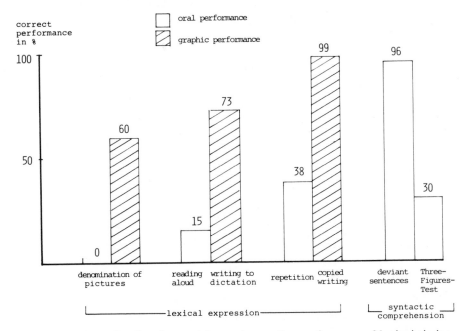

Figure 11.7. Profile of expressive and receptive performance: Neologistic jargon (Stage 2).

nation. For the rest, her lexical performance displayed the same discrepancy between speech and writing as 15 months ago.

Although there was only a minor change in her syntactic comprehension (deviant sentences, DFT), her repetition scores indicate an ameliorated capacity for decoding the speech of other people and controlling her own verbal output. In comparison with the results from 1979, her oral naming had become worse. But the fact that she did not utter 1- or 2-syllable jargon words, as in repetition or reading, but sentence-like neologistic chains, pointing at the same time to details of the pictures (e.g., the four legs of a table), may be interpreted as indicating increased awareness of anomia. She knew that it was impossible for her to name pictures and therefore substituted description for naming. (One could translate her neologistic description of the picture of a table in the following tentative way: "This is something with four legs.") She also wrote the corresponding words with her finger on the table, demonstrating that, in contrast to 1979, she was fully aware of the better quality of her graphic performance.

As she was obviously convinced of the accuracy of her reading aloud, she did not hesitate to read the fable of the voracious dog, giving a fluent, predominantly neologistic word-for-word translation of the original text. But this time she manifested an increased tendency to render function words of the original text by (incorrect) function words of the normal inventory. This may be interpreted as the beginning of an evolution from neologistic to semantic jargon.

Text 10:   reading of the fable by Mrs. K. on 13.6.1980

er [geoˈlɛ ˈdoː] ein [ˈgɛloseɔn]

[ˈɪk ˈglɑdusə] gut [ˈateuk ˈguːtvɪl] sie [ˈaŋɪoːn
ˈɪgvɔdɪːr] so [ˈbɔndrɪu ˈjɑːlɪç ˈiːθ ˈoːnən ˈhalɪːəvət
ˈkagləvaɪ]//
so [ˈkambaˈɪdəm ˈgok ˈkaɪ ˈɪŋk geːnˈdraɪ ˈvagɪr ˈkalɪdɪs]
so [ˈɪŋk] der [tɔˈveɪt bɪˈgavlɪu duˈkɑm//
ˈoː ˈvaɪ ˈdrɪnə diːˈɛrɔt dɪgəvuvuˈɛl ˈglɪːusɪt] er im
[ˈtrɪgəlaɔt ˈsɑːgə ˈkɛfaldɪ ˈvɔzəvɔn] ein [ˈtoːrədɪf]
so [yn] die [ˈkaɪ ˈsoːdəvɔn] die [ˈɛŋəvuθ ˈiːθ ˈɛmblɪu
ˈboːtsə ˈboːtən//
ˈoː faˈhɪːəθ] hier im [maɪərˈɛnəsɪs ˈtoːlɪəvuθ ˈdɪːgɑ
ˈvoɪ] er [ˈlagɪːəvusu ˈeːdɪvut] so [ˈkɛvəla ˈvɑːdɪm//
ˈvaɪ] ihr [ˈdavələ damˈnagəvɪs ˈgɪgəvɔsum ˈmeː ˈɪŋəvɔsvut]
da [ˈaɪgələt] so [ˈaɪgələsovutdeːˈɪkfɪr ˈbajələtsɪvɪr]//

Auditory Self-perception and the Concept of Anosognosia

At the beginning of the chapter we discussed the behavior of our patients from a psychiatric point of view and concluded that there was no evidence for anosognosia. Another explanation for jargonaphasics' apparent unawareness of their defective speech was proposed by Alajouanine *et al.* (1952), who compared the behavior of jargonaphasics with the reduced self-monitoring of normal speakers during the speech act:

> Mais l'apport le plus significatif du jargon aphasique, c'est qu'il ne s'écoute visiblement pas parler. Le faisons-nous, nous-mêmes dans l'expression normale? Probablement très peu, et c'est une surprise d'entendre, retransmises par le magnétophone indiscret, les formules que nous avons, quelques instants plus tôt, prononcés, sans même avoir remarqué les termes que nous utilisions [p. 166].

In March 1979, when both patients were at our clinic, we examined their reactions to delayed auditory feedback (DAF). Such investigations have been conducted by Alajouanine, Lhermitte, Ledoux, Renaud, & Vignolo (1964), Boller, Vrtunski, Kim, & Mack (1978), and others, with the main result that fluent aphasics with phonemic jargon or poor repetition and/or disturbed comprehension showed no change in their speech with DAF. Our procedure was the following: In the course of a spontaneous conversation, we asked the patient to put on a set of stereo headphones, which was connected with a Uher Royal de Luxe stereo tape recorder. The speed of the tape provided the critical delay interval of 180 msec. After this we resumed the conversation, with the patient's spontaneous speech played back to him via the headphones. The patients' reactions differed: Whereas Mr. W. interrupted himself, continuing with louder and slower speech, Mrs. K. showed no reaction at all. This clearly showed that Mr.W., the patient with semantic jargon, had a relatively intact external feedback, whereas Mrs. K., the patient with neologistic jargon, had a completely disrupted external feedback in the moment of speaking. Unfortunately, we do not know anything about the state of the preceding and—as Alajouanine *et al.* (1952) rightly point out—perhaps even more important internal self-monitoring of the patient.

These findings are confirmed by the patients' attitude toward their written production: When the intensity of the graphic feedback (see Peuser, 1980) allowed them to control their verbal output, they recognized the faultiness of their production. The striking difference between writing and speech (which we found in many patients; see Peuser, 1978; Leischner, Mattes, & Mallin, 1980) may therefore, at least partially, be explained by the difference of auditory and visual feedback. Thus, what could be mistaken as anosognostic behavior in our case of neologistic jargon is in reality the consequence of a complete disruption of external self-monitoring in the moment of speaking to what seems an "understanding interlocutor."

The Problem of Neologism

Two conflicting hypotheses have been advanced to account for neologistic speech:

1. Lecours and Lhermitte (1969) and Kertesz and Benson (1970) advocate the so-called "conduction theory" of jargon, which states that neologisms are phonemic distortions of a target word.

2. Buckingham (1977), Buckingham, Whitaker, and Whitaker (1978), Butterworth (1979), and Duchan, Stengel, & Oliva (1980) advance what might be called the "anomia-theory" or "empty-slot-filling-theory" of jargon, which is based on the anomic condition of jargonaphasics evidenced by Kinsbourne and Warrington (1963), Buckingham and Kertesz (1976), and others. According to these authors "neologisms appear to serve as substitutes for the root form of lexical items, when presumably these cannot be retrieved from the lexical system [Butterworth, 1979, p. 15]." A similar statement is made by Buckingham *et al.* (1978) who suggest "that many neologisms may also be produced during the period of time in ongoing speech when the precise word called for by the context has not yet been retrieved [p. 151]." Perhaps, Alajouanine and his collaborators (1952) had the same theory in mind when they wrote, that "on ne peut pas dire que, pour le malade, les mots n'ont plus des sens, mais plutôt, de façon caricaturale, que le sens n'a plus de mots [p. 167]."

With regard to the neologisms of our two patients, we strongly support the second hypothesis for the following reasons: Both patients are anomic. During his first stay at our clinic in 1973, when he was relatively unaware of his disturbance, Mr. K. substituted neologisms for content words he could not retrieve. With growing awareness of his anomia, he stopped (with a few exceptions) the production of neologisms, replacing content words by gesture and pantomime. Mrs. K., our second case, produced entire neologistic texts. The conduction theory would make it necessary to explain the phonemic distortion of entire utterances, which seems to us a futile task. Furthermore, on the occasion of her second testing, in 1980, she demonstrated awareness of her anomic situation by giving jargon descriptions instead of jargon denominations.

Although in the spontaneous speech and, above all, in the readings of the fable, we may find some phonemic distortions of target words, this strategy cannot account for the majority of the neologisms that occurred. For such a strategy to be feasible, it should be possible to recognize and reconstruct the underlying target words, at least in the case of the readings (see Lecours & Lhermitte, 1969). As this is obviously not possible, what rules govern the production of neologistic jargon?

The Structure of Jargon

If neologisms and neologistic utterances are phonematic ad hoc programs that fill lexical gaps or entire syntactic frames, are they chaotic combinations of sounds that do not necessarily belong to the inventory of the speaker's native language or systematic combinations of normal phonemes governed by the phonotactical rules of that language? At a first glance, jargon does not give the impression of being a chaotic combination of sounds, but, rather, resembles a foreign language (recall that, because of his neologistic jargon, our first patient was mistaken for a foreign spy). This comparison with a foreign language can be extended in that the "languages" spoken by different jargonaphasics represent different degrees of complexity. If normal speakers could easily imitate the neologisms of our first case, it is nearly impossible to discriminate, let alone to imitate, the rapid neologistic flow of our second case.

But the reality of jargon is still more confusing, as each jargonaphasic not only speaks and writes his own jargon, but also possesses several jargons. [We described elsewhere (Peuser, 1978) the case of a German aphasic, who spoke neologistic and wrote semantic jargon.] Concerning the two cases described in this chapter, there is a striking difference between the spoken and written neologisms of Mr. W. during his first stay at our clinic. Furthermore, there is a difference between the spontaneous and provoked neologistic jargon of our second case, Mrs. K.: When she was asked to repeat mono- or bisyllabic target words, she stopped the flow of her spontaneous jargon, trying (with increasing success in the course of therapy) to adapt her production at least in length to the normal target word. The same was true in the other tasks of our 20 pictures/words program, where she produced multiple variations of simple structured neologisms like ['oː'sɛ] or ['ma'lɛk]. Her reading performance lies somewhere in between these simple structured bisyllabic neologisms and the complicated neologistic chains of her spontaneous speech. Although she nearly always gives a word-for-word translation of the original text, her reading jargon is characterized by complicated polysyllabic structures. In her case, one might therefore speak of at least three different jargons depending on the kind of stimulus.

Although in both cases there is a certain trend of lexicalization, that is to say, a tendency to reproduce the same or at least similar jargon words, most of the spontaneous neologistic structures are unstable ad hoc productions of a disinhibited phonological device. It was Pick (1931) who explained the literal paraphasias of fluent aphasics by the disinhibition of the intact sound-sequencing mechanism. Green (1969) observed the phenomenon of sequential repetition of various phonological segments in a jargonaphasic and referred to it as alliteration (the repetition of consonants) and assonance (the repetition of vocalic segments). These "clang associations" (Brown, 1972), which may be seen in sensory aphasics, dementias, schizophrenics, and sleep talkers (Brown, 1972; Cromwell & Dokeki, 1968) are explained by Buckingham *et al.* (1978) in terms of a general principle of neuromuscular activity such as inhibition and postinhibitory rebound (see McKay, 1970; Ohala & Hirano, 1967).

Stampe (1969) holds that the principle of reduplication (the strictest form of alliteration and assonance) dominates the early period of language acquisition, thus constituting a natural phonological law which is later on inhibited by the phonotactical rules of the particular language system. It therefore seems that the neologistic productivity of jargonaphasics may be explained by the disinhibition of such processes of natural phonology as alliteration, assonance, and reduplication, to which one might add the preference for CVCV structures, that is, a regular sequence of consonants and vowels which is also characteristic of glossolalic speech (Rensch, 1971).

But if the neologistic output of jargonaphasics was entirely dominated by the laws of natural phonology and the principle of least effort (Zipf, 1949), jargon would be reduced to a monotonous "honolulu" language. The neologistic texts of both our aphasics demonstrate that this is not the case. Upon examining more closely their provoked as well as spontaneous speech, one discovers consonant clusters and a tendency to avoid the monotony of alliteration and assonance by phonological variation. The principle of least effort and the laws of natural phonology are thus countered by a continued effort to maintain the distinctiveness of speech (see our detailed analysis of Case 1 and of another case of neologistic jargon in Peuser, 1978).

Does this tendency to maintain phonological contrasts and oppositions obey the phonological and phonotactical rules of the jargonaphasic's native language? There is agreement among aphasiologists that in the neologistic productions of jargonaphasics the phonological and phonotactic rules of the normal language are respected. But the neologistic productions of our cases do not entirely confirm this opinion. The phonemes, it is true, belong to the normal inventory of the German language. (A few exceptions can be found in the text of our second aphasic, who occasionally produces non-German phonemes, such as [θ] and [w].) Yet the frequency distribution of this inventory is not quite that of normal German. Table 11.2 compares the rank order and frequency of the seven most frequent phonemes of German with their distribution in the spontaneous speech and the reading texts of our two cases, showing correspondences and deviations. (The same phenomenon was observed in a bilingual German–English aphasic by Perecman & Brown 1979, this volume, Chapter 10.)

Concerning their spontaneous speech, only 3(4) of the 7 most frequent phonemes of the patients' jargon can be found among the 7 most frequent phonemes of German. Furthermore, we find a severe distortion of fre-

TABLE 11.2

Rank Order and Frequency (in %) of the Most Frequent Phonemes

Rank order	Spontaneous speech					
	Normal language	%	Semantic jargon	%	Neologistic jargon	%
1	n	10.1	ə	17.1	ə	12.1
2	ə	8.7	n	12.5	v	10.7
3	r	7.3	s	8.2	a	7.5
4	t	7.0	k	6.5	g	6.6
5	d	4.5	v	6.3	ι	6.6
6	s	4.5	aι	6.0	s	6.6
7	ι	4.0	t	5.7	o:	5.9

Rank Order	Reading aloud					
	Original text	%	Semantic jargon	%	Neologistic jargon	%
1	n	1.1	n	15.0	v	9.5
2	ə	8.4	s	7.1	ε:	8.5
3	t	7.3	aι	6.8	l	8.2
4	r	6.3	k	6.8	ə	8.2
5	l	5.9	r	6.5	g	8.0
6	aι	5.9	ə	6.5	e:	7.5
7	f	4.5	ɔ	6.2	ι	7.5

quencies, insofar as the gap between the most frequent phonemes and the rest is much larger in jargon than in normal language. The same applies to the most frequent phonemes in the reading of the fable: Here we find only a partial correspondence (4 phonemes) with the original text in the case of semantic jargon and even less correspondence (2 phonemes) in the case of the neologistic jargon. Although the semantic jargon is closer to the original text, at the same time, it displays a very severe distortion of frequency in that the gap between the first two most frequent phonemes is considerably enlarged.

Table 11.3 examines the relative frequency of vowels versus consonants. It shows that our case of semantic jargon is very close to normal language in his spontaneous speech as well as in his readings of the fable.

TABLE 11.3

The Relation of Vowels and Consonants (in %)

	Spontaneous speech			Reading aloud		
	Normal languate	Semantic jargon	Neologistic jargon	Original text	Semantic jargon	Neologistic jargon
Vowels	38.7	36.7	47.1	38.7	35.3	48.6
Consonants	61.3	63.3	52.9	61.3	64.7	51.4

Our case of neologistic jargon, on the other hand, displays in both modalities a nearly equal distribution of vowels and consonants, which reflects her preference for simple CV syllables.

If the preceding statistical data give a somewhat confusing impression of correspondence with and deviation from normal language, the same holds true for the data concerning phonotactical rules. Many aphasiologists agree that in jargon the phonotactical rules of normal language are preserved. However, this is not borne out by our data, which contain, especially in the texts of our neologistic jargon, many instances of non-German phoneme sequences. Apart from the phenomenon of vowel harmony which makes certain passages resemble Finno-Ugrian or Turkic languages, there are many other utterances that sound like Slavonic or Ancient Greek. One might, therefore, be inclined to look for the influence of a specific language known by the aphasic were such utterances not merely brought about by the application of idiosyncratic phonotactical rules.

One may therefore distinguish three different tendencies which determine the phonological, phonostatistical, and phonotactical structure of jargon: (a) the influence of normal language; (b) the laws of natural phonology and the principle of least effort; and (c) idiosyncratic rules. Of these three tendencies, it is the influence of normal language that explains the normality of the phoneme inventory. But this influence becomes increasingly weaker where the phonostatistical and phonotactical rules are concerned. Correspondingly, the laws of natural phonology and idiosyncratic rules dominate the frequency distribution and the combination of phonemes.

The Evolution of Jargon

If we compare our cases we can easily situate them on the continuum of jargon proposed by Alajouanine (1956) and Kertesz and Benson (1970): During the period of observation, our second case started at the neologistic extreme point of this continuum and displayed, after a 15-month evolution, some initial signs of semantic jargon. Our first case, on the other hand, passed very quickly through this stage of neologistic jargon and had to be classified as a case of semantic-neologistic jargon when he came to our clinic. His further developmental stages depend on the modality we take into consideration: With regard to his reading performance, he evolved in the course of a 3-month stay at our clinic from semantic-neologistic jargon to pure semantic jargon. With regard to his spontaneous speech, he evolved in the course of 6 years from semantic-neologistic jargon to circumlocutory, anomic speech—the final stage of jargon evolution described by Kertesz & Benson (1970).

This regular pattern of evolution is best demonstrated by the reading performance of the two patients. The following renditions of the title of the fable (*Der Hund mit dem Fleische*) show a smooth transition from neologistic to semantic jargon:

Mrs. K. (14.02.1979): 'dɛgegən gɛ'vɛvejɔ 'gəvɛrdan]
Mrs. K. (25.04.1979): [ʊgə'bo:s 'se:tʊ mal'mi:əvaltsʊ]
Mrs. K. (13.06.1980): *er* [geo'lɛ 'do:] *ein* ['gɛloseɔn]
Mr. W. (03.09.1973): *einen* [lɛgɔ'hʊnts] *mit dem* ['flaʊsɔn]
Mr. W (29.10.1973): *der* ['vaʊkən] *hat den* ['faʊkən]
Mr. W. (05.12.1973): *der haben das sind eines*

The rate and degree of this evolution obviously depend on the extent and nature of the lesion and the age of the patient. These factors, that is to say cerebrovascular lesion and old age, may explain the relatively slow evolution of our second case of neologistic jargon. Correspondingly, the fast evolution of the first case can be explained by his relative youth and traumatic lesion.

As both patients received the same amount of therapy, therapeutic influence does not seem to be a decisive factor in the evolution of jargon. When confronted with this type of patient, therapists must count on a relatively slow and autonomous evolution of oral jargon which follows its own course. Therapists should therefore concentrate on the training of speech perception and writing skills. As, unfortunately, the referential value of the oral speech of these patients remains nearly zero, even at the final stage of circumlocutory, anomic speech, therapists must develop side channels of communication, such as writing and pantomime (see Kotten, 1976). Of course, these side-channels or roundabout ways for communication cannot be forced on the patients but must be developed with respect to the patient's own initiative and inclination.

Finally, there is a third factor, in addition to age and the extent and nature of the lesion, that may strongly affect the evolution of a specific jargon: the professional and social surroundings of the patient. The rapid evolution of jargon and the development of ancillary channels for communication that we observed in our first patient may be due to the fact that he continued working in his own factory and stayed in contact with his premorbid social milieu. The slow evolution of our second patient, on the other hand, may be partly due to the fact that she is a pensioner who lives without social contacts amidst her family on a farm. Although she expresses herself in neologistic jargon, her family knows what she wants to say, so that there is practically no need to develop roundabout ways for communication.

The phenomenon and the evolution of jargon can best be explained on the basis of psycholinguistic theory. If we distinguish, in accordance with Fromkin (1971, 1973) and Garrett (1975), several stages of sentence production from "meaning selection" through the final "specification of phonetic segments," then the data presented in this chapter suggest the following 6-step model, illustrated by the different stages of production of the noun phrase *der Hund mit dem Fleische*. As we believe, in accordance with Alajouanine (1952) and Duchan *et al.* (1980), in a "semantic base of jargon," that is, that the jargonaphasic knows what he is talking about, we suppose that the first step of syntactic processing (i.e., the selection of meaning) is intact. The same holds true for the second step, which consists in the choice of the syntactic frame and the intonational contours for the message to convey (see Duchan *et al.,* 1980). In the case of neologistic jargon, the following steps, 3–5—that is to say, the programs that normally fill up the lexical and grammatical slots of the syntactic frame—are blocked. As a consequence of the breakdown of internal and external feedback systems, this disturbance stays undetected and the phonological system can therefore provide neologistic "fill-up programs," according to normal, natural, and idiosyncratic rules. With the slow transition from neologistic to semantic jargon, the mechanisms that provide function words—conjunctions, prepositions, *etc.*—at Stage 3 of the sentence production program start to work again, providing first the constituent boundaries with the corresponding conjunctions. Later on, the processes that furnish adjectives, adverbs, and—to a very limited extent—nouns and verbs start functioning again. But, even then, most of the content words slots remain unfilled, so that function words have to fill these gaps. Although there is some evidence for the independent functioning of the mechanism providing inflectional

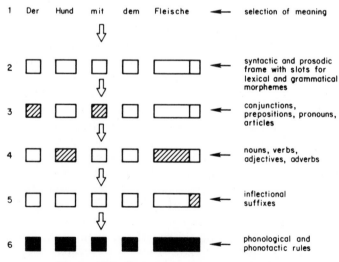

Figure 11.8. Stages of sentence production.

suffixes in Stage 5 (Caplan, Kellar, & Locke, 1972), this could not be observed in our patients.

With regard to the phonemic distortion of real words that occurred repeatedly in the spontaneous speech and/or reading of our patients, we must add that the mechanisms that furnish lexical entries and that in general seem to work on an "all-or-nothing" principle, nonetheless often provide partially correct word-programs, thus giving rise to phonemic paraphasia. But, in contrast to the great majority of the neologisms, these phonematic paraphasias are identifiable deviations of the target word.

We earlier characterized—in accordance with Buckingham et al. (1978), and Butterworth (1979)—the condition of our patients as anomic. With regard to this anomic condition, one might say that the evolution of jargon is dependent on the recovery from anomia. At the initial stage of neologistic jargon, anomia affects function words and content words equally, whereas, at the final stage of circumlocutory speech, anomia affects the content words in particular.

Several studies (Goodglass & Baker, 1976; Grober, Perecman, Kellar & Brown, 1980; Stachowiak, 1979; Whitehouse, Caramazza, & Zurif, 1979) have shed some light on the nature of the naming deficit, with the result that in posterior aphasics there seems to exist a partial breakdown and disintegration of semantic structure. It seems that the specific anomia of this type of patient consists in the inability to directly and consciously retrieve lexical entries stimulated by a pictorial representation or by semantic features of the corresponding object. (And it is this particularity of their anomic condition which makes them such difficult patients for the therapist.) The only way the patients have of retrieving at least some items of their disintegrated lexicon is to make use of the transitional probabilities of words in the course of speaking in an engaged and automatic—that is to say, a semiconscious—way. Perhaps it is more the awareness of this particularity of their anomia than compulsive loghorrea which makes Wernicke's aphasics in general and jargonaphasics in particular behave like the "indefatigable chatterboxes" described by Alajouanine.

REFERENCES

Alajouanine, Th., Lhermitte, F., Ledoux, M., Renaud, D., & Vignolo, L. A. Les composantes phonémiques et sémantiques de la jargonaphasie. *Revue Neurologique*, 1964, *110*, 1–20.

Alajouanine, Th., Sabouraud, O., & Ribaucourt, B. de. Le jargon des aphasiques. Désintegration anosognosique des valeurs sémantiques du langage. *Journal Psychologique*, 1952, *45*, 158–180.

Boller, F., Vrtunski, P. B., Kim, Y., & Mack, J. L. Delayed auditory feedback and aphasia. *Cortex*, 1978, *14*, 212–226.

Brown, J. *Aphasia, apraxia and agnosia*. Springfield, Ill.: Charles C Thomas, 1972.

Buckingham, H. W. The conduction theory and neologistic jargon. *Language and Speech* 1977, *20*, 174–184.

Buckingham, H. W., & Kertesz, A. *Neologistic jargon aphasia.* Amsterdam: Swets & Zeitlinger, 1976.

Buckingham, H. W., Whitaker, H., & Whitaker, H. A. Alliteration and assonance in neologistic jargon aphasia. *Cortex,* 1978, *14,* 365–380.

Butterworth, B. Hesitation and the production of verbal paraphasias and neologisms in jargon aphasia. *Brain and Language,* 1979, *8,* 133–161.

Caplan, D., Kellar, L., & Locke, S. Inflection of neologisms in aphasia. *Brain,* 1972, *95,* 169–172.

Cohn, R., & Neumann, M. A. Jargon aphasia. *Journal of Nervous and Mental Disorders,* 1958, *127,* 381–399.

Cromwell, R. L., Dokecki, P. R. Schizophrenic language: A disattention interpretation. In S. Rosenberg & J. H. Koplin (Eds.), *Developments in applied psycholinguistics.* New York: MacMillan, 1968.

Duchan, J., Stengel, M. L., & Oliva, J. A dynamic phonological model derived from the intonational analysis of a jargon aphasic patient. *Brain and Language,* 1980, *9,* 289–297.

Fradis, A., & Leischner, A. Vergleichende Untersuchung der morphologischen Kategorien bei motorischer und sensorischer Aphasie: eine Verlaufsbeschreibung. In G. Peuser (Ed.), *Studien zur Sprachtherapie.* München: Fink, 1979. Pp. 166–176.

Fromkin, V. The non-anomalous nature of anomalous utterances. *Language,* 1971, *47,* 27–52.

Fromkin, V. (Ed.). *Speech errors as linguistic evidence.* The Hague: Mouton, 1973.

Garrett, M. F. The analysis of sentence production. In G. H. Bower (Ed.), *The psychology of learning and motivation* (Vol. 9). New York: Academic Press, 1975. Pp. 133–179.

Goodglass, H., & Baker, E. Semantic field, naming, and auditory comprehension in aphasia. *Brain and Language,* 1976, *3,* 359–374.

Green, E. Phonological and grammatical aspects of jargon in an aphasic patient. *Language and Speech,* 1969, *12,* 103–118.

Grober, E., Perecman, E., Kellar, L. & Brown, J. Lexical knowledge in anterior and posterior aphasics. *Brain and Language,* 1980, *10,* 318–330.

Head, H. *Aphasia and kindred disorders of speech.* New York: Hafner, 1926.

Huber, W., Stachowiak, F.-J., Poeck, K., & Kerschensteiner, M. Die Wernicke Aphasie. *Journal of Neurology,* 1975, *210,* 77–97.

Kertesz, A., & Benson, D. F. Neologistic jargon: A clinico-pathological study. *Cortex,* 1970, *6,* 362–386.

Kinsbourne, M., & Warrington, E. K. Jargon aphasia. *Neuropsychologia,* 1963, *1,* 27–37.

Kotten, A. Die kommunikative Funktion nonverbaler Umweglgleistungen. In G. Peuser (Ed.), *Interdisziplinäre Aspekte der Aphasieforschung.* Köln: Rheinland-Verlag, 1976. Pp. 57–70.

Lecours, A. R., & Lhermitte, F. Phonemic paraphasias: Linguistic structures and tentative hypotheses. *Cortex,* 1969, *5,* 193–228.

Leischner, A., Mattes, K., & Mallin, U. Vergleich der oralen mit der graphischen Performanz bei 1975 Aphasikern. *Archiv Psychiatrie und Nervenkrankheiten, 1980, 228,* 213–222.

MacKay, D. G. Phoneme repetition in the structure of languages. *Language and Speech,* 1970, *13,* 199–213.

Monakow, C. von, & Morgue, R. *Introduction biologique à l'étude de la neurologie et de la psychopathologie.* Paris: Alcan, 1928.

Ohala, J., & Hirano, M. *Control mechanisms for the sequencing of neuromuscular events in speech.* Reprints from the Conference on Speech Communication and Processing, MIT, 1967.

Perecman, E., & Brown, J. W. *Phonemic jargon: A case study.* Paper presented at 7th Annual Meeting of the International Neuropsychological Society, New York, 1979.

Peuser, G. Der Drei-Figuren-Test: ein neues Verfahren zur qualitativen und quantitativen Bestimmung von Sprachverständnisstörungen. In G. Peuser (Ed.), *Interdisziplinäre Aspekte der Aphasieforschung.* Köln: Rheinland-Verlag, 1976. Pp. 143–161.

Peuser, G. *Aphasie. Eine Einführung in die Patholinguistik.* München: Fink, 1978.

Peuser, G. Gesprochene und geschriebene Sprache und das Verhältnis von lexikalischer Paraphasie und Paragraphie. In K. Gloning & W. U. Dressler (Eds.), *Paraphasie.* München: Fink, 1980. Pp. 121–168.

Peuser, G., & Schriefers, H. The "Three-Figures-Test": A new procedure for the assessment of syntactic comprehension. *British Journal of Communication Disorders,* 1980, *15,* 157–164.

Pick, A. Aphasie. In A. Bethe & G. V. Bergmann (Eds.), *Handbuch der normalen und pathologischen Physiologie.* Berlin: Springer, 1931. Pp. 1416–1524.

Poeck, K. Stimmung und Krankheitseinsicht bei Aphasie. *Archiv Psychiatrie und Nervenkrankheiten,* 1972, *216,* 246–254.

Rensch, K. Linguistische Aspekte der Glossolalie. *Phonetica,* 1971, *23,* 215–238.

Schuell, H. Aphasia theory and therapy. In L. F. Sied (Ed.), *Selected lectures and papers.* Baltimore, London & Tokyo: University Park Press, 1974.

Stachowiak, F.-J. *Die semantische Struktur des subjektiven Lexikons.* München: Fink, 1979.

Stampe, D. The acquisition of phonetic representation. In *Papers from the 5th Regional Meeting of the Chicago Linguistic Society.* Chicago: Department of Linguistics, University of Chicago.

Weinstein, E. A., & Kahn, R. L. Nonaphasic misnaming (paraphasia) in organic brain disease. *Archives Neurology and Psychiatry,* 1952, *67,* 72–79.

Weinstein, E. A., Cole, M., Mitchell, M. S., & Lyerly, O. G. Anosognosia and aphasia. *Archives of Neurology,* 1964, *10,* 376–386.

Weinstein, A., & Lyerly, O. G. Personality factors in jargon aphasia. *Cortex,* 1976, *12,* 122–133.

Whitehouse, P., Caramazza, A., & Zurif, E. Naming in aphasia: Interaction of form and function. *Brain and Language,* 1978, *6,* 63–74.

Zipf, G. K. *Human behavior and the principle of least effort.* Cambridge, Mass.: Adison Wesley Press, 1949.

Chapter 12

Vowel Timing and Linguistic Organization of Articulatory Sequences in Jargonaphasia

SAMUEL W. ANDERSON

INTRODUCTION

The patient who presents fluent, precisely articulated speech that is totally incomprehensible characterizes the purest form of jargonaphasia. To evaluate linguistic functioning in such a patient provides a formidable challenge.

Most workers who have attempted to develop methods for assessing functional level in jargon patients have dealt with cases in which a substantial portion of speech can be directly decoded into words, or at least into word fragments that permit reconstruction of the lexical items that may be missing or distorted. But in phonemic jargon, the possibility of lexical identification depends on two factors: (*a*) the number of features by which any given phonetic production deviates from a recognizable standard; and (*b*) the proportion of the patient's speech that is too opaque for a lexical standard to be recognized at all. If this proportion is low, identification of lexical units can be accomplished, after which it is not difficult to establish whether or not the capacity to formulate and execute syntactically organized utterances is intact. But if recognizable words are totally absent, lexical reconstruction is precluded, and some other method is required to evaluate the higher levels of linguistic functioning.

295

JARGONAPHASIA

Copyright © 1981 by Academic Press, Inc.
All rights in any form reserved.
ISBN 0-12-137580-3

Traditional linguistic theories have not been helpful in providing such a method. Most of them begin with the view that speech is constructed from the bottom up, that is, from phoneme to morpheme, morpheme to word, word to phrase, etc. I am not convinced that it is unfair to blame such theories for the common assumption that a patient without recognizable words can possess no more than the power of "thought," having necessarily lost all capacity for meaningful speech, even though his behavior may be rich in nonverbal evidence that he understands much of what is said to him, and he may vocalize in a manner that is conversationally appropriate and phonotactically fluent. In the following pages, the development of a nonlexical approach to the problem will be described and used to evaluate one such jargon patient, K.S. (see Perecman & Brown, Chapter 10, this volume, for clinical details, which need not be repeated here).

But the traditional bottom-up view of speech generation is not merely inadequate to account for jargonaphasia; there is now a growing body of evidence showing that it is simply wrong. A number of findings in acoustic and articulatory phonetics support the view that spoken utterances in any language are guided ballistically by motor programs prepared in advance. These programs have been found necessary to account for the intonation and syllabic timing pattern of the entire phrase, prior to and independently of the processes that control the retrieval and articulation of words (see Anderson, 1975, for a review).

This top-down view was anticipated as early as the nineteenth century in the work of Kussmaul, followed by Pick (cited by Critchley, 1970, p. 236; see also Pick, 1973). Pick proposed that the syntactic pattern (*Satzschema*) of an utterance is planned prior to word selection, and that the intonation pattern (*Betonnungschema*) is planned even before that. Recent work has identified the syntactic phrase as the domain over which preplanning functions operate to determine both fundamental frequency shifts and length changes in stressed vowels. As we shall see, these functions are specified independently of word selection, so that they could indeed be planned first, and may be preserved, in pure jargon.

PHONOLOGICAL CUES FOR SYNTACTIC BOUNDARIES

A number of coarticulatory conditioning factors have been investigated by Cooper and his associates (Cooper, Lapointe, & Paccia, 1977; Sorenson & Cooper, 1980) that identify distinctive transyllabic features for major syntactic boundaries. Two of these are of particular interest, because they not only define phonological conditions for the occurrence of a boundary between one syllable and the next, but also are based on the properties of ˌvowels. Because *every* syllable contains a vowel, these cues are very general, and can be expected to occur whenever phrase boundaries are established anywhere in every sequence of syllables. Pausing, which was once thought to be the only cue of such generality, has been found to co-occur with stressed vowel cues on some occasions as a secondary effect, but does not signal a phrase boundary by itself. Let us use the following terminology to capture these complexities: VOCALIZATION shall refer to any sequence of syllables without intervening pauses; a SYNTACTIC PHRASE is any sequence of syllables, with or without intervening pauses, bounded by stressed vowel cues; a PHONOLOGICAL PHRASE is a vocalization that is also a syntactic phrase. Unless stated otherwise, the word *phrase* shall be used to mean phonological phrase. Thus, a phrase is surrounded by both pauses and syntactic boundaries; it contains no internal pauses, but may contain internal syntactic boundaries signaled by vowel cues alone. A SIMPLE PHRASE is one that has no internal boundaries.

Fundamental Frequency Declination

In simple declarative phrases, fundamental frequency (F_0) has been found to show a tendency to drop as the utterance proceeds. Sorenson and Cooper (1980) report that the F_0 values of the stressed vowels define a "topline" for this declination that is rulebound as a function of phrase length (pp. 408–428). Because local F_0 maxima associated with the sequence of vowels must be determined with advance knowledge of phrase length, it is argued that the topline rule implies preplanning of the phrase. In any event, the topline rule entails that syntactic boundaries are cued by a RISE in F_0 when the function is reset. This rule is of more than passing interest, as it provides a theory of sentence intonation based directly on patterns of syntactic structure.

Vowel Length Effects

In work with numerous languages it is reported that the duration of stressed vowels is minimal in phrase medial positions (V_M) when compared with their durations at phrase initial (V_I) and phrase final (V_F) positions. Both the initial (postboundary) and final (preboundary) effects have been obtained with experimental sequence recitations by speakers of Swedish (Lindblom & Rapp, 1973) and from samples of English spontaneous speech (Anderson & Podwall, 1977). Preboundary lengthening has been reported for German (DeLattre, 1966), Russian (Zlatoustova, 1954, 1962; cited by Oller & Smith, 1977), Dutch (Nooteboom, 1973), and for experimental sequence recitations in English (Lehiste, 1973; Oller, 1973). The preboundary, or phrase final, effect appears to be the larger of the two, even when both are present. Lindblom and Rapp (1973) have proposed a stressed vowel length timing function that encompasses both effects. As with the topline rule, this function also requires advance knowledge of phrase length, again entailing that a characteristic of each stressed vowel in the phrase be planned in advance.

In Table 12.1, both effects appear in mean vowel durations sampled by computer from 15 speakers of English. Vowels were identified by rise and fall characteristics of the amplitude envelope as described in Anderson and Jaffe (1972). Only vowels of 60 msec or longer were considered to be stressed; shorter ones were excluded from the analysis. In order to maximize the opportunity to detect phrase structure cues, only vocalizations containing at least three syllables and two stress positions (V_I and V_M and/ or V_M and V_F) were included in the analysis. It should be noted that the thousand-odd vocalizations that contributed the data in Table 12.1 include an unknown number that are syntactically bounded. However, the V_F/V_M ratios support the hypothesis that many of them exhibit the phrase final effect, for which t is highly significant ($p < .0005$, one tail).

Cooper has shown that stressed vowels are also lengthened just before phrase-*internal* syntactic boundaries (Cooper et al., 1977). These investigators interpret the phrase final effect as the action of a "trochaic shortening rule" being blocked at the boundary. Preboundary length was found

TABLE 12.1.

Stressed Vowel Frequencies and Mean Durations (msec) at Vocalization Initial, Medial, and Final Positions in Spontaneous Speech Sampled from Normal Native Speakers of English ($N = 15$ 5-min Samples)

Subject	f_I	V_I	f_M	V_M	f_F	V_F	V_F/V_M ratio
1	143	220	592	184	102	192	1.04
2	126	189	695	180	151	219	1.22
3	175	188	1601	184	156	219	1.19
4	120	198	675	170	139	210	1.24
5	171	281	1131	222	133	247	1.11
6	161	242	761	220	141	281	1.28
7	37	254	208	193	40	244	1.26
8	43	222	161	220	39	229	1.04
9	62	228	514	192	64	294	1.53
10	52	213	350	214	55	266	1.24
11	31	216	147	187	43	252	1.35
12	43	173	163	172	40	203	1.18
13	23	186	69	184	27	227	1.23
14	45	164	230	197	47	195	0.99
15	32	150	105	150	20	112	0.75
f Sum	1264		7402		1197		
Grand Mean		216		195		231	1.18
SD: .18							

$t = 25.39$, $df = 14$, $p < .0005$.

to be no greater with following pauses than without, leading to the conclusion that preboundary vowel lengthening is "influenced by the status of the syntactic boundary *per se* as a juncture in the processing of timing relations, not via the mediating influence of a pause that may be induced by the syntactic boundary [1977, p. 1316]." It should be remarked that the trochaic shortening rule is an example of anticipatory compensation, and cannot account for phrase initial effects (Anderson, 1975, p. 239).

Oller and Smith (1977) have raised the question of whether or not there is any prepausal vowel lengthening at the ends of vocalizations where junctures are known not to occur. In order to rule out language learning altogether, vowel lengths were measured in infant babbling. A total of 108 instances of babbling were collected from six babies of about 10 months and compared with simulated babbling of specified reduplicative syllable sequences by adults. Lengthening occurred among the English-speaking adults ($V_F/V_{Non\ F}$ = 1.31, $p < .05$) but not for the infants ($V_F/V_{Non\ F}$ = .98). This result is consistent with the interpretation that the adults preplanned the boundaries of their syllabic sequences and the babies did not. However, it cannot be inferred from this outcome what would have happened if the adults had been asked to babble *spontaneously*. Smith (1977) also reported finding that another child as young as 14 months did show lengthening when uttering "meaningful" syllabic strings (p. 997).

Is it possible to elicit prepausal vowels without lengthening from normal adults at all? According to the theory, this could happen only under two conditions: (*a*) composition and preplanning of the syllable sequence do not occur; (*b*) nonsyntactic factors become dominant in determining when vocalizations will end.

Oral reading of running text under time pressure was selected as a task likely to favor both conditions, the first because linguistic content is available from the text, obviating the need to compose, and the second because reading speed is maximized if one stops speaking only when respiration requires it.

Of the 15 subjects in Table 12.1, 9 were instructed to read aloud for 5 minutes from a formal speech (Professor George Miller's Presidential Address to the American Psychological Association), a text that none were able to finish in 5 minutes. At the end of the specified time period they were interrupted and told to stop. The results, in Table 12.2, show that vowels in all positions were shortened by most subjects, and that V_F/V_M dropped significantly as lengthening disappeared.

It should not be imagined, however, that all tasks that require reading of material specified in advance necessarily create either of the two conditions mentioned earlier. Sternberg and his associates (Sternberg, Wright, Knoll, & Monsell, 1980, pp. 509 ff.) have successfully employed the recitation of a word list under time pressure to *facilitate* articulatory planning. In Sternberg's task, the subject is instructed to begin speaking and complete

TABLE 12.2.

Stressed Vowel Frequencies and Mean Durations (msec) at Vocalization Initial, Medial and Final Positions from Matched Samples of Spontaneous Speech and Oral Reading under Time Pressure—Normal Native English (N = 9 Paired 5-min Samples)

Subject no.	Spontaneous speech							Oral reading from text						
	f_I	V_I	f_M	V_M	f_F	V_F	V_F/V_M	f_I	V_I	f_M	V_M	f_F	V_F	V_F/V_M
7	37	254	208	193	40	244	1.26	54	177	496	180	53	166	0.92
8	43	222	161	220	39	229	1.04	80	174	521	163	64	155	0.95
9	62	228	514	192	64	294	1.53	54	188	586	181	61	212	1.17
10	52	213	350	214	55	266	1.24	71	174	391	157	88	160	1.02
11	31	216	147	187	43	252	1.35	55	180	242	191	47	189	1.00
12	43	173	163	172	40	203	1.18	64	152	347	145	64	152	1.05
13	23	186	69	184	27	227	1.23	60	212	263	191	48	196	1.03
14	45	164	230	197	47	195	0.99	55	145	197	146	50	161	1.10
15	32	150	105	150	20	112	0.75	73	171	377	168	66	183	1.09
f sum:	368		1947		375			566		3420		541		
Grand Mean:		203		194		236	1.17		175		170		174	1.04
SD:							0.22							0.07

Paired t-test on V_F/V_M ratios: df = 8, t = 2.995, $p < .01$ (one-tailed).

a single short list (never longer than six disyllables) as quickly as possible after receiving a signal to start. The subject is allowed to examine the items on the list in advance, and gets the opportunity to prepare and compose the correct syllable sequence. Under these conditions, it is probable that the subjects very actively and deliberately preplan the recitation as a phrase that can easily be managed within the span of a single breath group, establishing a terminal boundary at the end of the list that becomes an intrinsic part of this plan. At any rate, Sternberg found vocalization-terminal lengthening of stressed vowels, F_0 declination, *and* a direct relation between starting reaction time and the length of the list—the most comprehensive evidence in support of articulatory preplanning to date.

To summarize, the findings shown for normal speakers reported here, along with those of Cooper, Oller, Sternberg, and their associates, all support the theory that articulatory preplanning is involved in motor programs for speaking. The fact that these programs establish distinct phonological time courses for different syntactic structures, both simple and complex, further implies that this generative process has access to the planned structure of the entire phrase before execution is completed, and perhaps before it is begun. It would appear that children acquire the ability to plan articulatory sequences as early as they can attach meaning to them; for adults, it is apparently sufficient that a specified sequence be requested that it be uttered in isolation according to plan, but if such sequences are read from text under time pressure, juncture becomes desynchronized with pausing and may be diminished altogether. Almost nothing is known about the loss of this planning ability.

SYNTACTIC BOUNDARY CUES
IN APHASIC PATIENTS

In Table 12.3 are results of the stressed vowel timing analysis performed on speech sampled from aphasic patients with various diagnoses, including the jargon patient, K.S. In this table, a significant *t* score indicates a relative | *shortening* | of vowels in final position compared with spontaneous speech norms for the sex of the patient. Among the spontaneous samples, only the Wernicke, Korsakoff, and acute anomia cases exhibit significantly less final vowel lengthening than normals. The common feature linking these cases appears to be difficulty in organizing words into semantically consistent syntactic phrases. The Korsakoff patient performed oral reading from text without intrusive paraphasias or confabulations; this yielded the same low ratio obtained for spontaneous speech, where paraphasias and confabulations did occur. The jargon patient, on the other hand, was equally incomprehensible whether reading or speaking spontaneously, but his phrase marking contrasted between the two conditions, i.e., when he spoke

TABLE 12.3

Stressed Vowel Frequencies and Mean Durations (msec) at Vocalization Initial, Medial, and Final Positions Sampled from Patients.

Patient diagnosis and sample type[a]		f_I	V_I	f_M	V_M	f_F	V_F	V_F/V_M	Ratio
Broca's aphasia[b]	SP	120	288	83	265	74	344	1.30	ns
Cerebellar ataxia	SP	30	178	64	169	30	207	1.22	ns
Wernicke's aphasia	SP	19	328	55	246	19	221	0.90	$p < 0.05$
Anomia (sampled during first few months poststroke)									
First month	SP	52	280	117	305	37	243	0.80	$p < 0.01$
Second month	SP	67	258	179	251	49	281	1.12	ns
Fourth month	SP	98	208	103	177	72	205	1.16	ns
Fifth month	SP	175	224	93	185	165	249	1.34	ns
Korsakoff syndrome (confabulatory)									
	SP	8	132	22	190	8	179	0.88	$p < .05$
	RE	8	284	35	313	8	287	0.90	$p < .05$
Jargon aphasia (K. S.)									
	SP	31	209	200	222	31	250	1.12	ns
	RE[c]	6	578	27	282	7	246	0.87	$p < .05$
Bavarian normal control									
	RE[c]	61	148	195	140	61	145	1.04	ns

[a] SP = spontaneous speech; RE = reading aloud from text.

[b] Patient sampled several years poststroke, following speech therapy.

[c] Sample combines approximately equal amounts of exposure to English and German texts.

spontaneously, his final vowel lengthening did not differ significantly from normal. A complicating factor in this case is the fact that K.S. had been bilingual in English and German (see Perecman and Brown, Chapter 10, this volume, for an analysis of the extent to which his jargon was influenced by each language). In Table 13.3, readings in English and German are combined, both for K.S. and for a normal bilingual control. However, it should be noted that, if readings for English and German are analyzed separately for final vowel lengthening, in both cases the ratios are higher for English than for German. The reason is as yet totally unclear.

But the results confirm that a phonological cue for syntactic structure can be seen in a case of pure jargonaphasia.

REFERENCES

Anderson, S. W. Ballistic control of rhythmic articulatory movements in natural speech. In D. R. Aaronson & R. W. Rieber (Eds.), *Developmental psycholinguistics and communication disorders. Annals of the New York Academy of Sciences,* 1975, *263,* 236–243.

Anderson, S. W. *Intonation contours in jargon.* Paper presented at the 7th Annual Meeting of the International Neuropsychological Society, New York, 1979.

Anderson, S. W., & Jaffe, J. *The definition, detection and timing of vocalic syllables in speech signals.* (Scientific Report No. 12). Department of Communication Sciences, New York State Psychiatric Institute, 1972.

Anderson, S. W., & Jaffe, J. *Speech timing characteristics of normal, native speakers of English in New York City.* (Scientific Report No. 16). Department of Communication Sciences, New York State Psychiatric Institute, 1976.

Anderson, S. W., & Podwall, F. N. Scalar timing control in spontaneous speech. *Journal of the Acoustical Society of American,* 1977, *62,* Suppl. No. 1, S64.

Cooper, W. E., Lapointe, S. G., & Paccia, J. M. Syntactic blocking of phonological rules in speech production. *Journal of the Acoustical Society of America,* 1977, *61,* 1314–1320.

Critchley, M. *Aphasiology.* London: Edward Arnold, 1970.

Dahlberg, C., & Jaffe, J. *Stroke.* New York: Norton, 1977.

DeLattre, P. A comparison of syllable length conditioning among languages. *International Review of Applied Linguistics,* iv, 1966, *4,* 183–198.

Kellar, L. *Stress and syntax in aphasia.* Paper presented at the 16th Annual Meeting of the Academy of Aphasia, Chicago, 1978.

Lehiste, I. Rhythmic units and syntactic units in production and perception. *Journal of the Acoustical Society of America,* 1973, *54,* 1228–1234.

Lindblom, B., & Rapp, K. Some temporal regularities of spoken Swedish. *Papers from the Institute of Linguistics* (University of Stockholm), 1973, *21,* 1–58.

Nooteboom, S. G. The perceptual reality of some prosodic durations. *Journal of Phonetics,* 1973, *1,* 25–45.

Oller, D. K. The effect of position in utterance on speech segment duration in English. *Journal of the Acoustical Society of America,* 1973, *54,* 1235–1247.

Oller, D. K., & Smith, B. L. Effect of final syllable position on vowel duration in infant babbling. *Journal of the Acoustical Society of America,* 1977, *62,* 994–997.

Perecman, E., & Brown, J. W. *Case study of phonemic jargon.* Paper presented at the 7th Annual Meeting of the International Neuropsychological Society, New York, 1979.

Pick, A. [*Aphasia*] (J. W. Brown, Trans.). Springfield, Ill.: Charles C Thomas, 1973.

Sorenson, J. M., & Cooper, W. E. Syntactic coding of fundamental frequency in speech production. In R. A. Cole (Ed.), *Perception and production of fluent speech*. Hillsdale, N.J.: Erlbaum, 1980.

Sternberg, S., Wright, C. E., Knoll, R. L., & Monsell, S. Motor programs in rapid speech: Additional evidence. In R. A. Cole (Ed.), *Perception and production of fluent speech*. Hillsdale, N.J.: Erlbaum.

Thorsen, N. A study of the perception of sentence intonation: Evidence from Danish. *Journal of the Acoustical Society of America*, 1980, *67*, 1014–1030.

Chapter 13

Therapy with the Jargonaphasic

A. DAMIEN MARTIN

INTRODUCTION

Speech and language rehabilitation was a secondary consideration for the field of aphasiology in the nineteenth century and the first four decades of the twentieth. With the exception of a few individuals like Mills (1904), the primary goal of aphasiologists was to gain insight into the nature of normal functioning through determining the nature of the disorder. Therapy as a major consideration began with World War II. The advent of better medical treatment on the battlefield coupled with the commitment by some countries to the care of the veteran provided the impetus for a systematic and well-financed approach to rehabilitation.

Consequently, the need arose for specialists to develop programs in this relatively new field. Clinicians were drawn from several disciplines, including psychology, education, and speech pathology (Anderson, 1944, 1946; Huber, 1942; Wepman, 1951). The previous lack of attention to rehabilitation necessitated stopgap measures that sometimes indicated a failure to appreciate the complexity of both the disorder and the therapeutic process: "WACS are assigned part time to our service through occupational therapy (Arts and Crafts Department) as the need arises for instruction. These girls have usually had speech courses in colleges and adapt readily to our program with proper guidance (Peacher, 1946, p. 236)." However, the bulk of the new clinicians were professionals who, from the beginning, recognized the need to develop therapeutic rationales based on theory as well as clinical practice. The need for such rationales is as pressing today as it was then.

The purpose of this chapter is not to provide a manual of techniques but to present a rationale for therapy directed toward one recognized type of aphasia, jargonaphasia. Certain principles, premises, and suggestions will be offered. Their actualization will be left to the skill and imagination of the individual clinicians and their patients.

RATIONALES FOR THERAPY

Generally, rationales for aphasia therapy were taken from two opposing views, the "localizationist" model exemplified by the work of Neilsen (1936) and the "reduction of efficiency" view first suggested by Freud (1891). Each model gave rise to different approaches to therapy. A third model that had an important impact on the development of aphasia therapy was the psychometric model, especially as represented by the standardized test for aphasia.

The level of reference chosen for the focus of therapy was usually the linguistic processing abilities of the aphasic, although a second level of reference—communication—was sometimes implicit. The first part of this chapter will examine the general development of rationales for aphasia therapy as a background for the second part, which will attempt to specify an approach to be used with the jargonaphasic.

Learning Approach to Therapy

The localizationist view posits a loss of either information or function. Therapy then becomes the replacement of information (language) through teaching by the clinician and learning by the aphasic. That is, the aphasic has lost language, therefore the task of the aphasia clinician interested in rehabilitation is to teach language. The best known proponent of this view was Martha Taylor Sarno who, in a series of remarkably cogent articles, presented her rationale for therapy, the application of that rationale through programmed learning techniques, and finally, an evaluation of the approach (Sarno, 1968; Sarno, Silverman, & Sands, 1970; Taylor, 1963; Taylor & Sands, 1966)

One subdivision of the loss view held aphasia to be a form of regression, where impairment mirrored the development of language in the child, but in reverse (Jakobson, 1968). Higher, later developed forms of language behavior were lost first whereas those forms and functions that were lower on a developmental scale were more resistant to loss. Logically, therapy became an attempt to lead the aphasic through a series of developmental stages, an approach that lent itself quite easily to a pedagogical structuring of therapy. For example, Anderson (1944) among others, recommended the speechless aphasic should replicate the verbal developmental stages of "babbling, lalling, echolallia, and verbal utterance." The learning approach has always been unsatisfactory both as rationale and as guide for specific techniques. Evidence indicates that, aside from superficial resemblance to some characteristics of the development of the use of speech sound, the aphasic's linguistic deficit has no real relation to stages of language acquisition in children (Caramazza & Zurif, 1978).

The concept that language was lost, combined with various pedagogic techniques, led to an emphasis on the elements of language. Thus the aphasic was expected to learn the phonemes of English, to combine them into words, to learn a series of words, and, finally, to form syntactic utterances (Huber, 1942, 1946; Sarno, 1968). Basically a reductionist view of both language and language performance, this approach presented both theoretical and practical difficulties, as discussed in some detail elsewhere (Martin, 1974). To list just a few, no one learns a language in this way—neither the child acquiring a first language nor the adult learning a second language. The child produces meaningful, syntactically structured utterances long before he has mastered the phonology of the language; the adult uses words and phrases in his initial attempts at second language learning. Because normals recognize most words within a semantic and syntactic context, the isolation of phonemes or words makes them more difficult to learn. In addition, we know from a series of studies that frequency of occurrence, length, syntactic complexity, and other factors all contribute to the ease or difficulty of production. Thus the phrase *a cup of coffee* will probably be easier than a single phoneme for the aphasic to produce.

Stimulation Approach to Therapy

The second major influence on therapy, the "reduction of efficiency" model, led to what were called stimulation approaches. Within this framework, the aphasic is seen as having a reduced efficiency in the processing of language. Thus phonemes, words, and syntax are not lost. Instead, the aphasic has difficulty in processing these three levels of language because the necessary mechanisms are not operating with adequate efficiency. Therefore, if an aphasic does not name an object, his "retrieval mechanism" is not operating as efficiently, a construct that provided an explanation for the apparent variability in aphasic response capability.

One of the advantages of this approach was that the techniques developed could be used within both the structured therapy session and the outside environment. For example, some aphasics can handle stimuli of only a certain length. When stimuli surpass this length, the aphasic may lose part of the message because he is engaged in processing information that has already entered the system—a result Wepman (1972) called the "Shutter Effect." In the therapy session, the aphasic might be asked to repeat a series of utterances that gradually increase in length and syntactic complexity to improve his capacity for handling longer messages. On the other hand, a nonaphasic participant within a conversational setting can structure his speech to adapt to the reduced capacity of the aphasic. The message *What would you like for dinner?* will probably be easier for the aphasic to understand if the speaker phrases it as *What . . . would you like . . . for dinner?* (Schuell, Jenkins, & Jimenez-Pabon, 1964). [In all models, there is a danger of reification. Retrieval mechanisms, auditory retention span, shutter effects, and so forth are presented here solely as epistemological constructs. The basic premise is that, if varied information is presented in diversified ways, there will be varying effects on all the processes by which information is handled as the system attempts to deal with it (Martin, 1974, 1978; Schuell, Jenkins, Jimenez-Pabon, 1964).]

Standardized Tests for Aphasia

A third major influence on the development of therapy has been the standardized test for aphasia. Derived from intelligence tests (Benton, 1967), it has served as a means to define the nature and degree of aphasic impairment through a statement of deviation from a norm which itself is defined by the test through standardization procedures. A logical result has been to view therapy as an attempt to return the aphasic as close to the norm as possible (see Figure 13.1). Although logical, such a goal may not be appropriate, especially in the evaluation of therapy. The aphasic is outside the norm by virtue of the brain damage; he will not return. This is not to say that he will not improve, but the improvement must be in terms of his movement toward a better handling of his changed condition. For example, one widely used test for aphasia, the Porch Index of Communicative Ability (Porch, 1967, 1973), lists delayed response as a deviation from the norm. Time of response is also important on the Boston Diagnostic Aphasia Examination (Goodglass & Kaplan, 1972). A delayed response, therefore, is viewed as a deviation to be corrected. While it might be better to try to get one aphasic to speed up his response (Martin, 1974), a slowed response might be a better strategy for another. The agrammatic patient uses syntax in a manner outside the norm. However, the proper focus of therapy for a particular individual might be to get him to try to speak more often rather than to include function words and inflected endings in his speech. His speaking more frequently might better signify improvement than would movement toward an arbitrarily defined norm.

A second logical but perhaps limiting effect of the standardized test has been the direct derivation of therapeutic techniques from test tasks.

For example, confrontation naming is ubiquitous in tests for aphasia. It has also become one of the most common of therapy tasks, even though naming per se may be one of the most difficult procedures for an aphasic to perform. This is not to say that such derived tasks are not beneficial. It has been demonstrated that traditional therapy has a beneficial effect (Basso, Faglioni, & Vignolo, 1979; Wiegel-Crump & Koenigsknecht, 1973; Wertz *et al.* 1978).

Levels of Reference for Aphasia Therapy

Any rationale for therapy must answer three questions (Martin, 1979, 1980):

1. What is the nature of normal functioning?
2. What is the nature of the disorder?
3. What is the nature of therapy?

The answers to these questions will depend in large part on the underlying theoretical models and on the level of reference chosen for attention.

The most common level of reference in aphasiology has been the information-processing skills of the aphasic, especially the processing of linguistic information. Most therapy described in the literature has been directed toward improving the aphasic on this level. Within this framework there are clearly defined answers to the three questions posed above. However, there is another level of reference that can be a focus in therapy and that will provide different but equally valid answers. These answers will by necessity also affect the direction and techniques of therapy. This second level of reference is communication.

Both levels represent interactions: the interaction of individuals (see Figure 13.2) or the interaction of cognitive systems within the individual (see Figure 13.3). Although both levels of reference are important in therapy with the jargonaphasic, this chapter will deal primarily with the communication level of reference for several reasons. First, therapy structured according to parameters of a communication interaction will be easier for the jargonaphasic. Second, the nature and severity of the jargonaphasic's problems militate against the kind of structured task that has been developed in previous, information-processing-oriented therapies. This is not to say that such tasks are always inappropriate, but rather that such structure may be more appropriate when the jargonaphasic has attained a greater control over his own communicative behavior. Third, structured tasks evolved from an information-processing level of reference have already been detailed elsewhere (Sarno, 1968; Schuell, Jenkins, Jimenez-Pabon, 1964; Wepman, 1951). Any and all of these tasks can be adapted for use with the jargonaphasic, given the proper conditions.

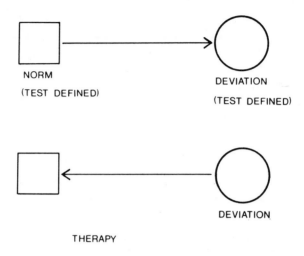

NORM
(TEST DEFINED)

DEVIATION
(TEST DEFINED)

DEVIATION

THERAPY

MOVEMENT TOWARD THE NORM

Figure 13.1. Test-defined therapy.

INFORMATION PROCESSING

When the aphasic's capacities as a processor of information are the focus of attention, the three questions posed earlier might be answered as follows:

1. Normal functioning is the efficient action and interaction of the cognitive process that support language behavior within and by the individual.
2. The disorder is the reduction, because of brain damage, of the efficiency of action and interaction of the cognitive processes that support language behavior.

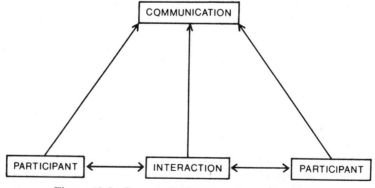

Figure 13.2. Communication as a level of reference.

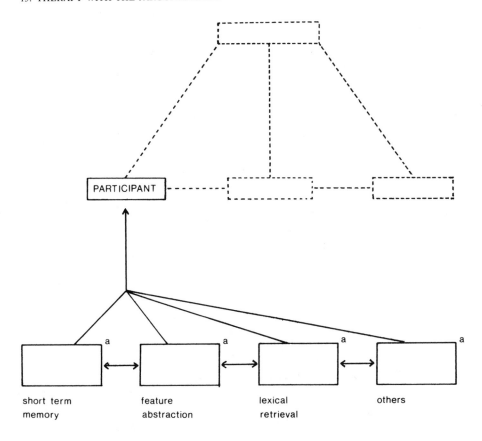

a selected hypothesized process

Figure 13.3. The participant as a level of reference.

3. Therapy is therefore the attempt to excite and manipulate the action and interaction of the cognitive processes that support language behavior so as to maximize their effective usage (Martin, 1979, 1980). (See Figure 13.3.)

A few comments may be in order about the approach underlying these answers. First, the term cognition is used here to mean all the processes by which sensory information is transformed, reduced, elaborated, stored, recovered, and used (Neisser, 1966). Second, such an approach does not view the impairment solely in linguistic terms. In other words, there is not a "syntactic" nor "lexical" impairment. Rather, the difficulty lies in the use of those processes which handle that particular type of information. As such, then, this approach partakes of the "reduction of efficiency" model. Third, it eliminates the tendency of therapy to be viewed as a movement back toward the norm. Therapy is not the curing of a disorder, but the maximizing of a potential within each individual aphasic patient.

COMMUNICATION

Damage to the brain resulting in aphasia does more than impair the information processing capabilities of the individual; it also disrupts communication. This is not to say that the aphasic does not or cannot communicate. The aphasic is often surprisingly good as a communicator. There are several reasons for this, reasons that have importance for therapy overall, but for therapy with the jargonaphasic in particular.

First, a communication interaction is a form of behavior in which there is an exchange of messages. As Watzlawick, Beavin, and Jackson (1967) have stated, "all behavior in an interactional situation has message values, i.e. is communication . . . one cannot *not* communicate [p. 48]." The logical consequence of this is that, when the aphasic interacts with another individual, he must perforce communicate.

Second, correctness or incorrectness of the form of the message may not necessarily be the major consideration. Again, to quote Watzlawick, Beavin, and Jackson: "Neither can we say that communication only takes place when it is intentional, conscious or successful, that is when mutual understanding occurs. Whether message sent equals message received is an important but different order of analysis [pp. 48–49]."

Third, because the essence of communication is interaction, the successful exchange depends not just on the performance of one of the individuals involved in the exchange—in this context, not just on the performance of the aphasic—but on the performance of the other individual as well. Each of the participants has roles to play, roles which, whether successful or not, complement or supplement each other (Muma, 1975). (See Figure 13.2.)

Fourth, communication does not depend on linguistic skills alone. Although language may be the most complex and efficient means of communication, language is not synonymous with communication. Several systems that supplement language behavior have extensive message value of their own. Let us take as one example the production of the neologism, [maɪ aɪrtɪd] by an aphasic. In this particular utterance, the aphasic has produced a message that is distorted linguistically, a distortion that must have an effect on the listener. In most circumstances, taken alone, the net effect of the utterance would be a lack of comprehension on the part of the listener. However, if the aphasic throws himself into a chair with a sigh as he says [maɪ aɪrtɪd] and the listener correctly interprets it as "I'm tired," communication has been effected, there has been a successful interchange of an intended message, and both participants in the interaction have succeeded in their roles.

Increasing communication effectiveness is a valid goal in aphasia therapy. It is also a viable goal for the reasons cited: the presence of communication in all human interactions; the possibility of communication even when a message is linguistically outside the norm; the participation and skills of the nonaphasic member in the interaction; the remaining communication skills possessed by the aphasic; and finally, the possibility of communication through behaviors and systems other than language.

If we use the communication framework as our level of reference, the answers to our three questions might be as follows:

1. Normal functioning can be defined as the maintenance, with maximum efficiency, of appropriate receiver–sender roles in a conversational exchange.
2. The disorder can be viewed as the disruption of communicative interactions, in which one of the participants is an aphasic, through the failure of either or both participants as a receiver–sender in the exchange.
3. Therapy is therefore the attempt to maximize the performance of both participants as receiver–senders in the exchange (Martin, 1978, 1979, 1980).

As in the earlier definition, therapy is not an attempt to cure but rather an attempt to maximize potential and performance. The critical difference, however, lies in attention to the other member of the communicative interaction, the nonaphasic partner. It is this focus that radically changes the form and direction of therapy, especially with the jargonaphasic.

THERAPY WITH THE JARGONAPHASIC

Historically, therapy with the jargonaphasic has been treated almost as an afterthought, in part because none of the therapies derived from the three models discussed earlier were addressed directly to the problems of the jargonaphasic. When therapy was mentioned, it was usually with vague reference to what became the apotheosis of therapy with the jargonaphasic—improvement of self-monitoring or auditory comprehension. Although there can be no argument with these goals, there is a need for specification of the means used to reach them.

There was another reason, perhaps, for the lack of attention. Often seen as a difficult patient with whom to work, the jargonaphasic was not expected to improve as much or as well as the "motor aphasic" (Huber, 1942). This perceived lack of improvement, as well as the unease shown by the clinician, probably arose more from the inappropriateness of the short-term goals and techniques of therapy rather than from the type of aphasia. For example, many tasks outlined in the literature were developed to elicit speech from the nonspeaking aphasic, an inapposite aim with one

who may exhibit a "press of speech." Symptomatic behavior, including
a lack of strong inhibitory skills and difficulty with auditory comprehension
and self-monitoring, probably militated against the jargonaphasic's success
with these structured tasks, at least at certain stages of the therapy. Many
techniques were also developed to teach linguistic elements, again an inapposite aim with an aphasic who uses all the elements, but incorrectly.

The rationale to be proposed here suggests some general principles
that can guide the clinician, principles derived in part from a consideration
of those symptoms that differentiate the jargonaphasic from other aphasics.
Again, the suggestions are not meant as techniques to be followed rigidly,
but rather as a series of guidelines for structuring therapy directed to the
specific problems of the jargonaphasic.

**Characteristics of
the Jargonaphasic**

One could say with some justification that there are as many types of
aphasia as there are aphasics. Classifications are not real descriptions of
individuals, but heuristic devices to aid the aphasiologist. Although the
need for taxonomies is self-evident, there are certain inherent dangers in
their use. When many types of behavior are grouped under one heading,
there may be a tendency to expect that all individuals so identified will
exhibit all those behaviors. There may also be a predisposition to certain
judgments of what is actually being observed. Recognition of these dangers
is very important in the therapy process as the clinician must always be
prepared to interact with each aphasic as an individual as well as a member
of a classificatory group.

With this caveat in mind, the jargonaphasic will be considered in this
discussion as one whose presenting symptoms include severe impairment
of auditory comprehension and self-monitoring abilities, so-called empty
speech, reduction in the ability to inhibit (sometimes called "press of
speech"), and speech characterized by the production of literal and verbal
paraphasias and neologisms. Under the rubric of jargonaphasia will be
included neologistic fluent jargon, phonemic jargon, paraphasic jargon, asemantic jargon—all those types of fluent aphasic speech where the utterance
is judged to be incomprehensible to the average listener. Excluded will be
stereotypical jargon such as the constant repetition of *me, me, me.* Consideration of the problems involved in the use of stereotypies would un-
necessarily lengthen and complicate the discussion. Alajouanine (1968) has
given a description of the course of recovery for such patients and a therapeutic approach can be derived from his outline.

The following discussion will examine these symptomatic behaviors,
defining them and outlining in each case both the premises on which the
therapy should be based and some techniques and approaches that can be
used.

Auditory Comprehension

A basic practice has always been to start therapy at a level where the aphasic will begin to have some success (Schuell, Jenkins, & Jimenez-Pabon, 1964; Wepman, 1951). However, traditional emphasis on improvement of auditory comprehension as a first and primary goal of therapy with the jargonaphasic has led to the peculiar situation where we present a damaged system, which is already having difficulty, with demands that increase the difficulty. A number of factors contribute to this paradoxical situation.

Auditory comprehension is but one aspect of comprehension, one specialized mode of receptive processing. Comprehension is holistic and depends, not just on linguistic coding within a particular modality, but on a multitude of codes and the simultaneous use of at least two modalities (Muma, 1975; Scheflen, 1974; Scheflen & Scheflen, 1972). If the auditory modality is the major focus of attention, concentration is on the most complex of all communication forms—language. (It must be stressed that language and communication are not synonymous.) The result may be a minimization or elimination of other forms of behavior that support language (for example, spreading the hands while saying the word *big*). This in turn reduces the redundancy that is always present in parallel nonverbal behaviors and that is necessary for normal comprehension (Scheflen, 1974). The increased difficulty in attending to the auditory modality alone can be attested to by anyone who has ever had to transcribe a tape-recorded conversation.

The problem can be further compounded by the way we view the nature of the comprehension problem, and by the tasks we choose to correct that problem. As mentioned earlier, the standardized test for aphasia has had a profound effect on our view of the aphasic and on the treatment offered him. Nowhere is this more apparent than in the way we approach auditory comprehension problems in the jargonaphasic. Assessment of the impairment depends largely on test scores rather than on actual conversational exchanges. For example, in the Boston Diagnostic Aphasia Examination (Goodglass & Kaplan, 1972), the one characteristic on the rating scale profile not based on nontest behavior is auditory comprehension because it "can be adequately measured by objective test scores [pp. 27–28]."

This contention is disputed by Wilcox, Davis, and Leonard (1978) who claim that the formal assessment of comprehension skills "fall(s) short of giving us information about an aphasic person's functional comprehension abilities [p. 252]." They base this claim on their examination of aphasic subjects' abilities to comprehend language within a context. Their conclusions are also supported by clinical experience. One may say to the apparently noncomprehending aphasic *Please pass the tissues* or *Would you like more coffee?* and he will pass the tissues or indicate he wants more coffee. But, because this behavior occurs outside the controlled situation of the test or experiment, it is seldom considered in the assessment of comprehension abilities. Even more important, it may not be considered in the planning or evaluation of therapy.

Tasks that were developed to eliminate context and other clues so as to test auditory comprehension are used intact as therapy tasks. For example, the aphasic is asked to recognize common words outside the context of the sentence. It is known that context and redundancy both contribute to the likelihood of comprehension of a message; by removing those factors, we are therefore making the task more difficult for the aphasic.

The preceding is not intended to suggest that the goal of improving auditory comprehension be abandoned. Severe comprehension difficulties in jargonaphasia must be dealt with if therapy is to be successful. What is suggested, however, is that improvement can be reached through means other than the traditional structured task and in a manner that will follow the usual guideline of starting with the easier and progressing to the more difficult.

As already stated, auditory comprehension is a component of comprehension. Improvement of the whole must perforce affect the parts (Martin, 1979; Miller, 1978). The total process—comprehension—can be affected through attention to the communication interaction, especially the role played by the nonaphasic participant in the conversational exchange. The clinician can increase the likelihood of comprehension by using, even exaggerating, all the means by which comprehension is effected in ordinary conversational exchanges.

Actual speech can include repetitions, rephrasings, pauses, and increased intensity (Muma, 1975; Schuell, Jenkins, & Jimenez-Pabon, 1964). Nonverbal behavior can be used to heighten and to support linguistic structure. This support can range from pointing to a patient when saying *you* or to oneself when saying *I*, to pantomimic gestures which mimic the word in some way (e.g., as raising the hand from a lowered position while saying *tall*). All these—and more—are normal behaviors in a conversational setting (Scheflen, 1973, 1974; Scheflen & Scheflen, 1972).

These nonverbal supports can be increased in number, repeated, made larger and therefore more intense, etc.; they are subject to the same kinds of modifications that are used with speech in order to heighten understanding on the part of normals (Muma, 1975) as well as aphasics (Schuell, Jenkins, & Jimenez-Pabon, 1964). The increase in redundancy and use of techniques to focus attention gives the aphasic a greater opportunity to scan the material for relevant features, to abstract those features from the clinician's behavior, and thus to comprehend.

The focus on the clinician's role as a speaker–sender represents the major difference between this rationale and others: In most aphasia therapy, emphasis is on the aphasic and his difficulties as an information processor. But, although this focus is different, it is not entirely new. Wepman (1972, 1976) proposed a conversational structure for therapy to stimulate "thought."

Martin (1980) suggested that Wepman's techniques involved not so much "thought stimulation" as an emphasis on shifting communication role. Davis and Wilcox (1980) describe a structure that allows for a wider acceptance by the clinician of the aphasic's varying responses.

The applicability of stressing the clinician's role rather than the aphasic's will be discussed further in the following sections.

Empty Speech, Neologisms, and Paraphasias

There are two ways to deal with jargon: first, to correct the faulty speech itself—the thrust of most speech therapy; and second, to improve the clinician as a listener.

According to the dictionary, jargon can mean the particular vocabulary of a trade, profession, or group; gibberish or unintelligible speech; or any talk or writing that one does not understand. The "emptiness" of any utterance then, depends primarily on lack of understanding by one of the participants—a lack that can result from unfamiliarity with the speaker's vocabulary or code as well as from a distortion or lack of apparent reference in the utterance. If one nonaphasic individual says to another *Get me the watchamacallit,* comprehension depends, not on the speech, but on the meaning the listener has been able to abstract from the total communication. If an individual aphasic says *I bike Perro,* it would be impossible on the basis of the transcription alone to decide the meaning, just as one could not understand *watchamacallit* by itself. However, if the aphasic is holding an album of Perry Como records, and if the listener knows that one of his distortion of form patterns is to combine the beginning and end of intended phrases into a single neologism, then the meaning becomes apparent.

The possibility that apparently empty speech is not without meaning and a belief that the clinician can reach an understanding of its content are two basic premises of therapy.

Most clinicians do, after a comparatively short time, develop the ability to "translate" jargon through an ongoing analysis of linguistic structure, identification of patterns within the jargon, observation of nonverbal behavior by the aphasic, and finally, recognition and use of context. Therapy with the jargonaphasic demands that the clinician develop these skills to as high degree as possible and use them to emphasize his own skills as a listener.

It should be stressed that this will not bring about change only in the clinician. Just as a manipulation and intensification of the clinician's role as a sender affects the probability of comprehension by the aphasic, so the manipulation and intensification of the clinician's role as a listener will affect the aphasic as well. Anything that interferes with a successful transfer of messages will have an effect on both participants in the exchange (see Figure 13.2). Anything that will aid in that transfer will also affect both participants. Increased understanding of the distorted form in jargon is as much a beneficial change in therapy as is a change in the speech of the aphasic, if only because it has enhanced the possibility and opportunity for successful communication experience. In addition, ability to translate the jargon and rephrase it into an acceptable linguistic form enables the clinician to use one of the most effective techniques in speech and language therapy—modeling.

MODELING

Modeling takes various forms and serves different purposes. Found in everyday conversational exchanges as well as in therapy, it can serve as a model for correct form, as when a mother repeats *spaghetti* after a young child has mispronounced it *pasghetti*; as a signal that one has understood; or as a vehicle to provide new information so the speaker can continue, for example, if one person were to say *I saw your new faculty member yesterday* and the second were to nod and reply *Harriet*.

In therapy with the jargonaphasic, modeling performs two major functions: to encourage and maintain a communicative interaction and to diminish literal and verbal paraphasias. It performs these functions by encouraging appropriate and necessary role taking by each participant and by providing a correct linguistic model against which the aphasic can compare his own production. Such comparison is essential to both development and change of behavior (Mysak, 1966).

Comparison can be affected in exactly the same manner with the aphasic producing the neologism [maɪ aɪrtɪd] while throwing himself into a chair with a sigh. The clinician can respond with *I'm tired, too*. The aphasic has immediate nonthreatening feedback of the correct utterance without an interruption of the exchange which would occur if an attempt were made to get him to say *I'm tired* correctly. Of course, individual examples are easier to deal with than the continuous flow of jargon sometimes faced by the clinician. To begin to be able to handle this flow, to try to understand it, and to provide modeling will require, not only the competence to perform the ongoing analyses described earlier, but also the ability to encourage what has been called "role taking attitudes [to reconcile] communicative obstacles [Muma, 1975, p. 296]," the subject of the next section.

Monitoring Skills and Press of Speech

There are two types of monitoring—intrapersonal and interpersonal. Both are essential to communication (Mysak, 1966).

Intrapersonal monitoring, or self-monitoring, is a combination of several highly refined skills. Generally unconscious and automatic, it involves the ongoing comparison of one's actual production with desired production effected through the use of a number of interrelated systems including proprioreceptive and auditory feedback systems (Miller, 1978; Powers, 1973). Interpersonal monitoring is attention to the communicative acts of another.

Impairment of self-monitoring is almost a given in jargonaphasia, and it receives—along with auditory comprehension difficulties—the bulk of the attention in most therapy. However, interpersonal monitoring is also often impaired and may be even more important.

INTRAPERSONAL MONITORING

The major reason for emphasis on self-monitoring and self-correction has been the recognition that they underlie the production of normal speech. It is also a remnant of learning-based therapies, where the fear was always that the aphasic would "learn" the error, a fear that has been demonstrated to be unfounded (Muma, 1978).

However, we again have a problem with degree of difficulty, especially in the initiation of therapy. Self-monitoring demands attention to fine points of language behavior through exceedingly exact discriminations and comparisons, all of which may be too difficult at first.

Although awareness of self-error is important in ongoing communication, it may not be the most important element. In fact, overemphasis on the errors of the aphasic can have a deleterious effect both on the individual aphasic and on communication. Some of the negative impact on the individual from an overemphasis on self-monitoring and self-correction has been detailed elsewhere (Aita, 1947; Martin, 1974) and will not be discussed here. An excellent example of interference with communication occurs in Kopit's play, *Wings*. In a group therapy discussion, one of the aphasics, fluent and communicating very well, says *cheesecake* for *cheapskate*. Given the content, context, and other factors, it is quite apparent to the group, the clinician, and even to the audience exactly what is meant. Yet the entire therapy session with its attendant communication interactions is disrupted while the clinician insists that the aphasic recognize his error and produce the word correctly. Often, in our desire for absolutely correct responses, we may make demands upon the aphasic that we would never make with a nonaphasic, even when he makes the same kind of error.

Of much greater importance to therapy with the jargonaphasic may be interpersonal monitoring.

INTERPERSONAL MONITORING

Interpersonal monitoring is essential to a communication-based therapy. Without the ability to attend to signals from the environment, including signals from the other participant in the exchange, the jargonaphasic cannot begin to benefit from therapy. If the aphasic cannot perform such basic monitoring acts as attending, orienting, and scanning, he cannot participate in a successful exchange of messages.

Let us assume that the clinician has listened long and patiently, has concentrated on all the clues available from the total situation, and finally thinks he understands what the patient is talking about. A logical next step would be to determine whether or not that understanding is correct. There are several ways in which this might be done, but perhaps the simplest would be for the clinician to stop and say *Is this what you mean?* and then state what he has understood. In other words, the clinician should change his role from receiver to sender. Implicit in this shift is a parallel shift on the part of the aphasic. That is, the clinician goes from receiver to sender, the aphasic from sender to receiver.

The patient who exhibits a press of speech may not be able to do this. His inability to stop talking long enough to assume the role of listener will be the greatest deterrent to interpersonal monitoring and to the application of the techniques that have been described. The first priority with an aphasic who experiences difficulty with this initial act of inhibition is to give him as many opportunities as possible to perform the act of role switching. All other techniques will depend on his developing the control necessary to stop speaking and attend to another.

Let us assume that the aphasic cannot or does not stop talking at the moment that the clinician asks him to do so. If an aphasic does not respond to a stimulus under one condition, he may respond if the nature, intensity, or size of the stimulus is increased, for example, if the clinician speaks louder, touches the aphasic, puts his hand in front of the aphasic's mouth in a shushing gesture, etc.

Again, the basic structure of therapy is derived from normal communication—in this case, from all the techniques we use when someone else is not listening to us and we wish them to stop and to attend. The difference lies in the severity of the aphasic's difficulty and in the exaggeration of the techniques which might prove necessary in the therapy situation.

In performing this basic act of role switching, we are also using all the approaches described earlier. If we succeed in getting the aphasic to stop talking and to listen, we then have the opportunity to apply the approach described under auditory comprehension. What we will say while he is quiet will depend on our analysis of the jargon. It is not really important at the early stages whether or not we have correctly understood. The simple act of having the aphasic stop and listen to what we are saying forces him to attend. If we are wrong, and he indicates we are, that is as much a plus as if we had been correct.

The basic concept can be used in a modified form with the more mildly impaired aphasic as well. One patient with whom the author worked no longer exhibited press of speech as a major symptom. A very social man, he and his wife enjoyed entertaining and visiting friends and relatives. Sometimes, when he became excited, he showed a tendency to revert to press of speech, with a corresponding increase in paraphasias. Part of therapy was directed toward developing a series of signals whereby the wife, in a social situation, could indicate to him that he was talking too much. If he felt it was too difficult to stop, for whatever reason, he would so indicate and they ended the evening.

Once the patient has reached the point where he can inhibit and attend in conversational role switching with comparative ease, one can then introduce structured tasks to refine these activities.

EXTENSION OF THERAPY

A communication-based therapy relies on the premise that increased opportunities to send and receive messages and to attend to others will affect the communication abilities and patterns of the aphasic. This premise receives support from studies of communication among nonaphasics (Lennard & Bernstein, 1970) as well as from work on functional communication therapy with aphasics (Aten, Caligiuri, & Holland, 1980).

However, if we accept the premise, we are faced with an immediate problem. Even under the best of circumstances, the clinician will be with the aphasic at most perhaps a total of 10 hours a week, usually less. This creates a need to expand therapy beyond the clinical session. I am not speaking here of carry-over, which is essentially a form of evaluation, but rather of the extension of therapy through interactions other than those with the clinician. It would seem logical to bring this about through the interactions that occur between the aphasic and his family, especially the spouse. This concept of family involvement in aphasia therapy is not a new one (Goodkin, 1969; Newhoff & Davis, 1978; Schuell, Jenkins, & Jimenez-Pabon, 1964; Turnblom & Myers, 1952).

Involvement of the Family

The clinician approaches the aphasic with both an academic and an experiential background in aphasia. He has, not only diagnostic skills which will aid in the recognition and interpretation of linguistically deviant utterances, but also a general understanding of other behavioral phenomena, such as perseveration and liability, and of how to cope with them. This is, of course, not true of the patient's family.

The first step, therefore, should be to provide the family with as much information as possible about the disorder. This must be done over a period of time and not in one or two sessions devoted to "family counseling."

The family needs time and help in order to interpret this information, to absorb it, and to be able to handle their own emotional reactions to it.

At the same time they must be reassured that, in many ways, the aphasic is the same person he was before. Fear that the aphasic has lost his mind is always present for the aphasic and those close to him. Such counseling can be done in individual sessions, in group sessions with other spouses, and in therapy itself.

Therapy may also be extended by including the spouse in the therapy session. Such inclusion would have several parallel goals: to illustrate to the spouse the content within the aphasic's speech; to demonstrate it is possible to understand the aphasic as well as to make the aphasic understand; to train the spouse in the techniques described earlier; and finally, to enlist the aid of the spouse in understanding what the aphasic is saying. The latter goal is feasible because the wife, as a result of the years she has spent with the patient, has learned many of the idiosyncratic aspects of the individual aphasic's communicative behavior, albeit unconsciously. In addition, she has a knowledge of the background to many of the utterances and can supply missing information to continue the exchange. For example, when one patient said *He's your/haid/, maybe a year or two, but fat,* his wife was able to identify the person as the patient's nephew.

The experience obtained by the spouse in the therapy session can be transferred to other situations. If, while at home, the aphasic says *You and me crossing the slimful whenever tonight* and she can respond with *I don't want to go to the movies tonight* (an actual exchange reported by the wife of an aphasic along with an explanation of how she was able to understand), there has been an interaction that is at least as helpful, if not more so, than repeating words.

There are instances, of course, where the inclusion of the family is either impossible or not advisable. These instances should be obvious in the individual case.

Structured Tasks

Although this chapter has deemphasized structured tasks, there has been no intent to minimize their desirability in aphasia therapy. What has been suggested is that the structured task may be most effective with aphasics other than the jargonaphasic. However, when the jargonaphasic improves to the point where he can switch communicative roles with comparative ease, structured tasks may be useful. Still, when used, there must be a clear specification of how the particular processing demands of any task will affect the patient. It is not sufficient to work with "recognizing common words" simply because the aphasic has difficulty with the task on the test. Nor is it sufficient to work on articulation simply because the patient has made articulation errors. The why of the task is more important than the how.

CONCLUSION

Therapy for the aphasic can be organized according to two levels of reference: information processing by the individual and communication interaction. Although these two levels are distinct, each is related to the other.

It has been suggested that a communication level of reference is more appropriate for the jargonaphasic during the initial stages of therapy. With such a focus, therapy is directed toward improving the aphasic's interpersonal and intrapersonal monitoring skills, as well as his overall comprehension skills, and toward providing correct linguistic models through an ongoing analysis of jargon in conversational exchanges. With such an emphasis, therapy can be expanded to include the life experiences of the aphasic, and to provide supportive therapy with and by the family.

There are several basic premises on which the therapy is based. First, apparently empty speech does have meaning and that meaning can be determined by the clinician. Second, changes within or by either of the participants in a communication will affect both the interaction and the other participant. Improvement by the clinician as a receiver of the jargonaphasic's distorted message therefore will have an effect on the aphasic as well. Third, increased opportunity for successful communication will have a beneficial effect on the aphasic, even on the level of information processing.

This has not been an attempt to define specific therapy tasks. Jargonaphasia is too complex a disorder, with too devastating an effect on both the individual aphasic and on those around him, for a therapy to be defined in terms of definite techniques. Muma (1978) put it very well when he stated:

> While it is understandable that clinicians want expedient procedures, they must recognize that more important issues are appropriateness and relevance to individual needs. Appropriateness and relevance are much more difficult to deal with than expediency, but are also much more rewarding since they end in more effective and efficient results. Clinicians are more challenged by the need to find the most appropriate procedure than by merely executing an easy program. A profession needs clinicians rather than technicians [p. 7].

What has been proposed in this chapter is a rationale for a particular approach to a particular type of aphasic patient. Hopefully, the rationale has been, not only appropriate and relevant, but also specific enough so

324 A. DAMIEN MARTIN

that techniques can be developed by the individual clinician in individual sessions.

ACKNOWLEDGMENTS

The author would like to thank Emery S. Hetrick, Margaret Han, and Nelson Moses for their suggestions, criticisms, and support.

REFERENCES

Aita, J. A. Modern considerations of the man with brain injury. *Journal of Neurosurgery,* 1947, *4,* 240–254.
Alajouanine, Th. *L'Aphasie et le langage pathologique.* Paris: J.-B. Bailliere et Fils, 1968.
Anderson, J. O. Aphasia from the point of view of a speech pathologist. *Journal of Speech Disorders,* 1944, *9,* 209–226.
Anderson, J. O. IS is not the verb for aphasia. *Journal of Speech Disorders,* 1946, *11,* 135–138.
Aten, J., Calgiuri, M., & Holland, A. The efficacy of functional communication for chronic aphasic patients. In R. Brookshire (Ed.), *Clinical aphasiology.* Minneapolis: BRK Publishers, 1980.
Basso, A., Faglioni, P., & Vignolo, L. A controlled study of language rehabilitation in aphasia: A comparison between treated and untreated aphasics. (F. Milanti, Trans.). *Aphasia–apraxia–agnosia,* 1979, *1,* 47–52.
Benton, A. L., Problems of test construction in the field of aphasia. *Cortex,* 1967, *3,* 32–58.
Caramazza, A., & Zurif, E. (Eds.). *Language acquisition and language breakdown.* Baltimore: Johns Hopkins University Press, 1978.
Davis, G. A., & Wilcox, M. J. Incorporating parameters of natural conversation in aphasia treatment. In R. Chapey (Ed.), *Language intervention for the adult aphasic.* Baltimore: Williams & Wilkins, 1980.
Freud, S. *On aphasia.* (E. Stengel, Trans.). London: Imago Publishing Co., 1953. (Originally published, 1891.)
Goodglass, H., & Kaplan, E. *The assessment of aphasia and related disorders.* Philadelphia: Lea and Febiger, 1972.
Goodkin, R. A procedure for training spouses to improve functional speech of aphasic patients. *Proceedings of the 77th Annual Convention of the American Psychological Association,* 1969, 761–766.
Huber, M. Re-education of aphasics. *Journal of Speech Disorders,* 1942, *7,* 289–293.
Huber, M. Linguistic problems of brain injured servicemen. *Journal of Speech Disorders,* 1946, *11,* 143–147.
Jakobson, R. *Child language, aphasia and phonological universals.* New York: Humanities Press, 1968.
Kopit, A. *Wings.* New York: Hill and Lang, 1979.
Lennard, H., & Bernstein, A. *Patterns in human interaction.* San Francisco: Jossey-Bass, 1970.
Martin, A. D. A proposed rationale for aphasia therapy. In B. Porch (Ed.), *Proceedings of the conference on clinical aphasiology.* Albuquerque: VA Hospital, 1974.
Martin, A. D. A critical evaluation of therapeutic approaches to aphasia. In J. Brookshire (Ed.), *Clinical aphasiology: Collected proceedings 1972–1976.* Minneapolis: BRK Publishers, 1978. Pp. 173–174.

Martin, A. D. Levels of reference for aphasia therapy. In R. Brookshire (Ed.), *Clinical aphasiology*. Minneapolis: BRK Publishers, 1979. Pp. 154–162.

Martin, A. D. An examination of Wepman's "thought-centered" therapy. In R. Chapey (Ed.), *Language intervention for the adult aphasic*. Baltimore: Williams and Wilkins, 1980.

Miller, J. *Living systems*. New York: McGraw-Hill, 1978.

Mills, C. Treatment of aphasia by training. *Journal of the American Medical Association,* 1904, *43,* 1940–1949.

Muma, J. The communication game: Dump and play. *Journal of Speech and Hearing Disorders,* 1975, *40,* 296–309.

Muma, J. *Language handbook: Concepts, assessment, intervention*. Englewood Cliffs, N.J.: Prentice-Hall, 1978.

Mysak, E. D. *Speech pathology and feedback theory*. Springfield, Ill.: Charles C Thomas, 1966.

Neilsen, J. *Agnosia, apraxia, aphasia*. New York: Hafner, 1936.

Neisser, U. *Cognitive psychology*. New York: Appleton, Century, Crofts, 1966.

Newhoff, M., & Davis, G. A. A spouse intervention program: Planning, implementation, and problems of evaluation. In R. Brookshire (Ed.), *Clinical aphasiology*. Minneapolis: BRK Publishers, 1978.

Peacher, W. G. Speech disorders in World War II: V. Organization of a speech clinic in an army general hospital. *Journal of Speech Disorders,* 1946, *11,* 233–239.

Porch, B. *The Porch index of communicative ability* (Vol. 1.: *Theory and development*). Palo Alto, Calif.: Consulting Psychologists, 1967.

Porch, B. *The Porch index of communicative ability*. (Vol. 2.: *Administration and Scoring;* Rev. ed.). Palo Alto, Calif.: Consulting Psychologists, 1973.

Powers, W. *Behavior: The control of perception*. Chicago: Aldine, 1973.

Sarno, M. T. Preliminary report: A study of recovery in severe aphasia using programmed instruction. In J. Black & E. Jancosck (Eds.), *Proceedings of the conference on language retraining for aphasics*. Washington, D. C.: Department of Health, Education and Welfare, 1968. Pp. 246–269.

Sarno, M. T., Silverman, M., & Sands, E. Speech therapy and language recovery in severe aphasia. *Journal of Speech and Hearing Research,* 1970, *13,* 607–634.

Scheflen, A. E. *Communication structure: Analysis of a psychotherapy session*. Bloomington: Indiana University Press, 1973.

Scheflen, A. E. *How behavior means*. Garden City, N.Y.: Doubleday, 1974.

Scheflen, A. E., & Scheflen, A. *Body language and social order: Communication as behavioral control*. Englewood Cliffs, N.J.: Prentice-Hall, 1972.

Schuell, J., Jenkins, J., & Jimenez-Pabon, E. *Aphasia in adults*. New York: Harper and Row, 1964.

Taylor, M. T. Language therapy. In H. Burr (Ed.), *The aphasic adult*. Charlottesville, Va.: The Wayside Press, 1963. Pp. 139–160.

Taylor, M. T., & Sands, E. Application of programmed instruction to the language training of severely impaired aphasic patients. *NSPI Journal,* 1966, *5,* 10–11.

Turnblom, M., & Myers, J. S. A group discussion program with the families of aphasic patients. *Journal of Speech and Hearing Disorders,* 1952, *17,* 393–397.

Watzlawick, P., Beavin, J., & Jackson, D. *Pragmatics of human communication*. New York: W. W. Norton, 1967.

Wepman, J. *Recovery from aphasia*. New York: Ronald Press, 1951.

Wepman, J. Aphasia therapy: A new look. *Journal of Speech and Hearing Disorders,* 1972, *37,* 203–214.

Wepman, J. Aphasia: Language without thought or thought without language. *ASHA,* 1976, *18,* 131–138.

Wertz, R., Collins, M., Weiss, D., Brookshire, R., Friden, T., Kurtzke, J., & Pierce, J.

Language rehabilitation in aphasia: An examination of the process and its effects. Paper presented at the American Academy for the Advancement of Science, Washington, D.C., 1978.

Wiegel-Crump, C., & Koenigsknecht, R. Tapping the lexical store of adult aphasics: Analysis of the improvement made in word retrieval skills. *Cortex,* 1973, *9,* 410–417.

Wilcox, M. J., Davis, G. A., & Leonard, L. B. Diagnostic and treatment implications of an analysis of aphasia adults contextual language comprehension. In R. Brookshire (Ed.), *Clinical aphasiology.* Pp. 247–254.

Subject Index

PERSPECTIVES IN
NEUROLINGUISTICS, NEUROPSYCHOLOGY, AND
PSYCHOLINGUISTICS: A Series of Monographs and Treatises

Harry A. Whitaker, Series Editor
DEPARTMENT OF PSYCHOLOGY
THE UNIVERSITY OF ROCHESTER
ROCHESTER, NEW YORK

HAIGANOOSH WHITAKER and HARRY A. WHITAKER (Eds.).
Studies in Neurolinguistics, Volumes 1, 2, 3, and 4

NORMAN J. LASS (Ed.). Contemporary Issues in Experimental Phonetics

JASON W. BROWN. Mind, Brain, and Consciousness: The Neuropsychology of Cognition

SIDNEY J. SEGALOWITZ and FREDERIC A. GRUBER (Eds.). Language Development and Neurological Theory

SUSAN CURTISS. Genie: A Psycholinguistic Study of a Modern-Day "Wild Child"

JOHN MACNAMARA (Ed.). Language Learning and Thought

I. M. SCHLESINGER and LILA NAMIR (Eds.). Sign Language of the Deaf: Psychological, Linguistic, and Sociological Perspectives

WILLIAM C. RITCHIE (Ed.). Second Language Acquisition Research: Issues and Implications

PATRICIA SIPLE (Ed.). Understanding Language through Sign Language Research

MARTIN L. ALBERT and LORAINE K. OBLER. The Bilingual Brain: Neuropsychological and Neurolinguistic Aspects of Bilingualism

TALMY GIVÓN. On Understanding Grammar

CHARLES J. FILLMORE, DANIEL KEMPLER, and WILLIAM S-Y. WANG (Eds.).
Individual Differences in Language Ability and Language Behavior

JEANNINE HERRON (Ed.). Neuropsychology of Left-Handedness

FRANÇOIS BOLLER and MAUREEN DENNIS (Eds.). Auditory Comprehension: Clinical and Experimental Studies with the Token Test

R. W. RIEBER (Ed.). Language Development and Aphasia in Children: New Essays and a Translation of "Kindersprache und Aphasie" by Emil Fröschels

GRACE H. YENI-KOMSHIAN, JAMES F. KAVANAGH, and CHARLES A. FERGUSON (Eds.). Child Phonology, Volume 1: Production and Volume 2: Perception

FRANCIS J. PIROZZOLO and MERLIN C. WITTROCK (Eds.). Neuropsychological and Cognitive Processes in Reading

JASON W. BROWN (Ed.). Jargonaphasia